DEGRADE
AND DESTROY

DEGRADE
AND DESTROY

//

THE INSIDE STORY

OF THE WAR AGAINST

THE ISLAMIC STATE,

FROM BARACK OBAMA

TO DONALD TRUMP

//

MICHAEL R. GORDON

FARRAR, STRAUS AND GIROUX

New York

Farrar, Straus and Giroux
120 Broadway, New York 10271

Library of Congress Cataloging-in-Publication Data
Names: Gordon, Michael R., 1951– author.
Title: Degrade and destroy : the inside story of the war against the Islamic State,
  from Barack Obama to Donald Trump / Michael R. Gordon.
Description: First edition. | New York : Farrar, Straus and Giroux, [2022] Includes
  bibliographical references and index. | Summary: "A history of the United States'
  war against the Islamic State in Iraq and Syria" —Provided by publisher.
Identifiers: LCCN 2021061241 | ISBN 9780374279899 (hardcover)
Subjects: LCSH: IS (Organization) | Terrorism—United States—Prevention—
  History—21st century. | Terrorism—Iraq—History—21st century. | Terrorism—
  Syria—History—21st century. | United States—Military relations—Iraq. | United
  States—Military relations—Syria.
Classification: LCC HV6433.I722 I85396 2022 | DDC 363.325—dc23/eng/20220118
LC record available at https://lccn.loc.gov/2021061241

www.fsgbooks.com
www.twitter.com/fsgbooks • www.facebook.com/fsgbooks

1 3 5 7 9 10 8 6 4 2

To Bernard Trainor, partner and friend

CONTENTS

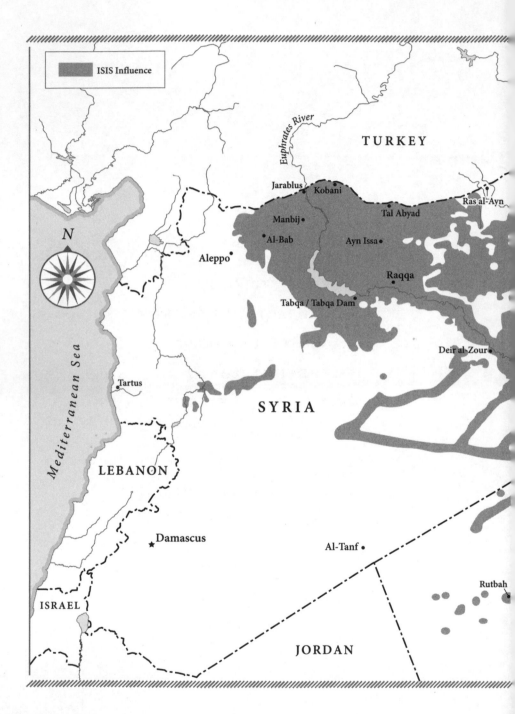

THE ISIS CALIPHATE AT ITS HEIGHT
September 2014

Al-Qamishli

Tigris River

Dohuk

IRAN

Al-Hasakah

Tal Afar

Mosul

Sinjar

Erbil

Dashisha

Makhmur

Al-Shaddadi

Qayyarah

Sulaymaniyah

Kirkuk

Hawija

AL-OMAR
OIL FIELD

Al-Mayadin

Bajji

IRAQ

Tikrit

Al-Bukamal

Samarra

Al-Qaim

Haditha

Euphrates River

Hit

Fallujah

Baghdad

Ramadi

Tigris River

0 Miles   100

0 Kilometers   100

Karbala

© 2022 Jeffrey L. Ward Source: CJTF-OIR

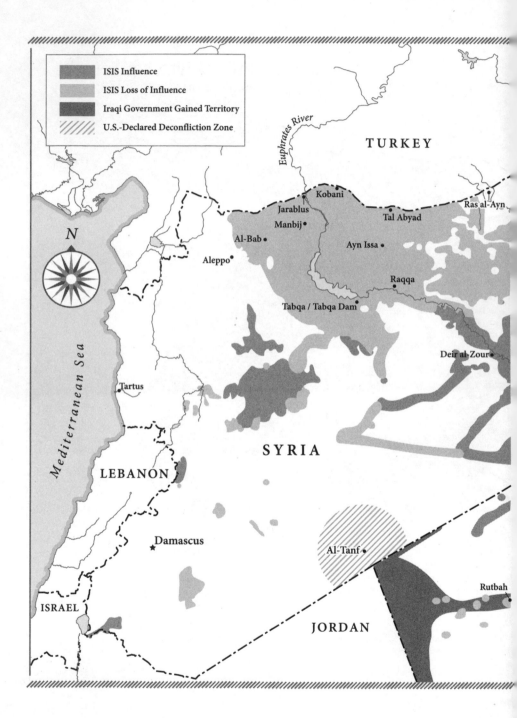

	ISIS Influence
	ISIS Loss of Influence
	Iraqi Government Gained Territory
	U.S.-Declared Deconfliction Zone

TURKEY

Euphrates River

Kobani

Jarablus

Manbij

Al-Bab

Aleppo

Tal Abyad

Ras al-Ayn

Ayn Issa

Raqqa

Tabqa / Tabqa Dam

Deir al-Zour

N

Mediterranean Sea

Tartus

SYRIA

LEBANON

Damascus

Al-Tanf

ISRAEL

JORDAN

Rutbah

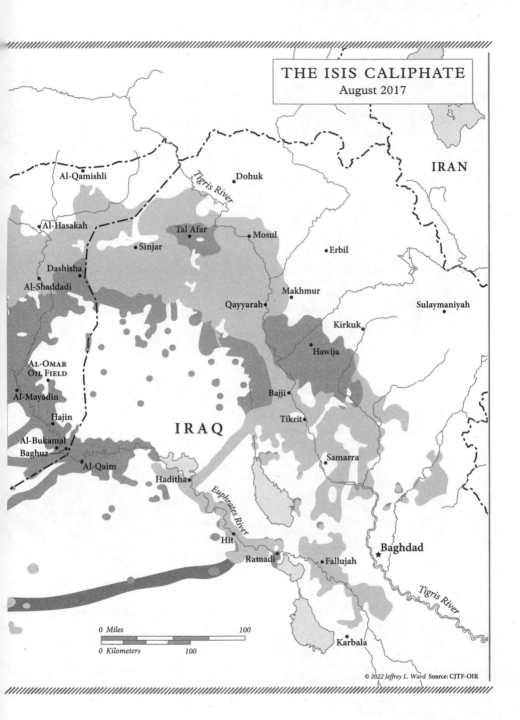

THE ISIS CALIPHATE
August 2017

IRAN

Al-Qamishli

Tigris River

Dohuk

Al-Hasakah

Tal Afar

Mosul

Sinjar

Erbil

Dashisha

Al-Shaddadi

Makhmur

Qayyarah

Sulaymaniyah

Kirkuk

Hawija

AL-OMAR
OIL FIELD

Al-Mayadin

Bajji

IRAQ

Hajin

Tikrit

Al-Bukamal

Baghuz

Al-Qaim

Samarra

Haditha

Euphrates River

Hit

Baghdad

Ramadi

Fallujah

Tigris River

0 Miles   100

0 Kilometers   100

Karbala

© 2022 Jeffrey L. Ward Source: CJTF-OIR

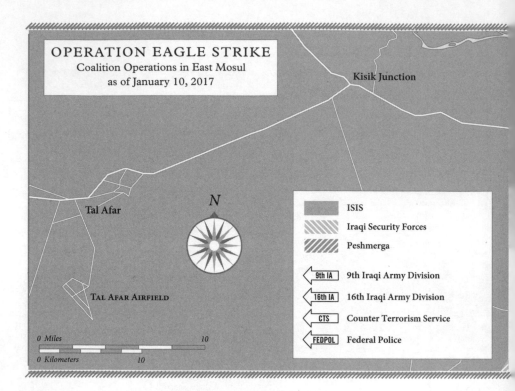

OPERATION EAGLE STRIKE
Coalition Operations in East Mosul
as of January 10, 2017

Kisik Junction

Tal Afar

N

Tal Afar Airfield

	ISIS
	Iraqi Security Forces
	Peshmerga
9th IA	9th Iraqi Army Division
16th IA	16th Iraqi Army Division
CTS	Counter Terrorism Service
FEDPOL	Federal Police

0 Miles   10
0 Kilometers   10

OPERATION EAGLE STRIKE
Final Weeks of Coalition Operations
in West Mosul

Tigris River

Kisik Junction

Badush

I R A Q

Tal Afar

N

Tal Afar Airfield

	ISIS
9th IA	9th Iraqi Army Division
16th IA	16th Iraqi Army Division
CTS	Counter Terrorism Service
FEDPOL	Federal Police

0 Miles   10
0 Kilometers   10

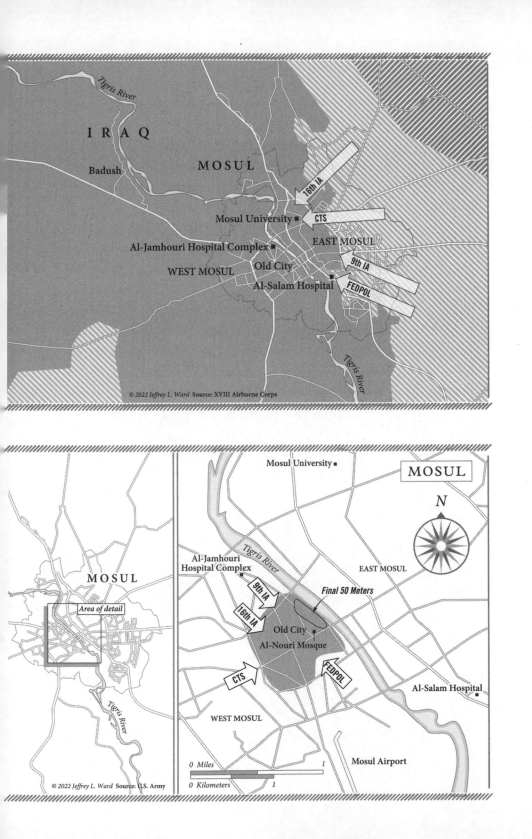

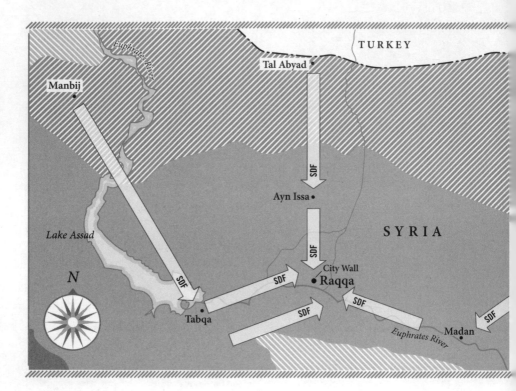

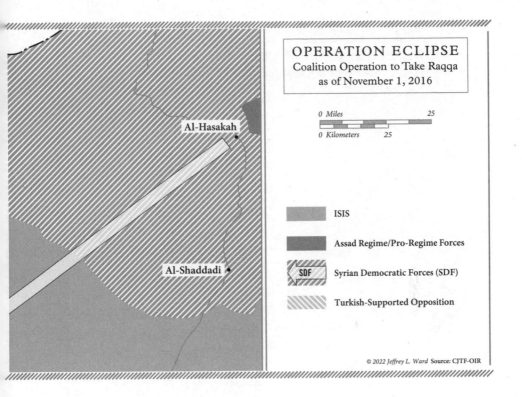

OPERATION ECLIPSE
Coalition Operation to Take Raqqa
as of November 1, 2016

Al-Hasakah

Al-Shaddadi

ISIS

Assad Regime/Pro-Regime Forces

SDF — Syrian Democratic Forces (SDF)

Turkish-Supported Opposition

© 2022 Jeffrey L. Ward Source: CJTF-OIR

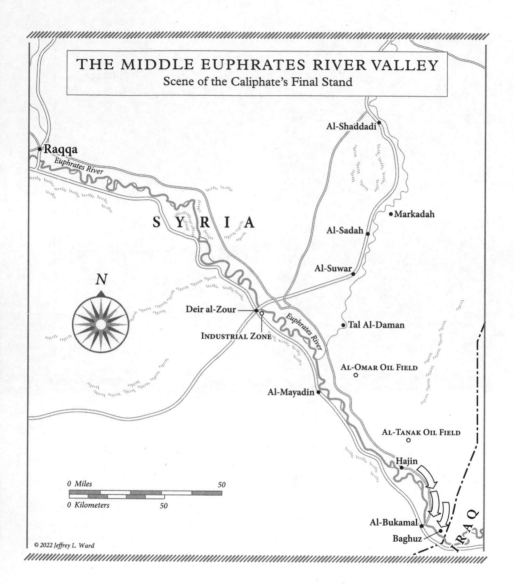

THE MIDDLE EUPHRATES RIVER VALLEY
Scene of the Caliphate's Final Stand

Raqqa

Euphrates River

S Y R I A

Al-Shaddadi

Markadah

Al-Sadah

Al-Suwar

Deir al-Zour

INDUSTRIAL ZONE

Euphrates River

Tal Al-Daman

AL-OMAR OIL FIELD

Al-Mayadin

AL-TANAK OIL FIELD

Hajin

N

Al-Bukamal

Baghuz

I R A Q

0 Miles 50

0 Kilometers 50

© 2022 Jeffrey L. Ward

DEGRADE
AND DESTROY

INTRODUCTION

This is a short book about a big war that upended the Middle East, killed tens of thousands of civilians, brought a new wave of terrorism to Europe, led three American administrations to send thousands of troops to a distant battlefield, and prompted the United States to pioneer a new way of war. The military gave the conflict a name that read like it was generated by a committee and never caught on: Operation Inherent Resolve. Most people simply know it as the campaign against the Islamic State and by the names of its signature battles: Mosul, Raqqa, Kobani, Ramadi, Sinjar, Tabqa, and Baghuz.

Numerous books have chronicled the rise of ISIS and of its diabolical leader, Abu Bakr al-Baghdadi. This book is different. My focus is on the American-led campaign, whose members were known somewhat grandly as the Global Coalition to Defeat ISIS. It is an intricate, dramatic, and largely untold story of policy wars in Washington and actual wars on the battlefield—one with important and hard-won lessons.

The campaign, waged principally from 2014 through the end of the caliphate in 2019, was unforeseen at the White House, where President Barack Obama presided over the withdrawal of U.S. forces from Iraq in 2011 and avowed repeatedly that the conflict there had been brought to a "responsible end." Once the battle was joined, however, the objective Obama established in September 2014 was unambiguous: the United States and its partners would "degrade and ultimately destroy" the Islamic State.

From its inception, this was no mere drone campaign in which targeted killings were directed by pilots a hemisphere away. But neither was it 1991's Desert Storm, in which General Colin Powell's overwhelming force chased Saddam Hussein's Republican Guards away from Kuwait after weeks of day-and-night bombardment. Rather, it was a bloody but politically low-risk form of war. What emerged by fits and starts was a strategy that relied principally on the use of proxy forces in Iraq; the recruitment of new forces in Syria, where none existed; the careful placement of American advisors; and the prodigious use of American and allied firepower in both countries: artillery, surface-to-surface missiles, attack helicopters, AC-130 gunships, and an armada of warplanes, ranging from tank-killing A-10s, stealthy F-22s, and Predator drones to lumbering B-52s. It was the new face of Middle East warfare for a United States that had grown weary of sacrificing so many of its own in seemingly unending confrontations with militant groups. The generals had a name for the unorthodox way of waging war: it was a "by, with, and through" strategy, in which operations were carried out against a common foe *by* a diverse array of local allies, *with* support from American forces and their coalition partners, and *through* a U.S. legal and diplomatic framework. U.S. forces had worked with proxies before, but never on such a scale or with such intensity.

As a presidential candidate, Donald Trump proclaimed that he had a secret plan to supplant this approach, throw away the old rules of engagement, and finish off ISIS. But as commander in chief, he essentially continued the Obama strategy. As his predecessor did in the case of Osama bin Laden, Trump presided over a raid that cornered and killed a top terrorist leader: Baghdadi. But also as with bin Laden, that operation did not end the movement, and the policies Trump put in place as the campaign wound down opened a new phase of competition for influence in the region among Russia, Iran, Turkey, and Israel while undermining Washington's ability to shape the outcome.

I observed much of this war firsthand on the battlefield and in the command centers as a correspondent for *The New York Times*. Later, as a correspondent for *The Wall Street Journal*, I spent more years peeling back the veneer of official Iraqi and coalition statements and boastful claims by ISIS. My effort to get at the truth led me to a Kurdish paramilitary force whose members brought me with them in November 2015 when they forged a path down a rugged mountain to retake Sinjar in western Iraq. It also took me to the October 2016 battle for East Mosul, where the Peshmerga from the Kurdistan Regional Government in northern Iraq allowed me to embed with their fighters. After ISIS struck back with suicide bombers in Kirkuk, I rushed there to interview combatants and civilians. Iraq's elite Counter Terrorism Service took me to their front lines during the battle for West Mosul in April 2017, and again in July for the climactic fight for the area known as the Old City.

I was also able to travel with Lieutenant General Steve Townsend, the commander of the American-led task force that helped the Iraqis retake Mosul, and Colonel Pat Work, who led the 2nd Brigade of the 82nd Airborne and advised Abdul Amir Rasheed Yarallah, the head of Iraq's counter-ISIS fight. On two occasions, I crossed the border into Syria, visiting Tabqa, which American-backed Kurdish and Arab fighters wrested from ISIS in May 2017, and command centers in the northeastern part of the country, where I met some of the senior leaders of the Syrian Democratic Forces and their commander, General Mazloum Abdi.

Along the way, I visited the American-led air war command center in Qatar, the Incirlik Air Base in Turkey, operations in Jordan, and U.S. military command centers in Baghdad, Erbil, and Kuwait. Trips in the region with Secretary of State John Kerry, Defense Secretaries Ashton Carter and Jim Mattis, U.S. Central Command (CENTCOM) leader General Joseph Votel, and senior State Department envoy Brett McGurk also gave me a look into diplomatic and military operations. I fleshed out the story with extensive reporting in Washington.

I was not able to interview Baghdadi or his top ISIS lieutenants, but I talked with Sunnis who were rescued from an ISIS prison in Hawija, Iraq; visited refugee camps near Mosul; studied the militants' texts; and learned about the inner workings of the caliphate from Western officials familiar with allied intelligence.

This volume is my best effort to assess the tumultuous events that brought the American military back to Iraq and onto the battlefields in Syria to combat a bold and cruel adversary the United States had thought it had all but defeated years earlier. The Pentagon has a poor record of probing and documenting its latest wars, especially in the years immediately following a conflict. These days, the military is focusing much of its attention on Russia and China, and much of the U.S. government appears to be trying to put its counter-ISIS war in the rearview mirror. Yet the tactics, procedures, and strategies that were forged in the conflict are likely to serve as a template for operations against terrorist foes in distant reaches of the globe. In that sense, this book is not just about the recent past: it is also a window into the future.

I am grateful to the members of the Iraqi and Kurdish forces who enabled me to join them on some of their most daring operations, and to the U.S., British, and other allied officials who took me into their confidence and brought me with them to newly reclaimed areas in Iraq and Syria. On a personal note, this is my fourth book on conflicts in and around Iraq, but my first without my friend and partner Bernard Trainor—a retired three-star general in the Marine Corps, former *New York Times* military correspondent, and Harvard University professor—who passed away in 2018 at the age of eighty-nine. I have sought to live up to the standard we set of making tough but fair judgments, free of ideological bias and grounded in assiduous reporting and research.

1

IMPALA RIDER

In February 2014, Major General Mike Nagata flew to Baghdad for a stocktaking mission. The head of special operations in the Middle East, Nagata had extensive experience in battling militant cells, lawless militias, and terrorists whose fanaticism magnified their lethality. Name the fight, and Nagata had been there. As a young trooper he had mastered martial arts, and after a stint in South Korea he had taken command of a Special Forces A-team at Fort Lewis, in Washington State. Forging a path in the world of special operations, Nagata had joined Task Force Orange, a classified unit that gathered human and electronic intelligence and in the years that followed worked with the Central Intelligence Agency in Mogadishu during the Black Hawk Down clash that had led to the deaths of nineteen American soldiers. That assignment had been followed by a stint hunting war criminals in the Balkans and eventually command of Orange as it gathered intelligence in Afghanistan, the Middle East, and Africa. By June 2013, Nagata had become the commander of SOCCENT, the special operations component of Central Command, which oversaw U.S. military operations throughout the Middle East and Afghanistan.

Also making the visit was an up-and-coming colonel: Chris Donahue, a West Point graduate who had forged his own path through the special operations community. After stints with the Army Rangers, special operations, and conventional units, Donahue had become the commander of Delta Force, one of the military's elite units for carrying out secret raids to kill and capture insurgents and conduct hostage rescues. That assignment was listed only euphemistically on Donahue's official résumé but was well known among the military's shadow warriors.

The trip to Baghdad by Nagata and Donahue had not been officially announced, but to the small circle of officials in the know, it was clear that this was an unusually experienced, high-powered, and operationally minded team.

What made the trip truly exceptional was that, more than two years before, Washington had declared the Iraq War to be over. After eight hard years, American forces had left the country at the end of 2011. The Obama administration's overarching strategy was summed up by a mantra that the president and his aides had recited in their speeches and included in their party's political platform: "The tide of war is receding." There was turmoil in Iraq to be sure—the very name of the country had, in the American mind, become synonymous with trouble—but nothing was taking place that the White House considered a danger to the United States.

Still, the situation in Baghdad was tense. Prime Minister Nouri al-Maliki had aggravated sectarian passions in the country and was struggling to hold off a marauding band of militants who deemed themselves participants in the new Islamic State. The group had profited from the civil war in Syria—a magnet for would-be jihadists who had flocked to the country to fight President Bashar al-Assad and those who were also drawn by ISIS's mission to build a caliphate there and in neighboring Iraq. In Iraq, the militants had orchestrated a series of brazen jail breaks at Abu Ghraib and Taji in July 2013, freeing thousands of their former comrades and demonstrating the fecklessness of the country's security forces. Their ranks bolstered by former prisoners of war, the fighters had moved on Ramadi and Fallujah, two of the bloodiest battlefields in the U.S. military's years of battling Sunni insurgents. The Americans had taken the cities at great cost, and now they were in danger of being lost again.

After arriving in Baghdad, Nagata and Donahue helicoptered to the U.S. embassy compound, the better to avoid the airport road, which Iraq's sovereign government was often not able to secure. Their meeting with a CIA hand at the embassy revealed few apprehensions about the militant threat. A different picture emerged, however, when they went to the headquarters of General Talib Shaghati al-Kenani, the commander of Iraq's Counter Terrorism Service, which the acronym-loving Americans dubbed the CTS.

Over the course of the Pentagon's many decades in the Middle East, Arab armies had been neither formidable foes nor powerful partners. The American military had rolled over Saddam Hussein's divisions in its 2003 invasion of Iraq and then dismantled the country's armed forces, only to mount a multibillion-dollar effort to rebuild them so they could deal with the hydra-headed threats that had sprung up. A bright spot in the endeavor had been the CTS, which the American military had created in the image of its own special operations forces. U.S. officers had selected many of the CTS's field officers and had equipped its soldiers with vehicles, assault rifles, machine guns, body armor, and tactical radios. Attached at the hip to their American partners, who often fought with them and whisked them to their door-busting missions on Black Hawk helicopters, the Iraqi commandos had been enthusiastic partners—so much so that some had taken not only to affixing patches of the U.S. Special Forces A-teams they had worked with to their uniforms but also to sporting baseball caps and sleeve tattoos. During the heyday of the collaboration, when General David Petraeus commanded forces in Iraq, the Special Forces teams had been supplemented by one hundred American advisors positioned at all levels of the CTS.

To ensure that its operations were not compromised by leaks from within Iraq's multisectarian government, the Americans had arranged for the CTS to have a unique chain of command: it reported directly to the nation's prime minister instead of to the minister of defense. The CTS cadre had been carefully vetted. Its members were not allowed to belong to political parties, and they received $800 a month in pay, far more than run-of-the-mill Iraqi soldiers or policemen earned. The Americans had insisted that the CTS recruits undergo high-level training, and to that end, they had revamped Area IV, a former regime compound at Baghdad International Airport that was modeled on the U.S. Special Forces schoolhouse at Fort Bragg—the Iraqis called it Academiya. But after the Americans left Iraq in 2011—taking their intelligence, air strikes, logistics capabilities, and medical care with them—the CTS had struggled. On the surface, it had maintained its elite identity, going so far as to repaint its Humvees black and replace its desert camouflage uniforms with menacing-looking black fatigues. The organization posted music videos on Facebook and reveled in its past glory as an elite fighting force. Without American air support and advisors, however, Iraq's army and police had begun to fray, and Maliki had responded by saddling the CTS with a burgeoning array of missions that included manning checkpoints, escorting convoys, protecting voting centers, and doing battle with militants in densely populated Iraqi cities. A specialized force that had been designed to carry out lightning raids against terrorist cells (with considerable American support) had become a jack-of-all-trades that was being tasked to deal with the upheaval in Iraq.

To take the measure of the force, Donahue headed west on an Iraqi convoy with General Kenani. The two officers disembarked on the outskirts of Ramadi to confer about the situation, while the vehicles drove on to resupply Iraqi units inside the embattled city. Within minutes, the convoy was ambushed. The Iraqi Humvees were ripped apart by armor-piercing rounds. Some of the soldiers were captured by ISIS militants, who demanded that they FaceTime their families on their cell phones to say their final goodbyes. Much of the mayhem was recorded by the surviving Iraqi troops on their iPads and cell phones, and Donahue set about collecting copies of their videos to share with the U.S. military.

Nagata, meanwhile, huddled with Major General Fadhil Jamil al-Barwari, a chain-smoking Kurd from Duhok, who led the 1st Iraqi Special Operations Force (ISOF) Brigade, which reported to the CTS. Barwari was no longer the confident commander the Americans had known in years past, Nagata later confided to one U.S. officer.

After Donahue returned to Fort Bragg that February, his Delta Force began to redouble its focus on the streams of jihadists who were flocking to the region to join ISIS. It renewed its contacts in the region, drew up contingency plans for joining the fight, and began to eye potential bases, even beginning to establish some in the region.

Nagata, for his part, drafted a memo that reported on the emerging danger and sent it up the chain of command. Years later, the visit was still seared in Nagata's memory. "I will say it very bluntly. It scared the shit out of me," Nagata told me. "My response was, 'What in heaven's name is going on here?' The Iraqis were now telling me about enemy tactics, weaponry, and a degree of combat sophistication that was alien to me even though I spent three years doing multiple rotations in Iraq."

Few officials involved in the policy wars in Washington sensed where events were headed, but for those special operations officers who had visited the battlefield two points seemed to be apparent: first, an old terrorist nemesis had been reawakened, and second, the United States was on a path toward yet another Middle East war.

WINDING DOWN THE Iraq War had been among Barack Obama's signature promises when he ran for president in 2008. His rhetoric was intended to mark more than just a pivot from the strife-ridden Middle East and toward the economic challenges in Asia. It also represented an effort to deemphasize the use of American military force and its potential for quagmires and distraction from the unattended problems at home. To carry out his agenda, the United

States could not simply withdraw its forces from Iraq but had to do so in a way that ensured the Iraqis could handle security on their own—what Obama called a responsible end.

Obama's opening gambit was to take the Bush doctrine and stand it on its head. George W. Bush had seen his American-led 2003 invasion of Iraq as a way to deal with the scourge of terrorism by implanting democracy in the heart of the Arab world; in this scenario, the overthrow of Saddam Hussein would turn a totalitarian Iraq into a catalyst for change in the region. "The defense of freedom requires the advance of freedom," Bush asserted. Obama, in contrast, vowed to engage personally with the leadership of Iraq's autocratic neighbors, including Syria and Iran; he would calm the situation from without. With a yellow legal pad in hand and a retinue of loyal aides standing by, Obama outlined the concept for me in his Chicago office in November 2007: "Once it's clear that we are not intending to stay there for 10 years or 20 years, all these parties have an interest in figuring out: How do we adjust in a way that stabilizes the situation." The idea, not an entirely new one, reflected a growing consensus among the war's skeptics and even the foreign policy establishment about how to bring the conflict to a close. Both the Bush and Obama theories, however, were more of a projection of Washington's hopes than a reflection of the hard realities in the region. Once in office, Obama was forced to confront the fact that the insurgency by al-Qaeda in Iraq (AQI)—the Sunni jihadist group formed in 2004 by the Jordanian militant Abu Musab al-Zarqawi—was reduced but not fully defeated and that Iraq's Syrian and Iranian neighbors were more interested in meddling than in cooperation. He tempered his heady campaign talk about removing all U.S. combat forces within sixteen months, and moved toward a policy that would enable him to declare an end to the U.S. intervention but that accepted the premise that some elements of the U.S. military might need to remain, at least temporarily, to train Iraqi forces so that they could stabilize the country.

There were no doubts in the upper ranks of the U.S. and

Iraqi militaries that Iraq's armed forces remained dependent on American training, equipment, intelligence, logistical support, and air strikes. In 2010, General Ray Odierno, the towering Iraq War commander, instructed Mike Barbero, the three-star general who oversaw the effort to train Iraq's military, to investigate that military's shortcomings. Barbero outlined his findings on the so-called capability gaps in a PowerPoint presentation that he delivered to everybody who was anybody in Iraq: Prime Minister Maliki; Maliki's principal Shiite rivals; leading Sunni officials; Kurdish officials; the heads of Iraq's defense, interior, and finance ministries; and the Iraqi generals themselves.

The Iraqi military had some strengths, including elite forces capable of carrying out counterterrorism operations. Still, for all the U.S. efforts, Iraq's special operations forces continued being flown to their targets on American helicopters and relied heavily on U.S. intelligence to plan their missions. Iraqi tank crews, artillery batteries, and infantry battalions had been trained separately and were not practiced in combined arms warfare. Logistics remained a challenge, and the Iraqi Army had an enormous and costly maintenance backlog. The Iraqis had no counterbattery radar system to pinpoint the location of rocket attacks on the Green Zone—the fortified sanctuary that served as the seat of the Iraqi government—or, as yet, an air force that could protect the nation's skies. In short, Barbero concluded, Iraq had a "checkpoint army" that was very much a work in progress. "The final part of the briefing was an assessment of their capabilities, and in this we were very blunt," Barbero recalled. "I told Maliki and all of the Sunni, Shiite, and Kurdish leaders that none of their security forces would be capable of providing adequate security by December 2011. Their almost universal response was 'General, then you must stay.' I told them that then they had to make it easier for us. Because of the tone coming from Washington, it was clear that it was going to be a hard sell to keep a force in Iraq."

For months, it was unclear if the president who had promised to extricate American forces from Iraq was prepared to extend their deployment, even for the relatively modest mission of mentoring and backstopping the Iraqi military. The status of forces agreement (SOFA) that Bush had concluded in 2008 with Maliki, which provided the legal underpinnings for the deployment of U.S. troops in a sovereign country, was due to expire at the end of 2011. Retaining forces in the country beyond then would require the Obama administration to work out an agreement for an ongoing troop presence through the next presidential election, notwithstanding its past campaign promise to turn the page on military involvement in Iraq.

For the Pentagon, at least, the soft landing it envisioned for post-occupation Iraq would depend on retaining a residual presence. During a swing through the Middle East, Robert Gates, Obama's first defense secretary, got an earful from King Abdullah of Saudi Arabia, Crown Prince Muhammad bin Zayed of the United Arab Emirates, and the Israelis, who were worried about the United States' staying power. Gates favored keeping a substantial presence in Iraq, as did his successor, Leon Panetta, who took over at the Pentagon in July, and their counterpart at the State Department, Hillary Clinton. To avoid signaling a decision that had yet to be made, the military's initial planning for a potential residual presence was heavily classified and carried out under the code name "Impala Rider."

Once the White House accepted the proposition that troops might remain, troop numbers were debated behind closed doors as officials sought to sketch out what America's future relationship with Iraq would entail. The U.S. military, which was intimately familiar with the Iraqi military's weaknesses and was intent on preparing for all eventualities, initially planned for a residual force of as many as twenty-four thousand troops: three brigades whose primary missions would be training Iraqi forces for counterterrorism operations, protecting Iraqi airspace, tamping down Arab and Kurdish tensions, and maintaining American influence. In the face of countervailing pressure from the White House for low troop numbers, Michael Mullen, the mild-mannered admiral who served as chairman of the Joint Chiefs of Staff and by law was the top military advisor to the president, shaved that number down to sixteen thousand troops—a force level that he told the White House in a confidential letter to Tom Donilon, the national security advisor, represented his "best military advice" on how to mitigate the risks. His view was endorsed by General Lloyd Austin, the top U.S. commander in Iraq, and Jim Mattis, the general who led Central Command. With an eye on Obama's campaign promises and the federal budget, Donilon had pressed the Pentagon to accept a force of no more than ten thousand troops. He was so distressed by Mullen's letter that he called over to the Pentagon and had Michèle Flournoy, the top civilian policy official at the Defense Department, pulled out of a meeting so he could complain to her that it should never have been sent, fearing that if the document ever became known, it could box in the president.

As the months passed, Obama and his aides drove the force level lower. Following a July 2011 trip to Iraq, Antony Blinken, who was serving as Vice President Joe Biden's national security advisor, and Denis McDonough, the White House chief of staff, explored whether the U.S. military could reduce troop numbers by dispensing with its mission of deterring conflict between Iraqi and Kurdish troops in northern Iraq. Biden, for his part, took a special interest in planning for a small military footprint. He met with General James "Hoss" Cartwright, a Marine aviator who was serving as the vice-chairman of the Joint Chiefs of Staff, and who had broken with other general officers by promoting the idea of a force just several thousand strong. The final number on which Obama settled—5,000 troops, 3,500 of whom would be stationed in Iraq permanently while the remainder would rotate through the country—was influenced more by U.S. politics than by a sober assessment of security requirements in Iraq, but it would allow the American military to at least keep its foot in the door.

In the end, the talks with the Iraqis foundered not over troop levels but over a separate issue: the White House's insistence that a new SOFA be reached with the Iraqi prime minister and also be formally approved by Iraq's parliament. Among former and current U.S. officials, the question was whether such approval was even necessary. Some of the U.S. officials who had negotiated the Bush-era SOFA had envisioned at the time that it might be extended by a future administration via a simple exchange of notes that left the guts of the original text intact while stipulating a new end date and and some necessary amendments, but dispensing with a fresh parliamentary debate. But the Obama administration insisted that its new SOFA be approved by the parliament to underscore that the accord was legally airtight and to demonstrate that there was broad political support in Iraq for some American troops staying on.

As the clock wound down on the talks, Maliki told James Jeffrey, the U.S. ambassador in Baghdad, that he was prepared to conclude an executive agreement authorizing American troops to stay but would not take the matter to his parliament, a move that would have required an Iraqi leader who had styled himself as the nation's protector to take on Sadrists and Iranian-backed delegates in the legislature to make the case for a continued U.S. military presence. "He said, 'I don't really want to go to the parliament. How about the alternative? We just sign an agreement,'" said Jeffrey, who recalled that Maliki noted that Saddam Hussein had once hosted thousands of Russian advisors without a formal legal agreement at all. By October 21, 2011, the diplomacy had ground to a halt and the effort to draft a new SOFA was abandoned. Reflecting the coolness between the two sides, the secure videoconference in which Obama and Maliki formally drew the talks to a close was only the second direct interaction the two leaders had over the course of the five-month-long negotiations.

At that point, the United States had about forty thousand troops in Iraq; all would need to leave by the end of the year.

The outcome heightened the tensions between civilian and military leaders in the United States and did nothing to ease the mistrust between the American and Iraqi leaderships despite their joint success in largely defeating their primary insurgent adversary, AQI. Jeffrey placed the blame on Baghdad. "Certainly, I got the impression that many in the White House would have been happy to see no troops stay on as long as they could blame the Iraqis. But in the end the Iraqis refused our conditions, and they were reasonable conditions," he said, referring to the requirement for the parliament's approval.

To some top U.S. military leaders, it appeared that the White House had mainly been going through the motions. "We were part of the process, but it was pretty obvious to me that their number was zero," Mullen recalled years later. "That was what the president promised the American people during the campaign. They did not put much effort into getting a status of forces agreement."

Publicly, the White House put the best face on the outcome—as if an unsuccessful negotiation that led to the end of a robust program to train and mentor the Iraqi forces had been intended all along. Nearly three weeks before the end-of-December deadline for the last American troops to leave Iraq, Maliki traveled to Washington to consult with Obama on the future of Baghdad's partnership with the United States. Following the one-on-one meeting, Obama said at a press conference that Iraq would host an Arab League summit. It would be a sign that the country was being accepted by other countries in the region. "A war is ending," the president said. "A new day is upon us."

2

PLAN B

Nobody who had spent time on the ground in Iraq expected the calm to last for very long, and even as the Obama administration expressed confidence in the country's future, it was quietly trying to hedge its bets. After retiring from the military as a four-star general, David Petraeus had moved to Langley, Virginia, as the CIA director. Obama had rebuffed Defense Secretary Robert Gates's suggestion that Petraeus be the next chairman of the Joint Chiefs of Staff, and the new arrangement served the White House well. The most celebrated proponent of counterinsurgency operations was no longer in the media glare or in a policymaking position, but he was still inside the fold, lest he harbor political ambitions of his own. Still, the CIA post also enabled Petraeus to keep his hand in the game and stay in the fight, albeit discreetly.

Neither the CIA director nor Secretary of State Hillary Clinton had been given a role in conducting the star-crossed SOFA negotiations, which were principally run out of the White House. That did not mean they were powerless to shape events. With the blessing of Obama, Petraeus had developed an alternative plan, which he and Clinton quietly proposed to Maliki at a dinner at Blair House, the ornate nineteenth-century home across the street from the White House that served as the presidential guest residence, during the prime minister's December 2011 visit to Washington. Under the plan, several dozen special operations personnel would be seconded to the CIA to deploy to Iraq and work under the agency's cover. Iraq's CTS would do the fighting, but the Americans would provide what the military called "enablers"—that is, people to help with monitoring enemy communications, analyzing intelligence, conducting reconnaissance, and even planning operations. Because the most sensitive aspects of the effort would be classified, and the U.S. special operators would be acting under U.S. embassy authorities, there would be no need for the Iraqi parliament to get involved and the White House could hew to its talking points about bringing an end to the American involvement in Iraq.

It was at best only a partial fix, but Maliki already had a good idea of what shadow warriors could do when they were armed with precise intelligence. When Petraeus was serving as the top general in Iraq, he had taken Maliki to Balad Air Base to meet with William McRaven, the vice admiral and Navy SEAL who led the Joint Special Operations Command (JSOC). Delta Force and Army Rangers had showed off their equipment and demonstrated their skills, much as they would have done for a visiting American VIP. In this case, the Americans would not be conducting the raids but would be enabling the Iraqis to keep tabs on the threats so that the Iraqis could conduct them. Maliki seemed receptive to the idea, enough so that Petraeus made plans to spell out the details later that month in Baghdad.

Maliki was already proving to be a challenging partner—so challenging that it was often difficult to believe that the United States had chosen him for the job. Steeped in conspiratorial politics from years of underground struggle against Saddam Hussein, Maliki had been serving as a parliamentary backbencher from the Shiite Dawa Party in 2006 when Zalmay Khalilzad, the entrepreneurial U.S. ambassador in Baghdad, reached out to him. The Bush administration had been eager to evict the incumbent prime minister, Ibrahim al-Jaafari, from his post, viewing him as passive, if not complicit, in the face of the sectarian tensions that were roiling the country. Khalilzad, who had been reading the CIA's intelligence on Maliki, had convinced himself that the Dawa Party operative was more or less uncorrupted and, given his long years of exile in Damascus, and not Tehran, sufficiently distant from Iran; he seemed to be somebody the United States could work with among an array of choices who were far from ideal.

Not everybody in the coalition shared that view. Sir William Patey, who served as the British ambassador in Baghdad, was convinced that Maliki had played a decidedly unhelpful role in fostering sectarian tensions when he served on Ahmed Chalabi's de-Baathification commission following the U.S. invasion, and that he was hardly prime minister material. The differences between the United States and Britain awkwardly came to the fore when Khalilzad brought Patey with him for the pivotal meeting at which he encouraged Maliki to run for prime minister. Turning to Patey, Maliki asked for the British view. Put on the spot and with no instructions from London, Patey muttered that the candidate should be the one chosen by the Shiite bloc, a diplomatic answer that did not disguise Patey's reservations. Years later, Maliki recalled the moment. "Khalilzad spoke with me and he said that 'we are ready to support you in case you accept the post,'" Maliki told me. "I met him and the British ambassador William, and, yes, he was disagreeing with Khalilzad."

The Obama administration made an effort to see if a politician other than Maliki might be put in the prime minister post. In the main, however, it accepted the premise that Maliki was somebody with whom Washington could do business. Vice President Biden himself had ventured at one top-level meeting in October 2010 that he was so convinced Maliki wanted U.S. troops to stay and would back a new SOFA to get them that he would bet his own vice presidency on the proposition. Though that had not come to pass, Plan B was designed to be an easier lift.

When Petraeus arrived in the Iraqi capital before Christmas in 2011 to seal the plan, however, the Iraqi political establishment was going through a series of convulsions. Fearful of threats real and imagined, Maliki had turned on leading Sunnis in his Shia-dominated government on the day after U.S. forces had departed, accusing them of planning a conspiracy against him now that American forces were gone. The Green Zone, which had been established as a fortified sanctuary for the Iraqi government, had come to resemble a war zone. M1 tanks, which the Iraqi military had acquired from the Americans, had been positioned menacingly outside the homes of top Sunni politicians, including Tariq al-Hashimi, an Iraqi vice president. In the months prior, there had been moments when Maliki saw himself as a target of dark conspiracies. During one October 2011 meeting of Iraqi and American officials, the prime minister had wondered aloud if assassins would murder him and drag his corpse through the streets, as had just happened with Muammar Gaddhafi, the Libyan strongman.

Now Maliki was acting on those fears, and the cross-sectarian government the Americans had struggled to stitch together during the years of occupation was at risk of being ripped apart. Deputy Prime Minister Saleh al-Mutlaq, the senior Sunni in the government, warned that Maliki was moving to create a dictatorship. Hashimi, whom Maliki accused of supervising terrorist death squads, escaped first to the semi-autonomous Kurdish region in northern Iraq and, ultimately, to Turkey, never to return. As he had during his years as the U.S. military commander in Iraq, Petraeus spent his first night back in Baghdad shuttling among the Iraqi factions, trying to soothe tensions.

Seeking to refocus attention on Plan B, Petraeus eventually got time with Maliki and his national security advisor, Falih al-Fayyad. Washington, Petraeus explained, was ready to provide the covert assistance Iraq required to fend off terrorist threats but needed a confidential letter from Maliki requesting the CIA's support.

Maliki assured Petraeus that he would sign such a request. The security challenges continued to mount. On December 22, Baghdad was rocked by the worst car bombings in eighteen months, a series of coordinated attacks that killed some seventy Iraqis and that AQI claimed as its own. But though the Iraqi prime minister had given every appearance of appreciating the offer to help, the letter was never signed.

Petraeus and Maliki stayed in contact. Worried that Sunni militants might try to attack religious pilgrims during a Shiite religious holiday, Maliki asked the CIA director the next year if the United States could fly reconnaissance drones over the event. Arrangements were secretly made for the drones to be flown into Iraqi airspace from Kuwait, but as soon as reports of the planned flight leaked, the Iraqi leader rescinded his request. As much as Iraq needed help with its security, Maliki was at pains to avoid the impression that he needed American assistance—at least in return for the limited capabilities that Washington was prepared to provide.

AS THE U.S. AMBASSADOR in Baghdad, Jim Jeffrey was not clued in on the CIA's Plan B, but he was pursuing his own ways to compensate for the American troop withdrawal. A blunt type with a Boston accent and a penchant for dropping the F-bomb, Jeffrey had an unusual pedigree for a diplomat—one that made him well suited to dealing with countries teetering on the brink of collapse. Before joining the diplomatic corps, he had served as an Army infantry officer in Vietnam and Germany. When Masoud Barzani, the president of the Kurdish Regional Government, hitched a ride to Baghdad in the fall of 2010 on the ambassador's plane along with his Peshmerga bodyguards, it was Jeffrey who removed the ammunition magazines from the fighters' AK-47s before they got on board.

Jeffrey's idea was to quietly expand on a practice that U.S. embassies carried out openly. Military officers were routinely assigned to U.S. diplomatic posts to facilitate the sale of American weapons, arrange military exchange programs, and generally boost cooperation between the two sides' forces, all under the tutelage of the ambassador. During a tour as the U.S. ambassador in Ankara, Jeffrey saw that the embassy maintained a particularly large security cooperation office populated with American military officers who worked with the Turkish general staff. As the SOFA talks faltered, Jeffrey began to formulate plans for a Baghdad security cooperation office on steroids, one that would be staffed by hundreds of military personnel who could network with their Iraqi counterparts at bases throughout the country. To glue the two nations' militaries together, Jeffrey envisioned regular exercises with Iraqi forces like the biannual "Bright Star" exercise the United States held with Egypt, and joint U.S. and Iraqi naval maneuvers near Iraq's offshore oil terminals in the Persian Gulf.

Jeffrey had a partner in Lieutenant General Bob Caslen, who had been assigned to run the Office of Security Cooperation in Iraq, or OSC-I as it was known within the embassy. Caslen had done a stint during the surge as the two-star commander of the American forces in northern Iraq, which gave him on-the-ground experience in dealing with Iraqi sensibilities. When he was selected for the three-star post, Caslen had assumed that Obama's SOFA talks would succeed and that he would be the commander of a follow-on force of thousands of troops who would train the Iraqi forces with a headquarters staff provided by the Army's 3rd Infantry Division. The collapse of the SOFA negotiations had made him an embassy staffer and a general without an army. By working with Jeffrey, he would at least have a real mission.

Making good on the vision for a robust OSC-I, however, was not easy. The core mission of the office was not controversial in Washington. Much of the security office's energy would be devoted to supervising more than $10 billion in arms sales to the Iraqi government. To fill out the Iraqi military, tie Iraq more closely to the United States, and provide some economic benefit at home in return for the vast treasure Washington had expended in its eight-year intervention, the Americans would sell M1 tanks, 155-millimeter howitzers, F-16 fighter-bombers, C-130 transport planes, and armored vehicles—all of which would be supported by thousands of American contractors who would not only deliver the equipment but also stay in Iraq to provide training and maintenance. To carry out those duties, the office initially was allocated a staff of 157. The question was how far to stretch the office's mission and staff beyond that.

Lieutenant General Joe Votel, who had taken over as head of JSOC in 2011, favored adding a small JSOC "in extremis" task force that could be employed for hostage rescue and hedge against what one classified briefing prepared by the U.S. military command in Baghdad described as a "dire immediate threat." One way to carry out this option, the briefing noted, would be to deploy a fifty- to one-hundred-strong special ops task force under "Title 50," the legal authority used for carrying out covert missions—essentially the same way Petraeus had hoped special operations advisors in Iraq would be part of the CIA mission. While administratively the personnel would be considered to be part of the embassy, the briefing noted, such a deployment might lead to accusations that the U.S. military was trying to "'hide' people in diplomatic structures," thus hampering cooperation with the Iraqi government.

Such an option was far more than the traffic would bear within the Obama administration. An early plan called for a security staff of 320, a tiny fraction of the more than 16,000 personnel and security contractors assigned to the embassy. On top of facilitating arms sales, Caslen's team would network with the Iraqi defense ministry and military intelligence officials in Baghdad, and would also be dispersed in half a dozen locations to monitor what was going on with the Iraqi forces in terms of ground and naval forces, logistics, and military education. In addition to the U.S. embassy complex in Baghdad, there were American consulates in the southern city of Basra and in the northern city of Erbil. Yet another consulate was being planned for Kirkuk, a city located in an oil-rich region rife with tensions between Kurds and Arabs. In Caslen's view, those sites and an array of Iraqi bases ranging from north of Baghdad to the port of Umm Qasr, at the head of the Persian Gulf, would form an American influence-projecting archipelago; there would also be a role for a small contingent of Green Berets to continue to train Iraq's CTS in basic skills.

Caslen's military brethren back at the Pentagon balked at such a large staff, and he had to settle for a security office of 262. That was not the end of the challenges.

Even on a reduced scale, the plan to disperse the OSC-I unnerved the Pentagon lawyers, who were still smarting over the failure to nail down a SOFA. To reassure Washington, Jeffrey persuaded Falih al-Fayyad to sign an agreement that spelled out the American assumption that U.S. security office personnel stationed throughout the country would have the same diplomatic status and legal immunities as if they manned a cubicle inside the embassy. Then the Pentagon and the State Department began to argue over who would pay the salaries of the U.S. military officers chosen to stay at northern command posts, a deployment that was intended to foster cooperation, or at least avert hostilities, between the Kurdish Peshmerga and Iraqi forces. The dispute was bumped up to Obama, who ruled that the Pentagon should pay, but it was telling that such a minor bureaucratic matter had to be brought to the president for adjudication.

As the months went by, the major military exercises Jeffrey envisioned never went forward. The U.S. Army was reluctant to conduct exercises with its Iraqi counterpart without a SOFA. The Navy, whose forces were shrinking under budget cuts, resisted keeping ships in the northern Persian Gulf to work with Iraq's small navy. Jeffrey later concluded that without American soldiers on the battlefield and in harm's way, it was all but impossible to get the White House, the State Department, and the Pentagon to keep the money flowing and, equally important, cut through the legalistic and bureaucratic obstacles to any unorthodox solutions. Washington talked a good game about the utility of "soft power," but it was military involvement that raised the stakes in Washington and got the administration's attention. Without that, even the best of plans could die by a thousand nicks.

After Jeffrey wrapped up his Baghdad tour in June 2012, he was replaced by R. Stephen Beecroft, an experienced foreign service officer. In Washington, the White House gave the word to Thomas Nides, the deputy secretary of state for management and resources: it was time to cut back on the use of expensive security contractors, a process the State Department called "rightsizing." Beecroft was tasked with continuing the new policy imperative, and concluded that much of the Iraqi government was also unhappy with a large embassy presence, including the appearance of uniformed U.S. military personnel outside the diplomatic compound, with its echoes of occupation. One of the biggest cuts entailed shuttering the Baghdad Police Academy, which eliminated about a hundred U.S. government positions and a thousand contractor ones. The State Department had a checkered record when it came to training police in Iraq, and the extremely costly program had run into resistance from officials in Iraq's Interior Ministry, which wanted the academy land for its own purposes. Caslen, however, viewed the closure as a major setback. As American forces had prepared to leave Iraq, thousands of former insurgents from Camp Bucca and other detention centers had been turned over to the Iraqi judicial system, only to be released because Iraqi courts lacked the evidence to convict them. Strengthening the Iraqi judicial system, including its ability to carry out forensic investigations, was one mission that Caslen believed was vital to mitigating what would otherwise be a process of catch and release.

It was not long before Caslen's own security cooperation office also began to shrink. The first step was to remove the small American military presence at the airfield in Kirkuk, which meant that the new American consulate there needed to be shut down as well. The administration's theory was that American diplomats in the city, which sat on the Kurdish/Sunni Arab fault line, could commute periodically to Erbil, a several-hour drive, but given concerns about security that was easier said than done. The next retrenchment involved the withdrawal of Caslen's personnel from a base near Tikrit, where the Iraqi Air Force trained its officers, and the departure of U.S. personnel and contractors from Taji, a major repair depot and the base where the Iraqi Army had many of its professional schools. U.S. personnel also left Besmaya, a huge Iraqi Army training site and the location of its armor school, and Umm Qasr, the base south of Basra that supported the Iraqi navy.

One of the most noteworthy casualties was a fifty-person directorate within Caslen's office that mentored Iraq's military intelligence officers to help them better gather and analyze information on the many threats the country faced. The initiative had been supported by Jeffrey and Lloyd Austin when he was the military commander in Iraq. It paid other dividends as well: this collaboration helped American officers develop their own intelligence picture of what was happening in Iraq, including within Iraq's military establishment, supplementing the picture that the CIA developed through its own sources, which the agency jealously guarded.

Another blow came with the curtailment of the legal authority that Caslen's team relied on to carry out its mission. Because the OSC-I was nestled within an embassy and its staff were technically diplomats, it could not train and advise Iraqi forces or help them plan military operations without specific approval from Congress. During the first year after U.S. troops left, the office had benefited from broader authorities, but complacency in Washington allowed it to lapse. By 2013, the OSC-I was allowed only to conduct "non-operational training activities" in "an institutional environment." No longer could Caslen arrange for his officers to be assigned on a day-to-day basis to Iraq's defense ministry, ground forces headquarters, air force headquarters, or navy to glean what they could about the Iraqis' abilities or mentor them as they struggled against AQI's efforts to reconstitute its forces. Instead, the focus would be on helping the Iraqis better manage their defense establishment. Caslen's team had gone from being a military partner, albeit one that played a limited role, to serving as a visiting management consultant. By the time Caslen left Iraq in 2013, the rightsizing had shrunk his office to a staff of 127, and additional cuts were projected to reduce it to 46. His personnel were mainly confined to Baghdad and Balad, where the Iraqis were to field their F-16s under a multibillion-dollar arms deal with General Dynamics. Caslen's own headquarters, across the street from the American embassy, was slated to be closed and its operations absorbed into the embassy compound after he left.

The harshest verdict about rightsizing was delivered in a thirty-seven-page audit by the State Department's own inspector general, who described it as a mechanistic cutback with scant regard for the missions that still needed to be performed in the country. By October, there was to be a 25 percent cutback in the embassy's staff and security contractors. By January 2014, the cumulative reduction was to be 61 percent, meaning there would be 6,320 personnel in the country. In some cases, the audit noted, the State Department reduced the numbers by not filling positions after their occupants had finished their tour of duty, regardless of their importance. "The Department's process to determine U.S. Mission Iraq staff reductions did not fully consider U.S. foreign policy priorities in Iraq," the audit concluded. "There was no mission priorities-based analysis supporting these reduction percentage levels." Worse, some officials who were canvassed for the audit believed that part of the rationale for the retrenchment was to demonstrate that the administration had indeed turned the page on Iraq— what the audit called "domestic political considerations." Those were strong words for an agency that was criticizing its own.

Even the worthiest projects to provide humanitarian aid and strengthen ties between the U.S. and Iraqi militaries were subject to the knife. This would lead to repeated frustrations for Colonel Aizen Marrogi, a U.S. Army doctor and Chaldean Christian who had been named after Dwight Eisenhower by his father and had emigrated to the United States as a young man. Marrogi believed that U.S. military physicians could be an instrument of soft power in the Arab world, but there was a practical reason to cooperate with Iraqi forces as well: the Iraqis had sent eleven pilots to the United States to learn how to fly the F-16s, only to see two washed out for medical reasons. What was celebrated as forward thinking by the military, however, was sometimes rebuffed by the U.S. embassy in Baghdad.

A major setback came after Marrogi was approached by Iraq's surgeon general, who asked for help in building a medical center to treat the tens of thousands of amputees from Iraq's costly war with Iran as well as the U.S.-led invasion. The hospital, which was to be modeled after Walter Reed Medical Center, would be paid for by Baghdad and would serve as a way for the two militaries to strengthen ties. Marrogi secured the support of the U.S. Army, which was eager to arrange a visit for a high-level Iraqi delegation to Walter Reed and the Brooke Army Medical Center, a world-renowned center for treating burn victims. Getting the U.S. embassy on board was another matter. Caslen had sent a November 11, 2012, memo to Beecroft noting that the projects represented a unique opportunity for the United States to deepen ties with Iraq. Soon after, a top deputy to Beecroft called Marrogi and said that the embassy was concerned the move would expand the U.S. military footprint in Iraq and could not support the initiative. Caslen discussed the idea with Beecroft, but was unable to secure his support.

Another disappointment came when Marrogi was approached by a contact at Iraq's Ministry of Health, which wanted to see how the United States might help it improve its medical care for pilgrims to the Shiite shrines in Najaf and Karbala. The health ministry was under the control of Muqtada al-Sadr, the fiery cleric who had railed against the U.S. occupation and whom the Americans had once planned to capture or kill, but who was moving to distance himself from his sponsors in Iran. Cooperation with the health ministry, Marrogi was told, could lead to a meeting with

Sadr himself. That initiative also went nowhere: When Marrogi sought to arrange a trip to meet the health minister, an embassy official said the risk was too great because the agency was run by Sadrists—overlooking the fact that, for Marrogi, forging some sort of working relationship with the Shiite group was precisely the point.

The final straw came when Washington fumbled an attempt to forge a relationship with a key Maliki aide: General Farouk Muhammad Sadeg al-Araji, who served as the director of Maliki's military office. Araji was in charge of security for the Green Zone, and suffered from a a variety of ailments. "General Farouk is the single most powerful military officer in Iraq," Caslen wrote in a February 20, 2013, memo to CENTCOM. "Building a positive relationship with General Farouk and exposing him to American values will continue to improve our relationship and potentially enable US engagement with Iraq during existing and future crises." Try as it did, the military could not get a U.S. visa for the Iraqi officer because U.S. authorities said he had ties to Shiite militias—the very ties Caslen had sought to weaken by providing him with access to the American health-care system.

After leaving Iraq in 2013, Caslen went on to become the superintendent of the U.S. Military Academy at West Point and was later one of the candidates called down to Mar-a-Lago to be considered as Trump's second national security advisor. He left Iraq convinced that the diminished U.S. military role had undermined American influence.

Caslen was succeeded by Mick Bednarek, a genial three-star general who set out to improve ties with Beecroft. Soon after Bednarek arrived in Baghdad, a member of the OSC-I suggested that he ask to be included in the morning meetings when the CIA station chief briefed the U.S. ambassador. That way, Bednarek could get the intelligence picture he needed to carry out his mission, while also demonstrating that he was a full member of the ambassador's team and offering an independent perspective. Bednarek made the request but was refused. The days in which General

Petraeus had worked as an equal partner in Baghdad with Ambassador Ryan Crocker, and when they had both met the CIA station chief to help defeat AQI and steady the Iraqi state during President George W. Bush's surge, were long gone. Beecroft would make sure Bednarek got the intelligence reports he needed, but he would not be in the room. One of Caslen's officers, Lieutenant Colonel Marty Terrill Butts, summed it up well: "The whole thing was about normalizing relations. They did not want us to wear our uniforms, so eventually we went along with that. The running joke was that we were being forced to normalize relations with a country that was not normal."

3

AN APPEAL FROM BAGHDAD

While the Obama administration was wrangling with itself over the U.S. role in Iraq, a familiar adversary was regaining strength in the Middle East. George W. Bush's troop surge had battered al-Qaeda in Iraq to the point that the weekly number of attacks—what the U.S. military called SIGACTs for "significant activities"—had declined from 1,500 to about 100 by the time of the U.S. troop withdrawal in 2011. Sensing an opportunity to re-establish control over towns and cities as U.S. forces surged into Iraq, Sunni tribes had made common cause with the Americans. Dislodged from their strongholds around Baghdad, the militants had been chased through Anbar, Diyala, Salah al-Din, and Nineveh provinces. The group's leader, the notorious Abu Musab al-Zarqawi, had been killed in 2006, and his successors, Abu Omar al-Baghdadi and Abu Ayyub al-Masri, had been finished off four years later in a raid Vice President Joe Biden called "potentially devastating blows to Al Qaeda in Iraq." The terrorist group, however, still retained some advantages, including a pipeline from neighboring Syria, a penchant for organization, and a political strategy to establish itself as an enduring presence.

Beyond detonating car bombs and creating mayhem, AQI had a vision some in the U.S. military were too eager to discount: They had declared an Islamic State in October 2006 and were determined to see the project through. That objective came complete with a flag, a letterhead, a governing structure, and a titular leader: Abu Omar al-Baghdadi, who held the title of emir and who aspired to govern the Sunni regions in western and northern Iraq. In a Green Zone briefing I attended in July 2007, the U.S. military had been quick to dismiss such talk as nothing more than an invention designed to put an Iraqi face on the terrorist organization—and even went so far as to assert that the voice of the leader on the audiotapes the group disseminated was the work of an actor. The briefing was delivered by the chief U.S. military spokesman in Baghdad, based on information gleaned from the interrogation of an insurgent who had been captured in Mosul. I wrote a straightforward news article about the presentation that carried the headline "U.S. Says Insurgent Leader It Couldn't Find Never Was." Years later, terrorism experts concluded that Baghdadi, in fact, had been a real person—so real that he had been killed in the same joint April 2010 Delta Force and Iraqi raid that finished off Masri. Terrorism experts have suggested that by belittling the titular leader of what was then the Islamic State in Iraq, the U.S. may have helped dissuade volunteers, encouraged Iraqi tribes and armed groups to turn their backs on it, and sowed chaos around the leadership succession following Zarqawi's death. However, in the long term, the misunderstanding of the evolution of the Islamic State and its history may have made it more difficult for Washington to discern the dangers posed by ISIS years later. With respect to Abu Omar al-Baghdadi, the Islamic State's first emir, it was later learned that his real name was Hamid Dawud Muhammad Khalil al-Zawi, and that he had been a police officer during the Saddam Hussein regime who was dismissed because of his Islamist views and became part of Iraq's underground Salafi movement before joining AQI after the U.S.-led invasion. Operating near his hometown of Haditha and also in Baghdad, he had been a dedicated operative before his elevation to the leadership post.

Though the Americans had been quick to discount the significance of the new Islamic entity, captured records revealed that its adherents saw its importance. "The resistance in Iraq was heading toward an abyss," the jihadist writer Sheikh Abu Yahya al-Libi wrote in some of the militants' pamphlets, until the announcement of the Islamic State of Iraq "gave the resistance its legitimacy and purpose." Importantly, the documents also showed the insurgents' interest in governance, including the establishment of local departments for legal affairs, security, media operations, and administration, as well as their schemes to raise funds through smuggling and extortion. To build support, the group sought to recruit representatives from prominent Sunni tribes, and diary entries of its members hinted at the scale of their ambitions, which went beyond controlling ground in Iraq. "Please, when you talk about the Islamic State, do not say Iraqi Islamic State; not in the beginning nor the end; not in the conversation nor the speech. You only say the Islamic State," wrote one fighter. During their long years in Iraq, the Americans had sought to usher in a democratic, multisectarian, and multiethnic Iraq, one that was aligned with Western norms and values. The Islamic State, however, would govern according to its harsh interpretation of the guidance emanating from the Prophet Muhammad, known as Wahhabism.

One ruthless operative who embraced its vision was Ibrahim Awad Ibrahim Ali al-Badri al-Samarrai, who was born in 1971 to a Sunni family in central Iraq. He did poorly in school but displayed such a talent for memorizing and reciting the Koran that he later earned advanced degrees in Islamic studies and jurisprudence. Swept up during a U.S. raid in Fallujah in 2004 and operating under the nom de guerre Abu Dua, he was detained in Camp Bucca. Released as a prisoner of no great significance, he worked his way up the ladder and, like others before him, assumed the leadership of the Islamic State in Iraq when the Americans provided an opportunity for upward mobility by killing his predecessor.

With the new position came a new moniker: Abu Bakr al-

Baghdadi, invoking Abu Bakr, the first caliph after the death of the Prophet Muhammad. The name thus harked back to the seventh century, and to burnish his credentials, the new leader claimed descent from Muhammad's tribe: the Quraysh. That lineage was formally required to serve as a "commander of the faithful," according to one of the group's 2007 treatises—"Informing Mankind of the Birth of the Islamic State"—which was later found in one of Baghdadi's last hideouts. It was an unabashed bid for leadership of the Ummah, the world's Islamic community, but Baghdadi's ambitions also ran closer to home.

As far back as December 2009, the militants had laid out their plan to make a comeback. Anticipating the eventual U.S. military withdrawal from Iraq, they sought to position the Islamic State to fill the vacuum. In the "Fallujah Memorandum," a senior Islamic State official outlined a strategy for unifying all of the Salafi and jihadist groups under the militants' banner and mounting assassination campaigns against tribal leaders, local officials, and high-ranking security officers who had cooperated with the Americans, especially those trained by U.S. Special Forces. "Nine bullets for the apostate, one for the enemy," the militants proclaimed. The civil war in neighboring Syria also provided the group with an extraordinary opportunity to anchor much of its operations in ungoverned territory across the border and to draw on a steady stream of volunteers who had come to fight Syrian president Bashar al-Assad but who could be repurposed for the Islamic State's designs.

The flow of jihadists from North Africa, Saudi Arabia, and other Muslim states through Syria had been an enormous problem during the American occupation, as it not only bolstered AQI's ranks but also provided it with the particular volunteers it needed to deploy the militants' version of precision-guided weapons: the vehicle-borne improvised explosive device (VBIED) or suicide car bomb that could be used to terrorize civilians or halt an Iraqi military advance. By 2005, U.S. intelligence estimated that 100 to 125 fighters were infiltrating Syria each month, many of them openly flying to the airport in Damascus. From there, many of the fighters would sneak into northern Iraq, using the back roads near the Syrian towns of Al-Shaddadi and Qamishli or the border crossing at Tal Kushik. In little time, they would find their way to the urban battlegrounds in Mosul or Tal Afar. Others took a southerly route from the Syrian town of Al-Bukamal through the Jazeera Desert and then to the Iraqi cities of Al-Qaim, Ramadi, and Baghdad itself.

U.S. intelligence believed that Bashar al-Assad's brother-in-law Assef Shawkat, who headed Syrian military intelligence, was directly involved in the effort, and that the foreign fighters were an important component of the Syrian regime's regional strategy to tie down U.S. forces in Iraq, lest Washington think of exerting pressure on the regime. This was not merely conjecture. Stephen Hadley, the president's national security advisor, noted in one classified memo that U.S. intelligence had evidence that Syrian foreign minister Walid Muallem had told the Iranians that their joint objective should be "the defeat of the United States" in Iraq.

By 2005, the problem was serious enough that John Abizaid, the CENTCOM commander, and Richard Myers, the chairman of the Joint Chiefs of Staff, approached Defense Secretary Donald Rumsfeld with a confidential memo that outlined a range of options from carrying out an air strike to signal to Bashar al-Assad that Washington would no longer tolerate the infiltration of militants to conducting cyberattacks and thus reducing the foreign fighter flow. "One thing Abizaid and I talked about is that we could bomb the Damascus airport," Myers told me years later. "You could do something that would be temporary, would be fixed fairly quickly, and would not hurt anybody. We had that kind of precision. But you would make a statement." Rumsfeld was not sympathetic to the request, and Bush, who had gotten more than he had bargained for with his invasion of Iraq, was reluctant to risk widening the war.

The full extent of the infiltration network became more clear in September 2007 when Army Rangers from the JSOC task force conducted a raid at a site code-named "Objective Massey" near the town of Sinjar in western Iraq. While there, they seized a five-terabyte trove of documents, including detailed accounts of the organization's finances and six hundred personnel files of foreign recruits. These documents also revealed that much of the cross-border infiltration was overseen by Abu Ghadiya, an Iraqi who split his time between Deir al-Zour and Al-Bukamal, a Euphrates River town near Iraq's Anbar province. In his waning months in office, Bush authorized a cross-border raid into Syria to kill Abu Ghadiya, a successful mission that the United States never officially disclosed and Assad never acknowledged. U.S. intelligence warned, however, that the same foreign fighters who were funneled into Iraq might linger in the region and even train their sights on Assad. Foreign fighters "who gained operational experience in Iraq return to their source countries through Syria," one report observed. "These experienced fighters returning from jihad pose a threat to the Syrian regime. Although Syria currently is mainly a transit point for AQI, Syria will be an AQI target in the future. AQI ultimately intends to conduct attacks in Syria." The militant problem was exacerbated in 2011 and 2012 when Assad released thousands of hardened Islamic militants from his prisons in a bid to tarnish the growing opposition to his rule.

As predicted, the militants set their sights on Syria, but on a scale few had anticipated. Abu Bakr al-Baghdadi's foray into Syria took the insurgents to Deir al-Zour, the country's easternmost province, and by late 2013 to Raqqa, which they took from other rebel groups and turned into the capital of a self-styled caliphate. Taking advantage of captured Syrian army equipment and the seizure of much of the country's oil infrastructure, Baghdadi's insurgents grew stronger.

As his ambitions expanded, so did his group's name: by April 2013 it had become the Islamic State in Iraq and al-Sham, an Arabic name for the Levant region that included Syria. American experts variously dubbed it ISIS or ISIL, while most of the Arab world knew it by its Arabic acronym, Daesh.

Baghdadi's foray into Syria had its difficulties, including a rupture with al-Qaeda's Syrian offshoot, Jabhat al-Nusra, whose leader declined to subordinate himself to ISIS and instead pledged fealty to al-Qaeda leader Ayman al-Zawahiri.

Notwithstanding his gains in Syria, Baghdadi's most important power center was in Iraq. His extensive experience in AQI's insurgency, particularly in and around Mosul, gave him a foothold from which he could expand his turf, gain revenue through extortion, and conduct raids to further expand his ranks. Between July 2012 and July 21, 2013, Baghdadi's "Breaking the Walls" campaign used twenty-four suicide car bombs in eight successful prison breaks, freeing thousands of veterans of his previous insurgency. The campaign culminated in the synchronized prison breaks at Abu Ghraib and al-Hawt prison near Taji, which enabled the escape of more than five hundred detainees, including Abu Abdulrahman al-Bilawi, who later helped plan the 2014 Mosul offensive. "If al-Qaeda can attack a prison, it means they can do whatever they want whenever they want," Meluk Abdul Wahab, an Iraqi lawyer, observed. Soon after, Baghdadi quickly announced "the Soldier's Harvest," a campaign to take the fight to Iraq's security forces. Its signature car-bomb attacks would be employed with devastating effect against the Iraqi units in Anbar and Nineveh provinces.

By that time, Plan B had been forgotten and the United States' capabilities on the ground were negligible. Still, as the situation began to unravel, some pro-Western Iraqi officials began to explore ways for the Americans to help. The statements out of the White House indicated that it would not be an easy sell. White House aides had already proclaimed the U.S. withdrawal from Iraq to be an unqualified success. In March 2012, Antony Blinken, who was still serving as the national security advisor to Vice President Biden, had delivered a major policy speech in which he complained the news media had been unduly alarmist in its coverage of the turmoil in Iraq. Blinken acknowledged that Maliki had purged Tariq al-Hashimi, the leading Sunni in his government, and extracted spurious televised confessions from his bodyguards about their involvement in terrorist activities. But that was just the rough-and-tumble nature of politics in Baghdad, and Iraq's government had been steadied by Biden's frequent phone calls and eight trips to the country as vice president.

"What is beyond debate—and what news coverage of Iraq too often fails to acknowledge—is that Iraq today is less violent, more democratic and more prosperous—and the United States more deeply engaged there—than at any time in recent history," Blinken said in the address, which was delivered in the friendly confines of the Center for American Progress, a think tank founded by John Podesta, who had served as President Bill Clinton's chief of staff and co-chair of Obama's transition team. When Tim Arango, my *New York Times* colleague in Baghdad, wrote an article in July 2012 about the growing violence, citing United Nations statistics, Blinken challenged the analysis in a letter to the editor, arguing that the U.S. government's metrics showed that violence remained low. Even given that 2012 was an election year, the White House had spiked the ball too soon.

IF THERE WAS anybody who could bridge the divide between Washington and Baghdad, it was Hoshyar Zebari. Iraq's affable foreign minister was one of the United States' favorite interlocutors. Zebari hailed from a Kurdish family in northern Iraq, had a master's degree from the University of Essex, spoke fluent English, and was the very picture of reasonableness. The Iraqi government was chronically mired in political squabbles and sectarian infighting, but Zebari had a disarming gift for mixing humor with candor and always seemed to rise above the fray. He had also experienced firsthand what terrorism could do: his own foreign ministry had been rocked by an enormous truck-bomb attack in 2009 that killed scores of his employees. Now four years later, the

Iraqis were picking up signals that the wolf was once more at the door. Sunni militants had established themselves in northeastern Syria and were beginning to extend their reach into western Iraq.

Zebari was hardly a military man, but he doubted that Iraq's forces could handle the threat. Even with the storm clouds gathering, there were rocky political shoals to navigate. Still, there had to be a way to secure some help in Washington, Zebari reasoned. Even a few drone strikes and some training for Iraq's special operations forces could help. Zebari's first step had been to confer with Nouri al-Maliki, who already had his eye on securing a third term as prime minister.

It would be politically awkward for Maliki, who had cast himself as a strongman able to protect his nation's security, to be seen asking for American help more than two years after U.S. troops had exited Iraq, but it would be even worse if the Iraqi leader lost ground to a terrorist army. His own political coalition, after all, had been dubbed State of Law. In a long meeting in the prime minister's Green Zone palace, Zebari tried to make his case. The Iraqi leadership needed to be honest with itself. There were dangers looming that were becoming increasingly hard for Iraq to handle, and the spillover from Syria was only making things worse. Iraq did not have a General David Petraeus, who could mount the Iraqi equivalent of a surge and roll the enemy back. It lacked the necessary intelligence capabilities, and most of Iraq's military capabilities had been allowed to atrophy. With his eye on the Iraqi election, Maliki began joking that Iraqis could manage somehow on their own. But Zebari argued he could test the waters in Washington and see if the Americans were prepared to help without Maliki taking a political risk. The timing was good because the prime minister was planning to visit Washington later in the year and could follow through. If Zebari was successful, Maliki would be pushing on an open door.

After getting Maliki to bless the trip, Zebari headed to Washington for an August 16, 2013, meeting with General Martin Dempsey, the chairman of the Joint Chiefs of Staff. Before head-

ing to the Pentagon, he hosted a lunch for a small group of reporters that I attended in a private dining room at the ornate Willard
Hotel, the Iraqi government's preferred hotel for official visits. Violence was on the rise, and the Iraqi authorities were worried that
AQI was trying to make a comeback. "There is greater realization
in the Iraqi government that we should not shy away from coming
and asking for some help and assistance," Zebari said. The United
States had been indifferent to the security problems in Iraq right
after it withdrew troops in 2011, but there were signs, Zebari said
hopefully, that Washington was coming around. Appeals for military help were matters that were generally discussed only behind
closed doors, but Zebari had friends in the Western media and he
was trying to get his message out.

In Dempsey, Zebari had an interlocutor who had extensive experience in Iraq. The general had come to Iraq in 2003 as the commander of the 1st Armored Division and then returned to lead the
effort to train Iraq's forces. But this same experience had left him
somewhat jaded about the country's politicians, and it was for this
reason that he had been skeptical of the surge of troops and the
new counterinsurgency strategy Petraeus later commanded that
eventually turned the military situation around. As a sign of his
seriousness during his Pentagon visit, Zebari was accompanied
by Fadhil Jawad, Maliki's legal advisor, and Lukman Faily, Iraq's
ambassador to Washington. "General, really we are here to ask
for help," Zebari said, coming right to the point. Iraqi forces were
facing some difficult challenges, but the Americans had many
ways to do more—by sharing intelligence, training Iraq's special
forces, providing drones to the Iraqis, or even carrying out drone
strikes on their own.

"Hoshyar, we are very disappointed," Dempsey responded.
"This was not the kind of Iraq we wanted to leave behind."
Dempsey said soothingly that he believed Iraq was one of the
most important countries in the world but he also wanted to be
sure Zebari was not freelancing and was speaking on behalf of
Maliki. "Is this a government position?" asked Dempsey, who had

long experience with a fractious Iraq and an ambivalent Maliki and wanted to know that the request came from the very top.

Zebari said that it was, but Dempsey said that the Iraqis needed to put the request in writing. He also had some further advice. Dempsey said that he knew all of Iraq's military men: Generals Abboud Qanbar, Ali Ghaidan Majid, and Saadoun al-Dulaimi, the culture minister who was also the acting minister of defense. They were nice enough, but Dempsey complained that they looked for easy answers and, too often, that meant looking for American help. If Maliki wanted a better relationship with Washington, he had to change his command staff and bring in new officers.

When he returned to Iraq, Zebari told Maliki that the groundwork had been laid for a more formal request for help. What he heard in the White House, the Pentagon, and the State Department was that the United States was willing to assist, but they needed to see some changes in Iraq, too. Maliki gave no hint that he was prepared to take any such steps and told his foreign minister that his commanders were confident they could handle the threat. "These commanders are lying to you; they are not telling you the truth about the situation," Zebari responded. That situation was an eerie reprise of the fumbled SOFA talks nearly two years earlier, when the two sides failed to make common cause against a persistent danger. To make matters worse, some of the hard-line Shia had attacked Zebari for even going to Washington to seek help from the former occupier.

AT THE WHITE HOUSE, the national security team had its hands full and ISIS seemed to be the least of its problems. All the demons lurking in the broader Middle East seemed to have been unleashed at once. Fearful of a bloodbath in Libya, Obama had used American airpower to support the Europeans' 2011 effort to rein in Muammar al-Gaddafi, which led to the demise of the Libyan strongman and a power vacuum in North Africa. That same year, the president had joined the chorus in urging Egyptian president Hosni Mubarak to cede power in the face of massive protests in Cairo, only to see General Abdul Fattah al-Sisi mount a coup two years later that killed hundreds of protesters, putting an end to Egypt's only democratically elected government and damaging Washington's hopes for an Arab Spring.

But the principal Middle East crisis casting a shadow over the White House was the one unfolding in Syria, where the administration had tiptoed up to the edge of direct intervention only to pull back in a series of twists and turns that seemed to consume the administration's energy. All the zigzags confused even some U.S. officials intimately involved in foreign policymaking. At first, Obama saw an opportunity to position himself on the right side of history by calling on Syrian president Bashar al-Assad in August 2011 to "step aside" as rebellion against his rule spread through the country—what some officials inside the government dubbed "the magic words." Following an explosion in Damascus in July 2012 that killed Assad's defense minister and other defense and intelligence officials, Denis McDonough, Obama's deputy national security advisor, ordered a study on how to pull Syria together if Assad was gone. Led by the State Department, the "Day After" working group involved dozens of officials and resulted in stacks of memos about what to do with the country's weapons and how to rebuild its economy. The rub came when Assad doubled down on his attacks on the Syrian opposition. Obama cautioned the regime against using chemical weapons in August 2012, stating that it would cross a "red line," while others in the administration began to face the fact that if there was any chance for the "Day After" scenario to happen, Washington would need to ratchet up the pressure.

The case for a covert role had been made forcefully by Robert Ford, who had a front-row seat to Assad's crackdown as the U.S. ambassador in Damascus. After returning to Washington, Ford traveled to Langley to speak with David Petraeus about how the CIA might arm and train the Syrian opposition to pressure the regime—and, at a minimum, provide the United States with a surrogate force that would prevent much of Syria from becoming a black hole dominated by extremists. This conversation was followed by an interagency debate over how to make good on a classified finding the White House had issued calling on the CIA to develop a plan to transition Syria away from Assad's rule.

Petraeus and Secretary of State Hillary Clinton argued for recruiting and arming moderate rebels, a position that was backed by the Pentagon. The president was skeptical of the idea that the United States could successfully tilt the battlefield through covert action, though he grudgingly agreed to help the rebels. That assistance did not come fast. As Obama pondered the question, Petraeus attended meetings in Turkey and Jordan with foreign intelligence chiefs at which he sought to dissaude Arab Gulf states from supporting rebel groups whose extremist affiliations made Washington uneasy while offering little in return.

Eventually, Obama backed a program to train and equip the Syrian resistance while stopping short of providing the surface-to-air missiles the rebels insisted they needed to turn the tide.

As the regime upped its lethal barrel-bomb attacks, enlisted the support of Hezbollah, and captured a key opposition stronghold, the question before the administration was whether to do more. A series of classified memos drafted by the State Department's Bureau of Near Eastern Affairs outlined the case for action. Militarily, the momentum was shifting against the lightly armed resistance and the refugee crisis was only getting worse. Diplomatically, U.S. allies in the region who wished to see Assad gone were getting frustrated. The Saudis and Jordanians, the bureau reported, were upset to the point that they had balked at cooperating with a new rebel training program, while the United Arab Emirates had been reluctant to host a CENTCOM conference for the U.S. and other regional military commanders.

"We are headed toward our worst case scenario: rebel gains

evaporating, the moderate opposition—including Salim Idriss—imploding, large ungoverned space, Assad holding on indefinitely, neighbors endangered, and Iran, Hizballah, and Iraqi militias taking root," read a memo, referring to the Free Syrian Army leader, that carried the anodyne title "Syria: Update on Fighting and Regime Airpower." To reverse the slide, the bureau was urging the White House to work with regional partners to provide more substantial weapons to the opposition and also to consider U.S. air strikes to knock out the Damascus airport and other airfields, which the Syrian regime was using to receive supplies from Iran and launch its own air strikes. That, however, was a distinctly minority view, and one of Obama's most trusted advisors, Denis McDonough, by then the White House chief of staff, privately questioned how much the United States had at stake in the fight. During a trip to the detention facility at Guantánamo Bay on June 7, 2013, McDonough told Senators John McCain and Dianne Feinstein that the internecine conflict in Syria might offer a strategic benefit to the United States by keeping two of America's foes—the Sunni jihadists and Assad's Iranian backers—at war with each other, McCain recalled.

On August 21, five days after Zebari's meeting at the Pentagon with Dempsey, a new government offensive in Syria revealed the crisis had no bottom. Syrian army rockets rained down on two areas in the Damascus suburbs that were controlled by the opposition. Hours later, the Syrian army moved in. For months, Syrian forces had engaged in small-scale chemical attacks, hoping they would be overlooked in the fog of war and testing the limits of what the United States and its allies were prepared to tolerate. But this time, the Assad regime went far over the line: More than 1,400 Syrian civilians were killed, nearly a third of them children, and more than 3,600 were treated for neurological symptoms in three hospitals run by Doctors Without Borders. Analyses of blood and urine samples later confirmed the presence of sarin. It was the biggest chemical weapons attack since Saddam Hussein's forces killed thousands in a 1988 attack on the Kurdish town of Halabja.

At Central Command headquarters at MacDill Air Force Base in Tampa, Florida, Lloyd Austin and his team scrambled to develop a series of options that would enable Obama to enforce the red line Assad had crossed, including firing sea-launched cruise missiles from four Arleigh Burke–class destroyers in the Mediterranean. The French, who had always been the most adamant among the allies that Assad had to go, signed up for the operation: They would fly Rafale fighter-bombers from a base in France and would fire long-range munitions. The United States sent a team to France to install special equipment so that the two militaries could have encrypted communications channels. To try to gain a measure of surprise, U.S. military planners developed a decoy plan that would give the impression that an attack might come from Turkish airspace. That plan was abandoned after Admiral James "Sandy" Winnefeld, the vice-chairman of the Joint Chiefs of Staff, objected to an act of deception that could implicate Turkey, a North Atlantic Treaty Organization ally, without its knowledge. Anxious about potential leaks, Austin's staff disseminated erroneous information at CENTCOM headquarters and waited to see if it turned up in the media. Nothing did, but as a further precaution Austin and Dempsey waited to input some of the real list of targets until right before the attack.

The biggest surprise, however, would be Obama's decision not to enforce his red line at all. The rethink began when the British Parliament voted against participating in the mission, which prompted the president to question his decision to strike without a congressional vote of support—a step that was not required constitutionally, but would provide political cover in case the operation went awry or led to a protracted intervention. While the administration made its case for military action to Congress, the Russians urged the White House to consider an alternative: an offer from Vladimir Putin to work together to dismantle Assad's chemical weapons, thus obviating the need for an American attack against Moscow's ally. Secretary of State John Kerry was initially skeptical of the proposal, which would require dismantling a hidden chemical arsenal in the middle of a shooting war. During a trip to London, Kerry ventured in a September 9 press conference that the Syrian dictator could avoid the hammer blows by getting rid of his poison gas, but then added that he did not believe Assad would do so. As I and other reporters were rushed in vans to Stansted Airport to board the secretary of state's plane back to Washington, Jen Psaki, the State Department spokeswoman, rushed to dispel any impression that Kerry had signaled a weakening of the resolve to punish Assad. "Secretary Kerry was making a rhetorical argument about the impossibility and unlikelihood of Assad turning over chemical weapons he has denied he used," she quickly told the media via email from her separate van as we hurtled down the highway. "His point was that this brutal dictator with a history of playing fast and loose with the facts cannot be trusted to turn over chemical weapons, otherwise he would have done so long ago."

The first hint that this was not the last word came on the plane when Kerry wandered back to the reporters in steerage and mentioned almost casually that he had been on the phone with Sergei Lavrov, the Russian foreign minister. Psaki's jaw dropped as Kerry volunteered the information, and she led him away from the media to the front of the plane. Kerry's debating point, which aides had so assiduously tried to walk back, had inadvertently furnished the White House with an off-ramp.

At the National Security Council, the dizzying series of policy reversals prompted a young official named Sam Parker to draft a classified analysis advocating a course correction more in keeping with Obama's apparent thinking. Parker, who spoke fluent Arabic and had spent time in Iraq, believed it was time to deal with the art of the possible, and that included what was possible in Washington. Robert Ford, John Kerry, and United Nations ambassador Samantha Power had argued at various points for stepping up military support for the opposition, but it was obvious the commander in chief had never been sold on the proposition. Parker argued that the administration needed to look for ways to de-escalate the fighting by pursuing local and even national cease-fires instead of prolonging the war, even if it meant punting on the question of who would run Syria in the future. Philip Gordon, Obama's top NSC hand for the Middle East, and Rob Malley, another NSC Middle East specialist who would succeed Gordon, agreed with Parker's take. Now the administration was split between two camps: those who wanted to step up the military pressure to try to force a political settlement, and those who had essentially concluded that Obama was not going to intervene in Syria and who wanted to turn down the temperature.

The president seemed reluctant to embrace either alternative. Ford saw the handwriting on the wall and resigned in early 2014. After putting in his retirement papers, he told Kerry in his seventh-floor State Department office that he could no longer defend the administration's Syria policy. Jihadists were flocking to Syria, but Washington was not prepared to give substantial military support to what moderates it could find, or to confront the regime whose actions had sparked the civil war in the first place.

"The only ones who are respecting the Sykes-Picot Agreement are the Americans," said Ford—referring to the national boundaries Britain and France had secretly agreed to draw in the Middle East during World War I. "That's a good line," said Jon Finer, Kerry's deputy chief of staff.

The debate over Syria had absorbed an enormous amount of the White House's energies, and those of the CIA as well. It also raised a question for those who were paying attention to Syria's neighbor to the east. If the Obama administration was not going to strike Assad after the worst chemical attacks in decades, was there any prospect the United States would intervene against ISIS in Iraq?

4

MAKE OR BREAK

In Baghdad, Captain Gabe LaMois was six thousand miles away from the policy discussions in Washington and saddled with the challenging task of helping Iraq's CTS hold the line. The commander of a Green Beret A-team from the 5th Special Forces Group from Fort Campbell, Kentucky, LaMois had been preparing to head to Afghanistan in the summer of 2013 when he was redirected to work with Iraq's premier fighting force under the auspices of the U.S. embassy in Baghdad. Operating without a substantial complement of troops and under the shrunken mandate governing the few soldiers stationed at the embassy, CENTCOM was doing what it could to buck up the Iraqi forces. LaMois was told that he and his Green Berets could provide "non-operational advisement of institutional training." That meant his twelve-man team could instruct the CTS in basic military skills but could not assist the Iraqis in planning operations against ISIS, let alone accompany them into battle. The U.S. embassy was not expecting any excitement, and LaMois and his soldiers were instructed to leave behind their personalized M4 carbines, sniper scopes, and other top-of-the-line gear.

After arriving in Baghdad in July, LaMois and his Green Berets were issued the basic kit for mundane training duties: old M4 carbines with iron sights and commercial walkie-talkies. The security was not everything LaMois's team figured it should be. The contractors who defended the State Department complex near the Baghdad airport had mounted a fake .50-caliber machine gun on the turret of one of their vehicles, as a heavy machine gun was not a piece they were authorized to use. Figuring that they would need better protection against potential risks, LaMois's team borrowed Glock pistols from the CIA Baghdad station and went on a scavenger hunt for weapons the U.S. military had left behind. The Green Berets, under strict orders not to wear their uniforms, had to don civilian clothes whenever they ventured to the non-militarized areas near the airport or drove downtown to the Green Zone to visit the CTS headquarters. One member of the team recalled that it was the first time he had gone on a military mission in a suit and tie.

It did not take the Americans long to see that they had a lot of work to do. The Iraqi military was suffering from many of the "capability gaps" Mike Barbero had warned of in 2010, and was further hampered by the corruption and cronyism at the top that had mushroomed under Maliki once American forces were gone and the United States no longer had the clout to push back against the politician's worst excesses. Maliki had sought to compensate for his forces' weaknesses by pushing the CTS to add a third brigade and grow its ranks from about eight thousand in 2011 to more than thirteen thousand in 2013. With the Iraqi Army and police struggling to hold the line, the CTS began to take on unfamiliar duties that the less-capable Iraqi forces could not be relied on to handle. After Baghdadi's Breaking the Walls campaign, the Iraqi government did not send the CTS to hunt down the escaped prisoners. Instead, it put the force in charge of the prisons and launched a prison guard course.

The overall erosion of standards was apparent at Area IV, the Baghdad airport base where the Green Berets did most of their work with the CTS. Though the headquarters building there was well maintained, the farther anyone ventured into the training area, the worse things looked. Some buildings had been stripped of their electrical and copper wiring, which had been sold off along with the air-conditioning units. To train the Iraqis in urban warfare during the American occupation, the U.S. military had constructed a shoot-house: a warren of prefabricated walls coated with special fire-resistant compounds. But the Iraqi soldiers were using tracer rounds inside the structure, which had been patched up with common building materials that could set the entire course aflame. The ventilation system was also broken, which meant that the practice sessions could subject the Iraqi soldiers to dangerous levels of lead. Worse, the "Operator Training Course" in which commandos had undergone ninety-eight days of intensive training before joining the CTS's most elite units had been dispensed with altogether in an effort to turn out fresh, if less proficient, recruits more quickly. What remained was just a shadow of the regimen the Americans had once instituted: During the U.S. occupation, a commando would shoot a couple of hundred rounds over two weeks of practice. But by 2013, ammunition was in such short supply that commandos were being allotted just thirty rounds a year. A force that had once been trained to shoot terrorists without harming their hostages was now barely able to fire its weapons.

The relationship between the U.S. military and the CTS had waxed and waned over the years, but LaMois's Green Berets and the CTS were quick to bond. The A-team stepped up training on room clearing, added a sniper course, and urged Fadhil al-Barwari, the commanding officer of the 1st ISOF Brigade, a CTS formation that was nicknamed the Golden Division, to open up stores of hoarded ammunition so that the commandos would have something to shoot in their exercises. Still, there were indications that corners were being cut. It was obvious to LaMois that the CTS was routinely graduating more people from its commando course than had been enrolled, a sign that well-connected Iraqis could find a way into the prestigious organization without enduring all of the training.

There was only so much, however, that could be done in a training area, and outside of Area IV, Iraqi forces were running into problems. In late December, Maliki's government suffered a blow when the commander of the Iraqi Army's 7th Division and more than a dozen high-ranking officers and their staff members were killed in an attack by three suicide car bombers during a visit to Rutbah, in western Iraq. It was an ominous sign. Rutbah was a key desert transit point to Syria, Jordan, and Saudi Arabia that AQI had fought to control between 2005 and 2007 but had ultimately lost. The town assumed renewed importance for ISIS, which was moving freely across the Syrian-Iraqi border.

Then a different challenge emerged closer to Baghdad. In January 2013, thousands of people from Anbar province had camped out on Highway 11, the main east–west highway, to demonstrate against Maliki's sectarianism and his forces' heavy-handed tactics against the Sunnis, including the arrest the previous month of the bodyguards who protected Rafe al Issawi, the finance minister. Things went downhill from there. As tensions between the Anbari protesters and the Maliki government mounted, and Sunni tribes clashed with Iraqi troops, Maliki sought to calm the situation by removing his army from Anbar. ISIS pounced at the withdrawal of government forces. Its fighters rushed from their desert hideouts to attack Fallujah and Ramadi, along with surrounding villages.

By January 2014, an escapee from the Tikrit prison and a Camp Bucca alumnus who called himself Abu Wahib was filmed in an ISIS propaganda video strolling around police headquarters in downtown Ramadi. Since joining ISIS, Wahib had become notorious for his brutality. In one 2013 video ISIS distributed, he executed three Syrian truck drivers after quizzing them on the tenets of Islam and determining they were Shiites. Now he was the Islamic State's new emir for Anbar province. In nearby Fallujah, Abdullah al-Janabi, a firebrand cleric who had been one of the first to organize resistance to the American occupation a decade earlier, took control after the mayor was assassinated. On January 3, 2014, during Friday prayers, fighters under Janabi's control cemented their victory by declaring Fallujah an Islamic State–held city. Janabi resumed preaching in the city's Saad bin Abi Waqas Mosque in the following days and established the Committee for the Promotion of Virtue and Prevention of Vice; this was the notorious Hisbah religious police that would become synonymous with ISIS rule over Mosul later that year. Some of the sermons at the mosques were focused on more pragmatic needs: calls went out for former military men who knew how to repair the American-made M1 tanks and M198 howitzers ISIS had captured at Iraqi bases outside Fallujah.

Not everybody in Fallujah had pledged their fealty to ISIS, but many of its residents appeared more tolerant of the devil they knew than of the nation's security forces, whom they saw as an occupying army.

The loss of the city was a damaging setback for Maliki and a powerful symbol of the crisis the country was facing. From the British occupation of Iraq in the 1920s to the American invasion in 2003, Fallujah had been a hotbed of resistance, and now that resistance was directed at the Iraqi government itself. The capture of the city was not without military significance, too, as Fallujah was a central hub on the route that ran from Baghdad to Amman, Jordan, and was only thirty-five miles from the Iraqi capital. Adding to the risk, the Fallujah Barrage, a dam just south of the city, regulated the water level of the Euphrates; if ISIS closed the floodgates, it could starve the areas downstream of the water they desperately needed for irrigation. While Fallujah was known for its many mosques, much of the city consisted of cinder-block homes and factories surrounded by concrete walls. In short, it was perfect terrain for the insurgents, who would have to be dug out street by street and, if they were not, could use Fallujah as a springboard for attacks closer to the capital.

Maliki handed the mission of retaking the city to Major General Barwari, who nine years earlier had led an Iraqi special operations battalion that participated in the American-led offensive that seized the city. But Barwari would not be fighting with the Americans this time. As the Iraqi commandos prepared for the difficult mission, Barwari reached out to Colonel David M. Witty, who worked out of the embassy as an advisor to the CTS and whose duties mainly involved facilitating arms sales, overseeing the training at Area IV, and dispensing generic advice alongside LaMois's A-team. A Special Forces officer, Witty had cut his teeth as an advisor to a Kuwaiti battalion during the 1991 Persian Gulf War, and later worked with Egyptian, Jordanian, and Bahraini forces before deploying on his second tour in Iraq. Like the Green Beret trainers, Witty wore civilian clothes for his interactions with the CTS headquarters staff. Unlike most U.S. officers, he spoke conversational Arabic and did not rely on interpreters, which enabled him to assume an even lower profile.

Huddling at the CTS's Green Zone headquarters with Major General Raed Lazim, the organization's chief operations officer, Witty tried to piece together what was happening from fragmented battlefield reports that were mostly conveyed by cell phone instead of by military radio. Before launching his assault on the city, Barwari had posed for a photo while holding up an AT-4 anti-tank rocket and vowing to quickly annihilate Daesh elements in the city. By the afternoon, the bravado had worn off. He reported that his men had entered Fallujah in the face of "heavy clashes." What Witty was hearing was not encouraging. Accustomed during the U.S. occupation to launching nocturnal raids with American support at times and places of their choosing, the CTS was struggling to gain control of the urban terrain and the surrounding roads in broad daylight.

As Barwari's Golden Division pushed toward the outskirts of Fallujah, its convoys of black Humvees stumbled into a classic insurgent kill zone: ISIS had laid IEDs and had booby-trapped homes and government buildings to slow down the CTS. Soon insurgent marksmen were shooting at turret gunners and the Humvees' tires, and pumping bullets into the vehicles' unarmored engine blocks, stranding many of the vehicles and the soldiers traveling inside. "They started strapping metal to the wheel wells because they were losing so many tires to sniper fire," Witty recalled. "They were begging for tires." Later, Witty was able to watch part of the fight from the Islamic State's perspective on YouTube, which only added to his worries. With casualties mounting, the CTS appealed to Witty for help in designing a plan to retake the city.

As much as Witty wanted to help, there were strict limits on what he could do. He could expound on the principles of urban warfare and could talk about the challenges of taking a hypothetical city. But he was not allowed to sit down with a map of Fallujah and help the Iraqis devise a way to contain, weaken, and expel the Islamic State. "There was an urgency and sense of desperation about the situation on their part, but my instructions were very clear. We would provide them with non-operational advice and training on clearing a city, but nothing that was directly applicable to Fallujah or any specific situation," Witty told me years later. "The situation was that the U.S. government was transitioning to a peacetime environment and the embassy was going to operate like any other embassy in the world. The Iraqis and the Americans who worked with them understood that the situation in Iraq was far from normal. It was apparent that things were rapidly going into the toilet. It did not take a Clausewitzian genius to understand that."

Nagata and Donahue later reported on the CTS battle losses during their February trip to Iraq, but that did not prompt an expansion of the American role. Operating at the limit of his mandate, Gabe LaMois began to conduct lectures for the Iraqis on how the U.S. military had captured Fallujah in 2004, hoping that Barwari and his officers might be able to extract some lessons from the case study.

Area IV emptied out as the CTS continued to make its push. As the weeks went by, General Barwari's battalions held regular memorial ceremonies there for their "martyrs," some fifty of whom were killed fighting in Anbar that winter. Some familiar faces returned: the walking wounded whom the Americans had trained and who had been evacuated from the fight. Some fresh faces appeared, too: troops from battalions of the 2nd and 3rd ISOF Brigades that were being rushed in as reinforcements. The Maliki government was not one to publicize its losses, but the United Nations estimated that the violence in 2013 led to the deaths of more than 8,000 Iraqis, more than 950 of whom were members of the Iraqi Security Forces, making for the greatest death toll since 2008.

ISIS's capture of Fallujah had been felt hard among Americans who had fought to take the city back from Sunni insurgents nearly a decade before. A year after the U.S. invasion of Iraq, Marines led by Jim Mattis had planned to use a mix of soft power and raids to secure the city, only to be ordered to mount a full-fledged assault after four American contractors were killed and strung up on the Fallujah bridge. The operation, which the Americans called "Phantom Fury" and the Iraqis dubbed "New Dawn," had led to the deaths of seventy-one Marines and soldiers, as well as hundreds if not thousands of insurgents, making it one of the iconic battles of the war. By the time U.S. troops withdrew, Fallujah had been declared a success, with security being provided by local police and, more important, by Sunni tribes who had cast their lot with the Americans. The cost in U.S. lives and treasure had been high, but the city was considered to be reasonably stable and certainly not a sanctuary for terrorists. Now, instead of remaining a symbol of perseverance, it had come to stand for futility. "I don't think anyone had the grand illusion that Fallujah or Ramadi was going to turn into Disneyland, but none of us thought it was going to fall back to a jihadist insurgency," said Adam Banotai, a twenty-one-year-old Marine sergeant at the time.

At the White House, however, Fallujah was still seen as a distant disruption best dealt with by local actors. During his years as senator, Obama had been unconvinced that AQI represented a major terrorist threat and had even fenced with Petraeus over the question during a July 2008 visit to Baghdad. The militants, he told the U.S. military's Iraq commander in a closed-door meeting in the heat of his political campaign, might be profiting from kidnapping and were certainly a menace to the Iraqis, but that did not necessarily make them an international terrorist pariah that needed to be countered by thousands of American troops. "If AQI has morphed into a kind of mafia then they are not going to be blowing up buildings," Obama said, according to notes from the meeting. Petraeus parried by arguing that a 2007 terrorist attack at the Glasgow airport had been carried out by a British-born doctor of Iraqi descent who claimed an affiliation with the group, that AQI had the potential to carry out terrorist attacks throughout the region, and that Iraq had emerged as a major front in the U.S. war on terror.

As president, Obama still held to the view that the Iraqi franchise of al-Qaeda was a pale reflection of what American counterterrorism officials dubbed "core" al-Qaeda—the bin Laden terror group that had plotted against the United States from its lairs in Pakistan and Afghanistan. When Obama was asked in February 2014 by *The New Yorker* whether he was concerned by the black ISIS flags flying over Fallujah, he echoed the argument he had made in private to Petraeus years earlier:

> The analogy we use around here sometimes, and I think is accurate, is if a jayvee team puts on Lakers uniforms that doesn't make them Kobe Bryant. I think there is a distinction between the capacity and reach of a bin Laden and a network that is actively planning major terrorist plots against the homeland versus jihadists who are engaged in various local power struggles and disputes, often sectarian. We have to be able to distinguish between these problems analytically, so that we're not using a pliers where we need a hammer, or we're not using a battalion when what we should be doing is partnering with the local government to train their police force more effectively, improve their intelligence capacities.

Al-Qaeda's varsity, as Obama saw it, was the core of the group in the ungoverned spaces of Pakistan and Afghanistan, along with its affiliate in Yemen, which had set its sights on blowing up airplanes. His administration's list of top terrorist targets for the CIA and JSOC to hunt started with Ayman al-Zawahiri, who had assumed the leadership of the group after bin Laden was killed, and a pair of his Afghanistan- and Yemen-based subordinates, not ISIS's Baghdadi.

In Baghdad, LaMois's A-team took ISIS more seriously, noting that the militant group not only had military skills and a cohesive leadership but also had a growing population from which to recruit. The soldiers worked to connect the U.S. Defense Intelligence Agency with dormant intelligence sources they encountered. But the Green Berets soon concluded that they needed more tools and sketched out a few ideas of their own, including sending small teams of U.S. advisors to accompany Iraqi units around the country and setting up supply hubs closer to the fight to help the CTS cope with its broken logistics. The recommendations pointed to a major gap in what Washington was providing. But nobody at the White House was asking the U.S. military for its input, and the suggestions contravened the all-important prohibition on non-operational advisement.

One person urging action, however, was Brett McGurk. A former law clerk for Chief Justice William Rehnquist, McGurk had begun his diplomatic career in L. Paul Bremer's Coalition Provisional Authority soon after the U.S. invasion, and through hard work and political skill had managed not only to survive the transition from the Bush to the Obama administration after a short interregnum, but also to establish himself as the State Department's point person on Iraq. As a member of Obama's negotiating team on the ill-fated SOFA talks, McGurk had advised the White House against demanding that a new agreement be approved by the Iraqi parliament, seeing it as an unnecessary and potentially insurmountable obstacle. After the talks failed, however, he had soldiered on and risen in August 2013 to become a deputy assistant secretary of state for Iraq and Iran. Detractors had painted him as a "Maliki whisperer" who had encouraged the

White House to believe it had a partner in the Shiite strongman; defenders insisted he was simply trying to work with Iraq as it was. McGurk was well connected with SOCCENT commander Mike Nagata and Joe Votel, the commander of JSOC, which oversaw Delta Force. All of them could see that ISIS was feeding on the turmoil in Syria and that Iraqi Security Forces were struggling. Iraq had endured five to ten suicide bombings a month in the years following the withdrawal of U.S. troops, but by 2013 that figure was fifty to sixty. After a deadly series of bombings in Baghdad in August, McGurk had pushed the State Department to issue a statement denouncing the attacks and reiterating that there was a $10 million reward for information that led to the death or capture of ISIS's leader, Abu Bakr al-Baghdadi. The reward was second only to that offered for Zawahiri.

In the fall of 2012, McGurk had traveled to Baghdad and conferred with the head of the country's border force. During the best of times, that force had its hands full trying to prevent jihadists from sneaking across the border from Syria. With the border itself now on the verge of being erased, McGurk sent a cable to the State Department appealing for help for the border units. Following another visit, he submitted a second report in early April 2013, titled "'Make or Break' Window in Iraq: Next Six Months Critical to U.S. Interests." It was clear that many in the administration, including the president and the head of the Joint Chiefs of Staff, were inclined to see the trouble in Iraq principally as a reflection of Maliki's sectarian agenda. McGurk argued that the United States still had friends in Iraq despite Maliki's sectarianism, as well as the potential to influence developments in a country that was situated strategically between Iran and Syria. All of that could be undermined by the inroads ISIS was making.

After extensive deliberation, the White House approved a flight by a Global Hawk reconnaissance drone, which confirmed the Iraqis' reports that five ISIS encampments had been established in western Iraq. To get a better intelligence picture, the CIA quietly dispatched a team to the U.S. embassy. One uncontroversial move the administration would take in response to the crisis was to sell arms. The Iraqis had yet to take delivery of the F-16s they had bought from the United States and were relying on Cessna Caravans to reach the ISIS encampments in the western reaches of the country. The Caravans were propeller-driven planes that had been designed to ferry passengers around rural areas in the United States or haul cargo for FedEx. U.S. personnel had helped the Iraqis jury-rig the aircraft to carry laser-guided Hellfire missiles, which the Iraqis were firing in abundance, though not with much effect. As a stopgap, the United States rushed the delivery of seventy-five more Hellfire missiles and approved the sale of low-tech Scan-Eagle reconnaissance drones to the Iraqi military. General Talib Shaghati al-Kenani, the head of the CTS, had been so eager to get a fresh supply of the Hellfires that he joked that he would be happy to carry them back on his private plane.

The move came in the wake of the Obama administration giving three sensor-laden Aerosat balloons to the Iraqi government, along with three reconnaissance helicopters. It was front-page news in the U.S. media, though hardly something that would tilt the balance of power. In a step that was not publicized, the United States also sent the Iraqis a million rounds of ammunition, intended to keep their security forces in the fight. To the frustration of the A-team in Iraq, the delivery was slowed by officious Iraqi customs inspectors, while some of the ammo mysteriously ended up being sold on the black market.

As ISIS sank its teeth into western Iraq, the Iraqis once again issued appeals for help. Maliki broached the matter in a phone call with Vice President Biden, and in a meeting with Lloyd Austin of Central Command. With the encouragement of McGurk, Iraqi ambassador Lukman Faily drove the point home in a confidential letter dated May 21, 2014. It was addressed to McGurk and to Jake Sullivan, who was serving as the national security advisor to Vice President Biden after working as a senior aide to Hillary Clinton when she was secretary of state. Citing Maliki's call to Biden, the letter underscored the risk of ISIS and made half a dozen specific requests. It asked for more U.S. help in training the CTS, including the deployment of elite American counter-terrorism experts. Similar training was requested for the Iraqi Army's 1st Division, an Anbar-based unit that was used by the Iraqi command to respond to security crises, as well as other army and border security units. The letter asked the U.S. military to carry out drone reconnaissance along the Syrian-Iraqi border and in the desert areas in Nineveh and Karbala provinces. Faily also sought bunker-busting bombs to destroy ISIS underground command centers.

Notably, the letter asked the White House to consider air strikes against ISIS staging grounds, safe havens, and training areas and to help Iraqi forces control the border. In an effort to assuage American concerns that Maliki would pursue his sectarian agenda in areas freed from ISIS control, it offered the prime minister's assurance that local leaders and local security forces would help safeguard the liberated areas. "We must act with dispatch to ensure ISIL cannot regroup in the border regions and sustain a steady support of weapons and fighters from Syria. My country is in urgent need of assistance to fully control its western border to mitigate the risks that ISIL presents to Iraq and the entire Middle East Region," it said. "Please deliver this letter to the Vice President as a formal follow up to his conversation with the Prime Minister." Faily never received a response.

By late May, Obama was focused on trying to end another war: the conflict in Afghanistan. After a trip to Kabul that month, the president had settled on a plan to curtail the U.S. involvement. By the end of 2015, the U.S. troop complement would be reduced from 32,000 to 9,800. The U.S. combat mission would end, with the remaining force playing an advisory role before a 2016 troop pullout as complete as the 2011 one from Iraq. Obama sketched out his vision in a May 27 speech, which he delivered from the Rose Garden. No more would troops accompany their allies into the field, help them plan military operations, or conduct air strikes on their behalf. Rather, the goal was to shrink the U.S. military footprint until it was limited to the U.S. embassy, where the military's role would be to provide general advice on security issues and to facilitate arms sales, as in Iraq. "By the end of 2016 our military will draw down to a normal embassy presence in Kabul, with a security assistance component, just as we've done in Iraq," Obama said, making the comparison explicit. "It's time to turn the page on more than a decade in which so much of our foreign policy was focused on the wars in Afghanistan and Iraq," he added. "I think Americans have learned that it's harder to end wars than it is to begin them. Yet this is how wars end in the 21st century."

5

ALL FALL DOWN

A curfew was called in Mosul in early June 2014. Washington was oblivious to the danger, but the security situation had been deteriorating for months and the city was on edge. Nominally, two Iraqi divisions as well as thousands of local police officers and members of the Iraqi Federal Police were in charge of protecting the city. Privately, Iraqi security officials acknowledged that their control over the city was slipping. "In the morning, we have some control, but at night, this is when we hide and the armed groups make their movements," one Iraqi officer observed.

Bisected by the Tigris River, spanned by five sturdy bridges, Iraq's second-most-populous city had never really been entirely in the grip of the Iraqi government. The capital of Iraq's northern Nineveh province, Mosul lay along the historic trade route from Syria to Central Asia, which during the Iraq War and in the years since had doubled as a route for infiltrating militants. The western half of the city featured an ancient quarter of narrow byways and old stone buildings, including the Great Mosque of Al-Nouri, a twelfth-century structure famous for its green dome and leaning minaret. The eastern half, less congested, was the site of one of the country's top universities. The greater Mosul area was home to a diverse array of ethnic and religious groups: Assyrians, Turkmens, Shabaks, Yazidis, and Kurds. The dominant group, however, was Sunni Arab—many of the Baathist officers who had served in Saddam Hussein's military had hailed from the city.

Major General David Petraeus's 101st Airborne Division had managed to control Mosul after the 2003 American-led invasion. That, however, had been the high-water mark for U.S. troops in the city and surrounding Nineveh province, and it had taken an entire U.S. Army division, some twenty thousand troops once all the attached units were included, to do it. Over the next eighteen months, the American military complement in the city shrank from six battalions to six companies, and the dangers began to resurface. When Jim Mattis moved to retake Fallujah in 2004, and U.S. reinforcements were pulled from northern Iraq, AQI took advantage of the situation to rampage through Mosul, sack government buildings, torch police stations, and attempt to break prisoners out of the Badush prison, northwest of the city. The American military and the Iraqi Security Forces mounted a furious counterattack to regain control of the city, with fighting so intense that one U.S. advisor found himself surrounded by sixty dead or wounded Iraqi commandos, while being pinned down by insurgents, until the enemy was finally beaten back.

After George W. Bush ordered a "surge" of reinforcements in 2007 to regain the upper hand over AQI, the additional combat forces never made it as far as Mosul, a situation AQI's leaders used to their full advantage. When I went there in December of that year, U.S. commanders acknowledged that 1,000 U.S. troops and 6,500 Iraqi personnel were enough to keep a lid on the city but not enough to clear it of the enemy. By diverting oil shipments from the nearby Baiji oil refinery, extorting funds from a local cement plant and car dealership, and engaging in fraudulent real estate transactions, the militants had managed to turn the city into a financial hub. In military-speak, it was still "a center of gravity" for the diminished insurgency. In the final years of the occupation, the U.S. embassy briefly considered establishing a consulate at the Mosul airport, only to recoil at how much it would cost to harden the facility against mortar fire and car-bomb attacks. The decision to abandon the project was one instance in which the green-eyeshade types did Washington a favor.

Iraq's Shiite prime minister evinced little concern for the Sunni-majority city. In May 2008, Maliki made his first and only visit to Mosul, where he met with Tony Thomas, the deputy commander of the U.S. Army's 1st Armored Division, who would later lead much of the fight against ISIS as the JSOC commander. With the encouragement of the Americans, Maliki talked of mounting a major military campaign to cleanse the city of insurgents. Instead, he opted that year to send those troops south to Basra, for an operation intended to shore up his Shiite power base.

After the departure of American troops, security for West Mosul was largely in the hands of Iraq's 2nd Army Division, whose soldiers had a well-deserved reputation for demanding bribes. Khalid al-Obeidi, a Mosul resident who was named Iraq's defense minister in October 2014 after ISIS's push into the country, said that corruption among the Iraqi forces was so extensive that residents viewed them more as predators than as protectors. "An officer in charge of a certain area in Mosul, who was supposed to collect intelligence about insurgents, was looking for chances to collect ransoms from wealthy people," Obeidi told me—a remarkable statement for a defense chief to make about his own military. Cells of extremists who had inserted themselves in the city had done much the same. One Mosul resident told me that his businessman brother had handed off a $5,000 payment to militants just a few hundred yards from an Iraqi Army checkpoint. An unpublished retrospective assessment of the Mosul debacle by Iraq's parliament, which I later obtained, concluded that ISIS had access to many of the same illicit income streams as its precursor, AQI, and quickly went from taking in $5 million to as much as $11 million a month in Nineveh province before it even moved on the city. The parliamentary report said the ISIS "deep state" had pursued "systematic extortion" in the province by setting a revenue goal for each population group and then collecting the *jizyah*, or protection tax, under the threat of death from everybody down to the lowliest vegetable and tea sellers.

Mosul's problems had only been aggravated by troubles in nearby provinces. When the fighting grew in Anbar the previous year, a mechanized battalion and some of Nineveh's better forces had been shifted there, only to be destroyed. A bloody government raid conducted in 2013 against protesters in Hawija, in Kirkuk province, had also reverberated, fueling suspicions between the authorities and the locals in Nineveh as well, and leading to further crackdowns. One provincial council member who visited the Nineveh Counter Terrorism Directorate found that 912 prisoners were held in a facility with a maximum capacity of 500. The deteriorating security situation had already unnerved Shabaks, Shia Turkmens, Christians, and other vulnerable minorities, many of whom had left the city. The proximity of the autonomous Kurdistan Region—whose capital, Erbil, was just sixty miles from Mosul—provided the Kurds with a window onto the city, and what their intelligence sources saw was concerning. Karim Sinjari, the Kurdish interior minister, began warning his American contacts that Mosul was becoming another Afghanistan.

The word on the street was that ISIS's priority was not seizing Mosul, but taking Samarra, more than 170 miles to the south. Samarra was home to Al-Askari Mosque, one of Shia Islam's holiest shrines, which had been rebuilt after AQI blew it up in February 2006 in a diabolical move that almost triggered an all-out civil war. In June 2014, ISIS militants, in fact, reached the outskirts of that city, blew up a police station, and used loudspeakers to urge residents to join their campaign, but they never penetrated the security belts around the shrine. The rumors were wrong—ISIS's biggest prize remained Mosul.

The 2014 assault on Mosul began when hundreds of vehicles manned by gun-toting ISIS fighters rolled in from Syria on Highway 47, through the towns of Sinjar and Tal Afar. The Nineveh Operations Command, which oversaw the hodgepodge of Iraqi units entrusted with the security of the city, received a call at 2:30 a.m. on June 5 reporting that Iraqi Security Forces west of Mosul were taking fire. Within two hours, the western and southwestern sections of the city were being attacked. Iraqi forces abandoned their checkpoints and, in anticipation of regrouping and mounting a counterattack, used loudspeakers to urge civilians to flee.

That first skirmish, however, was just a small taste of what was to come. The next day, ISIS began to move along two axes: one that ran from the highway into the neighborhoods surrounding the city's old quarter, and another that ran through an industrial area. When the commander of Iraq's 6th Brigade rushed to the fight in the 17th of July neighborhood (named for the 1968 coup that brought the Baath Party to power), he and his troops took fire from ISIS snipers who had taken up positions on the rooftops of surrounding buildings. Employing the tactics they had used so effectively in Fallujah and Ramadi, the snipers shot at the tires and windshields of the Iraqi vehicles until the soldiers withdrew. Unable to secure a supply of spare tires, let alone new vehicles, the Iraqi soldiers clambered to the tops of nearby buildings and jumped from roof to roof. Within several hours, they had reached a regimental headquarters that had been overrun and retrieved the bodies of Iraqi soldiers inside. The Iraqis had regained some ground, at least temporarily, but the episode was an object lesson in how difficult it would be to defend the city.

Although the city was ostensibly under the protection of the Iraqi Army, local police, and the Federal Police, the latter was a heavily armed paramilitary force under the Ministry of the Interior that had a reputation as a sectarian militia engaged in severe human rights abuses. For those security forces tasked with protecting Mosul, soon the situation began to further unravel. Around 6:00 a.m., the leader of an Iraqi police company called his battalion commander over the radio with the news that he was down to eleven men, was surrounded on all sides, and was considering surrendering. His superior urged him to fight on, but the besieged unit gave in to the ISIS fighters, only to be summar-.

ily executed. The distressing radio exchange had an unfortunate knock-on effect: Iraqi police units along Highway 47 and in the neighborhood of al-Najar had been listening in, and they quickly abandoned their posts. When the police battalion commander urged the Nineveh Operations Command to send what reinforcements it had, the head of its five Humvee security detail balked, insisting his mission did not include venturing deep into the city to join the melee in the 17th of July neighborhood. Eventually, the commander of a police SWAT unit took his four Humvees to the scene. "We saw two vehicles burning, an ambulance on fire, and the bodies of martyrs laying in the street," he later recalled. Under heavy fire, his unit retrieved some of the bodies and evacuated the wounded. By 11:00 a.m., the entire 17th of July neighborhood was under ISIS control.

From the start, Atheel al-Nujaifi had worried that Iraqi forces could not hold the line. Nujaifi, the governor of Nineveh province, was a proud man from a politically powerful Sunni family descended from the Ottoman ruling class. They were known for raising fine horses that were showcased internationally. His brother Osama was the speaker of the Iraqi parliament and a political operator who had much of the Iraqi government on speed dial. But Nujaifi, who had supported challengers to Maliki in Iraq's parliamentary elections, had his own political problems with the prime minister and some local officials as well.

Alarmed by the setback, Nujaifi called Major General Khalid al-Hamdani, the head of Nineveh's provincial police, to ask for an update. Hamdani told the governor that he was with his men, facing down the enemy. But when Nujaifi asked his other police contacts how he could meet up with Hamdani, he was told that the general was actually at the luxurious Mosul Hotel, which the police had decided to make its new battlefield headquarters, far from the fighting. When he drove there, however, Hamdani was nowhere to be found, Nujaifi recalled.

Later that day, Nujaifi called the commander of the Nineveh Operations Center, Lieutenant General Mahdi al-Gharawi, a commander who had been accused of human rights abuses by the Americans in 2007 when he was a police commander in Baghdad but had been protected by Maliki. Gharawi only offered excuses. The armored vehicles he controlled, Gharawi argued, would not be effective against ISIS snipers, and bad weather would preclude the Iraqis from using helicopters or planes. That night, Gharawi demanded that the Iraqi military and police provide the geographic coordinates of the headquarters they had abandoned. Then he gave his troops an order to shell the buildings with mortars, on the assumption that ISIS might be using them—a tactic that added to the risk of civilian casualties in the densely packed city.

Picking up his cell phone, Nujaifi appealed for help to Adnan al-Assadi, the deputy minister of the interior in Baghdad, using Iraqi officialdom's preferred form of communication: a text message. "We need to reinforce our forces today or tomorrow or else the operational leadership will be in danger," Nujaifi wrote in a series of texts that he shared with me. ISIS was making fresh advances, had burned the police headquarters in the Risala neighborhood, and was trying to prevent the Iraqi government from sending reinforcements by cutting off the roads toward Baghdad and Kirkuk. Assadi texted back that help was on the way. Ali Ghaidan Majid, the head of Iraq's ground forces, and Abboud Qanbar, a senior army commander who had long been close to the prime minister as well as the Americans, were headed to Mosul to take control. The entire command structure, Assadi allowed, needed to be reconsidered. The Iraqis had thousands of troops in the area and multiple security organizations, but they had "the ability of an ant."

On June 7, Nujaifi and Assadi texted again. What was happening in Mosul was no mere raid, in which ISIS might be expected to loot the city and then withdraw. The members of the group were building defenses, telling Mosul residents they were their true protectors, and blowing up decoy shells, claiming the explosions were indiscriminate fire from the Iraqi Army. Assadi, however, seemed confident that the tide would soon turn in the government's favor.

Ghaidan and Qanbar had told him that air strikes had been carried out against the Iraqi forces' abandoned headquarters in West Mosul, and that "the situation is under control."

Nujaifi underscored that Iraqi forces would risk being undermined by ISIS propaganda if they were not careful about how they used force. It was important that Ghaidan and Qanbar understand that they would need to gain the trust of civilians. After meeting with them, however, Nujaifi was worried that the top commanders Baghdad had sent would resort to the same blunderbuss approach as always, relying heavily on mortar and artillery fire, just as in the failed attempts to take back Fallujah. "I met with Generals Qanbar and Ghaidan, and it appears to me personally that I am in one wadi and they are in another," Nujaifi texted Assadi, invoking an Arabic metaphor for what the Americans would describe as a complete disconnect. "I am talking about a city with a million and seven hundred thousand people in it and they are talking about open ground."

Maliki was putting pressure on his forces to take the city back. Skipping several links in his chain of command, the prime minister expressed his frustration in a phone call to Brigadier General Fadhil Jawad Ali al-Obeidi, the Iraqi 2nd Division commander, and was angry to hear how much of the city had been lost. Maliki put the blame on the Nineveh Operations Command and made clear that he expected Ghaidan and Qanbar to fix things.

On June 8, Nujaifi drove to Erbil and met with Brett McGurk, who had been traveling through the region and by pure happenstance had ended up at the U.S. consulate there during one of Iraq's greatest moments of need. "I told him we need help from Peshmerga, from you, the United States, anybody, or Mosul will fall down," Nujaifi recalled. McGurk, who was serving as a deputy assistant secretary of state, had made any number of trips to Erbil to press the Kurdish leadership to mend fences with Baghdad over oil revenue splits, territorial claims, and Maliki's increasingly autocratic brand of leadership—important but second-order issues for U.S. officials in Washington. Now a terrorist army was heading toward Mosul and would soon be on the doorstep of the Kurds, who still enjoyed a reputation for being the most pro-American constituency in Iraq. Nor was Nujaifi being alarmist. McGurk received a phone call from a senior Turkish official in Ankara who reinforced the message. The Turks had a consulate in Mosul, and the staff had reported to their superiors at home that the Iraqi Army was doing nothing to defend the city.

In a series of emails and phone calls, McGurk urged the Obama administration to get remotely piloted drones and other forms of aerial surveillance over Iraq as quickly as possible. The Americans were flying blind, relying almost entirely on the reports of the Iraqis, Kurds, and Turks, who all had their own agendas. After spending years emphasizing that the Iraq War was over, there was little likelihood that the Obama administration would decide to rush to the rescue, nor was the U.S. military well placed to intervene. Ray Odierno, the former Iraq commander, had secretly stored a company's worth of M1 tanks in Erbil under a classified program to reassure the Kurds during the American occupation. That armor, however, had been removed when the U.S. military left Iraq. Pending a reversal of American policy, there was a long-shot option: persuading the Kurdish government's Peshmerga to join the fray on the side of the Iraqi Army. The relationship between the lightly armed Peshmerga and the Iraqi military was a tense one. In 2008, the two forces had almost come to blows in Khanaqin, a disputed area along the Kurdish frontier, and after U.S. troops left Iraq, the Kurds complained that the Iraqis had confiscated some of the military equipment the Americans had intended to provide them. Even if the two forces wanted to work together, coordination would not be easy, as the communications post for the Iraqi Army's 2nd Division in West Mosul was shut down.

Politically, the idea was even dicier. The Kurds had made it clear that there was no way they would intervene without a request from Maliki directly addressed to Masoud Barzani, president of the Kurdistan Regional Government (KRG). The mistrust between the two was so profound that Barzani's aides had privately appealed to the Bush administration to replace the Iraqi prime minister. Now that they had a violent enemy in common, however, McGurk hoped that fences could be mended. Steve Beecroft, who was manning the embassy in Baghdad, advised McGurk to start with Falih al-Fayyad, Maliki's national security advisor, who had ignored David Petraeus's Plan B offer. McGurk, said Beecroft, should make the case that it would be better to get the Kurds into the fight, lest they try to take advantage of the situation by expanding their turf while Iraqi forces were clashing with ISIS.

Still, it was not an easy sell. Fuad Hussein, Barzani's chief of staff, had broached the prospect of a Peshmerga intervention with Tariq Najim, Maliki's chief of staff. The aide agreed to take the matter to the prime minister, but he raised the question that appeared to be paramount for Maliki and his inner circle in Baghdad: If the Peshmerga pushed into East Mosul, would they ever leave? Even in extremis, Maliki could not think beyond his fraught relations with Erbil.

The proposition, in fact, was quickly becoming academic. In an effort to halt the ISIS juggernaut from spilling over into the government sector in West Mosul and the eastern sector of the city, Iraqi commanders ordered that a defensive line be established forward of a major hospital and the Mosul Hotel. On the morning of June 9, General Fadhil drove to the Mosul hospital, climbed to the sixth floor of the building, and asked his on-scene commanders to point out the defensive line. "They said, 'This street is the defensive line,'" he recalled. He saw two burning Humvees that had been attacked during the previous day's operations. "The dead bodies were still lying in the street."

ISIS was determined to puncture what remained of the line at all costs. Employing the group's signature shock attack, at 3:45 p.m. one of its suicide bombers drove a captured tanker truck into the SWAT vehicles in front the Mosul Hotel. The very fact that the truck could penetrate that far showed that the main routes through the city were no longer under the Iraqi military's control.

When the tanker exploded, among the wounded was the commander of the police battalion in the western part of the city. As word spread that the line was buckling and units were retreating, Abboud Qanbar sent a senior officer to confirm the disposition of the units. "I didn't notice any terrorists," the officer said later. "But I noticed the empty checkpoints that had been abandoned." After returning at 5:30, the officer reported back that he had been shocked by what he had observed. "The matter was over," he reported. The defense was collapsing fast.

Nujaifi returned to Mosul and noticed the same distressing quiet. For years, the Iraqi military had been plagued by the problem of "ghost soldiers," fictitious soldiers who were only on the rolls so that their commanders could pocket their pay. In Mosul, it seemed, Iraq had a ghost army, and the area near the city's government buildings was ripe for the picking. "It was empty," Nujaifi recalled. The parliamentary inquiry report noted that one of the battalions entrusted with reconstituting the defensive line could only deploy seventy-one men out of the standard five hundred. By 9:00 on the evening of June 8, Nujaifi was surprised to discover that the generals were no longer at their operations center, a departure that the dwindling number of Iraqi soldiers took as a signal to flee.

Nujaifi texted the news to Assadi the next morning. Assadi sought to reassure Nujaifi by noting that he had been in touch with the Kurdish interior minister, Karim Sinjari, about the possibility of deploying the Peshmerga. But Assadi was not Maliki, and he was not authoritative enough to persuade the Kurds to rush toward the sound of gunfire. In any event, it was now too late. "If nobody has told you, I think that the left flank is no longer in the hands of the army," Nujaifi texted back.

ISIS seized the Iraqi Army's American-made Humvees, raided its ammunition stores, and busted into Mosul's notorious Badush prison, freeing criminals and former insurgents just as it had done in its Breaking the Walls campaign. The Iraqi tricolor flag was being replaced with black ISIS banners. As feared, the Kurdish region was swamped with Mosul residents, including Nujaifi, whose parting message to his constituents, made during a phone interview with one of Mosul's television programs, was that the city was lost. "I told them that Mosul will fall down," Nujaifi recalled, "and there was no possibility that anybody would help, that everything was gone."

IRAQ WAS NO longer front of mind for most Americans. Nor was Mosul any longer a household name—the city where Saddam Hussein's sons had been killed by U.S. forces, and where American troops had struggled at an enormous cost, had faded from the collective memory. "Sunni Insurgents Drive Iraqi Army from Big City," read the headline in *The New York Times* on June 10, 2014. But this was no Fallujah, a situation Washington could try to ignore while the Iraqis tried to cope with the threat. If ISIS tightened its grip on Mosul, it would have an unobstructed supply line to Syria. The semi-autonomous Kurdistan Region would be swamped by tens of thousands, if not hundreds of thousands, of refugees. Nor was Mosul the limit of the Islamic State's ambitions. With the Iraqi military pervaded by confusion, ISIS prepared for a lunge to the south.

In Tikrit, Ahmed al-Karim, the chairman of the local provincial council, had a firsthand view of the government's panicky response. After hearing that the police headquarters in nearby Baiji had been burned to the ground, he figured that ISIS had torched the building, only to learn from his contacts that the Baiji police had stripped off their uniforms and burned their own headquarters—a message to the militants that there was no need to hunt down and kill the local security forces because they would not interfere. Soon Tikrit gave way as well. Karim and Governor Ahmed Abdullah al-Jabouri left the provincial palace complex for the security of the Iraqi 4th Division headquarters, where they were met by the region's top military and police commanders. Hundreds of vehicles were arrayed at 4th Division headquarters for what looked at first like a convoy to roll back the ISIS tide. The Iraqi soldiers, however, were not headed north to Mosul to confront the Islamic State. Instead, Lieutenant General Ali al-Fraiji, the commander of the Salah al-Din Security Operations Center, explained that they were falling back to Samarra, where they would try to rally the locals to their cause.

In Kirkuk, the provincial governor was Najmaldin Karim, an American-trained neurologist. He was reassured by the commander of Iraq's 12th Division that the line would be held at Tal Alwad, a village southwest of the city. But Karim doubted that the commander, Major General Muhammad Khalaf al-Dulaimi, had even ventured onto the battlefield. Soon the general fled to Kirkuk, where the governor arranged for him and his staff to change into civilian clothes and then travel to Sulaymaniyah so they could catch a flight to Baghdad.

Hundreds of cadets at the Iraqi Air Force academy at Camp Speicher were not so fortunate. As in Mosul, their senior officers had fled. Afraid and confused, many of the leaderless recruits decided to go by foot to Baghdad, more than a hundred miles to the south. No sooner did they get on the road than ISIS fighters intercepted them, offered to give them a lift, packed them into trucks, and hauled them to some of Saddam Hussein's former palaces. The Sunnis were permitted to repent for their service to the Iraqi government, while hundreds of Shia—ISIS claimed the number was 1,700—were pulled aside and shot.

Abu Nabil al-Anbari, who had been sprung from the Abu Ghraib prison during the ISIS jailbreaks a year earlier, was involved in the operation, which ISIS photographed and posted about on social media. Anbari, whose actual name was Wissam Najim Abd Zayd al-Zubaydi, would later be dispatched by ISIS to Libya, where he died in a U.S. air strike on November 13, 2015. However, in June 2014, the killings he directed ranked as one of the largest mass shootings in modern times and had a devastating effect on the morale of Iraq's reeling army. The Iraqi commanders had long had to endure a creaky logistics system in which ammunition resupply and reinforcements were never guaranteed, and orders were given by cell phone. Now there was a bloody example of what could happen if Iraqi units were cut off and relief did not come in time. After the massacre, many Iraqi soldiers began taking civilian clothes in knapsacks—so they could change and make a quick getaway.

Years later, Maliki still refused to concede any mistakes on his part—neither the cronyism that he had allowed to infect his army, nor his anti-Sunni policies that had provided fertile ground for ISIS propaganda, nor his failure to ask the Peshmerga to help protect Mosul when it was first endangered. Rather, he insisted that the defeat was the result of collusion and intrigue. "The people who were in charge of the fall of Mosul were the Sunnis and the Kurds," Maliki told me. "Mosul had fallen by conspiracy, not by a fight."

In the aftermath of Mosul's fall, ISIS exploited its quick victory. On June 12, it issued a statement hailing its "divine conquests," boasted of the prisoners it had busted out of the Badush prison, and said that it would govern the city on the basis of Sharia law: alcohol and cigarettes would be banned, women would need to cover up, prayer would be mandatory, and thieves would have limbs amputated. A new era of the Islamic State was beginning under the authority of a new caliph. ISIS's social media went to work, showing videos of fighters replacing Iraqi flags with black ISIS banners.

On June 29, Abu Muhammad al-Adnani al-Shami, the group's spokesperson and a senior leader, announced that the caliphate had been established and the group would henceforth be known as the Islamic State. It would be the birth of a new order. The announcement made clear that the group claimed to have reversed the 1924 Turkish decision under secular national leader Mustafa Kemal Atatürk to abolish the Ottoman caliphate. In keeping with the theme of overturning the post–World War I order, the Islamic State's media wing released a video of Adnani with another of the group's most distinctive fighters, the red-bearded Chechen jihadist whose nom de guerre was Abu Omar al-Shishani, standing at the recently bulldozed Sykes-Picot border between Iraq and Syria. For all the symbolism of that event, the Islamic State had even more in mind. In preparation, the nominated caliph released an audio message on July 1 titled "A Message to Mujahidin and the Muslim Ummah in the Month of Ramadan."

The most dramatic gesture came three days later. Dressed in black, the state color of the storied Abbasid caliphate, Abu Bakr al-Baghdadi climbed to the pulpit of the Great Mosque of Al-Nouri on July 4—the first Friday of Ramadan—and delivered a thirteen-minute-long sermon to the people of Mosul. No terrorist leader had ever undertaken such a brazen gesture: a militant with a multimillion-dollar price on his head had defied the world to proclaim himself a head of state. "I was appointed as a leader for you, although I am not the best of you, nor am I better than you," he said. "Obey me as long as I obey Allah in your regards." The event was recorded and disseminated on ISIS social media accounts. When the group had called itself a state in 2006, it was derided and mocked by many fellow jihadists. Since then, it had suffered setbacks and rebuilt in relative obscurity, far from the minds of most American policymakers and the cameras of the international media. Now it had burst onto the global stage.

Atheel al-Nujaifi watched the video from his sanctuary in Erbil. ISIS had seized his family's estates, killed and eaten their purebred Arabian horses, and ransacked his Mosul residence. Nujaifi noticed one vestige of his former life in the ISIS production: the Rolex watch he had left behind in his home was on Baghdadi's wrist.

6

BACK TO THE FUTURE

The fall of Mosul and the delivery of much of northern Iraq into the hands of ISIS came as a shock to the White House. Obama had touted 2014 as a turning point in the United States' long military entanglement abroad. Troops in Afghanistan were to be drawn down, Obama had told the nation in his Rose Garden address, adopting the rough exit strategy the White House had pursued in Iraq. With ISIS's seizure of Mosul, not only did Obama have a new crisis on his hands but his paradigm for ending the "forever wars" had collapsed.

In Baghdad, the U.S. position was already beginning to erode. The American embassy building had been intended, at its conception, to be the largest U.S. diplomatic outpost in the world and a durable symbol of a new Iraqi-American alliance. Now the State Department feared that the facility, a beige fortress with its back to the Tigris River, might be besieged if ISIS swept south. At a town hall meeting, the embassy staff was urged to remain calm in the face of a danger that was still more than a hundred miles to the north. Hours later, in the middle of the night, the embassy staff was woken up and informed that many of them would soon be leaving by charter aircraft or commercial flights. The State Department acknowledged that many of the embassy personnel were being "temporarily relocated" while the diplomatic post would continue to carry out its mission.

But the move decimated the embassy's already modest Office of Security Cooperation, which shrank overnight from more than a hundred to thirty, and spooked the small army of Western contractors who were working to maintain the costly weapons the Iraqis had bought from the United States. The United States produced some of the most sophisticated aircraft and armored vehicles in the world, and its defense industry was expert at selling them. Iraq's newly acquired M1 tanks were a vast improvement over its old Russian-made T-72s. But like its Bell reconnaissance helicopters and other advanced systems, they required substantial maintenance, which Iraq outsourced. "As ISIS came in, U.S. contractors left the country," said one former U.S. military officer who did business with Iraq. "Gone." The exodus took a toll on the already battered Iraqi military, leaving it that much weaker in its hour of greatest need. The United States' approach to arms sales was feasible in peacetime, but the response to the loss of Mosul showed that it did not work that well in war.

As Obama pondered his hand, Lloyd Austin's planners at CENTCOM's headquarters in Tampa rushed to identify targets in case the president ordered air strikes. One major worry was the Haditha Dam, a massive structure that stood astride the Euphrates and generated hydroelectric power for western Iraq. Iraqi Army troops, equipped with a smattering of artillery pieces, several Soviet-made armored personnel carriers, and one infantry-fighting vehicle, had a toehold at the dam and were defending the installation with the help of some nearby tribes. ISIS fighters, however, were in the surrounding area and were issuing ultimatums that the tribes surrender. If ISIS gained control of the dam, U.S. military planners feared, they might become self-styled water lords who could regulate the flow to punish their opponents and might even destroy the structure to cause catastrophic flooding that could extend to Ramadi.

CENTCOM also drew up plans for strikes to defend the Baiji complex north of Baghdad, which housed the country's largest oil refinery, as well as Balad Air Base, north of the capital. A plan was also devised in case a full evacuation of the embassy was ordered, along with contingency plans in case ISIS managed to take the Baghdad airport or "Route Irish," as the road to the airfield had been dubbed. The initial attacks, the planners indicated, could be carried out by F/A-18 Navy fighters launched from the USS *George H.W. Bush*, dispensing with the need to get approval from Persian Gulf states where U.S. warplanes were deployed—if and when the strikes received "POTUS approval."

The larger question was how the president might fit any action against ISIS into his broader strategy for fending off terrorist threats while avoiding Middle East wars. Unlike Bush's Iraq and Afghan conflicts, a new conflict with ISIS would not be a war Obama inherited but an intervention all his own. As he sought to define the terms of a new confrontation, Obama led an off-the-record brainstorming session with a group of former Middle East hands in a conference room off the Oval Office, during which he took pages of notes. Echoing Robert Ford's quip during his final meeting with John Kerry, John R. Allen, a retired Marine general who had worked with Sunni tribes in the fight against al-Qaeda in Iraq, argued that ISIS had given the region such a shake, on top of the civil war in Syria, that the Sykes-Picot Agreement itself might possibly be dead. Obama could well be faced with a decision between trying to restore the status quo ante, which would mean reinforcing the Syria-Iraq border and keeping Iraq together, or abandoning the borders drawn by the French and British a century prior. Iraq was already being subjected to centrifugal pressures, noted Allen, who had been talking to Sunni tribal leaders who were thinking about establishing their own autonomous region. Ryan Crocker, the former U.S. ambassador in Baghdad, added that military intervention would not help if the United States did not find a way to address the political turmoil in Iraq and the region. At the end of the session, Obama said that the thrust of his policy would be to accept the legal borders as they were drawn and not to embrace an alternative to Sykes-Picot. The administration was still hoping to eventually pivot away from the Middle East, not to redraw its map.

HOW PRECISELY THE United States might intervene and when, however, remained open questions, including for U.S. military leaders who were waiting for instructions. Fresh from consultations with the White House, Martin Dempsey, chairman of the Joint Chiefs of Staff, filled in Austin on June 19. The president was adamantly opposed to taking ownership of the security situation in Iraq as long as the country was ruled by a sectarian government led by the likes of Maliki. Until Maliki was replaced by a new prime minister and a new Iraqi government was formed, Obama was prepared to take only limited steps, such as assessing the status of Iraq's faltering forces; the evaluation would enable Washington to launch a training and advisory program if the political pieces fell into place. Small teams of U.S. Special Forces and other personnel would be sent to examine the Iraqis' ability to defend the northern and western approaches to Baghdad, but the president was adamant that their duties would be limited to writing report cards. They could not get involved in mentoring the bedraggled and demoralized Iraqi units. The teams could only spend a few days with the units and would be under orders to avoid forming a "habitual relationship" or anything that might imply the two sides were again partners. After the assessment was complete, and if the president decided to authorize additional military steps, the Special Forces teams could rejoin the Iraqi forces in a genuine advisory role.

To open the door for action, Vice Admiral Frank Pandolfe, Dempsey's chief planning officer, sketched out the legal rationale.

ISIS could be designated an "associated force" that was linked to al-Qaeda, so that it could be targeted under the authorizations Congress enacted after the September 11, 2001, terrorist attacks—a designation that overlooked the fact that Jabhat al-Nusra, al-Qaeda's affiliate in Syria, had broken with ISIS, but reflected the fact that the Islamic State had its origins in the terrorist movement spreading across the Middle East. If U.S. advisors were dispatched to Iraq, he noted, the Pentagon would need to work with Congress to expand the limited authorities that had hemmed in David Witty and the U.S. Special Forces who had trained the CTS. A new SOFA seemed to be out of the question; Maliki had balked at seeking approval from the parliament, and quickly drafting and securing such an agreement from a group of quarreling lawmakers was a bridge too far. An interim fix, Pandolfe told his superiors, could be an exchange of notes indicating that U.S. advisors were there at the invitation of the Iraqi government and would have diplomatic protections. Maliki had suggested a similar approach during the Obama administration's fraught SOFA negotiations, only to be rebuffed—but facing a new terrorist danger, the White House was likely to be more flexible.

Pending a decision to take on an Iraqi training mission, Obama would authorize air strikes to safeguard U.S. personnel at the embassy in Baghdad and at the consulate in Erbil. Otherwise, he would retain tight control over any air strikes, and was unlikely to delegate the authority to carry out bombing raids to U.S. military commanders, Dempsey told Austin. Rather, it would be up to the military to propose targets to the White House as it identified them. Obama, Dempsey ventured, was likely to authorize an air strike if he thought that ISIS was on the verge of an action that could dramatically escalate sectarian passions in Iraq, or put the Iraqi government in an even deeper hole, such as attacking the Shiite shrine in Samarra, the Baiji oil refinery, the Taji military complex, or a major prison that housed dangerous militants. Dempsey also thought Obama would approve air strikes against top ISIS leaders—what the military called a "high-value target"—if the case could be made that it would decisively weaken the militants. A broader array of strikes, however, appeared to be out of the question for the time being.

Still, the situation remained fluid. Dempsey told Austin that the military should develop two "excursions"—contingency plans for training Iraqi troops and using force against ISIS fighters. One excursion envisioned that there would be a new, pluralistic Iraqi government led by a pro-American prime minister other than Maliki. The other presupposed that politics in Baghdad would remain plagued by sectarian divisions. Obama, Dempsey confided, was not persuaded that the United States could find an acceptable partner in Iraq and thought Iraq's problems would probably intensify. The president acknowledged that Iran might continue to take advantage of his cautious approach by rushing military support and even troops into Iraq while the Americans were still deliberating. That, however, was a risk Obama was prepared to take, Dempsey told Austin.

In Amman, Jordan, and other Arab capitals run by Sunni leaders, Iraq's neighbors were free with their advice. As a weak state in a tough neighborhood, Jordan had long cooperated closely with Washington and was also the site of one of the CIA's largest outposts in the Middle East. Jordan's king, Abdullah II, told the U.S. ambassador in Amman, Stu Jones, on June 17 that he was prepared to help as long as Jordan's role was obscured to reduce the risk of retaliation. According to an undisclosed cable Jones sent the State Department, the king was prepared to let the United States conduct reconnaissance from his bases and might even throw his own helicopter gunships into the fight as long they operated out of the Kurdish areas in Iraq. Beyond that, Abdullah had some pointers for the Americans. The United States should get the Iraqi Kurds into the campaign and should take the time to improve its intelligence picture in Iraq before striking. The Americans had been out of Iraq for a while, and ISIS had moved into areas controlled by Sunni tribes, many of whose leaders had taken refuge in Amman or regularly visited there. The last thing the

United States needed was a strike that hit some of Jordan's tribal allies by mistake.

Qatar had a more far-reaching recommendation. During a meeting in Washington with Dempsey, Qatari foreign minister Khalid bin Muhammad al-Attiyah urged the United States to strike ISIS in Syria and only later in Iraq. That, Attiyah argued, would show that the administration was serious about taking the fight to ISIS in heavily publicized strongholds, and was not just supporting Iraqi Shiites over Sunnis. Qatar was already supporting Syrian rebels who were fighting Assad and saw the battle there as a priority.

As it turned out, the Iraqis could not afford to wait for the Americans to help. On June 13, just days after the fall of Mosul and with the nation's security on the line, Grand Ayatollah Ali al-Sistani issued a fatwa calling on all able-bodied Iraqis to defend the state—an edict that thousands of Shia took as a literal call to arms. Sistani hailed from the quietest school of Shiite theology, which held that religion needed to be kept apart from politics. He led a secluded life in the holy city of Najaf, hardly ever left his apartment, did not meet with American officials, and rarely interceded in the nation's affairs. When he did give an order, it had the force of law. Ayad Allawi, Iraq's first post-invasion prime minister and a secular Shiite who had ties to the Sunni community, had summed up Sistani's critical role during the early days of the American occupation: when Iraq's politicians held their closed-door deliberations in Baghdad, Sistani was in the room.

With the United States' willingness to intervene unclear and much of the Iraqi Army in disarray, Sistani's edict was an understandable attempt to fill the vacuum. Dempsey told Pentagon reporters that Sistani's fatwa complicated the situation, but Brett McGurk was relieved. McGurk had not been a fan of Obama's strategy of conditioning American military assistance on political changes in Iraq, believing that the president had the logic reversed: American military action against ISIS would build up Washington's standing in Baghdad and thus its ability to effect change. With Obama determined to move carefully, the ayatol-lah's actions had built a barrier against a national psychological collapse and bought Iraq and its partners some time. Even General Ghaidan was heartened by Sistani's move. Soon enough, the fatwa would spur the creation of al-Hashd al-Shaabi, known in English as the Popular Mobilization Forces (PMF), a collection of mostly Shiite militias, some Iranian backed, that was not yet an official arm of the state but would come to rival the Iraqi Army in terms of prestige and political power. But when your boat is sinking in the middle of a lake, Ghaidan later told an American advisor, you need a life raft.

Iran also exploited Washington's prolonged deliberations to rush in support. Qassem Soleimani, the head of Iran's Quds Force, had once assured Maliki that if his government were in danger, Tehran would help, according to U.S. intelligence. Now Iranian transport planes began to make twice-daily flights to Baghdad with military equipment and supplies, seventy tons per flight, for the militias it backed. To gather battlefield intelligence, Iranian soldiers set up a small command center at Rasheed Air Base in Baghdad, from which they flew Ababil surveillance drones. American forces had deployed an aviation squadron at the base during the early phase of the U.S. occupation, calling it Camp Redcatcher, and the Iranian drone operation marked the first time a former American forward operating base in Iraq had been repurposed for Iranian use. Iran also deployed a signals intelligence unit to intercept ISIS communications, sent ammunition to the Kurds, and positioned troops near the Iran-Iraq border, ready to come to Maliki's aid if Baghdad or Samarra was threatened. It was part of a longer-term Iranian strategy to nurture an Iranian-sponsored security structure inside Iraq.

TEN DAYS AFTER Sistani's fatwa, Secretary of State John Kerry arrived in Baghdad to try to orchestrate the political changes that would meet Obama's criteria for intervention. After decades in Congress, where he held the prestigious chairmanship of the Senate Foreign Relations Committee, Kerry had a broad international network of top-level contacts and considered no diplomatic problem too hard to solve, to the point that he had dedicated enormous amounts of time and energy in a fruitless effort to negotiate a peace deal between the Israelis and the Palestinians. Maliki, however, was one leader Kerry never had on speed dial.

In March 2013, Kerry had headed to Baghdad on an Air Force C-17 to take on another seemingly intractable problem: the Maliki government's complicity in allowing Tehran to use its airspace to fly military equipment to Damascus to bolster Bashar al-Assad's forces. Iran's cover story was that it was merely flying relief supplies, and after a call to Maliki from Biden, the Iraqi government promised to inspect the flights for military contraband. Iraq's transportation ministry, however, was run by Hadi al-Amiri, a hard-line Shiite politician who was close to Iran and who also led the Badr Corps, one of the groups that made up the PMF. The inspections were largely a sham: the Iraqis had arranged that one plane be inspected when it was on its way back to Tehran after delivering its cargo in Syria.

Huddling with Kerry before his meeting with Maliki, Beth Jones, the assistant secretary of state for Near Eastern affairs, advised the secretary of state to become Maliki's "new best friend"—someone who would call the prime minister on a weekly basis and keep up the pressure on him to act. Maliki received Kerry at his ornate presidential palace, an imposing structure, which was located in the "Little Venice" area of the Green Zone, a lush expanse of gardens, pools, and stone balustrades. Kerry began the meeting by joking about the tensions between the two sides. I was a pool reporter at that encounter, and the opening of the meeting was one of the most awkward attempts to break the ice that I had ever seen.

"The secretary told me that you're going to do everything that

I say," Kerry jested, referring to Hillary Clinton, the previous secretary of state.

"We won't do it," Maliki shot back, speaking through an interpreter.

"You will," Kerry teased.

Later, Kerry told the press that he had had a "spirited" conversation with Maliki about the Iranian overflights. Kerry was blunter in private, venting to his close aides that Maliki was a "thug" and that he did not want to have much more to do with him. He certainly was not interested in being his new best friend. The number of Iranian overflights declined for a while after Kerry's visit but picked up again after a lull, making the 2013 trip little more than an exercise in futility. Now Kerry would be trying to convince his troublesome interlocutor to relinquish power so a new government could be formed and Obama's condition for intervention would be satisfied.

Maliki, who was fighting for his political life after a contested election, had little use for Kerry as well. Sensing the growing opposition to him in Washington, Maliki was reluctant to meet with Kerry until Lukman Faily, the Iraqi ambassador in Washington, argued that the prime minister could not stiff the secretary of state during Iraq's hour of crisis, especially since the prime minister wanted American air strikes.

As the meeting got underway, Kerry sought to reassure Maliki that Obama was prepared to help Iraq and could push ISIS back. Understanding that Iraq faced an existential threat, the United States would be sending three hundred advisors to assess the state of the Iraqi military, which would soon receive a shipment of Hellfire missiles. Maliki had urged the Obama administration to launch some air strikes near the Syrian border to show ISIS that Iraq had a powerful ally in its corner. "I know you would have preferred symbolic strikes," Kerry said, according to notes taken at the meeting. "Our military doesn't do symbolic strikes. If Obama decides to strike ISIS it will change how it operates."

But the American intervention Kerry was talking about would not happen unless Iraq "accelerated its constitutional process," which was a polite way of saying that Washington wanted the Iraqis to field a new and more inclusive government, one that Maliki would no longer head. The Iraqi people need to see a new Iraqi government, Kerry added, noting that there were fears that Iraq could break apart if it didn't move quickly. The Kurds, he suggested, could be pushed toward independence. "Sure, Iraq could ask Iran for help," Kerry said rhetorically. "Yes, but it would guarantee the division of Iraq. We want to help, but we need you to help us help you."

Maliki rebuffed Kerry's concerns. "The situation is not as the lobbyists portrayed," the prime minister said dismissively. Iraq was following the proper constitutional process, and speeding it up or slowing it down was not an option. A majority of Sunnis, Maliki insisted, supported the current government, and the Iraqi command included Kurdish officers. "So where is the injustice?"

"So you think everyone is happy?" Kerry said with a hint of sarcasm.

Maliki responded with some irritation of his own. Iraq, he said, had believed in the Strategic Framework Agreement it concluded with the United States during the Bush administration. That accord called for close political and economic ties between the two nations, and, as Maliki saw it, that meant Washington had to defend Iraq in its hour of need, notwithstanding the fact that the two sides had failed to conclude a SOFA. It was an echo of the lament Maliki had voiced in December 2011 when terrorist bombings hit Baghdad and the prime minister wondered why the United States, whose forces were by then entirely out of Iraq, would not help.

"We counted on this," Maliki continued. "We believed that we would have fighter jets. That turned out to be an illusion. I believed in the security agreement that is not protecting us. We face grave dangers, provinces are falling, and you send twenty-five missiles and three hundred advisors. What am I supposed to do with your promises?" Maliki said that if ISIS attacked the Shiite shrine in Samarra, as al-Qaeda had done in 2006, it would unleash a sectarian bloodbath. "We can't wait for an assessment," he said. The U.S. might not want to strike Sunni areas, Maliki added, but that was where the threat was.

"Obama may decide any day to strike, but we won't bomb indiscriminately. We are identifying new targets every day," Kerry responded. "But the president needs guarantees on the political process."

Maliki pushed back. ISIS was infiltrating from Syria and the United States was not doing anything about it. "We know you have the power and capability to strike. We question your will," the prime minister said. Iraq would do the right thing politically, Maliki said, without offering specifics. "But the Baath and ISIS must be dealt with," a formulation that grouped old and new enemies.

Kerry's patience was wearing thin. Defending his country's efforts, Kerry said that the United States had lived up to the Strategic Framework Agreement. It had provided equipment, but the agreement did not cover mutual defense. Then Kerry reminded Maliki that it was his army that had collapsed in the face of a far smaller force of terrorists. "It folded and let them march in," he said. "That's not us. Let's understand where we are today."

"The army was not defeated," Maliki responded, repeating his oft-used refrain. "There was a conspiracy. These places were handed over to ISIS. We are investigating. They penetrated the army."

Kerry changed the subject to Iraq's stalled political reforms. There had been talk of a law that would govern the division of oil revenues, but it never happened.

"The government should not be blamed for the shortcomings of the parliament," said Maliki. Returning to his appeals for military help, he urged the Americans to mount air strikes against ISIS forces in and around Iraq's border with Syria. There was a lot of open desert there and little risk of civilian casualties, he pointed out, adding, "No one will be harmed."

Kerry said he hoped that the United States would do that, but stressed that he was expressing his personal view in confidence and that his thoughts were not to be shared publicly. "But I am here to bring back an assurance of a political solution. It won't work without a political solution. I must bring that back."

"Please tell the president not to heed rumors," Maliki said. "We will proceed by the constitution."

After the session, McGurk and other aides left so that Kerry could meet alone with Maliki, who reaffirmed that he was determined to seek a third term as prime minister and believed that he had the votes.

Continuing his rounds, Kerry met with Ammar al-Hakim, the leader of the Islamic Supreme Council of Iraq, a rival Shiite political group. Hakim had never been happy that Maliki had secured a second term in 2010, and had been surprised that the Obama administration so readily acquiesced to it. "The Great Satan and the Axis of Evil supported the same candidate," he had quipped at the time, alluding to Iran's support for the prime minister. This time, however, Hakim did not think Maliki had the support he needed. Kerry was slated to visit NATO headquarters after his trip to Iraq, and Hakim said that it was important that the Obama administration make clear its determination to help Iraq with security. Kerry said he would.

Kurt Tidd, a vice admiral who regularly accompanied Kerry on his trips as a representative of the Pentagon's Joint Staff, subsequently reported to Dempsey where he thought events were headed. There was no question that the Iraqi military was worried. Saadoun al-Dulaimi, the defense minister, had pulled Tidd aside and told him that an ISIS attack on Baghdad could take place in as little as four days and that the Haditha Dam could be in danger as militants advanced. Dulaimi thought that the Iraqi Army might be overhauled in a month, but he worried that Iraqi forces might not survive that long without American air strikes.

As for Kerry's role, Tidd told Dempsey that the secretary of state was leaning forward. If Obama's political conditions were met, Kerry could be expected to press for the rapid use of air strikes, and for having U.S. troops accompany Iraqi forces on the battlefield. Tidd added that Beecroft and McGurk had another concern: They did not want the three-hundred-person cap the White House had put on military advisors to apply to the two Special Forces teams training the CTS. There was not a lot of headroom in the ceilings the White House had already established.

Alerted that Kerry was likely to press for quick action, Dempsey made clear that he had a dim view of Iraq's leaders and believed in moving cautiously. Dempsey had done two tours in Iraq—he had led an army division and later had been in charge of training Iraq's military. Dulaimi was part of the problem and had been evicted from the post of defense minister only to return after his successor—Abdul Qadir al-Obeidi—was accused of corruption. These generals had led Iraq into decline, and if the United States rushed to rescue them, he feared it could be a mistake. The Obama administration should move slowly and deliberately before making the fateful decision to intervene. It was the same message Dempsey had delivered to Hoshyar Zebari in August: the JCS chairman did not have confidence in some of Iraq's top military leaders, and believed that broad political changes needed to be made if the United States was to serve as an active ally.

Though he did not share his views with Tidd, Dempsey had already given some thought to the question of how the United States might proceed if Maliki refused to budge and Iraqi politics remained hopelessly dysfunctional. On June 17, Dempsey told General Knud Bartels, the Danish chairman of NATO's Military Committee, that he saw three possible paths for Iraq: the restoration of the status quo; the creation of a loose federation, with Sunnis, Shia, and Kurds going their own way; and a stalemate. Of the three, stalemate was the most likely outcome, the chairman ventured.

Two days later, Dempsey told his aides that the preservation of a unified Iraq might not be the only way to protect American interests in the region. If Iraq became a failed state, the United

States could welcome the emergence of an independent Kurdistan and try to build a special defense relationship with Erbil, much as it had with Israel. Israel and the Kurdistan Regional Government could be the United States' main security partners in the region.

BEFORE LEAVING BAGHDAD, Kerry had some urgent business to take up with Foreign Minister Zebari. The Obama administration had decided to respond, but it wanted the world to know that the Iraqi government had invited the Americans back in. The Iraqi government, Kerry continued, had to send a letter to the United Nations by the next day saying that Iraq was under attack and that international help was needed. Any country that wanted to send advisors or personnel to Iraq to help in the fight against ISIS could cite the letter. If Obama eventually decided to strike ISIS inside Syria—and Kerry stressed that he did not know if the president would do this—he could also cite the letter in making the case that the United States was defending Iraq against an external terrorist threat. It was essential, Kerry advised, that the letter go to the United Nations secretary-general and not to the Security Council, where the Russians and Chinese wielded a veto, which they could use to block action, influence coalition decision-making, or perhaps even carve out a role for themselves.

Working with the American embassy, Zebari drafted the letter and implored Maliki to approve it. The country was in desperate need. Baghdad itself was under threat. It was, he argued, just a letter to the secretary-general that would enable foreign governments to coordinate with Iraq. But Maliki was wary. The Americans, he complained, were being difficult by asking for such a document: What if American forces used it to come back to Iraq and not just to offer temporary help? As with the SOFA talks, Maliki was worried about undermining his reputation for being a resolute leader, even if it meant putting his country at risk.

For days, Zebari was bombarded by messages from Washington asking about the letter, but Maliki sat on the request. Finally, Zebari gathered a group of influential officials—including Hussein al-Shahristani, the former oil minister who had been considered for the prime minister post during the early days of the American occupation; Falih al-Fayyad; and Saadoun al-Dulaimi, the defense minister—to confront Maliki. He could add to the letter or make changes, but the message that Iraq wanted help had to be clear. Finally, Maliki agreed that Zebari could send an appeal for international help to the secretary-general.

Zebari took an additional step to facilitate the American return by drafting a separate letter stating that any U.S. military advisors who would be deployed would have the same diplomatic status as U.S. embassy staff. Zebari considered the letter to be in his purview to draft as foreign minister, and he did not seek Maliki's approval before writing it. It stopped short of an airtight promise of immunity but was the next best thing. Thus, the issue that had proved to be the deal-breaker in the Obama administration's SOFA negotiations—the lack of parliamentary approval for a carefully negotiated accord providing a legal foundation for a U.S. military presence—was sidestepped. Administration officials were anxious about the arrangement, which illustrated how legal requirements could be bent depending on foreign policy and political considerations. They kept their fingers crossed that the media would not ask too many questions.

MALIKI HAD GIVEN no signs that he was prepared to yield to Kerry's entreaties to hand over power, but there was one person Maliki could not overcome: Ayatollah Sistani. As the Iraqis struggled to form a new government, the leadership of the Islamic Dawa Party, including Maliki, sent a letter to the ayatollah stressing that it wanted to form a government of national unity that would be open to all blocs—a plan that did not exclude a continuing role for the embattled prime minister. On July 9, Sistani responded in a letter to Maliki that was later made public. "Given the critical circumstances that our dear Iraq is experiencing and the need to deal with its intractable crises through a different vision," Sistani wrote, "I see the need to expedite the selection of a new prime minister who will enjoy broad national acceptance . . . to save the country from the dangers of terrorism, sectarian war, and division."

It took several days for Maliki to share the unwelcome news with other members of his party. When he did, the message was clear: Sistani wanted somebody new. The Iranians had been supportive of Maliki but also had a deep understanding of Iraq's dynamics and knew better than to directly challenge Sistani. The question now was who should succeed Maliki. The choice of some Obama administration officials was Tariq Najim, Maliki's soft-spoken chief of staff, who was a Dawa Party stalwart like Maliki and could be expected to keep the machinery of state running without alienating the Kurds or the Sunnis. Najim, however, decamped to London, put his phone on vibrate, and ignored the calls from the Americans and various Iraqi politicians. He was a behind-the-scenes player who was not anxious to face the cut and thrust of Iraqi political life at one of its most perilous moments.

With Najim out of the picture, the search continued for a new candidate. Mustafa al-Kadhimi, an intellectual and a journalist with extensive connections in Shiite political and religious circles, had introduced McGurk to Haider al-Abadi while other Iraqi interlocutors also began to float his name. Fluent in English and with a PhD in electrical engineering from the University of Manchester, Abadi had run an elevator servicing company in Britain that maintained the BBC's lifts—his Facebook page described it as a firm that specialized in "vertical transportation"—during Saddam Hussein's years in power before returning to serve as a midlevel parliamentarian. Like Najim, he belonged to Maliki's Dawa Party. Those Americans who had worked with him—including H. R. McMaster, who had encountered Abadi when McMaster was leading the 3rd

Armored Cavalry Regiment in the northern town of Tal Afar and Abadi was a parliamentarian—thought he was fair-minded.

As the administration laid the groundwork for a modest deployment, Dempsey and Austin continued to consult about the path forward. On July 14, Dempsey told the CENTCOM commander that the White House was pursuing two different approaches. The broad approach would not only aim to safeguard U.S. citizens and facilities in Iraq but also secure regional stability and seek to head off any terrorist attacks on American soil. The plan would be to "contain, disrupt, and defeat" ISIS and would involve some combination of training and advising in the field; the use of whatever partners the United States could find, which, depending on events, might not include the Iraqi government; and direct American military action, including air strikes on mobile and fixed targets in Iraq and Syria. The narrow approach would involve limiting the advisory effort to ministries and institutions away from the battlefield and restricting military support to planning, intelligence, and logistics. Air strikes would be carried out only to protect Americans. These were starkly different approaches, but Obama's defense secretary, Chuck Hagel, who had succeeded Leon Panetta in February 2013, wanted to wait and let the White House's own internal debate unfold before the Pentagon made a recommendation.

On July 27, Dempsey spoke with Susan Rice, who had followed Donilon as Obama's national security advisor, to try to gain some clarity about where the White House was headed. Obama saw ISIS as first and foremost a danger to the region but only a potential risk for the West. For the president, ISIS was less like al-Qaeda and more like the Taliban, whose ambitions were limited to controlling Afghanistan. In light of this belief, Obama did not see an urgent need to mount air strikes against an "insurgency." Killing "high-value individuals" would only lead ISIS to replace them with more militants. Obama would authorize air strikes to protect the U.S. embassy and the diplomats' main routes of egress, but otherwise American military power would be used only to back a new Iraqi government that had a credible plan to recover lost territory—and that was backed by an international coalition. To that end, Obama planned to instruct the State Department to name a special envoy to assemble a coalition that could be put to use if circumstance allowed; it would include the Arab Gulf states, Turkey, Jordan, and the Kurds. Obama also understood that any military campaign, if there was to be one, would need to deal with ISIS forces in Syria as well as Iraq.

Unlike Obama, Dempsey understood that ISIS was more than a Taliban-like organization. He and Austin would need to work with the intelligence agencies and get consensus about the threat. In the meantime, the contingency planning needed to proceed. Rice wanted to be able to present a plan to Obama by the middle of August. The president wanted to be in a position to announce his strategy if and when a new Iraqi prime minister was chosen. The White House, in effect, was calculating that it had the luxury of time and that there was no immediate need to prevent ISIS from digging in. There would need to be an international coalition, the Iraqi military would need to be in the lead, and it was important the plan be supported by Iraqi Sunnis. As for the United States, it would have only a light footprint. Rice had let Dempsey know in no uncertain terms, the JCS chief told Austin, that the president had no intention of sending five thousand troops back to Iraq.

7

IRAQ FIRST

Charged with running CENTCOM's office in Jordan, Major General Dana Pittard was traveling in the Sinai in June 2014 when he received a cryptic message from Lieutenant General James Terry, the top Army commander in the Middle East: "It looks like a go." Pittard had done several hard tours of duty in Iraq. His new mission was to oversee the initial twelve-day assessment of the Iraqi forces and set up the command structure in Iraq so the United States could hit the ground running if Obama gave the go-ahead to send military advisors. Even with the modest footprint the White House envisioned, the effort would be too substantial for it to be run out of the U.S. embassy's small Office of Security Cooperation. Much of the responsibility would also be shouldered by Pittard's one-star deputy, Robert Castellvi, a Marine officer who had led a team of military advisors to the 1st Iraqi Army Division in 2008 when it raced from Anbar to spearhead Maliki's campaign to secure the southern city of Basra from rampaging Shiite militias. That had been followed by a stint at Camp Lejeune, where Castellvi performed the more prosaic duties of overseeing Marine installations on the East Coast. A call from the top Marine commander in the Middle East, Lieutenant General Robert Neller, let him know that he had been plucked from that administrative role for more important things: Castellvi was to leave for the region within twenty-four hours.

Even with Iraq in a state of crisis, it took several days for the Iraqi government to provide the diplomatic clearances for the nearly one-hundred-member team Pittard and Castellvi led to fly from Kuwait to Baghdad. Owing to the partial evacuation of the U.S. embassy, there was plenty of room at the inn. The team initially set up shop in an embassy annex that had once been intended as a school for the children of American diplomats when the Bush administration had dreams of Iraq becoming a major democratic ally. In late June, Pittard and Castellvi traveled in uniform to the Iraqi defense ministry, where a cluster of Iraqi officers was huddling before an array of maps in a pop-up command center in which they were puzzling out their next steps. The sight of American military officers in their combat fatigues, a change from the embassy's practice of requiring U.S. military officers assigned to the diplomatic compound to wear civilian attire, prompted some of the Iraqi soldiers to applaud. A few individuals in the ministry were not smiling and quickly departed. Pittard was told later that they were Iranians. It was the beginning of a deployment in which the U.S. military would cross paths with their long-standing Iranian rival.

Pittard and Castellvi quickly determined that while Iraq's forces were in disarray, the fear that the capital might fall into ISIS's hands had been exaggerated. Not only had Ayatollah Sistani's fatwa yielded tens of thousands of gun-toting volunteers, but a substantial portion of the Iraqi Army in and around the capital was intact. The regional command centers the Americans had helped the Iraqis establish during their occupation were functioning. Some Iraqi units, including the 6th, 11th, and 17th Divisions, had never left Baghdad and had not been thrown into the fight. All this meant that the fall of Baghdad was not imminent. The United States would have some time to prepare for the mission that seemed likely to come.

Pittard transformed the defense ministry command center into a joint U.S. and Iraqi operation, and made plans to move it to Union III, the former American military compound across the street from the U.S. embassy. A second command center, which Castellvi would run, would be set up in northern Iraq and would facilitate operations with the Kurds. Castellvi set up his outpost at one of the Barzani family's guest houses on a small mountain outside the city before moving it to the military side of the Erbil airport.

Even before the fall of Mosul, Terry had had a plan to provide some measure of security for American diplomats in Baghdad. If the Baghdad airport were overrun, the contingency plans called for American civilians to be driven to Rasheed Air Base in Baghdad or to the air base near Tallil, in southern Iraq, and then flown by helicopter to Jordan or Kuwait. By June 28, the White House had given the green light to send several hundred U.S. troops to protect the embassy and airport in case an exfiltration was needed. After the CIA reported that ISIS fighters in Abu Ghraib and Yusufiyah might get within mortar range of the Baghdad airport, CENTCOM reinforced security by dispatching its "crisis response element," which included Army teams equipped with Shadow reconnaissance drones and Q-37 radar to pinpoint enemy mortar fire, and eight Apache AH-64s armed with laser-guided Hellfire missiles. The Apaches were based in Kuwait to respond to Iranian mine-laying ships and other possible subterfuges by Tehran, and it was easy to shift them north.

The weeks immediately following ISIS's attack on Mosul were haunted by another potential danger: there were fears within the U.S. intelligence community that militants might try to tunnel under the massive American embassy compound within the protected Green Zone in Baghdad and blow it up. At the Pentagon, a special tunneling working group was set up to figure out a way to foil the potential danger, but there was not a quick fix. Sophisticated acoustic and seismic sensors had been deployed to Afghanistan and to the border with Mexico, and had also been provided to Egypt to crack down on extremists' efforts to sneak weapons into the Sinai. There was a limited number of the sensor systems, however, and getting them to Iraq would take time. Nary a word was said publicly about this situation, which was never resolved but was eventually overtaken by more pressing problems. Nonetheless, it was an indication of the fears percolating through the national security community: the United States had once been the dominant power in the country but now faced an environment it no longer controlled.

To fill in the many gaps in its intelligence and prepare for potential air strikes, Austin directed the air war command at Al-Udeid on June 13 to begin surveillance flights over Iraq, which was no simple matter since its primary responsibility had been to support U.S. efforts in Afghanistan and to monitor Iran.

There were political hurdles to be overcome: Predator drones were directed over Iraq to conduct reconnaissance, prompting the Air Force to rush to the Kuwaitis, who provided the air base for those drone flights. Indebted as the Kuwaitis were to the United States for their liberation from Saddam Hussein's forces in the 1991 Persian Gulf War, formal notification had to be provided. U.S. Navy F/A-18s, equipped with "targeting pods" but not bombs or missiles, also took to the air from the aircraft carrier USS *George Washington*, which left its position in the Arabian Sea to move toward Iraq.

That mission became more complicated in early July when seven Iraqi Su-25 ground attack planes that had sought refuge in Iran during the Gulf War were flown back to Iraq to provide the Iraqi air force with additional firepower.

In theory, the Su-25s were being flown by Iraqis, but nobody could be sure that Iranians or even Russians were not flying the planes—or knew the full extent of Iran's new role in Iraq. That raised the question of whether the Americans could defend themselves if the F/A-18s were shot at from the ground or challenged in the skies by Iranian planes. Major General Jeff Lofgren, the deputy air war commander who was based at Al-Udeid Air Base in Qatar, quickly decided that U.S. planes, which were initially unarmed, should be equipped with air-to-air missiles—initially heat-seeking

Sidewinders, and then radar-guided AMRAAMs, which could strike targets beyond visual range.

To coordinate with the Iraqis, Colonel Michael Mathes, who was also working out of the Al-Udeid headquarters, arranged for two Air Force officers to be included in the fifty-person team that was headed to Baghdad. A lot had changed since the days of the U.S. occupation, when the American military controlled the skies in the country. The Iraqis now had their own air traffic controllers, beefed up by foreign contractors who directed civilian aircraft flying in and out of the country. There were also limits on how closely the Iraqis were prepared to work with the U.S. Air Force. If U.S. forces began pummeling ISIS, the missions would be laid out in an "air tasking order" that specified which U.S. and allied aircraft were to conduct which strikes and when, down to the precise altitude and time on target. The Iraqis made it clear that they had no interest in subordinating their air force to the U.S. effort, and would maintain the flexibility to conduct air strikes when and where they saw fit. The United States was not the only outside power gathering intelligence. When one senior U.S. officer visited Baghdad and climbed into the air traffic control tower, an Iranian reconnaissance drone whizzed by. The Iraqi hosts acted as if nothing had happened.

As the White House waited for a new Iraqi government to take shape, Pittard was concerned that the United States was missing an opportunity. The Islamic State's blitz across northern Iraq had left the terror group somewhat vulnerable. ISIS fighters were not only driving across open terrain but also hauling many of the artillery and armored vehicles they had captured to eastern Syria—which made them easy pickings for American airpower. Once that equipment was moved and the militants were hunkered down in Mosul, Tal Afar, and other cities, they would be far more difficult to target. "ISIL was temporarily overextended," Pittard recalled. "There was an opportunity at the operational level to conduct air strikes in July. We should have hit all sorts of equipment moving west from Mosul." The Obama administration, however, was determined not to make the fateful decision to intervene in the conflict until its political prerequisites were met.

In early August, however, events began to force the administration's hand. After securing its hold on Mosul and spreading its tentacles south, ISIS advanced on a remote mountainous region in northwest Iraq near the border with Syria. The town of Sinjar and the archipelago of nearby villages were inhabited by Yazidis, an ethnic minority whom the jihadists denigrated as infidels. Geography had been cruel to the Yazidis. The area around Sinjar had been a way station for AQI as it funneled foreign fighters into the country during the American occupation. Nearly 800 Yazidis had been killed and another 1,500 wounded in a day of coordinated car-bomb attacks that the insurgents carried out in August 2007, marking the largest single casualty toll of the war. Now history was repeating itself with an even crueler twist.

Sinjar was directly on Highway 47, the east–west route ISIS had taken to Mosul, and was essentially defenseless. The Yazidis had been left without protection by the Kurdish Peshmerga, who had fled the ISIS onslaught on Sinjar much as the Iraqi Army in Mosul had fled. Islamic State militants slaughtered thousands of Yazidi men and forced Yazidi women into sexual slavery, allocating the women to its fighters as a reward for valor in battle. The lucky few with vehicles tried to use them to flee, but thousands more trudged up rugged mountain roads only to find they were stranded without food or water, and potentially vulnerable to the ruthless ISIS fighters below.

Frantically, some Yazidis called their relatives in Lincoln, Nebraska, which improbably had become a major hub for the Yazidi diaspora and was home to a number of people who had served as translators for the U.S. forces in Iraq before being granted asylum in the United States. "My sister was yelling and screaming that they were all going to die if somebody didn't help them," one Yazidi recalled. At the State Department, Tom Malinowski's human rights office began fielding some of the calls and passing the information to Lloyd Austin's Central Command. Malinowski looked up Sinjar on Google Earth. It seemed like a scene out of a Tolkien novel: a massive mountain surrounded by gun-toting barbarians rising out of a vast expanse of desert, with defenseless civilians trapped at the top. On August 8, representatives of the Yazidi American community made the trek to Washington, where they met with Ben Rhodes, the top deputy for strategic communications at the National Security Council, who said that he planned to immediately bring the matter to the president.

In Tampa, Austin rushed to put together a plan. The U.S. Air Force could drop food and medicine to the Yazidis, much as it had done for refugees in the Balkans twenty years earlier. While there was only modest risk in sending lumbering cargo planes over the territory, getting the Yazidis off the mountain would be far trickier. Austin asked Masoud Barzani, the president of the semi-autonomous Kurdistan Region, to have the Peshmerga escort the rescued Yazidis to Duhok, in Kurdish-controlled territory, while Obama's National Security Council debated what to do. But it was clear that the Peshmerga were in no position to do much of anything. Bereft of a proxy force, Lieutenant General Frank McKenzie, the head of the Marine component of CENTCOM, was tasked with readying a plan to transport the Yazidis and headed to Erbil. If the word was given, a fleet of MV-22 tilt-rotor Ospreys would join him and then fly west to lift the besieged Yazidis to safety.

As audacious as the plan seemed, McKenzie's Marines would not have been the only U.S. forces in northern Iraq. In a clandestine deployment that the Pentagon never officially acknowledged, a portion of Chris Donahue's Delta Force, which was nearly two hundred strong, had already taken up positions in Erbil and would later move to a less conspicuous site, which military experts pinpointed as Bashur Airfield, thirty miles northeast of the Kurdish city.

In Washington, Obama convened an NSC meeting to discuss how to proceed. So far, not a single American bullet had been fired in anger. In Baghdad, the Iraqis were still trying to assemble a government. As president, Obama had stepped back from the "responsibility to protect" doctrine, according to which the international community has a moral obligation to intervene militarily abroad to avert a humanitarian catastrophe. The issue in Sinjar, however, was a narrow one: not a full-scale intervention, but the dropping of relief supplies with the option to send in McKenzie's Marines to evacuate the Yazidis to safer ground in northern Iraq if such a rescue was needed.

As one participant recalled, the moral case for action was clear: a buzzard was standing over a baby. Even so, there was a catch. If the aid was dropped, CENTCOM wanted permission to strike ISIS checkpoints to stop the militants from pursuing the recipients as well as the relief supplies. The goal was to help the beleaguered Yazidis, not to incentivize ISIS to kill more of them. Susan Rice, the president's national security advisor, was not happy with the idea of blasting the checkpoints, which could be the administration's first use of force and, she feared, a slippery slope leading to deeper military involvement. U.S. forces, Rice argued, could drop the aid and then revisit the question of whether to bomb ISIS positions at a later date. Obama made the call: the mission, including the air strikes on the checkpoints, could go ahead. As the meeting drew to a close, Rice again raised her concerns, again only to have Obama cut her short, saying the matter had been decided. Obama was known for his caution, but sometimes his White House advisors doubled down on this trait; they could be more Obama than Obama himself.

The air drop began on August 7 when a C-17 and two C-130s flew over Mount Sinjar, escorted by F/A-18s from an aircraft carrier in the Persian Gulf. All told, nine C-17s and sixteen C-130s dropped more than 35,000 gallons of water and—notwithstanding the fact that Yazidis were not Muslim—more than 114,000 halal ready-to-eat meals in the span of a week. As planned, two F-16s launched air strikes on several ISIS positions. As the drama was unfolding, Donahue and his Delta Force troops in Erbil began to receive reports that the Yekîneyên Parastina Gel (YPG), or People's Protection Units, a Kurdish militia based in Syria, was already on the mountain and had been loading civilians into dump trucks, driving them across the border to Syria, and then looping back into Iraq to take them toward Duhok.

The Kurds, it seemed, had their own ways of doing things, and McKenzie's mission would not be needed after all. To confirm that a rescue was not necessary, Delta Force commandos flew to Mount Sinjar along with a State Department official and confirmed that the population there was down to several hundred Yazidis who were determined to stay put. There was a sigh of relief in Washington—the operation had worked, and with only modest U.S. involvement. "Earlier this week, one Iraqi cried there is no one coming to help," Obama said in a statement he delivered on August 7 from the State Dining Room in the Old Executive Office Building. "Well, today America is coming to help." The operation had led to the first use of American force in Iraq in years, and the aid had been welcome, but it was the YPG that had played the critical role in escorting civilians to safety.

WHILE WASHINGTON WAS debating how much to help the Yazidis, an equally dramatic episode was unfolding to the east. Despite their fraught position, the Kurds had used the weeks after Mosul's fall to move into areas that were disputed between Erbil and Baghdad, and to establish a claim to the northern oil-rich city of Kirkuk—actions that risked overstretching the Peshmerga and that were based on the conceit that the Islamic State's fight was with the Shia-dominated Iraqi government and not Barzani's KRG. In early August, however, ISIS pivoted and began to move toward Erbil, which was home to a modern airport and a U.S. consulate, and was a hub for Western investment. An ISIS rampage through the city would be an enormous propaganda coup for the militants, would deal a devastating blow to the Kurds, and would deprive the U.S. military of the staging area it would need for its campaign to roll back the caliphate. Barzani and his aides called everybody they knew in the White House and Congress to ask for help. Chris Donahue's Delta Force troops saw the danger, too. The situation at the U.S. consulate, a warren of modest structures behind a barricade in the city's heavily Christian Ankawa neighborhood, was tense. If American diplomats pulled up stakes, the rest of the diplomatic community would certainly follow, isolating one of the few friends the Americans seemed to have in the region. As the danger approached, American diplomats began burning and shredding their cables and sensitive papers.

In Baghdad, Pittard also thought the situation was desperate. To convey the urgency of the matter to Washington, Colonel Ed Abisellan, a member of Pittard's team, took the map marking ISIS's most forward progress, which was about an hour's travel time from Erbil, and drew a bright red line over the positioning. A number of ISIS fighters and vehicles were perilously close to or even over the line. Virtually overnight, the White House had to decide whether to join the war or move to evacuate its Erbil consulate.

In a tense meeting in the situation room, Obama unleashed his frustrations on Martin Dempsey and Lloyd Austin. Most of the time, Obama lived up to his reputation for being calm and even detached. This time, he was visibly upset. How, the president demanded to know, could the military not have seen the new threat in Iraq coming and allowed the administration to confront such a dilemma? Dempsey, who had ridden over from the Pentagon while Austin was beamed in from Tampa, took the drubbing in stride. "I characterized it as he was very unhappy that the United States military had spent over ten years working with this thing called the Iraqi armed forces, only to see it collapse in forty-eight hours," Dempsey recalled. The ass-chewing was more of a blow to Austin, who was one of Obama's most loyal and unflappable generals.

At the Pentagon, word spread among the Joint Chiefs of Staff that the president was blaming the military leadership for having to go back into Iraq, and not all of the generals were as philosophical about it as Dempsey. Nobody took the setback harder than the officers who had spent years in the country, wore metal bracelets with the names of fallen troops, and had drawn up plans for thousands of U.S. soldiers to stay after 2011 to mentor the Iraqi force they knew was a work in progress. One senior officer confided that he was dumbfounded by Obama's response: the president seemed to be blaming the military for the chaos that had unfolded following the failed SOFA talks and the decision to exit Iraq. There was, however, no time to look back: the question was how to respond before a bad problem became even worse.

Within hours of fielding the request to defend Erbil, Obama gave the go-ahead to defend the Kurds. With limited reconnaissance, the mission was trickier than it seemed. In Baghdad, Pittard had identified three potential routes to Erbil, but the U.S. military had only two drones that launched from U.S. bases in the Persian Gulf to monitor them. As Pittard watched the screens at his command post in Baghdad, an F-16 identified hundreds of fighters on one of the routes that was east of the line, and asked for permission to strike. The force was a substantial one. It would take twenty-seven minutes to maneuver one of the unmanned aircraft over the site to take a second look, and if the fighters made a beeline for Erbil, the Americans would be all out of time. Pittard decided to wait for the drone, and it zoomed in only to determine that the "fighters" were actually Peshmerga. The United States thus narrowly avoided a significant episode of friendly fire.

On the evening of August 8, as the militants moved closer to the Peshmerga defending Erbil, a B-1B bomber arrived overhead and used its targeting pod to pinpoint an ISIS artillery piece, which was shelling the Kurds. The bomber was prepared to strike but was told to hold off. The B-1B had been reassigned from a planned mission over Afghanistan shortly before its takeoff from Al-Udeid base in Qatar. With no time to wait for consultations with the Arab partner on whether the United States could unleash the first blows of Obama's new war from an aircraft that departed their base, the

B-1B handed off the target to two F/A-18s from the *George Washington*. A few hours later, there were more air strikes, by an armed drone and four F/A-18s. The next day, Air Force planes took off from the Gulf after the diplomatic niceties were ironed out. On August 9, two F-16 fighters finally carried out the Sinjar mission Obama ordered and bombed ISIS barriers, armored vehicles, and an observation post, killing dozens of fighters.

When the Obama administration explained its air strikes, it sought to justify them in the narrowest possible terms. The strikes near Erbil, it said, were carried out only to defend the U.S. consulate, a legal argument that understated the foreign policy imperatives that drove the intervention, but that was intended to uphold the administration's stance that a major campaign to roll back ISIS was dependent upon a new government in Baghdad. "This was not an authorization of a broad-based counterterrorism campaign," an Obama official told reporters in the background briefing that was arranged to voice the administration's talking points.

That message was soon driven home for Castellvi when a U.S. drone zoomed in on a lucrative target. Hundreds of ISIS fighters were in Makhmur, a Kurdish town southwest of Erbil, near the Qarachogh Mountains, and were holding a rally that the military figured was probably attended by some of the group's leaders. Castellvi and Pittard were determined not to miss the opportunity to deal the militants another blow when Colonel Eric Timmerman, Pittard's chief of staff, let him know that the lawyers further up the chain of command had objected: the ISIS fighters were just to the west of the red line. Pittard was flummoxed. The line had been drawn to illustrate the situation on the battlefield; he had never intended for it to limit the scope of the air strikes that could be carried out against an adversary that was still active in the north. If the map had been drawn with a fat red marker instead of a fine line, the ISIS fighters might have even been inside the boundary. Pittard called James Terry, who told him he needed to call Austin if he wanted approval to strike. So Pittard called the CENTCOM commander, expecting a favorable ruling, but was told the administration would authorize strikes only on the Erbil side of the line. Intelligence later convinced Pittard that he had lost a chance to hit several ISIS field commanders.

With Erbil seemingly secure, the administration's focus turned to reclaiming control of Mosul Dam, which ISIS had seized in July. The massive hydroelectric dam along the Tigris River had been built on a weak foundation by a German and Italian consortium during Saddam Hussein's rule and had long been a maintenance nightmare. Because water was eating away at the gypsum under the dam, Iraqi teams had drilled holes in the foundation, which they pumped full of a cement grout mixture six days a week. It was a mission that required constant attention, but the workers had fled when ISIS swept through the area, which meant that the structure could be in jeopardy even if ISIS did nothing to harm it. That would pose an enormous risk, not only to Mosul but also to the cities and towns downstream, including Baghdad. Engineers estimated that if the dam gave way, a wall of water as high as eighty feet might rush through the center of Mosul, sweeping away the buildings and people in its path, before moving through Tikrit and Samarra down to the Iraqi capital. The areas in Baghdad near the Tigris included the U.S. embassy compound and prominent Iraqi government buildings, which could face a flood with water as high as thirteen feet. ISIS's capture of the dam had provoked anxieties at the White House. Joe Biden had called Masoud Barzani on August 8 and urged him to retake the dam as soon as possible.

With the Kurds on their heels, it fell to Donahue to organize the operation. The American plan to retake the dam required the use of two different forces: the Peshmerga, who had been charged with defending the dam before the ISIS onslaught, and Iraq's CTS, which had failed to take back Fallujah but had the best training, equipment, and armored vehicles among the forces in Iraq. In effect, the Kurds and the Iraqi commandos would be working together for the first time, much as Brett McGurk had hoped they would just before Mosul fell—only this time the U.S. military would provide the air strikes, advisors, and planning likely required for the operation to succeed. The mission also required a little diplomatic footwork since the Kurds were inclined to the view that they should lead operations on their turf. Donahue and other Delta officers had long-standing relationships in the region, and it was time to use them. This was no time to get hung up on Kurdish pride, Donahue told Masrour Barzani, the son of the president of the Kurdistan Regional Government and the official in charge of its security forces. Did the Kurds want to win or lose? The lightly armed Peshmerga, which had yet to score a victory in battle against ISIS, could follow behind in their SUVs and unarmored vehicles. Austin weighed in with a call to Massoud Barzani, the KRG president.

Pulling the operation together would be no mean feat, and would require some improvisation. When the U.S. Air Force proposed that its Iraqi partner use its own rickety C-130 cargo planes to fly the CTS to its staging area in the north, Pittard arranged for U.S. advisors to be flown to the area on the U.S. Air Force's roomy C-17s—one per aircraft—so that the Iraqi vehicles and equipment could be crammed on board.

The more politically sensitive issue was the military's proposal that Donahue's troops accompany the CTS and Peshmerga forces on the battlefield to call in air strikes and reduce the risk of friendly fire. The Iraqi and Kurdish troops did not speak the same language, could not communicate directly with each other, had no history of cooperation, and had separate chains of command that led back to their home capitals.

Dempsey saw the merit in arranging an accompanying mission, but it was early days for the White House's new involvement in Iraq, and this was as yet a bridge too far. In the end, the military came up with a workaround that involved outfitting the Iraqi and Kurdish forces with communications gear, monitoring the fight with drones, and having U.S. advisors stay at what the Pentagon called the last point of cover and concealment, a piece of terrain that was a safe distance from the action. Every night, Donahue would fly out from his Erbil command post and review the next day's plan.

The operation began on August 16 and involved the use of punishing airpower. First, B-1B bombers from Al-Udeid in Qatar and F/A-18 fighters from the *George H.W. Bush* in the Persian Gulf pounded ISIS positions between the Rabia Crossing on the Syrian border and Tal Kaif, to the northeast of Mosul, to preclude ISIS from sending reinforcements to help defend the dam. The next day, the combined CTS and Peshmerga force advanced as American air strikes paved the way in what amounted to a rolling barrage. Within three days, the dam and several nearby towns had been taken back. The air strikes, however, continued for three more weeks as the United States sought to head off a reversal. All told, eighty-five air strikes were carried out in support of the Mosul Dam operation, an impressive, almost extravagant display of airpower that established the Iraqis' expectations for the fight ahead.

Not all of Donahue's plans were carried out. As it was developing contacts and gathering information in northern Iraq, Donahue's Delta Force troops learned that about three hundred Yazidi women were being held by ISIS at an installation south of Tal Afar, from which they would be handed over to militants for sexual servitude. Donahue and Castellvi proposed a U.S. raid to rescue them, drawing on Peshmerga counterterrorism forces—with whom Delta had a long-standing relationship going back to 2003—and U.S. air strikes. The officers were convinced that the mission was doable and advocated for the operation, though it could have involved a significant clash with the militants before the women were driven to safety. The plan was sent up the chain of command with support from Pittard and Terry but was never approved. Dropping bombs or relief supplies from an aircraft was one thing; sending American commandos into harm's way on the ground in ISIS-controlled terrain was not yet a mission the Obama administration was prepared to undertake, however noble the cause. As all of the deliberations were secret, the administration never faced any second-guessing about the mission that never was.

BY SEPTEMBER, THE new Iraqi government was beginning to take shape. Haider al-Abadi, the UK-trained engineer, would be prime minister. The Americans' preference for president was Barham Salih, a fluent English speaker who had worked closely with the Americans in Baghdad and Erbil. But Salih had strained relations with the family of Jalal Talabani, who had served as Iraq's president from 2006 to 2014 but had been incapacitated by a stroke in 2012. The new president would end up being Fuad Masum, who had a PhD in Islamic philosophy and was in his seventies. As for the speaker of the parliament, it would be Salim al-Jabouri. None of the top three figures in the new Iraqi government were known as dynamic political figures or major reformers, but they were acceptable to Washington, and their selection by the parliament opened the door to deeper American involvement and a full-fledged counter-ISIS military campaign.

On September 10, one week after Abadi was formally approved for the prime minister post by Iraq's parliament, Obama unveiled his new strategy in a speech to the nation. "Our objective is clear," Obama said. "We will degrade, and ultimately destroy, ISIL through a comprehensive and sustained counterterrorism strategy." The United States, the president added, had already carried out more than 150 air strikes and could now conduct a systematic campaign of air strikes while Iraqi forces went on the offensive. Nor would militants in Syria continue to be off-limits for air attacks. In its internal planning documents, the American military had talked about degrading, containing, and, years down the road, defeating ISIS. "Destruction" was a higher bar, one that meant that the enemy would not only be pushed back but also battered to the point that it could never recover, as AQI had done after American forces left the country. The qualification "ultimately" bought the White House some time.

Still, after the shock of seeing AQI 2.0 emerge in the Middle East, the White House had opted for a blunt articulation of the goal. Obama's address came to be known as the "degrade and destroy" speech. The word "destroy," White House aides later explained, had been chosen by Obama himself. To underwrite the new strategy, Obama announced that he was sending an additional 475 U.S. troops to add to the several hundred advisors who had already been sent. This would be a purely advisory effort that would steer clear of the grim dangers of land warfare. "These American forces," Obama said, "will not have a combat mission . . . But they are needed to support Iraqi and Kurdish forces with training, intelligence and equipment."

On September 17, Obama flew to Tampa to meet with Austin and was whisked to the fourth floor of the headquarters for a war council that also included Defense Secretary Chuck Hagel and Joseph Votel. NSC aides had initially envisioned a thirty-six-month campaign, which some officials had taken to calling "Iraq first." The idea was to start by clawing back control of territory in Iraq, a country the U.S. military knew well from its long years of combat and which had a government, however dysfunctional, with whom the Americans might partner. The problem of wresting control of northeast Syria from ISIS would be left for a later phase of the operation, meaning that it could well be deferred until the next administration. Still, initiating air strikes against ISIS fighters in Syria was already on the table and one of the topics Obama had come to discuss.

At CENTCOM, the timeline for the Iraq portion of the plan was extraordinarily ambitious. The first steps were to take the Baiji oil refinery southeast of Mosul, which ISIS had infiltrated, and then Qayyarah Airfield West, south of Mosul. The retaking of Mosul was projected to start by the end of December or the early part of 2015, with the ultimate goal of enabling Iraqi forces and the Peshmerga to secure the country. To carry out the strategy, as many as eight Iraqi divisions were to be trained and equipped, along with three Peshmerga divisions, which would be getting arms and ammunition. The ultimate goal was to "eliminate ungoverned spaces," "restore sovereign borders," and "create conditions for Syrian political agreement."

But there were, the plan noted, an array of risks. Iranian-backed militias might turn against the Americans, ISIS might attack the bases where the United States was training Iraqi forces, and Iraqi domestic politics might spin out of control. A major risk noted in the briefing slides was that "the mitigation measures required due to small numbers in theater will drive a deliberate tempo." In other words, the small U.S. presence and the numerous constraints on where advisors could go and what they could do meant that progress was likely to be slow, despite the optimistic schedule. There was a trade-off between assuming political and military risks and the speed with which an operation could be carried out, and the plan was deliberately shaded toward the avoidance of risk.

For months, the United States' new war against terrorism in the Middle East did not have a name. George H.W. Bush had called his enormous air and ground operation to evict Iraqi forces from Kuwait "Desert Storm." Promoting his agenda to bring democracy to the Arab world, George W. Bush's invasion to topple Saddam Hussein had been dubbed "Operation Iraqi Freedom." Barack Obama had pledged to bring an end to America's military conflict in Iraq and Afghanistan. American warplanes had carried out air strikes at Sinjar, near Mosul Dam, and outside Erbil, and Obama had now promised to do much more to roll back a foe the White House had largely dismissed as little more than a regional headache months earlier. Still, a name said a lot, as it elevated a scattering of air strikes into a full-fledged military operation— replete with newly minted medals, press briefings, public expectations, and, possibly, casualties.

While the Pentagon spokesman publicly insisted that a name was unimportant, Dempsey was privately lobbying for one, telling Chuck Hagel on August 12 that there needed to be a "named operation" instead of a concept of operations (CONOP)—Pentagon-speak for the limited bombing attacks the White House had approved. If the war had a name, it could be easier to form a coalition and squeeze money out of Congress. The absence of a name, Dempsey fretted, could also make the entire effort less coherent.

And so, as the weeks went by, CENTCOM began to grapple with what to call the operation. More than half a dozen generals and countless aides were involved in the deliberations. The guidelines were spelled out in the Joint Chiefs of Staff manual on code words, nicknames, and exercises. Any names devised by CENTCOM had to consist of two words, no more, and the first of those words had to start with a specific combination of letters: either EA, EB, EC, all the way through EF; IM, IN, all the way through IR; or NA through NF. Compounding the challenge, the command wanted to signal a sense of determination and optimism. The history of the command was marked by some notorious examples of how the naming process could backfire. When the war in Afghanistan began in 2001, CENTCOM initially dubbed it "Infinite Justice," only to be told that it had insulted its Islamic partners because Allah alone could be infinite—the name was quickly changed to "Enduring Freedom." Bill Clinton's four-day bombing raid against Iraq's supposed weapons of mass destruction in December 1998 was dubbed "Desert Fox," prompting criticism that his administration had inadvertently invoked the nickname of the Nazi general Erwin Rommel. The Iraq War furnished an even more embarrassing example. After the Bush administration's disastrous decision to dismantle the Iraqi Army and build an entirely new force from scratch, CENTCOM had to find a name for that new force. The name that was chosen, "New Iraqi Corps," seemed straightforward enough. But the acronym-loving American military immediately contracted the name into NIC, not realizing that when pronounced it sounded like an invitation to fornicate in Arabic. The Americans had dissolved one of the most venerable institutions in the country and had essentially proclaimed that it would be replaced by the "Fuck Force."

CENTCOM was determined that there would be no mistakes this time. The brainstorming officers came up with three candidates that met the alphabetic and public relations requirement: "Iraqi Resolve," "Iraq Unity," and "Earnest Partner."

"Iraqi Resolve" was the early favorite at the Tampa-based command and among some of the Iraqis who were sounded out. An internal CENTCOM memo noted that the name "evokes a sense of determination and strength in the Iraqi government, the ISF [Iraqi Security Forces], the population, and the allies." But "Iraq Unity" was a close second, the memo noted, since it reinforced the notion of a nation that was committed to overcoming its deep sectarian and ethnic differences. On the other hand, neither name seemed particularly accurate given that the Iraqi Army had fled Mosul in the face of a foe that fed on Maliki's sectarianism. But they underscored the goal. Mick Bednarek, the general who was running the U.S. embassy's Office of Security Cooperation in Iraq at the time of the ISIS attack on Mosul, tipped the scales in favor of "Iraq Unity." But then the command ran into the reality that the mission was not limited to defeating ISIS in Iraq, and that some Arab coalition partners had urged that it begin in Syria and not in Iraq's Sunni regions.

It was the Pentagon's Joint Staff that endorsed the politically correct answer: "Inherent Resolve." Nobody quite knew what it meant, and some senior officials were not impressed with it, but it avoided any reference to geography and did not seem to insult the Islamic faith. The emails churned as CENTCOM prepared the release and prepared for the inevitable queries, including inquiries into why it had taken so long to come up with a name for the operation in the first place.

The internal press guidance pointed the finger at the coalition: "In coordination with the Defense Department, U.S. Central Command has taken great care to thoroughly socialize the name with the Iraqi government and other partner nations prior to making this announcement." Thus, Operation Inherent Resolve was born.

8

TALON ANVIL

The day after Mosul Dam was back in friendly hands, Chris Donahue flew to Sulaymaniyah. Surrounded by mountains, the city was closer to the Iranian border than to Mosul. But the Kurds' clannish politics had resulted in it becoming one of their region's power centers—so much so that Donahue's Delta Force commanders had set up an outpost in the area. For decades, the Kurds in northern Iraq had been split between political parties that were controlled by the Barzani and Talabani families. The two groups had clashed violently during the mid-1990s but had put aside their animosities to make common cause against Saddam Hussein in the 2003 Iraq war. Still, tensions lingered. While Masoud Barzani and his Kurdistan Democratic Party (KDP) dominated politics in Erbil, which was the capital of the semi-autonomous region, Jalal Talabani's Patriotic Union of Kurdistan (PUK) held the reins of power in Sulaymaniyah. The competition between the rival factions was so intense that each controlled individual Peshmerga units. During the United States' long years in Iraq, Washington had urged the two factions to integrate their military efforts, with only incremental success. In the face of the threat from ISIS, there was no more time for peacemaking, however—and there was every need for the U.S. military to navigate among competing groups, which sometimes offered unusual possibilities.

An important opportunity had been presented by Lahur Talabani's Counter Terrorism Group. The organization's beginning went back to 2003, coinciding with the invasion of Iraq, when the U.S. Special Forces were looking for a Kurdish partner for an operation dubbed "Viking Hammer," to be carried out against Ansar al-Islam, a terrorist faction established by former al-Qaeda members, in northern Iraq. The U.S. special operations community, especially Delta, and the CIA had continued ties to Lahur and his brother, and to the counterterrorism unit they established in 2004. After ISIS emerged, the Talabanis had established ties with Polat Can, a YPG commander, in the Sinjar area, figuring that the Syrian Kurds could be a useful ally against ISIS. One hundred YPG fighters were smuggled to Sulaymaniyah, given weapons and training, and then sent back to northeastern Syria in the hope of tying down at least some of Baghdadi's fighters there.

"We were facing very difficult times after ISIS took over Mosul and was very close to Kirkuk. The idea was to find a force in Syria to engage ISIS to stop them from reinforcing the front in Iraq," Lahur Talabani recalled. Polat Can was brought to Sulaymaniyah for discussions about the budding alliance between the two Kurdish factions. Lahur Talabani also pressed the idea of having the Americans work with the YPG. It would be a modern-day Viking Hammer operation, only this time the fighting would be in neighboring Syria.

Donahue was already thinking along the same lines. After his February 2014 visit to Iraq, the colonel and his Delta team had begun preparing a strategy for a U.S. intervention they felt was all but inevitable, and he had positioned soldiers in the region. The goal was to preclude ISIS from conducting operations abroad by eliminating its sanctuaries in northern Iraq and Syria and, importantly, cutting off the flow of foreign volunteers and especially operatives who could carry out attacks abroad.

During the Mosul Dam operation, Donahue had seen the potential, as well as the limits, of what the CTS and the Peshmerga could do. The Iraqi Kurds in the Peshmerga were licking their wounds after the initial ISIS offensive and concentrating on defense closer to home, and the Iraqi military lacked the manpower and logistical capabilities needed to defend northern Iraq—and it was certainly not going to Syria. Surveying the situation, Donahue saw one force that might be able to fit the bill: the YPG militia that had led the Yazidis to safety from Mount Sinjar and which Delta commandos had observed during their own forays there. On August 18, the day after Mosul Dam was retaken, Donahue met near Sulaymaniyah with the military leader of the Syrian Kurds, a man who went by the nom de guerre Mazloum Abdi.

Donahue quizzed Mazloum about his fighters and his goals in the region. For several years, Mazloum had done what he described as political work in Turkey and Europe for the Kurdish cause before returning to Syria, where he helped create the YPG and was imprisoned multiple times by the Syrian government. The Turks knew him as Ferhat Abdi Sahin, and insisted he was a devotee of the radical and violent separatist leader Abdullah Öcalan, who had founded the Partiya Karkerên Kurdistanê (PKK)— Kurdistan Workers' Party—and had been imprisoned in Turkey since the 1990s. The PKK was on the U.S. government's official list of terrorist groups.

Neither Donahue nor Mazloum was eager to dwell on the past. "You know my background," said Mazloum, insisting that taking on Turkey was not going to be part of his agenda. Then Donahue sketched out his vision. There needed to be a way to curtail the thousands of foreign jihadist volunteers, the majority of whom were sneaking into Syria and Iraq from Turkey, carrying out the brunt of the suicide bombing missions and replenishing the militants' ranks faster than the United States and its Iraqi and Peshmerga partners could possibly kill or capture them. Back in Baghdad, U.S. commanders were focused on rebuilding the Iraqi forces so they could retake ground in the years ahead. Donahue's plan was to help the campaign by stopping militants from getting to the fight in the first place. As a practical matter, that meant controlling the border in northern Iraq and areas of northern Syria up to the Euphrates River, including Jarablus, which was on one of the main Syrian thoroughfares used by the foreign fighters. Mazloum's forces, aided by Delta Force advisors and American airpower, would be the hammer. The Euphrates River would be the anvil. Any ISIS fighters who stood in the way would be destroyed.

Donahue had a name for the mission he was proposing that encapsulated the strategy: Talon Anvil. Mazloum was surprised by the audacity of the plan, but if there was to be an offensive in northern Syria, he wanted to go further. The Syrian Kurds had long dreamed of building a canton in northern Syria, but Donahue made clear that the Americans were not signing up for that and envisioned pivoting south to the ISIS capital in Raqqa after the forces reached the Euphrates River. Any forces venturing west of the Euphrates risked being enmeshed in a tug-of-war with the Assad regime and, potentially, the Turks, who would not abide a Kurdish enclave on their doorstep. Donahue laid down another requirement: whatever land the Kurds occupied, they would need to treat minorities fairly and not abuse prisoners.

Donahue had given the Syrian commander a lot to think about, but he was not the only suitor. Mazloum had met earlier that day with Qassem Soleimani, the head of Iran's paramilitary Quds Force and a longtime nemesis for JSOC commanders like Donahue, who was looking for partners to help spread Iran's influence westward. Soleimani offered weapons as well as financial support; by contrast, the Americans were not authorized to offer lethal weapons as of yet. A few days later, Mazloum's choice became clear. Returning to Sulaymaniyah with a group of military commanders, the YPG worked with Donahue's team to plan the offensive, and a joint headquarters was established to run the operation.

There were three operations centers now: one each in Baghdad and Erbil, which the United States openly acknowledged, and a secret one to the east, which was planning a mission the White House would still need to bless. Whether the White House's approval would ever come, however, was far from clear. Ankara was not prepared to turn a blind eye to Mazloum's activities in his early years and considered his YPG to be an offshoot of the PKK, which Ankara saw as a mortal enemy. Appeasing the Turks would be difficult, since by Ankara's reckoning the United States had gone from facilitating attacks on its foe to consorting with one of that foe's offshoots. Still, the Obama administration had drawn the line at sending U.S. combat forces to Iraq, and a proxy force of some kind was needed to shut the door to foreign jihadists infiltrating from the north. The YPG was an unlikely ally but not a disagreeable one. In the short interaction with Donahue, Mazloum had given the appearance of being a man of his word. He commanded forces that were willing to fight and represented a community that, while not a full-fledged democracy, embraced women's rights. For now, however, a military alliance with Mazloum remained but a mere possibility.

AS THE U.S. MILITARY continued its efforts to train the Iraqis, the Obama administration moved to expand its air campaign to Syria. Apart from ratcheting up the pressure on ISIS, the air strikes had some diplomatic advantages: they were an opportunity for the multilaterally minded administration to demonstrate that it had support from Arab nations in the Gulf. The possibility that the Shia-dominated Iraqi government in Baghdad would allow Sunni Arab air forces to bomb Iraqi territory was out of the question, but ISIS targets in Syria posed no such political quandary. Still, coaxing Sunni Arab states to join the air campaign was a difficult undertaking. During the years he led CENTCOM under Obama, Jim Mattis had arranged for Arab nations to send liaison officers to the U.S. air war command at Al-Udeid in Qatar. Iran had been the main focus then, and Mattis's calculation was that including Arab Gulf states in the command center would facilitate efforts to deter Tehran and, if need be, fight the Iranians. That had laid the groundwork for better cooperation, but it was still up to Austin, Mattis's successor, to do the political spadework with Arab leaders.

The Saudis were "in." They had been prepared to join the United States and France in air strikes against Bashar al-Assad's forces in 2013, had Obama enforced his "red line," and did not need any convincing. The Saudis also used their influence over Bahrain to get more Gulf states to participate in the operation. Austin urged the United Arab Emirates to join the strikes in a phone call to Muhammad bin Zayed, the monarchy's crown prince. "MBZ," as he was known by the Americans, made it clear that he would find it easier to act if the Turks and Qataris also participated. The Turks were a nonstarter, but an entreaty was made to the emir of Qatar, who finally decided to join but made the decision so late that the Qatari pilots did not have time to be briefed on an attack role and thus could not drop any bombs. They were assigned the mission of "defensive counterair" in the unlikely event that Syrian aircraft tried to intervene and the more capable American pilots could not handle them.

The Iraqis, meanwhile, had their hands full at home. They had tolerated the Iranian overflights ferrying arms to Assad and kept their distance from the U.S.-led Syria operation. Shortly before the American-led air armada carried out its first air strikes against ISIS in Syria, Prime Minister Abadi sent Falih al-Fayyad, his national security advisor, to Damascus with a message for the Syrian president that relations between the two countries were still on track.

The September 22 air strikes were a public relations boost for the White House, which sought to portray the dominant American role as part of a broader international response. A setback came in December, however, when a Jordanian F-16 pilot was forced to eject before his plane crashed near Raqqa. He was captured and was later set on fire by ISIS militants, who filmed the grisly spectacle and posted it online. Over time, the Saudis and the partners they had recruited also lost interest in bombing ISIS and turned their air forces against the Houthis in Yemen. The bigger problem, however, was that the air strikes did little to stem the flow of ISIS volunteers from Turkey or hamper the militants' operations on the ground.

After moving across northern Iraq, ISIS had spent the ensuing weeks sweeping through the towns and villages of northern Syria, and by October was closing in on Mazloum's hometown of Kobani, just across the border from Turkey. Mazloum's YPG fighters had kept Assad's troops from getting near the city since they had taken over the area in 2012, but ISIS was a far more formidable threat, not least because of its violent tactics and the inventory of armored vehicles and artillery it had captured from the Syrian and Iraqi militaries. Moving through the countryside, ISIS began squeezing the majority-Kurd area in the summer of 2014. Before the Turks shut the border, a flood of refugees—more than fifty thousand from Kobani alone—had fled to Turkey, abandoning hundreds of their cars on the Syrian side of the frontier. Surrounded and out-numbered, YPG fighters were waging a last stand.

In the time that Chris Donahue had known him, Mazloum had not asked for much, but now his fighters were in desperate need of arms, ammunition, and American air strikes. The Turks had positioned tanks on the Turkish side of the border but had no intention of intervening. This was a battle neither Washington nor CENTCOM had planned to fight, but unlike Mosul or Fallujah, this clash was being monitored hourly by American and international television crews, who had assembled near Sanliurfa, a small town on the Turkish side of the frontier. With the media watching the clash, Kobani would be seen as a barometer of the broader counter-ISIS campaign.

Having dropped aid to the Yazidis, the United States faced the question of how many humanitarian interventions it would take on. As the Obama administration debated its options, U.S. officials sought to counter the narrative that the fall of Kobani to ISIS would matter to Washington's larger military campaign. The United States had an Iraq-first strategy, one that anticipated the overall campaign would last thirty-six months; the hard part in

Syria would be put off for the next administration. The Obama administration's message was that there was a risk in being thrown off stride. Kobani, John Kerry remarked on October 8 during a visit to Cairo, "is not of strategic importance." Lloyd Austin said at a Pentagon briefing a week later that it was "highly possible" that Kobani might fall but that fighting ISIS required "a certain strategic patience." If the United States responded to every ISIS assault that the media was covering, he added, it could "tug you in ways that are not all that helpful."

Behind closed doors, however, Obama administration officials came to the view that their plan had collided with the political and military realities of the region, and that a course correction was needed. ISIS was determined to retain access to the Syrian-Turkish border, along with the fighters and supplies that were being funneled across it, and Kobani had become integral to that strategy. By turning its attention to Kobani, the administration could also wear down the enemy in what the Pentagon liked to call a target-rich environment—and just possibly avoid a media black eye. It was a David-and-Goliath situation. ISIS had an estimated four thousand fighters who were moving on the city with tanks they had captured from the Iraqis and Syrians, as well as pickup trucks with large-caliber weapons and artillery. The YPG fighters numbered in the hundreds. A connection of sorts had already been made in Syria between the YPG and French special operations forces, who were coordinating with Delta. Lahur Talabani had flown to northeastern Syria on a plane with a small French team who provided the YPG with some basic instruction in using GPS and other battlefield systems. But if the defenders in Kobani were going to hold out, Washington would need to help.

To extend the YPG a lifeline, Obama approved air strikes and air-dropping supplies. The strikes began on September 27 in the face of considerable logistical challenges, as Turkey would not allow its bases to be used for any of the bombing operations. The first big airdrop was carried out on October 20 by C-130s carrying twenty-four tons of ammunition and small arms, along with ten tons of medical supplies. It was a tricky operation—made worse by high winds—that required airdropping supplies near the Syrian-Turkish border without flying through Turkish airspace or allowing any of the shipments to reach ISIS fighters nearby. While the airdrop helped, one shipment of rocket-propelled grenades (RPGs) landed right in ISIS's lap, Lahur Talabani recalled.

An important figure in the effort was Abu Layla, the nom de guerre of a commander in the Free Syrian Army, which rose up against Bashar al-Assad in 2011. Now he was leading a resistance group against ISIS in northern Syria and had taken up a position in Kobani with the YPG and some of Lahur Talabani's own fighters. Equipped with satellite phones and computer tablets with a Google Earth–like application, they were sending back detailed coordinates of enemy and friendly positions to a joint Peshmerga and Delta command post in Sulaymaniyah.

It did not take long, however, before it became clear that the YPG fighters, who were holed up in the battered buildings and alleyways of Kobani, would need heavier arms to hold their increasingly vulnerable positions—a requirement that involved some sensitive triangular diplomacy at the highest levels. For Ankara, the only thing worse than helping their Kurdish nemesis was arms supplies they could neither monitor nor control. Meanwhile, officials in Erbil were determined to help. Media coverage of the Syrian Kurds' plight was a consideration not only in Washington—in Turkish villages and in northern Iraq, Kurds could see that their compatriots in Kobani, women among them, were fighting for their lives and the situation was not being helped by Turkish president Recep Tayyip Erdoğan's decision to shut the border. "People sitting at home could see through TV reports that there was shelling and bombing going on," recalled Fuad Hussein, President Barzani's chief of staff. "There was a huge discussion in Kurdish society about what we would be able to do for Kobani."

In response, the United States sketched out a workaround:

Iraq's Kurdish authorities in Erbil could send a small number of Peshmerga fighters into the Kobani maelstrom equipped with the heavy machine guns and anti-tank weapons that the YPG lacked. Brett McGurk had broached the idea to the Turks during a visit to Ankara and then called Fuad Hussein to tell him the door was open. A series of meetings between the two sides was held, including one in Duhok, Iraq. The arms themselves were diverted from the weapons shipments European nations had sent to Erbil. A Turkish plane flew to Iraqi Kurdistan and picked up 156 Peshmerga troops. After flying to Sanliurfa in late October, the Peshmerga relief column headed toward the border, with Turkish Kurds cheering them along the way. It was the first time that the Turks had allowed Kurds to cross their border to defend other Kurds.

For all that, Kobani might have been lost had the United States not adjusted the rules of engagement. In Iraq, the Americans carried out air strikes under procedures that allowed the liberal use of airpower for collective self-defense of Iraqi troops, Peshmerga fighters, and U.S. forces. But the United States was still feeling its way in its embryonic relationship with the YPG, and no such partner force had been formally designated. That anomaly led to some important constraints. U.S. drones and warplanes could strike ISIS's military equipment and vehicles that were out in the open. But structures within the city could not be bombed without extensive and time-consuming precautions to ensure they were not inhabited by civilians. It was a reasonable procedure for conducting counterterrorism strikes at a distance, but it was ill suited to a dynamic battlefield where the enemy was advancing by leaps and bounds and where virtually all of the civilians had fled. ISIS was quick to figure out the rules of engagement and began hugging the buildings as it advanced. For months, Kobani had been a meat grinder. Now it appeared that the American help might be too little, too late. "We were probably twenty-four to forty-eight hours from the fall of Kobani before we said that we've got to open it up," one senior U.S. officer said.

Advised of the predicament, Lloyd Austin decided that the people of Kobani should be designated as a partner force. Mazloum's own house was pulverized by a U.S. satellite bomb—ISIS had seized the building, apparently figuring that the coalition might be reluctant to destroy it. According to U.S. calculations, 89 percent of the American bombs that were dropped landed "danger close," meaning there was a considerable risk that ordnance dropped on the enemy might hurt friendlies as well. In one notorious case, ISIS militants and YPG fighters clashed inside a single six-story structure for a week. All told, more than six thousand ISIS fighters were estimated to have died in the battle. To try to spook the enemy, Delta Force, which was not allowed to set foot in Kobani, had leaflets dropped saying that ISIS militants who were killed by female Kurdish snipers would not ascend to paradise.

In February 2015, the limited cooperation between the Kurds and Turkey did set the stage for an unusual joint operation in Syria. One of the geographical quirks of modern-day Syria was that it housed the tomb of Sulayman Shah, the Turkic tribal leader and grandfather of Osman I, who founded the Ottoman Empire. Turkish troops had been posted around the tomb under the terms of a treaty the Turks negotiated with France when it was the colonial power in Syria. It was Turkey's only foreign exclave. In February, the YPG escorted an armored Turkish column to the site so that it could remove the remains and rescue the small cadre of Turkish troops who were still guarding the tomb and who had effectively been trapped there. The remains were transported to a village close to the Turkish border where a new mausoleum was built. The Turks blew up the old one to prevent ISIS from defiling it. The operation, carried out with the help of U.S. surveillance, was the high point in cooperation between the Turks and the Syrian Kurds. A few months later, the YPG took the villages of Tal Abyad and Ayn Issa from ISIS, expanding their footprint outside Kobani, and the Turks began to agitate for their own intervention.

The looming question was whether the U.S. alliance with the YPG had reached its limit or whether it might continue.

SYRIA WAS NOT the only place where the United States was looking to see if it might find additional partners. During the long U.S. occupation of Iraq, the Americans had achieved important gains by aligning themselves with the Sunni tribes and working with them to reclaim Anbar province and other contested regions from AQI. The tribes had been motivated to work with the Americans in no small measure because the militants had infringed on their turf and the U.S. military brought a lot of lethal capability, air and ground, to the fight. For an administration that was gingerly making its way back to Iraq, the prospect of working with the tribes beckoned again. Brett McGurk had already floated the idea with Falih al-Fayyad, who said that the tribes near Haditha were prepared to fight ISIS and were still holding out in Ramadi.

The Sunni tribes had long complained that Prime Minister Maliki had starved them of weapons and funding after American troops left Iraq in 2011, and Maliki's crackdown on Sunni protesters had only aggravated the situation. But with the wolf at the door, Fayyad seemed to welcome an effort to get the tribes' help.

To set the conditions for remobilizing the tribes, McGurk devised a framework for a new awakening. Each Iraqi province would have its own national guard units, which would be recruited locally and receive government funding. The units would relieve the largely Shiite Iraqi Army of the burden of securing the predominantly Sunni cities in northern and western Iraq, and provide the tribes with a way to secure their own towns and cities. There was no Delta Force commander like Chris Donahue in western Iraq to work with the tribes, but McGurk thought General John R. Allen could do the job. "This will take time to organize and Iraqis need U.S. advice and assistance," McGurk reported in a cable from Baghdad. "What has been inchoate ideas are coalescing into what can be a national strategy," he added optimistically. If the White House went forward with his scheme, the next step, McGurk advised, would be for Allen to come to Baghdad to meet with Fayyad; Talib Shaghati al-Kenani, the head of Iraq's CTS; and Nickolay Mladenov, the United Nations representative in Iraq.

There was no question that Allen had the credentials for the job. As a one-star Marine Corps general in Anbar province during the Iraq War, Allen had developed working relationships with Sunni tribes in the fight against AQI. As the deputy commander of CENTCOM under David Petraeus, he had worked with nations throughout the region. And as the four-star military commander in Afghanistan, he had overseen NATO and other international forces that had been deployed to supplement the American effort. After retiring from the military, he had served as a quasi-diplomat, developing a plan to help secure the West Bank for John Kerry's ill-fated effort to forge a peace settlement between the Israelis and the Palestinians. After Mosul fell, Allen had written an impassioned article for a defense publication in which he praised Obama for dropping supplies to the Yazidis and described the conflict as nothing less than a struggle for the civilized world. "The president deserves great credit in attacking IS," Allen continued, using a military abbreviation for the Islamic State. "It was the gravest of decisions for him. But a comprehensive American and international response now—NOW—is vital to the destruction of the threat." More than 4,400 American troops had died in the Iraq War, and if ISIS prevailed it would be for naught, he told his wife.

Selling the Pentagon on the idea of using Allen as an envoy was harder than dealing with the Iraqis. While Allen was in good standing with the White House, the very mention of his name raised the hackles of Martin Dempsey, who told Elissa Slotkin, a senior civilian Pentagon official and former CIA analyst, that he was adamantly opposed to the move. Having Allen serve as an emissary to the tribes or an advisor to Fayyad, Dempsey argued, would diminish the Pentagon's role and that ˙of Lloyd Austin's CENTCOM as well. He also thought that the idea of setting up national guard units presumed a degree of decentralization that the Iraqis in Baghdad had yet to accept.

Dempsey took his concerns to Chuck Hagel, the secretary of defense, in the hope that Hagel would put his foot down. Slotkin, meanwhile, passed on Dempsey's concerns to the White House, but Antony Blinken, who was then the deputy national security advisor, explained that the White House was attracted to the idea of working with the tribes, which would empower the Sunnis to take on the militants in their midst and limit the need for a substantial U.S. military role in the country. To mollify Dempsey, Slotkin promised to ask the Pentagon's Joint Staff to recommend other candidates. Obama later endorsed the national guard strategy in his "degrade and destroy" speech on September 10, though Iraq's parliament had yet to approve the legislation that would be needed to implement the plan.

That same month, Allen had been driving along Constitution Avenue when he got a call from Denis McDonough, Obama's chief of staff. The White House wanted to hire him, but for a different position: he was to serve as a special envoy to assist John Kerry in forming an international coalition to support the American-led campaign, and McGurk would be his deputy. Obama had long touted the virtue of collective action, which he saw as a way to share the military burden, establish the legitimacy of military operations internationally, and rebut the notion that Washington was imposing a new Pax Americana. "Multilateralism regulates hubris," Obama famously declared. Allen had a long record of working with coalitions within the Middle East and beyond.

As the envoy to the coalition, Allen had some success, not least in helping to facilitate the Kobani arms supply operation in a trip to Ankara that he made with McGurk. During long months of globe-trotting, Allen helped assemble a coalition of more than sixty-five nations and international organizations, including the

European Union and the Arab League. Working groups were established to crack down on ISIS's finances, stem the flow of foreign volunteers, and respond to ISIS's propaganda. A "stabilization" working group led by Germany and the United Arab Emirates discussed ways to ensure that areas retaken from ISIS would have electricity and other essential services, no small consideration since nobody wanted Sunni discontent to be exploited by what would remain of ISIS, or its successor. After Allen made a quick trip to Rome, the Italian Carabinieri was tapped to train Iraq's federal and provincial police forces. The multilateral framework that Obama envisioned as an essential complement to the American effort was established. Still, there was no disguising the fact that it was the United States that was the Iraqis' principal Western partner and was doing the heavy lifting.

Allen's long associations in Iraq enabled him to quietly defuse a touchy situation. In a misguided attempt to gain an edge on ISIS, a U.S. team had mounted a covert operation in 2014 to drop empty boxes of ammunition in the desert to lure the militants out into the open so they could be tracked. The operation backfired badly when the Middle East rumor mill began to accuse the United States of secretly flying arms to ISIS so it would have an excuse to send troops back to Iraq. Allen sought to put that rumor to rest when he was asked about it by Ammar al-Hakim, one of Iraq's leading Shiite political figures, who had been fed a heavy dose of disinformation during a visit to Tehran. There was a lesson to be learned about how to do psychological operations in the Middle East. The one saving grace for CENTCOM was that the scheme never made the news in Washington.

He also found, however, that it could be hard to satisfy all the expectations his appointment had raised in Iraq. Interpreting his coalition-building mandate broadly, Allen flew to Amman, Jordan, to meet with some of the Anbari sheikhs he had worked with during his years in Iraq. He then flew to Erbil to meet with other tribal leaders who had fled the ISIS onslaught. The meetings had the air of a friendly reunion, but the sheikhs became downcast when they learned the terms of the administration's intervention. This time, the United States would not be sending combat brigades to fight alongside them or facilitating shipments of weapons to the tribes. For the sheikhs, this meant that a Sunni tribal uprising against ISIS was all but off the table, especially as in Baghdad the Shia-dominated parliament showed no interest in passing legislation to authorize the national guard approach.

Allen's bigger problem, however, was at CENTCOM, where Austin did not see the reason for involving a former general in a region for which his command had responsibility. When Allen visited Tampa to meet with Austin before an October trip to Iraq, the CENTCOM commander, who had been told erroneously that he would be working with Iraq's national security advisor, said that he had all the help he needed. ISIS, Austin added, was just a "flash in the pan," and if the United States started breaking things, it would be hard to control the flow of events.

Strains also emerged with the Pentagon. Allen cautioned Dempsey that some of CENTCOM's briefings showed the battle to reclaim Mosul beginning in a matter of months, an impossibly fast timeline. Then, during a stop in Erbil for a visit to the operations center Robert Castellvi had set up, Allen was struck by the fact that the classified maps in the Erbil and Baghdad operations centers showed different locations for the Iraqi Army, which suggested it was possible that the commanders were not entirely in sync. Allen communicated this discrepancy to Dempsey, who said he would pass on the information to Austin but made clear that he thought Allen had strayed out of his lane and should let CENTCOM fight its own war. When Obama convened an October 14 meeting at Joint Base Andrews for military leaders from more than twenty countries, the envoy was conspicuous by his absence. McGurk had been included in the session, but the Pentagon left Allen off the list of invitees.

The Americans were not the only ones who were having difficulty gaining traction in the campaign against ISIS and working effectively with their Iraqi partners. After ISIS militants took

Tikrit, Ahmed al-Karim, the provincial council chairman in Salah al-Din, huddled at the university outside of the city with Lieutenant General Ali al-Fraiji, the commander of the Salah al-Din Security Operations Center. After a breakfast of biscuits and tea, the general told him that he had an important visitor he wanted him to meet: Abu Mahdi al-Muhandis, the leader of Kataib Hezbollah, an Iraqi Shiite militia that was established with the backing of the Quds Force years earlier to fight U.S. troops. With graying hair and wire-rimmed glasses, Muhandis looked at first glance like a professor. But he had plotted against the Americans during the U.S. occupation, when his militia smuggled in explosively formed penetrators (EFPs), the deadliest form of IEDs, as well as Katyusha rockets and other explosives from Iran that his fighters used to attack American troops.

Muhandis wrapped Karim in a bear hug, and after a kiss on each check led him into a conference room where he was joined by a man with a cap and a close-cropped beard, who whispered advice to the militia leader from time to time but otherwise stayed out of the deliberations. When Karim later checked the news photos, he discovered that they had been meeting with none other than Qassem Soleimani, the commander of Iran's paramilitary intervention in Iraq and Syria. Najmaldin Karim, the governor of Kirkuk, had his own meeting with Soleimani, who came to inform him of operations he planned to conduct against ISIS near the Hamrin Mountains. Karim found him to be polite and professional.

Soleimani's role, and that of the Iranians generally, created a dilemma for the American military. U.S. intelligence reported that Soleimani initially feared that the emergence of ISIS would be an excuse for the U.S. military to return to Iraq. But he soon concluded that it was wiser to let the Americans do the heavy lifting against their common foe and then resume the jousting with the United States afterward. It was unthinkable that the Americans would directly coordinate with their long-standing nemesis, but Major General Dana Pittard pushed the envelope by dropping hints about how the Iranian-backed forces might contribute to the overall effort. In September, he had told his contacts at the Interior Ministry—an Iraqi institution that had long had close ties with Shiite militias and Iraqi politicians close to Iran—that it would be helpful if somebody could take on ISIS in Jalula and Al-Sadiyah, two towns in the eastern part of Diyala province, which bordered Iran. Within two weeks, Iranian artillery and drones appeared to be operating in the area.

Nor could all Shiite militias be painted with the same brush. The Americans were not averse to deconflicting their military operations with the less anti-American factions like the Badr Corps, whose leader, Hadi al-Amiri, wanted to have a working relationship with the United States, and who for all of his unsavory ties with Iran was on nobody's terrorist list. Major General Richard Clarke, the Inherent Resolve land-component commander, once met with Amiri when his militia was fighting ISIS in the Baiji area. It was an ironic encounter for Clarke, who as the commander of the 75th Ranger Regiment had once led Task Force 17, whose mission during the Iraq surge of 2007 and 2008 was to capture or kill Shiite extremists. But the Americans were carrying out air strikes and helping Iraqi forces plan their own operations, so it was vital to know who was operating where. The odd couple pored over Amiri's cloth map of the battlefield, which Clarke later had Amiri sign for him as a souvenir.

For all that, the Americans steadfastly drew the line at providing air support for the Shiite militias. That became evident in March 2015, when the Badr Corps mounted an attack to retake Tikrit, promising to have the city under control in a matter of days, only to stumble badly. By late March, Soleimani had left the area and Prime Minister Abadi had turned to the Americans, who insisted that they would only provide air strikes for Iraqi Army and police units that were directly in the Iraqi government's chain of command. It was a painful lesson for the Shiite militias, who sought to represent themselves as the vanguard of the effort to oust ISIS. At times they tried to game the system, sometimes positioning themselves near Iraqi Army units in the Tikrit operation and, in a later episode in Fallujah, even donning Iraqi national police uniforms in order to masquerade as government forces. But there was no disguising the fact that there was only one outside power that had the firepower, targeting systems, and real-time intelligence to enable the Iraqis to reclaim Mosul and other major population centers from ISIS. Iran was influential in Iraq, and whoever served as the Iraqi prime minister would need to balance interests in Tehran and Washington. But the Iraqi leadership understood that if it wanted to drive out ISIS, the Americans would need to play the key role.

As for the Americans and Soleimani, they had an unstated live-and-let-live policy that eschewed loose coordination but that led to some awkward close encounters: On one occasion Tony Thomas, who had become head of JSOC in July 2014 and oversaw Chris Donahue and his troops, flew to an airfield in northern Iraq on a visit from his Fort Bragg headquarters, only to discover that his military jet was parked near Soleimani's plane. In the early part of 2015, Castellvi was back in Baghdad and overseeing the joint operations center at Union III when he was told that General Abdul Amir Rasheed Yarallah was on his way there with a visitor. Jaws dropped in the command center when the Iraqi commander's guest, who was wearing civilian clothes, turned out to be Soleimani himself. The standard protocol when visitors arrived was to turn off the computer screens and video feed that showed classified data. Soleimani seemed as surprised as Castellvi by his unanticipated encounter with a U.S. Marine general, and the two men carried on a professional conversation about the military situation and disposition of Iraqi units. Afterward, Castellvi sent a report up the chain of command: he had been paid a visit by Iran's Quds Force commander.

9

THE DARKEST HOUR

In February 2015, Chuck Hagel handed over the reins at the Pentagon to a new player in Obama's war cabinet: Ashton Carter. A former Republican senator from Nebraska, Hagel had been a loyal supporter of Obama and had accompanied him in 2008 for a meeting with David Petraeus in Baghdad, where he had pressed the case for hastening the reduction of the U.S. military footprint in Iraq. Though he was an Army veteran who earned a Purple Heart for his Vietnam service, Hagel had done little to demonstrate to the White House that he had firm control of the Pentagon and a strong vision for how to pursue the Inherent Resolve campaign the administration had taken on.

Carter, a physicist by training who cut his teeth analyzing the "Star Wars" missile defense system, had never served in the armed forces. Still, he brought a lengthy résumé to the post. He had moved for decades between academic posts at Harvard and the Pentagon. During the Clinton administration, with the Cold War deemed over and America still an unrivaled superpower, the wonkish Carter had coauthored a book titled *Preventive Defense*, which asserted the United States faced no urgent perils but had to contend with contingencies that could grow into more serious dangers if left unattended. The problem was not so much threats as threats of threats, Carter had told me at the time. Since then, he had assumed more high-level duties overseeing the Pentagon's chronically overbudget weapons programs and managing the sprawling bureaucracy, eventually becoming the deputy defense secretary. Now Carter had no opportunity to prepare a preventive defense against ISIS: the group had already emerged from an incipient menace to a full-fledged danger to American allies and interests in the Middle East. He would need to do what he could to roll back and defeat a terrorist army.

Soon after becoming defense secretary, Carter planned a fact-finding trip to the Middle East to huddle with the team that was leading the fight against the Islamic State. The war council was convened at James Terry's headquarters at Camp Arifjan. Cobbled together out of old aluminum warehouses in a remote stretch of desert outside Kuwait City, Arifjan had once stored some of the armored vehicles the U.S. Army had used in its 2003 invasion of Iraq. Since then, the base had morphed into the headquarters for the U.S. Army Central (ARCENT), the command Terry led, which not only oversaw Army forces in the Middle East and Afghanistan but also doubled as the nerve center for newly minted Operation Inherent Resolve (OIR). The players at the February 23 session included most everybody who was anybody in the operation: James Terry, Lloyd Austin, Brett McGurk, John Allen, Joe Votel, and Mike Nagata. Carter observed after the six-hour session that he had presided over a veritable meeting of "Team America." Despite the bravado, the new defense secretary left Arifjan convinced that the American war effort was splintered, far too modest, and being run in a way that ignored hard-learned lessons about the need for unity of command. Viewed from the inside, the plan was largely an improvised effort to help the Iraqis and Syrians fight an adversary that was proving to be far more resilient than Washington had anticipated.

The problems Carter discerned were fundamental. The very structure of the war effort appeared to be laid on a rickety foundation. Terry was leading the fight while juggling his ARCENT mission, which meant that the commander could not give the campaign his full attention or even spend the bulk of his time in Baghdad. Geographically, Terry's responsibilities also made little sense. The commander's writ was confined to Iraq, which reflected the Obama administration's early anxiety about getting involved on the ground in Syria. But while Iraq was within the military's comfort zone, ISIS's caliphate did not respect international borders. Chris Donahue and the JSOC team that was working with General Mazloum understood that, but as members of JSOC they reported to Tony Thomas at Fort Bragg and not to the Kuwait headquarters from which Terry oversaw regular Army and Marine troops in Iraq and non-JSOC special operations forces like the Green Berets. It was a stovepiped arrangement Carter hoped could be streamlined. As for the air war, it was being run out of an operations center at Al-Udeid, Qatar, and was only loosely coordinated with Terry's effort. Carter hoped the new commander, whom the Pentagon would be rotating in that fall, would have some fresh ideas, but in the meantime the defense secretary hoped to strengthen the task force he would lead.

John Allen had an even broader set of concerns about the organization of the war effort. During his first week on the job, Allen met with Susan Rice, who asked him to read the strategy as it stood and give her his thoughts. It was clear that a lot of effort had been put into the strategy, though it was not quite as bold as Obama's vow to destroy ISIS had suggested and was drawn out over three years. The plan had nine facets—what were dubbed "lines of effort"—including a Treasury Department push to cut off the group's finances, State Department initiatives to counter ISIS propaganda, steps to somehow reduce the flow of foreign volunteers, and of course the deployment of U.S. air strikes and advisors. A lot of important U.S. agencies appeared to be doing something. What was missing, Allen argued in the White House Situation Room, was a detailed plan that would tie everything together and establish concrete benchmarks to evaluate whether the United States and the coalition Allen was supposed to help form were making headway.

Even day-to-day coordination was an issue. Treasury Department experts, he argued by way of example, might be seeking to unravel the workings of ISIS's oil infrastructure, trying to figure out where the fuel it produced went and who handled the revenue, only to see that infrastructure suddenly blown away by an air strike they had not known was planned. What was needed was a small cell of interagency officials to oversee the implementation of the strategy, and somebody to run it—namely, Allen. Allen's proposal to play the key coordinating role, however, had little appeal for Rice, whose NSC carefully guarded its prerogatives to the point that it was often accused of micromanaging the war. If a review of the ongoing effort was needed, Rob Malley, her senior deputy for the Middle East, could do that. In the meantime, Allen should build the coalition, Carter would attend to the military line of effort, and the White House would manage the overall war effort.

There were already signs that the U.S. military's mission was about to get much harder. The Marines had been given the mission of training the Iraqi military at Al-Asad, a sprawling base in Anbar that had been built for Saddam Hussein's air force. During the heyday of the U.S. occupation, Al-Asad had featured all the accoutrements of large American forward operating bases, including a coffee kiosk and a dining facility that once hosted a morale visit by the Denver Broncos cheerleaders. Those days were long gone. In November 2014, Marines had been among the fifty U.S. troops who had arrived to stand up the base for the larger force of advisors that was to follow. Only a small corner of the installation had been kept up, and much of the base needed considerable work just to make it habitable. When the Marines opened up one aging hangar, they found a plywood command center caked in five inches of dust. Master Gunnery Sergeant Katherine Scoffield recalled that cleaning supplies were in high demand at the bases the Marines initially opened up: they had been neglected for so long that much of the ground was covered with bird and animal feces.

It soon became clear that training the Iraqis was going to be a heavy lift. Basic equipment was lacking. In late December, some Iraqi soldiers showed up without hats, gloves, or heavy jackets—what Lieutenant Colonel Sean Hankard called "a Valley Forge scenario." Others seemed daunted by the mission ahead. Many of the troops had "a very fragile level of confidence" and "had a hard time seeing how they would ultimately push back ISIL," Hankard added.

The early months were marked by other frustrations. The base was subject to frequent rocket attacks, and all retaliatory air strikes had to be routed to a joint U.S.-Iraqi operations center where an Iraqi general had the final say on what strikes occurred, a process that First Lieutenant Samuel McGrury recalled could take anywhere from fifteen minutes to four hours. In early February, a number of steps were taken to upgrade the security of the bases where, as McGrury observed, the troops were the only group of Americans for perhaps a hundred miles. A Danish platoon arrived and beefed up the guard watch. Ground sensors were installed, as was equipment to fortify the entrance to the base. The Marines reported that ISIS had appeared to conduct probes near Camp Havoc, as the coalition part of Al-Asad was known.

Though the Iraqis were not yet ready to march, the war soon came to them. On February 13, 2015, a ten-man ISIS squad succeeded in infiltrating the Iraqi military section of the base. Hankard climbed onto the roof of one of the buildings the Marines were using and then came downstairs. Some sort of attack was underway, he told Colonel Jason Bohm, who commanded the Marine mission. The ISIS assault created a dilemma for the Marines. The Iraqis were asking for help, but reports came in that the militants might be wearing Iraqi military uniforms. "You want to get in there, you want to help them. But how do you step into the middle of that?" Hankard recalled. First Lieutenant Christopher Solop managed to rush some ammunition to 7th Division soldiers, told them to load their weapons, and then gave the Iraqis the unwelcome news that the Americans were leaving but could return if they were in trouble. A couple of the infiltrators got within fifty meters of the 7th Division headquarters before they were killed. No Americans were hurt, but there were other troubling signs that ISIS was becoming more active in Anbar province. The town of Baghdadi, near the base, which U.S. forces had eventually pacified during the occupation, was taken by the militants. Of even greater concern was the fact that ISIS was beginning to shift some of its operations toward Ramadi, the capital of Anbar province and location of the command center charged with directing Iraqi forces in the region.

Allen was particularly concerned about the deteriorating situation in the province. Just two weeks after President Obama hosted the coalition's military chiefs at Andrews, Allen received a text message from one of his longtime tribal contacts. Jalal al-Gaood, who ran a trading company in Jordan, hailed from the Albu Nimr tribe, which was based in Anbar province and had been under unrelenting pressure from ISIS. The tribe was not receiving any military protection from the Iraqi Army. Most of the tribesmen were relying on their own personal arms and had yet to be given any ammunition or weapons by the government. The one airdrop in the region had occurred at the nearby Al-Asad base, but the tribe had no access to that. "We have 4,000 people from our tribes sleeping in the desert tonight without food or shelter bcs ISIS asked to leave their home," Gaood wrote in an October 28, 2014, text. Allen forwarded the information and whatever coordinates he could obtain to CENTCOM, but he was not in the chain of command and had no authority over U.S. military operations. After Gaood went public with his complaints, Allen counseled him in an email to keep his criticism within confidential channels. The U.S. efforts were just getting underway, and Allen cautioned that Gaood's complaints could feed the narrative in Washington that the war was unwinnable and that the United States should get out now. By the spring, Allen was also receiving messages from Ahmed Bezaa Abu Risha, the brother of the slain leader of the 2007 Anbar Awakening movement that took on AQI, warning that Ramadi itself was in danger.

In a replay of Kobani, Martin Dempsey sought to inoculate the media against the potential loss of the city. Ramadi, Dempsey said

on April 16, 2015, "is not symbolic in any way. It's not been declared, you know, part of the caliphate on one hand or central to the
future of Iraq." Those comments provoked a scorching response
from John McCain, who pointed out that 187 U.S. troops had
been killed and another 1,150 wounded during a grueling push by
U.S. Marine, Army, and SEAL units to seize the city at the height
of the U.S. occupation. If Ramadi was worth fighting for before,
why was its security unimportant now? Dempsey's comments also
turned a blind eye to history: when AQI first proclaimed the Islamic State in Iraq in 2006, Ramadi was its putative capital.

Brigadier General Thomas Weidley, Terry's chief of staff, adjusted the message. In a Pentagon press conference, he did not
dismiss the importance of the city but asserted that any ISIS gains
were not significant. ISIS, he said, might have captured a "specific building" or taken photos for propaganda purposes, but the
militants' gains were bound to be ephemeral. "Daesh does remain
on the defensive," the general insisted. "We will see episodic temporary successes. But again, these typically don't materialize into
long-term gains. Our current strategy is working."

The ripening tensions in western Iraq sharpened a behind-the-
scenes debate. In Baghdad, Dana Pittard had pushed to reverse
ISIS's seizure of Mosul as quickly as possible, which meant beginning the counteroffensive before the end of 2014 and trying
to wrap it up in 2015. Sure, the Iraqi Army would squawk that
it needed more time to get ready; its commanders were always risk-
averse, Pittard figured, but Mosul would be the war's Gettysburg.
The U.S. Civil War had gone on for two years after that iconic battle, but the loss there put the Confederacy on the path to defeat.

At CENTCOM, Austin also saw the need to keep the pressure on the Iraqis, lest they put off the Mosul operation. The
CENTCOM commander told Qubad Talabani, the deputy prime
minister of the semi-autonomous Kurdistan Region, that if he
waited until the Iraqis considered themselves to be fully prepared,
Mosul would not be retaken until he was in the old soldiers' home.

Allen and McGurk thought the timetable was utterly unrealistic. Instead of starting with a push north to Mosul, the Iraqis would be better served to first reclaim western Anbar province, which is what Abadi also favored. Reclaiming Anbar would not require logistical somersaults that seemed to be beyond the Iraqi military capacity in 2014 since Fallujah and other Anbari cities were within reach of Iraqi troops around Baghdad. Beyond that, the province bordered Saudi Arabia and Jordan, two allies that were anxious about having ISIS near their frontiers. If the United States put all of its focus on Mosul, it could leave the Sunnis in Anbar under ISIS's dominion for yet another year and might lose them to the extremist movement altogether. "Anbar was the dying patient and Mosul was the dead patient," said one State Department official. "Our view was let's save the dying patient." The American military could make a start by establishing a presence at Al-Taqaddum Air Base east of Ramadi and begin working with the tribes near there. John Kerry himself was supportive of the "Anbar First" plan.

AUSTIN WAS MEETING with Prime Minister Abadi in Baghdad when the first reports of the fall of Ramadi started to come in. He urged the prime minister to order the Iraqi troops to hold fast, despite reports that ISIS was mounting suicide car-bomb attacks against the Ramadi government center, the Anbar Operations Center, and Camp Ramadi, where Iraqi troops were based. It was one of Abadi's darkest hours. Mosul had fallen on Nouri al-Maliki's watch and brought an end to his years as Iraq's prime minister. Fallujah was still in ISIS's hands. Now a third city was about to fall to the militants. The main force defending the city was a beleaguered unit from Iraq's CTS that had had its hands full trying to defend a sprawling city for eighteen months, and now was being hit by dozens of suicide vehicles. Compounding the dilemma, a column of reinforcements had come under fire and pulled back.

In a frantic effort to rally his forces, Abadi rushed to the joint Iraqi-American command center at Union III, one of the two operational headquarters the United States had established, where he watched drone feeds showing the CTS's retreat. Under the Iraqi constitution, Abadi was the commander in chief, but the prime minister was acting like an engineer who was yanking a lever that was disconnected from the rest of his machine. He was trying to halt the retreat, but none of his orders were being obeyed.

As Abadi steamed, Peter "Gunz" Gersten, an Air Force major general and the new deputy commander of operations for Terry's counter-ISIS task force, walked into the command center. It was his first day on the job.

"Welcome to the fight," said Robert Castellvi, the one-star Marine general who was one of Gersten's classmates at the war college.

Seeing a U.S. Air Force officer, Abadi put down the phone, pointed to locations on the map, and yelled, "You! You are in charge of the air and you need to stop this attack. I need air support here and here, and I need it now."

Gersten said that he was working on the problem, but that the imagery transmitted by the drone flying over the battlefield showed Iraqi soldiers getting out of their U.S.-supplied tanks and Humvees and climbing into personal vehicles or running away. ISIS, meanwhile, was grabbing their weapons, vehicles, ammunition, and other abandoned military supplies. It was clear to Gersten and Castellvi that it was no longer possible to save the city from ISIS. The best they could do was to control the damage. Gersten was planning to bomb the captured Iraqi tanks and weapons before ISIS absconded with them and used them to become stronger still.

Abadi objected vehemently. The Iraqi Army badly needed that equipment, and it would be expensive to replace. After he issued the order not to bomb the equipment, however, his soldiers failed to take back the tanks and Humvees they had abandoned, and ISIS drove them into Ramadi. Twenty-four hours later, Abadi had a change of heart. Reentering the command center, he directed Gersten to find and destroy the lost tanks and Humvees. It took two more days and all the intelligence support at Union III to complete the task, but all of the equipment was eventually destroyed.

After the dust settled, it became clear that ISIS had captured another provincial capital, one heavy with symbolism for both Iraqis and Americans, and Obama faced another moment of truth. When he convened an NSC meeting on May 19, the question on the table was about more than Ramadi—it was about whether the Iraq mission itself was still viable. If the Iraqis did not want to fight for their country, what could the United States actually do? Usually, Obama waited until the end of an NSC meeting before chiming in, but this time he opened the session. "We have a strategy problem and not just a tactical problem," said Obama. The president then referred to the war in Vietnam, which had become fixed in the American mind as an example of a quagmire in which the United States backed a partner that did not have the will to fight. Was the United States again backing an ally who could not win?

Adding to Obama's frustration, the United States had not been able to muster a large cadre of tribal fighters, as the Bush administration had done during the surge. It seemed like the only capable Sunni fighters belonged to ISIS or other extremist groups like Syria's Jabhat al-Nusra. "We can't just win the fight from the air," the president added. "We need to step back and ask ourselves should we be doing more of the same even though it doesn't look like it is working. Do we have to look at other options? I don't want a sectarian war, but I don't want ISIL either." Thinking aloud, Obama wondered if the United States should support the Shiite militias as the lesser of two evils.

Jim Clapper, the director of national intelligence and a Vietnam veteran, was critical of the Iraqis' will to fight and asserted that the force had significant discipline problems. "Politically, the fall of Ramadi could significantly weaken Abadi's credibility," he added. "Nobody appears to have the ability to break the stalemate."

John Brennan, the CIA director, also expressed concern that the best of the Iraqi forces were being chewed up.

Ash Carter was worried that the counter-ISIS campaign might

be going disastrously wrong. "I am concerned that the ISF commander ordered the withdrawal of their forces despite Abadi telling them to stay and fight," said Carter, referring to the Iraqi Security Forces. "I am worried that it all could be unraveling. We could think about giving up on a unified Iraq or we could double down by joining the ground campaign."

Austin, who was participating by videoconference from Cairo on his way back from the Middle East, sought to put the reversal in perspective. Ramadi, he said, was just part of a bigger fight. The United States was ahead in some areas—the Syrian Kurds, for instance, had made gains in Syria. "We need to be patient," he said. "We are only in month eight of a thirty-six-month campaign. I recommend that we stay the course and get the Iraqis back on their feet." Austin said there were some things the United States could do, like deploying more close air support aircraft and reconnaissance assets. The Americans had trained two new Iraqi brigades and needed to get them into the fight. They would have to push the Iraqi government to create more combat units if it was not willing to divert forces that it was currently using to secure Baghdad.

Brett McGurk sought to buttress Austin's cautious optimism. The problem, he argued, was not that the Iraqis weren't committed to the defeat of ISIS. The problem was that the unit in Ramadi had been attacked by massive car bombs driven by foreign suicide bombers and there were no American advisors anywhere remotely near them to help. To drive home his point, McGurk passed around a color printout of the ISIS suicide vehicles that had been used in Ramadi, including a dump truck that had triggered a massive blast. To turn the conflict around, McGurk argued for his plan to shift some of the weight of the U.S. effort to Anbar. He suggested placing advisors at Al-Taqaddum, an Iraqi military base between Ramadi and Fallujah that had been a hub for U.S. Marine operations during the occupation. The small contingent of U.S. Marines and Danes who were then in Al-Asad were too far away from the Anbar-based tribes who might play a role in Ramadi.

James Winnefeld, the admiral who served as the vice-chairman of the Joint Chiefs of Staff, pointed out that the particular Iraqi CTS unit that had fled the fight was not composed of U.S.-trained soldiers. "I still think we have a willing partner," he said.

Allen stressed the need to position U.S. advisors at Al-Taqaddum to stabilize the area west of Baghdad. Ramadi, he said, "was a tactical but not a strategic setback," but the United States had to move quickly before ISIS dug in.

Stu Jones, who had succeeded Beecroft as the U.S. ambassador in Baghdad, reported that while Abadi was frustrated with his commanders, the fall of Ramadi had galvanized military leaders. Abadi believed that the Iraqi Security Forces and Shiite militias could still take the city back, he advised. The ambassador was giving his views but also believed that Austin's assessment had been vital in countering the sense of defeat that had threatened to overshadow the meeting.

Kerry agreed with the proposal to put advisors at Al-Taqaddum. He said that the United States should get a commitment from Abadi that he would stand up a force of twenty thousand Sunnis, seven thousand of them from Anbar. They would not be part of the Iraqi Army but could serve as police or as a tribal security force to augment the Iraqi military's efforts.

"History suggests that if we can mobilize the tribes, they will fight," Antony Blinken chimed in. The observation was true on the surface but ignored the fact that the United States had deployed an Army armored brigade and tens of thousands of Marines in Anbar during the occupation, and had supported the tribes' efforts with airpower. Now the administration had forsworn a combat role and had even prohibited its advisors in Iraq from leaving the wire. The conditions for mobilizing the tribes were not being set.

Jones cautioned that Kerry's idea of standing up a Sunni force was much trickier than it sounded. The prime minister had to balance the political cost of arming Sunni tribesmen, a move many of his Shiite allies would be sure to protest, against the potential security benefits. Abadi tended to be cautious.

Throwing his weight behind the Al-Taqaddum plan, Vice President Biden backed up the optimistic talk about unleashing the Sunnis against ISIS. The fall of Ramadi, Biden argued, had gotten the attention of Baghdad. It was a moment of opportunity to support the Sunnis without the usual political blowback.

After the freewheeling meeting, Obama decided to send advisors to Al-Taqaddum and agreed to increase the U.S. role. "I am prepared to resource this in a significant way short of ground troops," he said. "I am looking for somebody to do the fighting. Right now, the pieces don't fit together and that makes it look like a strategic defeat." The U.S. might be able to build momentum if a way was found to get the Iraqi government on board with arming the Sunni tribes and the Shiite militias prowling the battlefield did not interfere. "This also needs to be tighter. We need to do a better job of describing what we are doing. A steady-as-she-goes approach may underestimate the challenge," he added. "It is not clear to me who we are supporting in Sunni land. So show me on paper how this fits together. I am all in. I will authorize significant resources, but I need a clear plan."

Susan Rice was tasked with producing a paper on the way forward with the Sunnis. Obama approved the deployment of U.S. advisors to Al-Taqaddum: Some 450 troops were to be dispatched, a combination of Marines and special operations forces, though the vast majority were assigned to secure the base and handle logistics. Of the total force, only about fifty were advisors, and they were under orders not to leave the base—which they would have to share uneasily with Kataib Hezbollah, an Iranian-backed militia that acted as if it owned the installation.

Later that month, Green Beret Colonel George Sterling and a small group of Special Forces drove to Al-Taqaddum, which was built on a plateau overlooking the Euphrates and which was known by the military simply as "T.Q." One of his first orders of business was to meet the Kataib Hezbollah militia that had laid claim to a section of the base. The militia's vehicles were parked military-fashion in orderly rows, and their buildings appeared well maintained. But the rest of the base was a mess. The portion of the base Sterling and his troops used had no electricity, no beds, and no functioning bathrooms, forcing them to pull out their shovels and dig latrines. Once the American advisors were in place, several hundred Sunni tribesmen were brought in for training. Sterling, who had helped stand up tribal militias in Afghanistan a few years earlier, thought the lightly armed Sunni fighters should be used in small formations to conduct reconnaissance, set up snap checkpoints, and disrupt ISIS's operations while generally avoiding becoming decisively engaged.

The Iraqi military, which set up its own operations at the base, had different ideas and wanted to use the tribes as shock troops in conventional attacks to hold down the Iraqi military's own casualties. The tension was not fully resolved, and the modest tribal force ended up playing a modest role. But Al-Taqaddum played an important role nonetheless as a training base for the Iraqi Army and as a platform for the American Marine and Army units that rotated in to work with them, which included the Army's self-propelled artillery. The base was also used to provide medical care for the Iraqi troops wounded in the battle to retake Ramadi. Between November 2015 and April 2016 alone, the United States treated 350 Iraqi battle casualties, recalled a Marine combat surgeon. The riskiest part, he added, often happened once the Iraqi casualties left Al-Taqaddum for longer-term care in Iraqi hospitals. One Iraqi intelligence officer who had been treated for a gunshot wound to the abdomen and then sent to Baghdad for follow-on care returned to the base three weeks later, so sick from an infection that he was almost in septic shock.

THE CHALLENGE THE Obama administration faced went well beyond Ramadi and led to another series of conversations between the president and his war cabinet. Obama's scrupulous management of military operations left an impression among some of his senior aides that the president was as worried about doing too much and becoming ensnared in a Middle East quagmire as doing too little. "The situation was confused. Nobody would have felt that if they came up with anything out of the clear blue sky it would be approved," recalled one Defense Department official. "We had been at this for a year, and cities were still falling to ISIL. It did not feel like we were in a great position." Obama himself was concerned that a climate of self-censorship had set in— one that he had inadvertently cultivated but that he now needed to take steps to reverse.

In July, Obama went to the Pentagon to convene a meeting of his National Security Council, a symbolic gesture that signaled the White House was interested in ramping up the military effort. Meeting in a conference room across from Ash Carter's third-floor office on the Defense Department's "E Ring," the president told his team he was open to new ideas, according to notes taken by a participant. Ray Odierno, the Army's chief of staff, had the most experience in the room in fighting Sunni militants in Iraq: fifty-five months commanding a division, a corps, and finally the entire U.S. and allied effort in the country. He outlined an option to expand the American role by putting more boots on the ground in Syria and Iraq—a suggestion that ran smack up against the president's initial hope to minimize to the risk to U.S. forces. By deploying special operations forces like Delta Force and the Green Berets in Syria, Odierno also argued, the American military could develop networks among the Kurds and anti-Assad Arabs, secure better targeting information, and begin to sketch out a strategy for maintaining stability in the liberated areas if and when ISIS was defeated—the "day after" problem that had bedeviled the Bush administration in post-Saddam Iraq. And by having a limited number of American artillery and infantry units accompany the Iraqi military on the battlefield, and deploying more special operations forces, the United States could speed progress and give the Iraqis a jolt of confidence. Odierno had let Austin know before the meeting that he would discuss sending U.S. advisors and perhaps even a battalion or two to Iraq, and the CENTCOM commander had not objected.

Challenging another administration assumption, Odierno argued that the United States should step up its efforts to send weapons and military equipment to the Iraqi Kurds. If everything else went wrong, the Americans would still have a military alliance with the Kurds and a strategic platform for projecting power and influence in the Middle East. Such steps had potential political ramifications for Iraq, but Odierno also urged the president to rethink whether the U.S. strategy should even be to maintain a unified Iraq. If the Kurds took the fateful step to become independent, the United States could still have an alliance with them.

Obama was willing to put more troops on the ground, provided that the Pentagon could show that it would make a critical difference while also keeping local forces in the lead, but he indicated little interest in taking on a direct combat mission. As for Iraq's territorial integrity, Obama said that he wanted to stick with the American policy of favoring a unified Iraq, though he acknowledged that the situation had deteriorated to the point where that might no longer be tenable.

After the meeting, Obama went to the Pentagon briefing room and explained that he had met with his military team to assess "what's working and what we can do better" and had asked for "blunt and unadulterated, uncensored advice." Even so, he sought to deflate expectations that there would be a rapid turnaround on the battlefield. There had been gains at Mosul Dam, Tikrit, and Kobani, he noted, as well as setbacks in Ramadi and central Syria. "This will not be quick," he said. "This will be a long-term campaign."

10

COMBAT

The officer Ash Carter picked as the next commander of the war against ISIS was Lieutenant General Sean MacFarland, who headed the Army's III Corps at Fort Hood, Texas. A West Point graduate, MacFarland had served as a deputy to John Allen in Afghanistan. Like most Army officers, however, MacFarland had also done time in Iraq. In 2006, he led a brigade of the 1st Armored Division to Iraq, replacing H. R. McMaster's regiment near Tal Afar. "He's like me, only with hair," McMaster reassured the locals. But he arrived only to be redirected to Anbar, at the time the most formidable stronghold of al-Qaeda in Iraq. MacFarland succeeded in retaking Ramadi and its environs from the insurgents who had captured it by forging an alliance with Abdul Sattar Abu Risha, the charismatic Sunni tribal leader who masterminded the Anbar Awakening. For years, the Marines had been given credit for ushering in the Anbar Awakening, but the early work had been done by MacFarland's brigade. Success, however, had come at a price: Abu Risha himself was assassinated by an IED that AQI managed to plant near the gate of his compound.

After Ramadi was retaken, MacFarland was optimistic that the victory would last. "I am more convinced than ever that having come so far the people of Ramadi will never allow Al Qaeda to force them to return to the dark days of early 2006," he wrote in his diary. With the advent of ISIS, that prediction had been upended. Now MacFarland would need to figure out a way to liberate Ramadi, Fallujah, and Mosul from AQI's successor as the head of Combined Joint Task Force Operation Inherent Resolve, whose resources and scope had never quite matched its impressive-sounding name.

Before leaving for the region, MacFarland went to Washington to get U.S. officials' take on Iraq and Syria and met with Lloyd Austin, who would be his direct superior, at the CENTCOM headquarters in Tampa, Florida. Austin, who was still hoping to begin the long-awaited Mosul operation by the summer, urged his new task force commander to spend most of his time in Baghdad. He also had another piece of advice: MacFarland should be careful not to associate himself with people who were pushing their own agenda—an allusion to John Allen, the retired Marine general whose influence on counter-ISIS policy still stuck in the throat of the CENTCOM commander.

MacFarland had not been at Obama's Pentagon meeting. Nor was he ever included by videoconference when the president later convened his National Security Council to discuss the fight against ISIS. Instead, the administration's protocol called for Stu Jones, the U.S. ambassador, to be beamed into the NSC meetings. Gone were the days when a commander like Petraeus had direct and easy access to the president via classified teleconferences from the field, and MacFarland would finish his tour as the Inherent Resolve commander without talking directly with Obama. Mac-Farland would have to rely on secondhand reports in order to assess the president's wishes, and his recommendations for how to make the campaign more effective would need to be processed through the chain of command.

Carter, however, had big hopes for the new commander. Lanky, cerebral, and generally unflappable, MacFarland had skills Carter wanted, and the III Corps command he led could focus exclusively on the ISIS fight, leaving Terry's ARCENT to focus on the day-to-day task of managing Army forces in the Middle East. "Rather than three generals responsible for different aspects of the campaign, as had been the case, I have empowered Lieutenant General MacFarland as the single commander of counter-ISIL activities in both Iraq and Syria," Carter said when MacFarland assumed his duties at Camp Arifjan on September 22, 2015. "His efforts will be critical in the coming months." Three days later, the four-star general Joseph Dunford took over as chairman of the Joint Chiefs of Staff. With a new defense secretary, a new commander, and a new Joint Chiefs head, Inherent Resolve would get a new look.

Soon after MacFarland took the reins, Dunford paid an October visit to Iraq. Flying in a C-17, the better to maneuver around anti-aircraft fire and make tactical landings, Dunford had planned to meet first with the Kurdish leadership in the north before heading to Baghdad. But after his plane entered Iraqi airspace, Iraqi air traffic controllers in Baghdad insisted it be routed through the capital first, acting on rumors that it was carrying weapons for the Kurds. For an hour, Dunford's C-17 lingered over Iraq until his air crew finally persuaded the Iraqis that the plane was carrying the top U.S. military officer and not arms. The incident was a sign that tensions persisted between the Kurdish and Iraqi authorities over who called the shots on sovereignty, even in the midst of a shooting war. It was the last time that Dunford made the mistake of starting his Iraq trips up north.

In a one-on-one with MacFarland, Dunford asked what victory would look like and how the United States might achieve it. MacFarland, who had worked for Dunford in Afghanistan, indicated that he was still working on a new campaign plan and could provide only a sketchy answer. In Iraq, victory meant that ISIS as a fighting force would be pushed out of the country and would be reduced from an insurgent army to a terrorist organization. In Syria, defining a successful endgame was more complex, as the United States had neither bases nor an obvious proxy force it could work with beyond Mazloum Abdi's Kurdish fighters, which it had yet to arm, and the country was bound to be in a state of upheaval as long as the civil war between Bashar al-Assad and his opponents raged. It was a preliminary response, and MacFarland promised a fuller one with specific recommendations on the way ahead.

MacFarland's early efforts to answer Dunford's question put him on the wrong foot with Austin. During his years in Baghdad, David Petraeus had pulled together a team of military and civilian advisors, including H. R. McMaster, to sketch out his campaign plans. Ray Odierno had done the same. MacFarland assembled a small team that included Joel Rayburn, an Army colonel and former Petraeus aide who would later become the Trump administration's special envoy on Syria; Ken Pollack, a former CIA analyst and think-tank expert on Arab armies and the Middle East; Jim Isenhower, a brainy Army colonel; Michael Knights, an expert on Iraqi security forces who reviewed the training effort at the Taji military complex; and Derek Harvey, a former Defense Intelligence Agency (DIA) official who had alerted the Bush administration that a change of strategy was needed if it wanted to succeed in Iraq.

When Austin heard about the move, he let MacFarland know that he was unhappy that the commander had not run the names by him first. The last thing Austin wanted was any controversy in the media. Austin complained about Harvey, who had had some run-ins at the DIA. A chastened MacFarland instructed Pollack to avoid any high-level meetings with Iraqi officials, which negated much of the purpose of putting him on the team in the first place, while Harvey was frozen in place once he arrived at Camp Arifjan in Kuwait, and never made it to Iraq.

Rayburn completed his assessment, which made the point that pushing ISIS into Syria would not end the war and that the United States needed to have a plan to stabilize the situation in northeastern Syria if it wanted to see the last of the militants. Taking Austin's counsel to heart, MacFarland outlined his report for Dunford and submitted his proposals through the CENTCOM chain of command. When the Joint Chiefs of Staff chairman made a return trip to Baghdad in April, he asked whether MacFarland had ever supplied the recommendations he had asked for. Where

MacFarland's proposals had been sent in the military hierarchy was something he never learned.

MacFarland also ran afoul of Austin by responding to queries from senior Pentagon policy officials like Elissa Slotkin and for sharing information with John Bass, the U.S. ambassador in Turkey. These were the sorts of interactions MacFarland had routinely had while working for Dunford and Allen in Afghanistan, but Austin was trying to control expectations in Washington. MacFarland later faulted himself for not anticipating his superior's approach and resolved to follow Austin's orders. Austin ran a tight ship, and it did not allow for the sort of direct interchange with the Pentagon that MacFarland had benefited from during his years in Kabul.

It did not take long for MacFarland to discover that not everybody was on a war footing. To establish a forward command post in Baghdad, MacFarland wanted to move as many as one hundred of the staff he was bringing with him from Fort Hood to the Union III compound in Baghdad. But those plans ran afoul of the cap the White House had set on the number of troops in Iraq, so the Inherent Resolve commander ventured to Baghdad with a skeleton staff while communicating with the rest of his headquarters at Camp Arifjan by videoconference. The experience reminded him of David Bowie's "Space Oddity": the new commander felt like Major Tom, orbiting in a tin can that was tethered to Camp Arifjan by a satellite link.

To get some headroom, MacFarland resorted to a bureaucratic workaround. The "force manning level," as the White House troop cap was known, did not count personnel who were deployed on a "temporary duty assignment," which the military defined as 120 days. By rotating much of his staff every four months, MacFarland could beef up his Baghdad team. This procedure resulted in some turbulence, but at least it enabled the new commander to put his team on the field and give them some familiarity with the country they were supporting while staying within the limit. Meanwhile, it took the better part of a year for the State Department to furnish MacFarland with a POLAD, or political advisor, one of the diplomatic advisors regularly assigned to military commands to help them navigate foreign policy and internal political issues.

Other battles proved harder to manage. A unit of U.S. Army Gray Eagle reconnaissance drones had been sent from Fort Hood to Ali Al-Salem Air Base in Kuwait to support ARCENT's "Spartan Shield" mission—if Iranian gunboats and mine-laying ships created trouble in the Persian Gulf, the U.S. military would take them on. Tasked with fighting ISIS with a minimal U.S. force, MacFarland arranged for half of the Gray Eagles to be moved to Al-Asad Air Base in Iraq. But try as he might, he could not persuade ARCENT to send the rest. Frustrated, MacFarland called Admiral Kevin Donegan, the head of U.S. Naval Forces in the Middle East, who agreed there was no pressing need to keep the Gray Eagles in Kuwait to deal with a hypothetical Iranian threat at a time when ISIS was still marauding across much of northern and western Iraq. Donegan backed MacFarland, but the OIR commander was still unable to prevail.

Nonetheless, MacFarland was able to overcome some problems closer to the battlefield. Since there were special operations personnel spread across Syria and Iraq, he had the idea of establishing a headquarters for them in an empty warehouse adjacent to his own rear headquarters at Camp Arifjan. The move, he thought, would help the special operations forces coordinate among themselves, and would make it easier for MacFarland to integrate them into his own plans. The Camp Arifjan fire marshal, however, vetoed the idea because the warehouse lacked a sprinkler system. So MacFarland ordered that the tents his staff had brought from Fort Hood be set up in the motor pool parking lot as an alternative. And, after much effort, MacFarland also prevailed in his quest to secure direct control over the numerous contractors the Americans were sending in to fix up the bases they would occupy in Iraq. It took many appeals before ARCENT ceded that responsibility to MacFarland's task force. Taking over the war against ISIS, a MacFarland aide quipped, was like a messy divorce in which your ex-wife was still clinging to the checkbook.

The bigger challenge was more fundamental: finding a way to speed up the "by, with, and through" strategy of relying on local forces to do the brunt of the fighting while supporting them with U.S. and coalition advisors and firepower. The problem was evident to Colonel Scott Naumann, the commander of an Army brigade from the 10th Mountain Division that was overseeing the advisory effort under MacFarland. The Obama administration had signed off on using Al-Taqaddum, but there was only so much the United States could do from the base since the advisors were not allowed to leave it. The Iraqi fight to reclaim Ramadi was dragging on because U.S. advisors were not where they needed to be to help. Naumann put together a plan that MacFarland developed further and sent to CENTCOM with his imprimatur.

The Inherent Resolve commanders sought the authority to have U.S. and coalition advisors accompany Iraqi Army brigades and CTS battalions on the battlefield. With the advisors constrained to operating inside the wire, MacFarland's officers were forced to rely on reports from Iraqi field commanders, which were not always reliable, or on overhead imagery. By accompanying Iraqi forces, the United States could provide air, artillery, and other firepower more quickly and identify the obstacles that were slowing down the campaign. An important element of MacFarland's proposal was the authority to use Apache attack helicopters as needed.

The Apaches had been stationed at the Baghdad airport since the early days of the campaign, when the CIA became concerned that ISIS might make a run on the capital and therefore diverted some of the Apaches from the Spartan Shield mission in Kuwait. Unless the airport was genuinely in danger, the Apaches were not to attack the enemy. When Ramadi fell to ISIS in May 2015, CENTCOM kept the Apaches on the sidelines, to the great frustration of John Allen, who believed they could have been used to repel the militants' advance. The Pentagon had been worried about a Black Hawk Down scenario in which a chopper might be shot down and its crew captured.

The restrictions made no sense to MacFarland, and he put considerable work into plans to get them into the fight. The Iraqi Army did not like to fight at night, when the Apaches could operate with the least risk. But MacFarland could use the Apaches safely nonetheless by employing them along with small teams of U.S. advisors who would accompany select Iraqi brigades on the battlefield and call in Hellfire missile strikes. The Apaches would not cross the front line, but they could provide firepower for any Iraqi units that needed it and could escort medevac helicopters as well. Quick reaction force teams were already stationed in Iraq to rescue pilots in case a U.S. warplane was shot down, and they would do the same if an Apache was lost. MacFarland presented the idea to Prime Minister Abadi, who had one important reservation. If the Apaches were positioned at Al-Taqaddum, there was a risk of a confrontation with Kataib Hezbollah, and the last thing Abadi wanted was a clash between American forces supporting the Iraqi Army and CTS and Shiite militias trained and equipped by Iran. MacFarland had a workaround for that problem: he would base the Apaches at Al-Asad, well away from the cluster of PMF forces east of Ramadi and Fallujah. MacFarland pitched his idea for the use of the Apaches along with an appeal to deploy advisors alongside the Iraqis on the battlefield. He would wait for months for a response from his own government.

In November 2015, John Allen resigned his post and handed off his responsibilities to his deputy, Brett McGurk. During his thirteen months on the job, Allen had succeeded in building a substantial coalition. For all that, he had been deeply frustrated by the impossibility of convincing the White House of the need for a war czar. The lack of an overarching plan that tightly coordinated the economic, information, and military lines of operation, he told confidants, meant the administration was pursuing a "suboptimal campaign," and the persistent friction with the Pentagon was not helping. In an exit interview with Obama, Allen told the president that he had been assailed by Senator John McCain and others for not having a counter-ISIS strategy. The criticism, Allen said, was unfair. But what the administration was still lacking was a detailed plan for U.S. and allied efforts and a system for implementing it. The war could not be fought by convening meetings of the NSC principals and deputies every time a decision needed to be made. The White House responded by directing that Rob Malley, the senior director on the NSC for the Middle East, review and oversee the strategy, which was not the sort of management Allen had in mind.

IN EARLY OCTOBER, MacFarland was briefed on what was to be the first major raid by JSOC commandos in Iraq since the 2011 pullout. Since the United States resumed its military involvement in the summer of 2014, Delta Force operators had been mounting occasional raids in Syria, planning campaigns with Mazloum Abdi, and working with the counterterrorism forces the Iraqi Kurds had fielded. It was, by design, a war in the shadows, one that rarely broke into the open and had resulted in misses as well as hits. In their first foray into Syria since 2008, Chris Donahue's Delta commandos had raided a hideout near Raqqa in July 2014 in an attempt to find James Foley, a freelance journalist who was abducted by ISIS and later beheaded in Syria, and Kayla Mueller, an aid worker who was later taken by Abu Bakr al-Baghdadi as his personal property—only to discover they had been moved just days before. Nearly a year later, in May 2015, another Delta strike force had flown from their base near Erbil to Syria on CV-22 Ospreys and MH-60 Black Hawk helicopters to capture Abu Sayyaf, described as ISIS's "emir of oil and gas" and a pivotal figure in financing the organization. Abu Sayyaf was killed in the assault, but his wife and a Yazidi woman were flown back to Iraq. More important, seven terabytes of data were seized. The Pentagon was eager to have some good news to announce, and Ash Carter put out a press release disclosing the find the next day. That raid told the Americans a lot about ISIS's inner workings, including how the militants' wives passed messages on social media, figuring the coalition would not be wise to their communications. There was much gnashing of teeth at the Special Operations Command in Tampa and JSOC at Fort Bragg when information about the wives' network made it into the media weeks later. Nonetheless, the raid was counted as a success, though there had been no similar raids in Iraq.

The operation that Delta Force briefed MacFarland on would be the first raid on the Iraqi side of the border since Inherent Resolve had begun a year earlier. The Kurds had information that twenty of their Peshmerga were being held in an ISIS prison in Hawija, a Sunni town west of Kirkuk that was under the dominion of ISIS, and were about to be massacred. Time appeared to be of the essence, and the Americans wanted to stand by an important ally. The plan was to carry out a surprise rescue mission and quickly leave. Five Black Hawk and MH-47 Chinook helicopters of the 160th Special Operations Aviation Regiment would fly in a rescue force of Kurdish special operators and their Delta advisors. MacFarland had been briefed that the commandos would form an outer cordon and protect the landing zone but would not participate in the assault, which was to be carried out by Masrour Barzani's counterterrorism force. Despite Carter's effort to streamline operations, MacFarland was never given direct authority over the secretive world of JSOC raids. It was agreed, however, that Mac-Farland would be briefed in advance on major JSOC operations and could "red card" any raids he thought were ill-advised. Mac-Farland signed off on the October 2015 operation, as did Carter, who informed the White House. It was, strictly speaking, an advisory mission but with this difference: Americans and their Kurdish allies would be venturing into a fiercely defended ISIS stronghold. ISIS had recently executed eleven young men who were sons or relatives of Iraqi police officers and soldiers, and displayed their bodies on a nearby bridge, so a fight was to be expected.

Stu Jones had been instructed to notify Abadi before the raid, which was a politically sensitive operation for a Shia-dominated government that sought to protect Iraqi sovereignty. Jones repeatedly called the prime minister's office but was told he was not available. Finally, with the operation just hours away, Jones and MacFarland notified the Iraqi defense minister, Khalid al-Obeidi, a Sunni from Mosul with whom the Americans worked closely but who was hardly in the prime minister's inner circle. For months, the Iraqi prime minister had placated hard-line Shiite critics by downplaying the American role in fighting ISIS and stressing that U.S. forces were merely mentoring the Iraqi military. Now U.S. commandos were battling militants in a sizable Iraqi town without Abadi's knowledge. There was no more sensitive issue in Iraqi politics than respect for Iraqi sovereignty. Moving ahead without the prime minister's permission would make him vulnerable to the charge from the Sadrists and a chorus of Iranian-backed politicians that he was weak and that the Americans had stepped over the line.

The operation began on October 22, when the United States bombed the bridge near Hawija to block the Islamic State's ability to send reinforcements. The ISIS prison itself was in a walled compound that had been owned by a local doctor and that residents of the town simply knew as "Prison No. 8." Kurdish commandos initially took the lead but were quickly pinned down as the raid turned into a firefight. Alarmed that the in-and-out operation could bog down, Master Sergeant Joshua Wheeler rushed forward, only to be shot in the neck and fatally wounded.

When the prisoners were freed, the Kurds were stunned to see that no Peshmerga fighters were among them. Instead they found sixty-nine Iraqi prisoners, whom they whisked away to Erbil along with half a dozen captured ISIS fighters. In a year of misfortunes, the detainees were the luckiest men in Iraq: if the Americans and Kurds had known that only locals had been jailed, they would never have mounted the operation. It was the opposite of a friendly-fire episode; civilians had been rescued by mistake. As for the Peshmerga, Kurdish intelligence later concluded they had been quietly moved to Mosul before the mission got underway.

Even if it had been carried out with lightning speed, the operation would have been all but impossible to hide. After whisking the former prisoners to safety, an F-15E had dropped a bomb on the prison. I was tipped off by Abu Malik at *The New York Times*'s Baghdad bureau, who seemed to know everybody who was worth knowing in Iraq, and initially thought the story was almost too fantastic to chase. But when I called Najmaldin Karim, the governor of Kirkuk province, he told me that Kurdish intelligence had informed him the account was true. "They cut off roads and raided the place," he said. ISIS's ruthless rule would continue in Hawija for another eighteen months, but Prison No. 8 would not be part of it. Only later that day did I learn about Wheeler's death.

MacFarland flew unannounced to Erbil for the "fallen angel" ceremony in which the casket with Wheeler's remains was loaded onto a cargo plane and flown to the United States. The Hawija mission had not unfolded as MacFarland had expected, but the general did not second-guess the on-scene Delta commander. The coalition had suffered other casualties: a Canadian soldier had been killed in northern Iraq in March in a friendly-fire incident, and there was also the Jordanian pilot who had been burned to death by ISIS after his plane crashed in Syria. Still, it was the first time that a U.S. serviceman had been killed in action since Obama sent troops back into Iraq. Far from flexing its muscles and casting the episode as a renewed push to roll back the caliphate, the Pentagon portrayed it as an exception. "This was a unique circumstance in which very close partners made a specific request for our assistance," Peter Cook, Ash Carter's spokesman, said. "I would not suggest that this is something that's going to now happen on a regular basis." For all the frustration with the slow pace of the campaign, reassuring the American public that the military's intervention would be virtually cost-free seemed to be a higher priority for the Pentagon's public affairs team than striking fear into the hearts of the enemy.

Days after the operation, I flew to Erbil, preparing to embed for what was to be the Kurds' largest battle to date against ISIS: the long-awaited push to retake Sinjar. As it became clear that the waiting game was going to last a little longer, I asked Masrour Barzani's aide if I might see the now-freed prisoners from Hawija, who had been kept from public view. The next day, I drove north to Salah al-Din, a mountain town north of the Kurdish capital, to meet four of the former detainees and, over sweetened tea, hear a firsthand account of life under the Islamic State. One, Muhammad Hassan Abdullah al-Jabouri, a police officer who had worked with the American soldiers during the U.S. occupation, spoke some basic English. The rest spoke in Arabic, which meant the Kurds needed to come up with two interpreters: one to translate their accounts into Kurdish and yet another to translate from Kurdish to English. Tinker to Evers to Chance.

ISIS had run Hawija with an iron fist from the day it stormed into the town in 2014. It was a world in which some Iraqi Sunnis brutally imposed their will on fellow Iraqi Sunnis. When the militants barged in, they had gone house to house, seizing weapons and money. Disarmed and impoverished, Sunni men in the town were offered $50 if they joined the invaders. Trying to leave the Islamic State's "area of control" was forbidden, and Hawija's residents were subject to an array of exacting restrictions. Local residents were told down to tiny details what to wear—the cuffs of men's trousers had to be rolled up over the ankle—and precisely how to position their hands and fingers when praying. Disobedience or carelessness in following the rules stirred suspicion. Anybody who had served in the Iraqi police or army, or who might have had contact with Americans or Kurds, no matter how long ago, was thrown in prison. There, new prisoners were subject to a methodical program of abuse: electrically shocked, beaten with hoses, smothered with plastic bags until they lost consciousness. Food was meager: pieces of bread pushed through cell doors.

Prisoners were kept in their cells day and night, and the rooms were jammed. The Islamic State's messaging was relentless: television sets played videos of beheadings, which the captives were forced to watch.

Jabouri's troubles had begun when his younger brother, who taught English, came under suspicion and escaped from the town. In retaliation, ISIS detained Jabouri, three of his other brothers, his cousins, and his eighty-year-old father. After a week, all but one was set free: an older brother was killed as a warning to the family. The family was told never to mention the killing, but soon the militants came looking for Jabouri again. After confiscating his cell phone, the militants discovered contact numbers for two American soldiers who had worked with the Iraqi police in Hawija in 2008, which was enough to land him back in jail.

Saad Khalif Ali Faraj, a thirty-two-year-old police officer, came under suspicion because one of his two wives, the mother of five of his children, was Kurdish. His brother had already attracted the attention of the militants and had been beheaded. "They gave me his head, not his body," he recalled. Accused of supplying information to the Peshmerga, Faraj was jailed by the Islamic State and ordered to divorce his Kurdish wife, which he refused to do. Told by ISIS guards that he, too, was facing execution, Faraj wrote a letter to a nephew, urging the nephew not to risk his safety by going in search of him. "I told him: 'Look after your brothers and your family,'" he recalled. "'Don't go out looking for me. They will kill me. Do not look for me.'"

As I prepared to leave, Jabouri asked if he could make a statement: he was grateful for being rescued and dismayed that Joshua Wheeler had sacrificed his life in the operation. The deeper moral of the story, I thought, was that there were Iraqi Sunnis, perhaps many of them, who chafed at ISIS's draconian rule and would be glad to see them crushed. I tried to insert that thought into a "Reporter's Notebook" the *Times* asked me to write, but it was struck by an editor who thought it was editorializing.

As grateful as the former prisoners were for their narrow

escape, the episode also created some problems in Washington. On October 30, President Obama called Prime Minister Abadi to make amends for the failure to notify him about the raid and assured him that there would not be a repeat. But the White House struggled with how to explain the episode at home, as it punctured a hole in Obama's pledge in his September 2014 "degrade and destroy" speech that he would not send American forces back into ground combat. The day the president sought to reassure the Iraqi prime minister, Josh Earnest, the White House press secretary, insisted in the face of a barrage of skeptical questions that neither the Hawija operation nor a fresh decision to send fifty American Delta Force commandos into Syria to support the Talon Anvil operation—the first American troops ever officially deployed in the country—reflected an expansion of the "train, advise, and assist" mission. "These forces do not have a combat mission," Earnest said. "The mission hasn't changed."

In Baghdad, Colonel Steve Warren, an Army spokesman, decided that the best way to deal with the question was to meet it head-on. Warren had been dispatched to Baghdad to serve as MacFarland's spokesman after the White House determined that it needed to improve its strategic communications. It was a challenging assignment—one that required explaining the war to an American audience without running afoul of Iraqi sensitivities. Warren figured that if Earnest and Cook felt constrained from calling things as they were, he would take the heat and put an end to the persistent questions from the media about the "c-word": combat. Before joining a weekly teleconference with Pentagon reporters, Warren consulted with MacFarland and asked if he thought the U.S. military was engaging in combat. Fresh from his ramp ceremony for Wheeler, the general said he did.

"We're in combat," Warren later said to the reporters. "That's why we all carry guns. That's why we all get combat patches when we leave here. That's why we all receive imminent danger pay. So, of course it's combat." The burst of candor ended up as a segment on Comedy Central in which it was contrasted with the staid recitals of the party line at the Pentagon and White House. The White House press operation let Warren know that he considered his comments to be highly problematic. Worried that this blunt message might be his last, Warren reached out to his former boss, John Kirby, a retired Navy rear admiral who had left the Pentagon to serve as Kerry's spokesman at the State Department. "I think you are okay," Kirby responded. These were not the strongest words of reassurance. Warren, who had long before abandoned any idea of climbing the greasy pole, was stoic about the exchange, but the episode was telling. If the White House was still anxious to maintain its distance from anything that smacked of a ground war, how was MacFarland going to secure support for sending Apache gunships and U.S. advisors onto the battlefield?

11

DWELLER

In the year and a half that followed the fall of Mosul, the Kurds separated the northern tier of Iraq from the ISIS-controlled lands to the south by a long line of trenches, sand berms, barbed wire, and fortified outposts. Manned by Peshmerga fighters, the outposts stretching from Sinjar to Mosul to Kirkuk looked like a scene from World War I. During a visit I made to Mount Alfaf, overlooking Mosul, a small band of Peshmerga were augmented by an unusual assortment of allies, including Kurds from Iran and a small number of volunteers from Scotland and Eastern Europe. It was a polyglot coalition of the willing. In Baghdad, MacFarland sought to explore the "by, with, and through" strategy by looking for ways to bring in Apaches and have U.S. troops accompany proxy forces on the battlefield in Ramadi and beyond. But in the north the Iraqi Kurds and their American allies were preparing to claw some territory back within their existing mandate. Mosul was as yet too formidable to approach, but the Kurds and their Yazidi partners still had their eyes on retaking Sinjar, which had been occupied by the jihadists since the earliest days of their push into Iraq.

Sinjar was in disrepair. The city's Yazidi population had fled, leaving behind a maze of battered neighborhoods occupied by militants who had fortified their redoubts with tunnels, belts of

IEDs, booby-trapped houses, and a long line of concrete T-walls they used to shield themselves from sniper fire coming from the Kurds and Yazidis at the top of Mount Sinjar. On the outskirts of the town, a mannequin that ISIS had outfitted in a military uniform as a decoy stood watch over the apocalyptic landscape. Some of the biggest dangers were not visible. According to U.S. Army intelligence, ISIS had spent much of its time building a tunnel system that connected houses, provided protection for the fighters, and functioned as an underground system of command and control. Lined with sandbags, the tunnels were about the height of a militant and were filled with ammunition, prescription drugs, blankets, and electrical wires. There were thirty to forty of them, and they were intended to enable ISIS fighters to pop up when least expected.

Sinjar's occupation astride Highway 47 had allowed trucks to ferry fighters and supplies to Mosul ever since ISIS took that city in June 2014. Plastering the vehicles from the sky was not an option: it was hard to distinguish between military and civilian traffic. The best way to sever the link was to occupy it. That would not isolate Mosul, as there were more circuitous routes ISIS could still take to get there. Recapturing Sinjar, however, would begin to squeeze ISIS, and would be the coalition's first major countermove in northern Iraq.

More than seven thousand fighters, mostly Kurdish forces, but also Yazidi fighters looking for payback against the militants, were mobilized for the operation. While the Kurds were gathering in November 2015, I went to see Major General Aziz Waisi, the commander of the Zeravani, one of the Iraqi Kurds' premier paramilitary units, at his headquarters near Mosul Dam. His strategy was audacious. He would avoid the IEDs on the push to Sinjar by taking an unexpected path—forging a way down the rugged Mount Sinjar, a route so rough that his forces would need to put a bulldozer at the head of their column to create a road. After reaching the base of the mountain, the column would rumble over a rocky riverbed until it arrived just east of Sinjar on Highway 47, and presumably find itself inside ISIS's outer defenses. Meanwhile, other forces farther to the east and to the west would make a parallel push until they reached the highway. It would be a three-pronged attack, and Waisi would be leading the sneak assault up the middle. The United States, which would provide air support, called the operation "Dweller." In an appeal to Yazidi sensitivities, it was also dubbed "the Fury of Melek Taus," an homage to the Peacock Angel, one of the principal figures in the Yazidi faith. Waisi's forces were often called "elite," but they had little of the kit that the Iraqi military possessed.

The Zeravani had some armored Humvees, but many of their fighters traveled in a hodgepodge of SUVs, jeeps, buses, motorcycles, and light trucks with jury-rigged machine-gun mounts in the back. Waisi's fighters themselves were lightly equipped, mostly with AK-47s and small arms, and many lacked body armor. In addition to worrying about IEDs and clearing Sinjar of ISIS diehards, the Kurds would need to consider the possibility of an ISIS counterattack from its strongholds in Tal Afar to the east and Ba'aj to the south. Waisi's plan was for bulldozers to pile mountains of sand on the roads to and from Sinjar. The U.S. strike cell in Erbil, the command center that orchestrated the air strikes in northern Iraq, ordered one such attack to crater the road west of Tal Afar. If the operation succeeded, it would represent a big step toward breaking the stalemate in the war and perhaps building some momentum.

The U.S. military's "by, with, and through" strategy had its advantages, not least of which was that proxies were doing the fighting. But one of the drawbacks was that it left the United States at the mercy of local politics, of which there was plenty in northern Iraq. Masrour Barzani, the top security official for the semi-autonomous Kurdistan Region, was overseeing the operation, and his government had pretensions of extending its writ westward to the border with Syria and southward to encompass Sinjar itself. In the northwest, however, Barzani's Peshmerga were not the only players and were grudgingly sharing Mount Sinjar with Mazloum Abdi's YPG and even its cousin organization, the PKK, which sought Kurdish autonomy in Turkey.

I waited along with a crew from *Vice News* in a two-star hotel in Duhok for the weather to improve while the Kurds sought to wrap up the final preparations for the Sinjar offensive. The launch of the operation would require several days of clear skies so that the United States could mount strikes by A-10 attack planes, which were flying in from Turkey's Incirlik Air Base, and so that other allied nations could launch strikes as well. Once the clouds lifted and the operation remained on pause, however, it became clear that the remaining impediments might be political, including who would lay claim to Sinjar after the town was liberated. Masrour Barzani would not be able to dissuade the rival forces from joining the attack. Deconfliction would be the best he could do.

Adding another layer of complexity to the operation, the tensions among the Kurds themselves had found an echo in the tensions between the Iraqi Kurds and the Yazidis. Even before the emergence of ISIS, there had been strained relations between the Yazidis and the Kurdish authorities in Erbil. When David Petraeus traveled to Sinjar during the American occupation, one Yazidi leader presented the general with a book of grievances on life under the Kurds. This ill will was only aggravated when the Peshmerga abandoned Sinjar during ISIS's initial onslaught in June 2014, leaving the Yazidis to fend for themselves until the Syrian YPG led them to safety.

Nonetheless, one Yazidi commander, Qassem Shesho, remained aligned with Barzani's Peshmerga and vowed to reclaim Yazidi lands with the help of the American-funded and -armed force. Complicating the family dynamics, his nephew Haider Shesho, a Yazidi expatriate whose family fled to Germany when Saddam Hussein was in power, and who returned to defend his homeland against ISIS, recruited a 2,500-strong militia of his own. He dubbed it the Protection Force of Sinjar and was later contacted by the

Shiite militia leader and Iranian ally Abu Mahdi al-Muhandis, who sent equipment, guns, and ammo, as well as salaries for a thousand fighters for three months. In January 2015, the Iraqi government began sending money as well, which was used for weapons, ammunition, vehicles, and uniforms.

Barzani's government was not amused by the Yazidi commander's alliance with forces it deemed hostile to its project for control of northern Iraq. Several months later, Haider Shesho was arrested and thrown into a jail in Duhok, where he was forced to share a cell with two ISIS fighters, who in an act of compassion gave him two blankets. He eventually managed to persuade the warden to put him in a cell by himself lest the militants figure out his identity, but his problems were just beginning. Taken before a judge, he was accused of establishing an illegal militia and conspiring with an outside entity, he recalled. Meeting with Masrour Barzani, he promised to cease all cooperation with Baghdad and presumably any of the militias it backed. Instead, his own Yazidi force would be folded into Barzani's larger effort.

Apparently, there was still some settling up to do with Muhandis. When I met with Haider Shesho months later at a conference in Sulaymaniyah, he asked me to assure Muhandis, should I ever meet him, that he had never received all of the funds and weapons that had supposedly been sent to him. As Muhandis rebuffed my initial attempts to interview him and was later killed in the January 2020 American drone attack that did away with Qassem Soleimani, I never delivered the message.

ON NOVEMBER 11, the effort to retake Sinjar got underway. Embedding with the Zeravani was not like attaching oneself to U.S. forces. It required hiring a truck and a driver, and stocking the truck with food, water, gas, toilet paper, and medical supplies. Sinjar was cold at night, but we would need to shut down the engine to conserve fuel as we slept in the truck. We began to move in a long column, maneuvering within sight of the Syrian border before taking up our attack positions in a cluster of unheated stone buildings.

Before dawn the next day, as we started our descent, I noticed one telltale sign that I was part of the main attack: a Kurdish television truck was just ahead to document what the authorities in Erbil hoped would be a great battlefield success. Our Yazidi driver had never taken the route before because, in fact, there was no road to speak of. Once we began to move, there would be no turning back. It was no more possible to drive back up the mountain than to swim against a rushing tide. "We were ordered to take this route," Hamid Khudir Ahmed said. "Otherwise, I would never have taken it." Simply reaching the foot of the mountain unscathed was cause for celebration. Blasting music from their vehicles, Peshmerga fighters got out and danced. After a hasty meal of bread and canned fish, they were on the march again. A caravan of ambulances staffed by paramedics brought up the rear. Getting the wounded back to the hospital in Duhok would take hours, assuming Highway 47 was cleared. The U.S. military liked to talk about the "golden hour," the sixty minutes when emergency treatment was critical and it was vital to evacuate the wounded to a combat surgical hospital in the rear, but that was a foreign concept on this mission. I was told later that some two dozen U.S. Special Forces members were serving as advisors to Peshmerga forces. But they had taken up positions away from the immediate fighting, and I never saw them.

As we approached Highway 47, General Waisi's Peshmerga force came upon the first of many IEDs that ISIS had seeded around the city. "TNT!" one fighter called out, using the force's catchall nickname for the bombs. Lacking sophisticated mine-clearing equipment, Waisi's vehicles detoured across a rocky hillside, as it was easier to forge a new path than to clear the planned one. As soon as the Peshmerga got to the highway, they brought in a bulldozer with armored plates bolted to the driver's cab to erect a massive earthen wall across the road to guard against suicide car bombs—ISIS's version of precision-guided weapons. Before the sand wall had been finished, however, a Kurdish fighter screamed, "It's coming!" A truck was barreling down the road. "The explosion is coming!" As the truck approached, the Peshmerga unleashed a barrage of machine-gun fire from the armored Humvees and fighting positions that had been set up beside the highway, in order to avoid the full force of a truck explosion. But the bullets stopped neither the ISIS driver nor his truck: a heavy piece of armor had been bolted across the front of the vehicle. The American A-10 attack planes and B-1B bombers could not get there in time. MILAN anti-tank missiles the Peshmerga had acquired from Germany were the only recourse the Peshmerga had. "Shoot it! Shoot it!" a Peshmerga fighter yelled.

"Let it come closer," a commander said over the tactical radio. The Kurds had a limited supply of the missiles and did not want to miss.

With the truck racing down the road, a Kurdish fighter unleashed a MILAN, which streaked down the highway and exploded— behind the oncoming truck. There was little time left for a second shot, and the fighters had only one other missile. "Hamodi, get out!" a fighter implored a comrade. "Hamodi, hurry up!"

The truck was virtually upon the Kurds when the second Milan found its mark, turning the explosives-laden truck into a massive fireball that could be seen from miles away. In that moment, the Kurds did not seem to know if they would survive to fight another day or join the ranks of the more than one thousand Peshmerga who had perished in the war with ISIS.

"God is great! God is great!" one fighter yelled over and over. "There is no god but God, and Muhammad is his Prophet!"

As the debris settled, a commander was heard over the tactical radio: "Is everybody OK?"

"We are all OK," another fighter responded in a radio transmission. Somehow, all of the fighters had survived. One had a broken hand, but there were no major injuries.

The next day, the Peshmerga set up a temporary command

post at the site of the attack, where they planned the next stage of the fight while they grabbed a quick lunch of lentil soup among the twisted metal debris and bits of human remains. By this time, the dirt barrier had been completed. Now the armored bulldozer was called in again, this time to forge a path for the Peshmerga. In the ebb and flow of the battle, it was their turn to seize the initiative and push west down the road to retake Sinjar.

Eventually, the Peshmerga pushed their way into the battered city. Amid deafening bursts of celebratory gunfire, a Yazidi militia fighter with a walrus mustache who had joined the Kurdish offensive, Edo Qasim Shamo, proclaimed excitedly that the moment of his people's liberation was finally at hand. The victory did not put an end to the casualties, however. Homes in the newly reclaimed city were booby-trapped with bombs. Mass graves of ISIS victims, some of which were rigged with explosives, were also found.

Even as the American-backed offensive appeared to have achieved its goals after just two days, the politicking continued unabated. President Masoud Barzani held a news conference at the top of Mount Sinjar to hail the retaking of the town and made clear that it would be formally incorporated into the semi-autonomous Kurdistan Region. "Sinjar is part of the Kurdistan Region," he said. "Aside from the Kurdistan flag, no other flag will rise in Sinjar." As he uttered those words, however, different flags were being prominently displayed in Sinjar—those of the rival YPG as well as the PKK, along with the banners of its Syrian Kurdish offshoot. After weeks of efforts by the Iraqi Kurdish government to sideline the Syrian Kurdish militias, the rival fighters insisted that they had in fact led the fighting for months.

"We have been fighting in this city for fifteen months," said a PKK fighter who went by the nom de guerre Adil Haroon. "We fought. They don't fight. Now they say that we should leave." Compounding the dilemma, Iraq's prime minister considered Sinjar to be an Iraqi city and was not about to cede it to the Kurdish leadership in Erbil. It was apparent that the resentments in the region would outlast Sinjar's liberation. As we drove back up the mountain after the operation, smoke was rising from Arab villages east of Sinjar that had been set on fire, while trucks full of looted furniture could be seen driving north. "They took our possessions, now we are going to take theirs," said one Yazidi man, whose truck was carrying a wooden wardrobe and metal sheeting.

Months after Sinjar was liberated, Mark Odom, the one-star American general in Erbil who supported the Sinjar operation by approving the U.S. strikes, briefed Ash Carter on the tensions over Sinjar. For the Pentagon chief, the key thing was not what color flag flew over Sinjar. The important thing was that the town was no longer in the hands of the Islamic State. It was a lot easier to remove ISIS than to put in place a local government to replace the extremist group. Tensions might flare up again, but in the meantime the United States had taken a step toward putting pressure on the ISIS fighters in Mosul.

AS THE KURDS were moving on Sinjar, Obama convened an NSC meeting to take stock of his counter-ISIS campaign. There had been some progress since the May 19 NSC meeting—when Obama and his principal aides had confronted the question of whether the United States had a genuine partner in Iraq and if the campaign against ISIS was even viable—but there were also frustrations. Following pressure from John Allen and Brett McGurk, the Turks were now allowing American warplanes—including F-15As, F-15Es, and A-10 close air support planes—access to their bases. Starting in July, the Turks had also allowed the Americans to station armed drones on their territory. But despite having one of the largest armies in NATO, Turkey had not locked down its frontier with Syria. As the November 10 meeting got underway, Obama asked why the Turks were not doing more to seal the border with Syria and prevent the flow of jihadist volunteers to ISIS, according to notes taken by a participant. Turkish forces could at least clear their side of the border. The United States, the president said, should be pushing them harder. It was their country to defend.

John Kerry ventured that the Turks were recalcitrant "because their quid pro quo with ISIS is not eliminated." The secretary of state did not believe that there was a formal understanding between the militants and Turkish intelligence. Rather, his contention was that Erdoğan's government was operating on the assumption that if it did not interfere with militants who were traversing Turkish territory to join ISIS, the group would leave Ankara alone. In light of two suicide bombings at an Ankara train station the previous month that killed more than a hundred people, which some Turkish authorities blamed on ISIS, the calculus was beginning to change—or so the Americans thought. But Kerry's assertion was that Turkey's hands-off approach still held sway.

Obama was also concerned about the Iraqis' slow pace in retaking Ramadi, which he saw as another example of a partner's faltering will. To take back the city, the Iraqis had begun an attack on four fronts. The lack of coordination between the CTS, the Iraqi Army, and the Federal Police had initially led Lloyd Austin to worry that Iraqi forces might converge in a jumbled mess inside the city, with enormous potential for friendly fire. In reality, the progress had been glacial. So slow was the Iraqis' advance that MacFarland had pressed Abadi to replace one particular Iraqi Army commander, whom the Americans figured must be taking bribes from either the militants or Iranian-backed militias. As the months went by, the Iraqis embraced a familiar talking point: the CTS was to do the heavy lifting of clearing the city, with the Iraqi Army trailing behind. But the Sunni tribal fighters the White House kept hoping would materialize never did, at least not in any significant numbers.

"I remain concerned that the basic planning and execution is stalling out," said Obama. "We need to do more to engage the Sunnis."

Seeking to reassure the president, Austin noted that the encirclement of Ramadi was almost complete, and that Abadi might be willing to bring in the local Sunni police as a holding force. Reinforcing that point, McGurk said that eight thousand Sunni tribal fighters were being trained and that another twenty thousand had been identified.

Joseph Dunford, however, cautioned that the United States needed to tread carefully in trying to mobilize the Sunnis in Anbar. Going around the Shia-dominated government in Baghdad would only complicate the United States' dealings with Abadi. One step the administration could consider, the chairman of the Joint Chiefs of Staff added, was pressing the Iraqi prime minister to allow Washington to deploy more special operations advisors. More than his civilian counterparts, Dunford understood that encouraging the Iraqis to move forward would be much easier if they did not have to operate alone.

"Abadi is not a great politician," Obama observed. "And he is under huge constraints, but we are not going to do any better in Iraq. So we need to do all we can to fortify him, including on the economic side, and do what we can to give him as much space as possible."

One challenge that was well within the Americans' bailiwick was finding a way to expedite air operations across Iraq and in neighboring Syria. In a conventional conflict with a foreign adversary, U.S. military intelligence would dissect the enemy threat by identifying the adversary's command and control centers, weapons depots, and other important infrastructure. The process was called the "intelligence preparation of the battlefield," and it was usually the prelude to a major, fast-paced offensive operation.

The Islamic State was a hybrid enemy. It declared itself a caliphate, administered territory, extracted and sold oil, had a military command structure, and fused terrorist tactics like suicide car bombs with standard conventional tactics like laying minefields and building sand berms, which it covered with machine guns, artillery, and mortars. But the overwhelming majority of U.S. air strikes had targeted small vehicles, fighting positions, mortar teams, and suicide bombers on the front lines. The numbers told the story. The air strikes that were run out of Al-Udeid were roughly grouped into two categories: "deliberate" strikes that were planned in advance against key targets in the rear, and "dynamic" attacks in which American and allied warplanes hit Islamic State fighters tangling with Iraqi or Kurdish troops. During the summer of 2015, 90 percent of the strikes were dynamic.

"The first three to four months of my life over there were short-range targets, and we were trying to stop the rapid expansion of ISIS. There was no strategy in place or deep strike," Gunz Gersten recalled. "Everything we had was in the five-meter target zone—Baiji, Ramadi, Sinjar Mountain." There was a role for close air support, he acknowledged, but too much of the emphasis was spent on striking what the Air Force dismissively called "nefarious dirt." What MacFarland and Gersten wanted was a strategic air campaign that would also go after targets that allowed the caliphate to function: its locations for raising money, disseminating propaganda, and commanding operations. Part of the problem was the process for approving proposed strikes. When MacFarland took command, any significant deliberate strike had to be vetted by all of the relevant U.S. intelligence agencies, which could take as long as ten workdays, not including weekends and federal holidays. If one of the agencies had little information about a particular target, it could "non-concur." As the intelligence world liked to operate on the basis of consensus, that required MacFarland to file an appeal. To speed up the process, MacFarland asked the intelligence agencies to embed representatives with his staff. Some agencies sent them; most did not.

Other difficulties resulted from the way the military looked for targets in the first place. At the start of the campaign, it was CENTCOM, not the air war commander, that controlled one of the most in-demand assets on the modern-day battlefield: the all-important remotely piloted vehicles that were used to find the preponderance of targets. The command had an entire building at its headquarters at MacDill Air Force Base in Tampa, Florida, that was filled with intelligence analysts. Few of those analysts appeared to be convinced there was much of a payoff in searching for targets deep in the caliphate.

Working within these constraints, MacFarland and Gersten were able to expand the scope of the air strikes to some extent. During ISIS's first months in control of Mosul, the militants kept local services going with some inadvertent help from the Iraqi state, which initially kept paying government salaries on the assumption that the ISIS occupation would soon end. The Americans eventually convinced the Iraqis to cut off the flow of money. Now the objective was to find ways to target the oil infrastructure, banks, and administrative centers that ISIS depended on to govern its territory—and to do so without unduly endangering civilians.

Some of their ideas did not pass muster at home. In studying ISIS's control of Mosul, Gersten determined that much of the electricity for the city was generated by the Mosul Dam, which thanks to the CTS and the Peshmerga was now in friendly hands. When winter came, however, the water level fell to the point that the dam could no longer produce power. Mosul then relied on a gas-oil generation plant west of the city. By striking that plant in September, Gersten reasoned, the city would be left bereft of electricity by December and ISIS would be presented with a choice: either divert funds away from the main war effort and repair the electrical production facilities, or be blamed for a failure of governance. In the end, CENTCOM rejected the plan to target the plant on the grounds that the U.S.-led coalition might be blamed for destroying the country's infrastructure and aggravating the hardship of Mosul's already suffering residents. So Gersten proposed to go after the fuel supply in Syria that fed the plant. In Syria, the United States had more leeway to target the gas-oil separation plants that ISIS used to produce what it sold on the black market in Syria, but it also wanted to go after the distribution network.

The location of the plants, however, meant that hundreds of trucks gathered each week to fill their tanks near Deir al-Zour, Syria, before driving east to Mosul and other ISIS possessions.

MacFarland and Gersten wanted to strike them. But this meant involving Washington, which insisted on reviewing any plans for ambitious air strikes deep in ISIS territory, whether they were supported by CENTCOM or not.

Gersten had learned this lesson the previous summer the hard way. After ISIS announced it would attack the United States on the Fourth of July, he had sought to answer that threat by ordering a series of air strikes that would for the first time reach far into the heart of the self-proclaimed caliphate in Syria. The operation, which was designed with the help of Major General Scott Zobrist, the Al-Udeid deputy commander, would target eleven of the main bridges that led to Raqqa, the ISIS capital. Gersten would have liked to strike even more of the spans, but American intelligence officials explained that some would be needed for the U.S.-backed proxy force to eventually retake the city. The U.S. Agency for International Development, meanwhile, insisted that another be preserved to facilitate the humanitarian assistance it hoped to arrange after Raqqa's liberation. In the end, B-1B bombers, F-15E "Strike Eagles," and Navy F/A-18s participated in the raid to strike the targeted spans, which in a bit of symbolism ISIS may not have appreciated was timed to occur just as the first Independence Day fireworks were set to go off in Washington. The message the military intended to send was that there was no place in the caliphate that the United States could not reach. The White House, however, had been surprised that the military had acted so boldly without getting the administration's explicit permission, and made it very clear that this sort of operation should not be repeated.

While striking trucks was not as bold as striking ISIS's capital, the issue was that the bombing raid would kill not only ISIS soldiers but also some of the drivers, who were not hard-core members of ISIS but simply hired hands. To acknowledge the messiness of war, the Obama administration's initial goal of avoiding all civilian casualties had been slightly relaxed for top-priority targets. Under the rules of engagement that strictly regulated projected civilian casualties, MacFarland had what the military called a "non-combatant cutoff value" of five for rural areas and ten for urban targets. That meant any strike in which more than five civilians were likely to die would require that CENTCOM and most probably Washington sign off before it was executed.

For weeks, MacFarland and Gersten were stymied until the CIA reported that the truck drivers went to a nearby town at night to sleep and hired a handful of locals to move the trucks that were in line to fill up near Syria's oil fields and rustic refineries—a kind of valet service. If the air strikes began at the rear of the column and then moved to the front, it was reasonable to conclude that the valet drivers would be sure to run away. If the plan was designed and executed correctly, only a small number of valet drivers would be killed.

On the night of November 16, two F-15Es dropped thousands of leaflets about an hour before the attack, with cartoons of planes dropping bombs and big arrows pointing to safe areas to the left and right. Strafing runs were also conducted to reinforce the message. Then four A-10 planes attacked with five-hundred-pound bombs and 30mm cannons, while two AC-130 gunships equipped with 40mm Gatling guns and 105mm cannons also moved in. At least 116 of the 150 trucks at the scene were thought to have been destroyed. The attack was part of a larger deep battle campaign MacFarland dubbed "Tidal Wave II" after the bombing campaign the United States had carried out against the Romanian oil refineries the Nazi war machine had relied on during World War II. It was not the most appropriate name, given that more than three hundred U.S. airmen had perished in the Tidal Wave I raids against the heavily defended refineries in Romania, but the name was selected to hark back to the use of strategic airpower.

After Tidal Wave II was carried out without any political clamor, the door was opened for a much more ambitious operation. The coalition had intelligence that ISIS was using three buildings in Mosul to pay its fighters and fund its war machine. All told, the banks, or what the military called "bulk cash storage units," were believed to hold anywhere from 100 million to 600 million in U.S. dollars, the unofficial currency in the region, and a stack of plates for making counterfeit bills.

Gersten's idea was to strike the banks simultaneously. That way ISIS could not try to shift the money to yet another location after the first bombs fell. Gersten developed the plan, which was code-named "Robin Hood," and MacFarland sent up the targets for approval by CENTCOM, which forwarded them to Washington. The intelligence showed that the banks were usually filled with cash around the tenth of the month, and that they paid out the money to foreign fighters on the twelfth, so the timing was key. The military used a computer program to generate casualty estimates, which projected the radius of a blast against the local infrastructure and was known irreverently in the military as "bug splat." It projected that dozens could die, though MacFarland and Gersten were convinced that if a small bomb was picked and the right choices were made with respect to fusing so that the bomb detonated in a specific part of the structure, the actual number would be a handful—perhaps only a night watchman whom the Americans rationalized could be judged to be complicit in ISIS's activities. Incendiary bombs would not be used to reduce the risk of what the military called "collateral damage"—the unintended killing or wounding of civilians.

Given the apprehension in Washington about such a significant strike, the military decided to attack only one of the banks and to do so at night, after the streets had cleared out. The rest of the targets would have to be taken on later. Soon before the strike was to be carried out, the NSC met to discuss the campaign, and John Kerry remarked that some of the targets the military was considering looked interesting. Ash Carter had just returned from a trip and was upset that his staff had not drawn the impending attack to his attention. Why was the State Department getting the request before the defense secretary? Carter put a hold on the request until he had the time to sort things out himself.

On the eve of the strike, Gersten was waiting for a green light from Washington when he got a call informing him the attack had yet to be approved. It was the tenth of the month, which meant he would need to wait another thirty days at a minimum. Another complication was that the air command center at Al-Udeid had just issued an Air Tasking Order, which laid out all of the coalition missions for a several-day period. It was a necessary mechanism for conducting air strikes and deconflicting operations, but it had been shared with Arab partners, which raised the possibility that the plan might leak if there was a protracted delay.

Adding to the pressure, Gersten was told that British intelligence, which had sources inside the city, had determined that if the strike did not go ahead that night, one of the banks would be emptied out the next day and the hundreds of millions of dollars stashed there would be gone. It was 10:00 p.m. in Tampa when Gersten got on the phone and called CENTCOM headquarters, which woke up Austin. Austin called Carter. "No" turned to "yes," and the operation was approved.

A U.S. drone was aloft when F-15Es and F/A-18s carried out the strike, which scattered much of the $400 million that was believed to have been stashed in the bank vault across the street like confetti. One quick-thinking Mosul local pulled out a sack and began scooping up as much cash as he could carry. "Ladies and gentlemen, your Robin Hood moment," Gersten told his team. Within five minutes, however, ISIS vehicles showed up and cordoned the whole area off. Gersten wanted to hit the other two banks the next day before the money was moved.

At Al-Udeid, Zobrist had the planes armed and ready to go, but it took seven more days to get permission from Washington, and by that time intelligence analysts assessed that much of the money had been moved elsewhere. What was seen as prudence at the White House and a requirement to minimize the risk of civilian casualties was seen in the field as a reluctance to press the initiative. Weeks later, American intelligence traced some of the money to a house in southwestern Mosul. Spies on the ground reported that several bags containing millions of dollars in cash were lined up in the hallways. But there was a problem: the wife and children of ISIS's banking emir also lived in the house. MacFarland wanted the money destroyed as soon as possible, so Gersten came up with a plan—one that depended on precise execution and was designed to give the civilians in the house a chance to get out but not enough time to take the money with them. In the campaign's first use of tactical cyberoperations, the military would hack into the local cell phone network and send a text message that said, "Those people who were in a house filled with bags full of money needed to leave immediately . . . The house is about to be destroyed." Thirty seconds after the text message was sent, leaflets would be dropped by F-16s in the neighborhood with the same message. After another thirty seconds, a Predator drone would shoot a single Hellfire missile that would be timed to explode in an airburst fifteen feet above the roof of the structure, so that bomb fragments would rattle the roof but not penetrate it. Forty-five seconds after that, four small-diameter bombs from an F-15E would hit the building. U.S. commanders used a drone to monitor the scene, and the plan unfolded like clockwork. Right after the text was sent, two men bolted out of the side door of the house. Shortly after that, a woman who was carrying a baby and dragging a young boy by the hand ran out the front door. Petrified, the boy broke free and ran back into the home. With the bomb already in flight and just seconds away from pulverizing the structure, the woman hesitated and then ran back into the house with the baby to try to get her son. The operation had been meticulously planned, but it was still war.

For the Air Force, the strikes were a start at addressing strategic targets. The idea of going after deep targets received another push when Lieutenant General Charles Q. Brown, Jr., assumed command of Al-Udeid and in August appealed successfully to Austin at a commanders conference for more control over the use of reconnaissance drones and aircraft. Still, the Air Force believed more could be done. Colonel Jason Brown, General Brown's director of intelligence at Shaw Air Force Base in South Carolina, did what he could to help. The base served as U.S. headquarters for the Air Force units deployed in the Middle East and backstopped the command center at Al-Udeid. Colonel Brown, too, believed that there were more targets out there but that CENTCOM was not doing enough to exploit the enemy's weak points.

In the years after the 9/11 terrorist attacks and the U.S. interventions in Afghanistan and Iraq, the command had pressed U.S. intelligence agencies to support counterinsurgency and counterterrorism operations. This meant the focus was on manhunting and supporting U.S. troops in harm's way instead of what the Air Force considered to be high-payoff targets like command and control, logistics, and finances—the functions that kept ISIS operating as a whole. "CENTCOM was still fighting ISIS like merely an insurgency when it was a pseudo-nation-state," he said, referring to ISIS's self-styled caliphate. "It struggled to identify the vulnerable places ISIS resources flowed from and through."

In an attempt to drum up support for a deep targeting effort, Colonel Brown flew to Tampa in September 2015 and made a pitch to CENTCOM for a crash effort to search for strategic targets, including those near Al-Qaim and Al-Bukamal—two border cities in Iraq and Syria, respectively, where ISIS was believed to have located much of its logistics and command and control. The CENTCOM intelligence shop was not persuaded that focusing on that area was more important than battlefield interdiction. But as a sop to the Air Force, CENTCOM did propose a series of classified conferences of senior military officials to review the target selection process extending through June of 2016.

That was much too late for General Brown, who decided to organize his own targeting discussion at the Pentagon in December, which would include top Air Force officers and senior officials from U.S. intelligence agencies, whom Brown intended to lobby personally. CENTCOM officials would participate, but they would have to defend their decisions in front of a broad array of top officials, who were all anxious to make more progress. At the Pentagon, General Brown and Colonel Brown made the case for greater intelligence support for the air command's deliberate targeting effort. Those efforts began to pay off when the Air Force struck fifteen targets around Al-Qaim and Al-Bukamal in a single day in February 2016.

A bolder idea that some had flirted with in the early days of the fight against ISIS was to have an Air Force general assume command of Operation Inherent Resolve instead of leaving it under the control of an Army general. The idea appears to have been floated when Lieutenant General John Hesterman was the commander at Al-Udeid, according to a RAND report commissioned by the Air Force and an officer who served at Al-Udeid. At the time, the headquarters was short-staffed and the Air Force lacked a unit that had been trained and equipped to serve as a task-force headquarters. In 2015, General David Goldfein, the Air Force chief of staff, drafted a plan for the Air Force to lead a joint service command and submitted it to Joe Dunford, arguing that this approach might engender some fresh thinking about how to go after ISIS. The initiative, however, went nowhere. The wars in Afghanistan and Iraq were multiservice campaigns, but it was the Army and the Marines who had the vast majority of the troops on the ground and the experience in running regional commands to lead them. For now, Inherent Resolve, like all of the other American interventions in Iraq, would be led by an Army general.

12

THE WAR ROOM

On November 13, 2015, several gunmen barged into the Bataclan, a theater in Paris where the Eagles of Death Metal were performing in concert, and began shooting into the crowd. It was one of a binge of mass shootings and suicide bombings across the city that night. In all, 130 people were killed and 416 injured. The Islamic State claimed credit for the carnage, which French president François Hollande denounced as an "act of war." Though the attacks were nearly four thousand miles from Washington and occurred in a European nation with a substantial Muslim population, the event struck at the White House's core assumptions about how to confront ISIS. American intelligence indicated that the attacks had been planned in Raqqa, the ISIS capital, and in Manbij, a city in northern Syria that was still in ISIS's hands. Most of the assailants in Paris had French or Belgian citizenship, and some had fought in Syria. This was not the Taliban-like group that the White House had mused about soon after the fall of Mosul— that is, a group that was a regional threat within the Middle East rather than an international terrorist group that could carry out mass casualty attacks in foreign capitals and perhaps even the United States. The Obama administration had allocated thirty-six months to weakening and largely defeating ISIS, with the bulk of the American effort at first taking place in Iraq. But ISIS had its own timetable, and it was taking its struggle to the West.

It was more than a military problem. A November 13–type attack in the United States, the president's aides fretted, could even strike a blow at his domestic agenda. Obama's theory held that the cure could be worse than the disease. The 9/11 attacks on the World Trade Center and the Pentagon had killed nearly three thousand people but had also spawned a massive surveillance program at home and two wars in the Middle East and southwest Asia, which was one more intervention than Obama deemed necessary. If the Obama administration did not show that its strategy against ISIS was working, and if the United States was hit again, there could be another backlash.

Two days after the Paris attacks, the air war command in Qatar arranged for a dozen French aircraft to drop sixteen bombs on ISIS targets near Raqqa, which the French government said included a training camp and a munitions dump, but which Syrian activists said included some abandoned bases. The strike enabled the French to make a political point, but at the pace the military campaign was going, there was no prospect of quickly collapsing Abu Bakr al-Baghdadi's caliphate.

Obama convened an urgent meeting after the Paris attacks, which was followed by a more thorough discussion on November 24. The president was leaving for a nine-day trip to Asia, one that supported his administration's foreign policy goal of pivoting to the Pacific region and eventually winding down the U.S. involvement in the Middle East. Now that the terrorist threat was spilling over into Europe from the Middle East, however, Obama wanted to do more. The intelligence assessments, in fact, were concerning. The United States would later uncover some alarming plots, including a scheme in which a Bangladeshi ISIS recruit who was a former pilot would try to commandeer an aircraft in Turkey.

Setting the stage for the meeting, Nicholas Rasmussen, the director of the National Counterterrorism Center, asserted that as many as six thousand Europeans had joined extremist groups in Syria and Iraq, and that many of them could return to their home countries. Europe had a double problem: fighters who came back to their countries might carry out attacks at home, while radicalized civilians who never left the continent might engage in terrorism as well. Militants holding European passports might also try to carry out attacks on American soil, and some U.S. citizens might be influenced by ISIS propaganda to adopt the terrorist cause.

Ash Carter gave a rundown of what the Pentagon dubbed its major lines of effort, which by that point included resupplying Arab members of Mazloum Abdi's forces with light arms, using air strikes to help the Kurds shut down some of the key roads ISIS used near Sinjar, conducting the Tidal Wave II strikes against the militants' oil tankers, and building up the special operations force in northern Iraq. The latter effort included both advisors working with CTS and Kurdish commandos and an "expeditionary targeting force" that despite its bland-sounding name was intended for raids against ISIS leaders of the sort JSOC had routinely carried out during the U.S. occupation of Iraq but had avoided since reentering the country. The Pentagon was also working with Jordan to train anti-ISIS militants in southern Syria.

Obama noted that in the wake of the Paris attacks the risk of "external plotting" had grown and there was increasing pressure for faster action. "The more they entrench, the harder it is going to be to get them out of there," Obama added. "The stakes are higher and frankly the public risk tolerance may be higher after Paris, and the coalition may be willing to do some more." Obama hinted that he, too, would be open to making some fresh decisions.

Carter reported that he had written to forty members of the coalition about steps they could take. The British would soon join the air campaign, and the Italians were already training Iraq's Federal Police. But the Paris attacks would give the United States the opportunity to press for more, particularly from the Europeans, who were fearful that more ISIS attacks could be in store for them.

"Should we be putting in more SOF?" asked Obama, referring to special operations forces.

Joe Dunford, the chairman of the Joint Chiefs of Staff, said that he could come back to the president with a detailed assessment of that possibility. "I think the aperture is open," Dunford said.

More boots on the ground? Obama continued.

"We might need some, and I don't feel inhibited. But it is not my assessment that it would help right now," Dunford responded.

Obama asked about coordination between the intelligence agencies and the Pentagon. Dunford and CIA director John Brennan both insisted that it was fine.

Austin said that the greatest opportunities to make headway in the ensuing months might be in northern Syria. The CENTCOM war plan had come a long way since the "Iraq first" strategy his headquarters initially devised, with its emphasis on taking Mosul. The Iraqis were moving slowly, and much of ISIS's plotting was now happening in Syria.

Joe Biden chimed in at the end with some political advice. With decades in the Senate, Biden had more sensitive antennae than any other member of Obama's foreign policy team when it came to the political ramifications of national security deliberations.

"Mr. President, we need to give you the space to make the right decisions. It is really important for people to understand that you are not blocking any good options," Biden said.

There was a perception that Obama was cautious to a fault. The president had drawn the line at sending conventional combat troops, had yet to allow U.S. advisors to accompany Iraqi troops into battle except during Delta Force's Hawija raid, and was still explaining his 2013 decision not to enforce his red line in Syria. Biden was underscoring the point that it was not in the White House's interest to see stories in the press that it was turning down good ideas and prolonging the campaign if there were more aggressive options that did not require it to depart from the basic logic of its "by, with, and through" strategy. The impression that Obama was tiptoeing his way into the conflict could be damning if ISIS was now in the business of exporting terror. To counter it, the administration would need to find a way to expedite its campaign and, importantly, be seen to be doing so.

AUSTIN'S RECOMMENDATION THAT the administration look at stepping up the pace in northeastern Syria followed some painful twists and turns over the course of a couple of years. The original plan had been for Mike Nagata to rustle up a scrappy force of largely Arab Syrian fighters who were prepared to do battle against ISIS. The scheme had a complicated backstory. During his time as head of the U.S. Special Operations Command Central, Nagata had been asked by CENTCOM to put together ideas for pressuring Syrian president Bashar al-Assad to step down. Under David Petraeus, the CIA had launched a small program to train Syrian rebels, but the question was whether to establish a parallel and more substantial effort that would be run by the Green Berets under Nagata's command. Nagata drafted a classified three-page memo that described in general terms how his command could recruit, train, and arm a paramilitary force that would be infiltrated into the country. With little concrete data on potential recruits, Nagata wrote that there would need to be course corrections along the way. By fielding rebel fighters to go up against Assad's army and air force, and the foreign powers that were backing him, he noted, the United States would be inheriting a moral obligation to the Syrians it trained and sent into the fray.

Nagata's plan sat on a shelf for months while the White House pondered whether to intervene in Syria. After the captured journalist James Foley was beheaded by ISIS in August 2014, however, the Obama administration had changed its tune. Nagata was asked if his plan could be retooled to confront ISIS instead of the Assad regime. Nagata said it could, but he reminded his chain of command that he had never been given any money to establish the program and was uncertain as to what legal authority he had to run it. Coming up with the necessary resources proved to be difficult. Nagata had never specified how many Syrian fighters might be trained, but Washington now did: 5,400 combatants over three years. To develop the capacity to train such a substantial force, John Kerry flew to Jeddah, Saudi Arabia, in September 2014 to secure King Abdullah's approval for opening a training base in Saudi Arabia to supplement the ones the Americans planned to establish in Turkey, Jordan, and Qatar. The only way to get the program underway fast was to take weapons and equipment from U.S. stocks. The Eastern European arms market was the go-to source for many cash-strapped armies and militias, but with the Russian intervention in Ukraine heating up, not to mention various other insurgencies around the world, Nagata concluded that it would be difficult to get Soviet-bloc weapons quickly.

Nagata had never ventured a cost estimate, but some administration officials estimated that the cost of arming and training volunteers abroad could reach $500 million. Then there was the matter of the lawyers: while the Obama administration had justified its intervention against ISIS as an extension of its war against al-Qaeda, the Pentagon's general counsel determined that Congress would still need to approve what the military called "1209 authority" to train and equip the Syrian opposition. Nagata began making the rounds in Congress in the fall of 2014, but the money was not approved until the following year, which meant that he could not begin recruiting Syrian volunteers until the spring of 2015. Back in 1972, Robert "Blowtorch" Komer, who was charged with reinvigorating the counterinsurgency effort in Vietnam, had written about "institutional inertia" in a RAND Corporation study titled "Bureaucracy Does Its Thing." A similar tome could have been written about the plan to train Syrian opposition fighters, but Nagata dutifully pressed ahead.

In Turkey, a suitable training site was found at an old security compound near Hirfanli Dam, the country's first hydroelectric plant, in Ankara province. The Jordanian training camp was ready first, however, and so the recruits would be flown there for training, before being flown back to Turkey so they could be infiltrated into Syria from the north. Nearly a full year after ISIS's execution of Foley, Nagata's Green Berets were ready to train his first class of sixty fighters. The selection of recruits required careful vetting, using lists from Gulf partners and American intelligence agencies, which never seemed to quite match. People under the age of eighteen could not join: the American military was not one to hire "child soldiers." Volunteers with unhealed war wounds also had to be turned away.

It proved hard to attract recruits in the first place, however. From the start, plenty of Syrians were eager to take up arms against the regime, but how many of them would be willing to leave their families and homes, be trained at a foreign base, and then return to fight ISIS, not Assad? It did not help that there was no assurance the United States was willing to medevac wounded fighters after they clashed with ISIS in Syria: if the fighters managed to drive their wounded comrades to the Turkish border, the Americans would evacuate them from there. Nor could Nagata initially assure prospective volunteers that they would be protected by American airpower once they were in the fray. Permission from Washington to support the fighters with air strikes came only days before the first class was to slip back into Syria. Sending American advisors to accompany the fighters in battle was as yet out of the question.

By the time Nagata turned over command, he had trained several hundred Syrian fighters. When the first thirty were inserted into Syria northeast of Aleppo, the program received a very public and humiliating black eye. Armed with small arms, machine guns, and communications, the fighters fended off an attack by Jabhat al-Nusra, a jihadi group aligned with al-Qaeda, thanks in large measure to the Hellfire missiles fired by U.S. Predator drones circling overhead. Spooked by their first encounter, however, the fighters decided to move to safer terrain, only to disband while the Nusra fighters took over their warehouse of supplies. The timing could not have been worse for Austin: under grilling from Congress in September 2015, Austin told the Senate Armed Services

Committee that only four or five of the initial cohort were still active inside Syria. Even so, Nagata did not think this should sound the death knell for the program: from the start, he had cautioned that there would be a period of trial and error.

Far from being frustrated by the lack of an effective proxy force in Syria, the White House almost seemed relieved that it had no way to easily intervene. The administration cast the faltering training program as a vindication of its policy of providing only limited and belated covert support in the parallel effort against Assad. "The administration knew on the front end that this would be a quite difficult task, and it's proved to be even more difficult than we thought," Josh Earnest, the White House press secretary, said. "Many of our critics had proposed this specific option as the cure-all for all of the policy challenges we're facing in Syria right now." The White House was still on the defensive about its decision not to intervene forcefully against Assad's killing machine in Syria—so much so that its spokesman cast Nagata's tribulations as a vindication.

On October 1, the White House formally suspended the much-pilloried training program. The program had not been canceled, but the difficulties it had encountered meant that it was not an expeditious way to influence events in northern Syria at a time when ISIS's ability to create mayhem abroad had become a major worry. There was another Syrian force, however, that was active in northeastern Syria and had nothing to do with Nagata's train-and-equip effort: Mazloum Abdi's fighters. By default, they were becoming the administration's only recourse for taking on ISIS inside Syria, though the United States as yet had no commitment to arm and equip the most capable fighters under Mazloum's command: the YPG.

THROUGHOUT 2015, AS the Obama administration considered its options in Syria, the Russians significantly narrowed its room for maneuver. Despite Russia's annexation of Crimea in 2014, Kerry had argued that the United States needed to include the Kremlin in a search for a diplomatic solution to the conflict in Syria. In May 2015, Kerry flew to Sochi for a meeting with Vladimir Putin. After making an obligatory visit to a World War II memorial, Kerry met for more than four hours with the Russian leader, who was disarming at times. In one aside, Putin marveled at how the defenders had parted like the Red Sea when he drove to the net to score in a VIP hockey game at the Black Sea resort. Kerry's State Department had been so determined to cast the meeting as productive that it jumped the gun and posted a Twitter message in the secretary's name hailing the "frank discussions" on key issues while the meeting was still underway.

The visit that seemed to matter the most to Russia, however, was not Kerry's but rather the unannounced trip to Moscow that was taken in August by Major General Qassem Soleimani, who had been directing Iran's military support for Assad. Though shrouded in mystery, the reasons for the trip became clear in early September when Russia sent an advance team to Syria and began assembling prefabricated housing at an air base near the Assad family's ancestral home near Latakia, Syria's principal port city. Russia, it seemed, had its own version of Obama's "by, with, and through" strategy of working with local partners: the Russian military would provide airpower and some special forces troops, while Hezbollah and its Iraqi Shiite allies would join Assad's army on the ground.

With an alacrity that caught the Obama administration by surprise, Russia began to deploy an air wing and the forces to support and protect it. Alarmed by the deployment, the State Department rushed to stop it in its tracks. Russian aircraft initially flew over Bulgaria and Greece, using the cover story that they were transporting humanitarian supplies. The State Department quickly persuaded the Bulgarians to close their airspace to the flights. Flying over Turkey was not an option for Moscow at that point: the Turks had forced Russia to land planes for inspection in the past. While his aides were trying to stop the Russians from getting to Syria, Kerry got on the phone with Sergei Lavrov, the Russian foreign minister, and urged the Kremlin to stand down. Disposing of the customary niceties, Kerry's spokesman took the unusual step of making the rift public. The Russian intervention in Syria, the State Department announced, "could further escalate the conflict, lead to greater loss of innocent life, increase refugee flows, and risk confrontation with the anti-ISIL coalition operating in Syria."

Putin, however, was not about to be deterred, and even if the United States' NATO allies would not open their airspace to Russian planes, he had other options. No sooner had the Bulgarians closed the door on Moscow than huge Russian Condor transport planes began to lumber over Iran and, crossing Iraq, make their way to the Latakia base. Russian fighter escorts, which were not accustomed to flying such a long distance from home, followed closely behind like goslings.

Stu Jones, the U.S. ambassador in Baghdad, was directed by the State Department to take up the issue with Iraqi prime minister Haider al-Abadi. But when Jones contacted him, Abadi insisted that he was not aware that Russian planes were using his country's airspace as a corridor and would need to look into the matter. As in the days of Nouri al-Maliki's rule, the Iraqi government was not eager to interfere with air traffic emanating from Iran, no matter how concerning it appeared to the United States. The next day, Jones called Washington to ask how hard the administration wanted to press the Iraqi leader, and learned that the White House did not think much could be done now that the Russian deployment was underway.

In a quest to find a silver lining, some NSC officials argued that the Russians would now be vested in the conflict and might try to pave the way toward a political solution. At worst, the conflict would become a Russian quagmire. Obama himself later adopted this latter point, stating at a White House news conference, "An attempt by Russia and Iran to prop up Assad and try to pacify the population is just going to get them stuck in a quagmire and it won't work." All told, the Russians flew more than a thousand sorties to establish an air expeditionary force in Syria, and to deploy the forces to protect and sustain it—and the Russian military foothold took shape faster than the Obama administration anticipated. Russian Su-34 fighters and Su-35 multirole planes operated out of Latakia, along with An-30 reconnaissance aircraft and Forport drones—an Israeli-designed system that was manufactured in Russia. The Russians also flew in artillery, air defense, and Spetsnaz (special forces), as well as signals intelligence units to intercept communications from rebel forces that were fighting Assad. Gone were the days of Putin's appeals to the readers of *The New York Times,* when he explained in a September 11, 2013, op-ed that "we are not protecting the Syrian government, but international law," while admonishing the Obama administration, which was still debating how and whether to enforce the president's red line on Assad's use of chemical weapons, saying, "We must stop using the language of force and return to the path of civilized diplomatic and political settlement." Acting rather than writing two years later, the Russian leader would use force to pursue a military victory for Assad that secured Moscow's interests.

Another surprise came in September when a delegation of Iraqi military officials arrived in Moscow for a visit. The Kremlin announced it was setting up a joint operations command with the Iraqi military in Baghdad to share intelligence. When Abadi met with Biden on the margins of the United Nations General Assembly, the Iraqi leader said that the defense ministry team had traveled without his knowledge but that it would have been too awkward to pull the plug. The idea of giving the Russians a seat at the table in Baghdad to discuss intelligence or military operations was too much for the United States, and the Americans used their influence to snuff out the initiative. But the Russians had every intention of flexing their muscles in Syria.

On the morning of September 30, Stu Jones was having breakfast at his ambassador's residence when he was informed that a Russian general was at the gates of the American embassy with a message. Jones told the embassy security to invite him in, but the general balked and merely left behind a letter. Addressed to the U.S. defense attaché, the letter said that Russia intended to carry out its first air strikes in Syria in a matter of hours and warned American warplanes to stay out of Syrian airspace. Jones sent the letter up the chain of command. The U.S. military had no intention of calling off its air strikes and reconnaissance in Syria, but its operations there would never be the same.

Syrian fighters in the CIA's covert program immediately felt the impact. While the Russians maintained publicly that they were going after terrorists, they targeted the CIA-backed rebels, including their weapons depots. The strikes infuriated the Gulf states that had backed the uprising against Assad. Adil al-Jubeir, the urbane Saudi foreign minister and the kingdom's former ambassador in Washington, told the Americans that the Russian actions would inflame the Sunni world. "Even Sunnis that drink will come to jihad," his Qatari counterpart, Khalid bin Muhammad al-Attiyah, observed.

In the end, Russia's Syria deployment was a fait accompli, one that boosted Moscow's importance in the region and gave the Russian military a chance to demonstrate a global reach and to use the Syrian conflict as a weapons test site. In October, four Russian warships in the Caspian Sea fired more than two dozen cruise missiles at targets in Syria, nearly a thousand miles away. On November 30, two Blackjack bombers took off from a base on Russia's Kola Peninsula, flew around Western Europe, lumbered over the Mediterranean, fired their cruise missiles at targets in Syria, and then continued over Iraq and then Iran before turning north again to land in Russia. In August 2016, Russian Backfire and Fullback bombers launched air strikes at targets in Syria after taking off from Hamedan Air Base in Iran. Russian Bear and Blackjack bombers also fired cruise missiles from Iranian airspace.

With the coalition's struggle against ISIS moving slowly, the naked display of Russian military might was applauded in Najaf, the Shiite holy city I visited in 2015. "What the people in the street care about is how to get Daesh out of Iraq," Ibrahim Bahr al-Ulum, a member of Iraq's parliament, said. "Now, Putin is more serious than the United States." One of the most popular Facebook posts in Iraq's Shiite heartland was a photoshopped meme of Putin dressed in the robe of a southern tribal sheikh. For American commanders, on the other hand, the Russian military was one more problem to be managed. After a flare-up with Turkey, the Russians deployed an advanced S-400 air defense system in Syria—the first time that the Russians had taken such a sophisticated air defense system and used it abroad. The system had the range to cover the approaches to Incirlik, which had become a hub for American operations in Syria and Iraq. There was nothing the Americans could do about that, though after the Russians activated an SA-17 surface-to-air missile battery, Kerry managed to persuade the Russians to turn it off during a visit to Moscow. The potential for confrontation was the push of a button away.

THE PRESSURE ON the White House to make headway against ISIS escalated further after December 2, 2015, when a mass shooting at a government building in San Bernardino, California, resulted in the deaths of fourteen people. The culprits, a U.S. citizen of Pakistani descent and his Pakistani-born wife, had not been directed by ISIS, but they had become radicalized by reading jihadist posts on the internet and had pledged allegiance to Baghdadi. The presidential candidate Donald Trump exploited the episode at a campaign rally in South Carolina, where he called for a "total and complete shutdown" of the country's borders to Muslims, notwithstanding the fact that the main perpetrator had been born in the United States. This was the very scenario that Obama and his team had worried about: a terrorist attack that would shift public attitudes at home. The sooner ISIS was destroyed and the sooner the American public understood that the militants' fate was sealed, the better, the Obama administration officials thought.

On December 14, Obama returned to the Pentagon to convene another NSC meeting. The Obama administration's "by, with, and through" strategy was fifteen months old. It had been moving forward, but the progress was incremental, while ISIS had a flair for the dramatic. From the start, the White House had been as worried about getting too heavily involved in a potential quagmire as taking too long to vanquish its foe. The White House was not trying to wage a war as much as manage one. But the November 13 Paris attacks and the prospect of homegrown terrorism were changing the president's calculation. "We need to have a sense of urgency," Obama said. "We need to be aggressive and surface new ideas, and I want an assessment of what is and is not working."

Austin gave a dutiful rundown of how the campaign was proceeding. In Syria, Mazloum's fighters were operating northeast of Raqqa, had turned to Al-Shaddadi, and would continue to defend their frontline position against ISIS. In Iraq, the government forces could, Austin felt, clear and hold Ramadi. After that, he said, the Iraqis could move on Hit, another ISIS stronghold in Anbar province. Austin, however, wanted the Iraqis to hold off on taking Fallujah so that they could maintain a focus on Mosul. The goal now was to put pressure on ISIS at multiple points simultaneously. That would require the use of more U.S. forces, specifically advisors at the brigade level. So far, U.S. advisors had only operated within bases, and assigning them to Iraqi brigades could finally move them outside the wire, though it would still keep them well away from the fighting.

Obama, however, wanted more than a tactical update. He had vowed to degrade and destroy ISIS. Going into the final year of his presidency, he wanted to break the back of the militants' resistance. "Tell me how this fits together over the next six months to generate momentum?" Obama asked.

Stepping back from the details, Ash Carter responded that the United States was trying to put pressure on ISIS simultaneously in Syria and Iraq. That would force the militants to fight on multiple fronts and prevent them from shifting reinforcements back and forth. "We are trying to sever Iraq and Syria," he said. Carter added that the Americans still needed to stand up a Sunni constabulary to hold the liberated towns, a project on which they had made little progress but that was a constant preoccupation at the White House.

The operations that are coming up, Joseph Dunford added, would really challenge ISIS's aura of invincibility.

"What will ISIL do to adjust?" asked Obama.

The president then posed a sensitive question on how the United States might expedite the offensive. The United States and Iran were staying out of each other's way based on a common interest in defeating ISIS. But they were not talking to each other about the campaign and there was always a risk of an inadvertent run-in between U.S. troops and the Iranian-backed militias. Would it help to get Iran and the Tehran-backed Shiite militias on board with the evolving U.S. strategy?

The out-of-the-box thinking went too far for the military men who had contended with Iran during the eight-year-long U.S. occupation of Iraq and had hundreds of troops killed at the hands of Iranian proxies. Austin saw nothing to gain by consulting with the Iranians. Iran, he said, wanted ISIS to be defeated, but it also did not want the United States to rack up too many wins. Far from helping, the Iranians, Austin cautioned, would find ways to slow down the U.S.-led coalition's progress against ISIS so that their Shiite militia proxies in Iraq could play more of a role. There was a general consensus among the president's team to leave the situation with the Iranians as it was, and Obama agreed.

Shifting to Syria, Carter asserted that Raqqa was a more brittle target than many people thought. He took note of Kerry's dogged efforts to secure a cease-fire in the nation's civil war.

Obama asked if the Raqqa offensive depended on negotiating a diplomatic end to the other fighting in Syria. The president was skeptical that Kerry could ever deliver on that initiative and did not want the campaign to be further delayed. "I don't want our strategy to be completely dependent on diplomacy," he said.

Carter said a Syrian cease-fire would undoubtedly make it easier for the United States and Mazloum's fighters to operate against ISIS, but that it was not essential. The two were not linked.

Dunford noted that Mazloum was trying to recruit more Syrian Arab fighters to join his Kurdish-led force. If Mazloum succeeded in mobilizing an additional two thousand Arab fighters, he would have more manpower to isolate Raqqa, and the recruiting efforts might also encourage other Arabs to join. There could be a snowball effect, which could also be useful in showing that the U.S. Syrian ally was ethnically diverse.

Austin added that it would require a great deal of effort to mobilize enough forces to take Raqqa, but that any pressure Mazloum and the United States could put on the ISIS capital would be useful.

Directing the discussion back to Iraq, Brett McGurk said that Abadi believed that retaking Ramadi was pivotal. The city had been lost on the prime minister's watch and was close to Baghdad. But it would be important to keep Iranian-backed militias out. Abadi, McGurk continued, wanted to retake the Anbar town of Hit after that. The Iraqi prime minister, McGurk said, was open to the deployment of U.S. Apaches and more special operations forces at Al-Asad. The closer one got to Baghdad, he said, the more visible the American presence would be to Iraqi politicians, and the harder it would be to send U.S. advisors with Iraqi forces in the field, a bridge the Obama administration had not yet crossed.

Then the conversation shifted to what the C-ISIL coalition—as the assemblage of nations John Allen had helped organize to counter ISIS had been dubbed—could do to help speed things up. Carter was scheduled to meet with his fellow defense ministers soon and noted that he had prepared a list of "tailored asks."

Expressing frustration with the United States' allies, Obama said that, with the possible exception of France, the others were not showing up. Obama wanted to know if there were "game-changing" asks that he could make at the head-of-state level.

Blinken, who was about to be elevated to the role of deputy secretary of state, suggested that the United States ask for more special operations forces from the British, French, Dutch, Danes, and United Arab Emirates. Kerry chimed in with his own suggestions, including asking Sweden to do more. Obama stressed that he did not want the State Department to get ahead of the Pentagon in seeking out additional military partners.

Obama then returned to the theme Biden had sounded in a previous NSC meeting: the United States needed to tell a better story about what it was doing. The purpose was not only to dispel any impression that ISIS was on the march but also to show the American public that the administration was on the case at a time when polls revealed that public approval of Obama's ISIS policy was about 35 percent. "We need to do a more effective job of telling our story," the president said. "We need to package this in a coherent narrative."

During the NSC meeting, Carter had come up with a way to persuade the public that Operation Inherent Resolve was making headway toward a decisive victory. Recalling the World War II newsreels that showed the march of the Allied Powers across Europe and the Pacific, Carter showed Obama a Pentagon map with bright red arrows pointing to Mosul and Raqqa. The Inherent Resolve task force had a plan to mobilize Iraqi, Kurdish, and Syrian fighters to advance toward each objective. Obama instructed Carter to work with Ben Rhodes, the top NSC aide for strategic communications, to lay out the scheme for the American public, but Rhodes pointed out that the presentation would be more persuasive if it came from the Defense Department.

"We need a lot more people out there, and it can't just be the White House," which would be seen as overly political, said Rhodes.

"There needs to be more of a war room mentality," added

Obama, invoking the campaign trail for an all-out messaging effort. "My key takeaway on the C-ISIL campaign is that we need to do more to pull all these threads together with a clear narrative. I want this articulated to me by January 1. I want this in a box by the time I hand over the keys. I want ISIL to be on a clear path to defeat, and I want to go at them hard. It is not just the threat they pose to the homeland, but it is the distortionary effect they could have on our politics if we have an attack here. There is no higher priority for me."

The next day, December 15, Obama approved more special operations deployments in Syria, the use of Apaches in carefully planned operations, and an increase in the force manning level in Iraq. The White House press office spun into overdrive, even enlisting the support of Rob Malley, the senior NSC Middle East hand, who carefully avoided the spotlight but dutifully tweeted everything the White House Office of Digital Strategy prepared. Overnight, article roundups echoing the administration's themes started piling up in the media's in-boxes with subject lines like "Relentlessly Pursuing ISIL's Leadership and Shrinking ISIL's Safe Havens"; "Enhancing and Enabling Partners"; "Counter-Financing, Foreign Fighters, and Protecting the Homeland"; "Expanding Humanitarian Support"; and "Diplomatic Track."

BUILDING ON THE establishment of the Al-Taqaddum base, the United States had been prodding the Iraqis to reverse ISIS's May 17 capture of Ramadi. Brigadier General William Mullen, a Marine officer who had coauthored a book on the U.S. military's old success in Fallujah, took over from Robert Castellvi and spent long planning sessions with Abdul Amir Rasheed Yarallah and other senior Iraqi officers. The plan was for the Federal Police to attack from the east while the Iraqi Army and the CTS moved in from the north, west, and south. When Austin first heard of the plan, he fretted that the Iraqi forces might collide in the heart of the city in a sprawl of confusion. But the offensive moved at a snail's pace—when it moved at all. After failing to get the Federal Police, who clung to their defensive positions, to move, Mullen plucked two Iraqi brigades—the 73rd and 76th—that were being trained as part of an eventual Mosul assault force and suggested they join the attack.

Fresh problems arose when the head of the Anbar Operations Command, which was supposed to oversee the effort, balked at advancing until U.S. airpower destroyed everything in his path. Sean MacFarland went to Abadi and got the commander replaced with a more assertive officer so that the offensive could lurch forward again. Even so, the offensive ran into obstacles when Iraqi troops were attacked by a band of ISIS fighters who had shaved their beards and donned Iraqi police uniforms, the better to sneak up on their foes. In the end, it was the CTS that did the heavy lifting and ventured into the city. By late December, the CTS had raised the Iraqi flag over the government compound in Ramadi and declared the city to be liberated, although the urban center and its suburbs would not be completely recaptured until February 2016.

The Ramadi offensive was carried out with some disadvantages. U.S. and Australian advisors did not accompany Iraqi units but rather stayed within the confines of Al-Taqaddum, where they sought to translate battlefield requests from their Iraqi partners into timely air strikes. U.S. Apache helicopters were not used in the fight: by the time the Obama administration gave its approval, Abadi calculated that the battle could be won without them. There were also, however, some lessons to absorb. The CTS was still the most reliable and courageous unit, Iraqi Army and police forces were reluctant to undertake operations without copious U.S. air support, and a behind-the-scenes American role was essential, including in advising the Iraqis on their plans and their choice of leaders.

Soon after the December 14 NSC meeting, Carter decamped for the Middle East to see what he could do to move the campaign along. The secretary of defense traveled in an E-4B, a flying com-

mand post the media had dubbed "the doomsday plane," which
included a crew of military officers who worked behind banks of
terminals that connected the Pentagon chief with the latest intelligence and enabled him to direct orders to the U.S. conventional
and nuclear forces, if it came to that.

For all of the public confidence about Operation Inherent Resolve, Carter's travel arrangements reflected the apprehensions
the Pentagon had about security in Iraq. I was on the trip, and the
plan called for us to stay overnight in Bahrain and then make
day trips via a C-17 to Baghdad and Erbil. Even so, Carter got a
taste of war. As we got off the plane at the Erbil airport on December 17, a military officer who was attached to the consulate
muttered to me, "The shit hit the fan tonight." Sure enough, we
soon learned that ISIS had mounted a multipronged attack just
hours before Carter arrived—its most determined attack against
the U.S.-backed coalition in five months. Brigadier General Mark
Odom, who ran the Erbil strike call, had been up all night coordinating the battle. ISIS fighters had caught the Peshmerga by surprise by attacking in the late afternoon instead of waiting for the
cover of darkness. It was what Odom called a "spoiling attack," an
ISIS attempt to unhinge the coalition's preparations for an eventual Mosul offensive.

The coordinated attack had been directed at the Iraqi Army
bases at Nawaran, Bashiqa, and Tal Aswad, with 80 to 120 militants equipped with armored bulldozers, trucks outfitted with
machine guns, and suicide car bombs hitting each location. Some
of the ISIS militants had succeeded in infiltrating the Peshmerga
lines, and at least eighteen Peshmerga had been killed, including a
couple of local commanders. Some ISIS fighters had lobbed mortars at a Turkish compound north of Mosul that was being used
to train some of Atheel al-Nujaifi's fighters. In a sign of what was to
come, they used small hobby-kit drones to direct their fire. American, British, and French aircraft responded with strikes that
lasted until 9:00 a.m. on December 17. In the confusion, a team
of Canadian Special Operations Regiment soldiers who had been

sent to northern Iraq to mentor the Peshmerga joined the fighting to push ISIS back, taking advantage of the more accommodating guidance from Ottawa about participating in combat, if necessary, than their American counterparts enjoyed.

Keeping to his schedule, Carter drove to Barzani's mountaintop palace outside Erbil and promised that Iraqi forces would vacate any Kurdish territory they used to stage their Mosul attack once the fighting was over. The Americans had another sweetener to offer as well. The Kurdish economy, which was already burdened by mismanagement and corruption, had been battered by the conflict and a sharp downturn in foreign investment. The enormous construction projects in Erbil had been stopped in their tracks, and the government was woefully behind in paying its teachers and civil servants. The financial strains were so acute that there was even a two-month lag in paying the Peshmerga fighters who were defending Kurdistan against ISIS along a six-hundred-mile front. The highway between Erbil and Sulaymaniyah was decorated with the portraits of the Peshmerga martyrs who had died fighting ISIS, but their government was having trouble paying the force. To keep the war going, the Pentagon quietly promised to provide the salaries to the tune of some $50 million a month, and to contract for food and other supplies to sustain the Kurdish army. Carter also promised to send two brigades' worth of equipment for the Peshmerga. The United States had been holding on to the equipment until the Peshmerga moved to integrate units that were beholden to the rival KDP and PUK political parties and created more of an apolitical force, but there was no time for that now. In return, Barzani assured the United States that the Kurds would not use the looming offensive against ISIS as an opportunity to claim still more territory in their tug-of-war with the Iraqi government. Carter, however, did not ask the Kurds to relinquish their claim to Kirkuk and other disputed areas they had occupied when Iraqi forces fled after the fall of Mosul. Those issues would still need to be hashed out with the Iraqi government.

After returning to the United States, Carter did his best to support the White House's public information campaign during a January 13, 2016, visit to Fort Campbell, Kentucky, the home of the 101st Airborne Division. The division's senior officers and several hundred of its soldiers would soon be headed to Iraq to advise and train Iraqi forces, and Carter used his address to the troops to spell out the administration's goals for a broader audience, comparing the Islamic State to a cancer that had metastasized. "The ISIL parent tumor has two centers—Raqqa in Syria and Mosul in Iraq," he said, displaying a diagram. "That's why our campaign plan's map has got big arrows pointing at both Mosul and Raqqa."

Two days later, Carter told Obama at an NSC meeting that the United States should plan on taking both cities by the end of the year.

13

THE NEXT TEN PLAYS

In Baghdad, Sean MacFarland was tasked with turning Ash Carter's red arrows into an actual operation. The effort entailed as much negotiation as military planning. MacFarland had taken to calling the counter-ISIS campaign a "marbled" war. That was a shorthand way of saying the United States had multiple partners with their own timetables, equipment, and agendas that had to be corralled to fit MacFarland's strategy. There would be a lot of zigzags on the road to Mosul and Raqqa.

Compounding the challenge, the U.S.-led coalition had only enough reconnaissance assets and airpower to press ahead with one main offensive and one secondary attack at a time, which would make coordination all the more important. To advance the offensive in northeastern Syria, MacFarland flew to meet with Mazloum Abdi near the Lafarge Cement Plant. Situated south of Kobani, the plant had been run by a French company that was later charged by French prosecutors with paying off ISIS so that it could keep its factory running in the midst of the Syrian civil war. By the time MacFarland arrived, the French were long gone and the plant had been turned into a makeshift headquarters, complete with a tactical operations center, a dining facility, a garage for tactical vehicles, a weight-lifting area, and an interior metal walkway that I maneuvered along during a stay there in 2017.

The purpose of MacFarland's meeting was to talk with Mazloum about what it would take for his fighters to seize Raqqa, and the American commander had some ideas about how the Syria campaign should unfold. Some steps had already been taken. Mazloum had mustered several thousand fighters for the battle for Kobani, and by the spring of 2015 his force was estimated to have grown to fifteen thousand. At the Americans' behest, Mazloum also rebranded his force to send a message of inclusiveness: the Syrian Democratic Forces (SDF) were born.

The next step, MacFarland thought, should be for the SDF to take Tabqa Dam, a major source of hydroelectric power that sat beside Lake Assad near Raqqa. That would enable the U.S.-led coalition to seal off the western approaches to the city. As with the seizure of Mosul Dam a year earlier, this would preclude ISIS from sabotaging the installation. Tabqa, MacFarland continued, should be followed by a push to retake Manbij, the multiethnic city where U.S. intelligence believed that the Paris terrorist attacks had been planned.

Mazloum had his own priorities, which had to do with cementing control of his canton in northeastern Syria before taking on objectives farther afield. Mazloum's immediate goal was to chase ISIS out of Al-Shaddadi, a move he told MacFarland was needed to build up his fighters' confidence. The city was also located in a region that had oil resources, and was home to an Arab tribe that the SDF had recruited. MacFarland went along with Mazloum's plan but secured a promise that future objectives should pave the way for the retaking of Raqqa.

Mazloum's fighters had been working with Delta Force, or Task Force 9, as it was known at JSOC. But to avoid aggravating the Turks' anxieties, the Americans promised that Task Force 9 would only train and arm the Arab members of Mazloum's expanding force, which the Pentagon dubbed the Syrian Arab Coalition (SAC). To try to assuage Turkey, MacFarland made an unpublicized trip to Ankara, where he met with the Turkish general staff and insisted that none of the weapons would fall into the hands of

Syrian Kurds or end up with Kurdish separatists in Turkey proper. It was an argument that the Americans would make time and time again, but that Erdoğan challenged and never bought.

While MacFarland was pushing Mazloum to advance in the northeast, he was also putting the pieces in place for a parallel move in the south. The idea was to train and equip Syrian Arab fighters who had been pushed out of the Euphrates River valley by ISIS and had taken refuge at an outpost on the Jordanian side of the border called Tower #22, which consisted of little more than an old radio beacon. The fighters called themselves the Jaysh Maghawir al-Thawra (Revolutionary Commando Army)—a name the Americans abbreviated to MaT—and had come from the southern city of Al-Bukamal. The MaT did not have a leader as charismatic as Mazloum and were virtually unknown in the West. They did not have the military experience and organization of the Syrian Kurds, but they also lacked a foreign neighbor who viewed them as an existential threat, which meant there would not be a large price to pay for supporting them. Significantly, they wanted to get Al-Bukamal back, and MacFarland hoped to help them do just that.

If all these efforts bore fruit, U.S.-backed partners would be squeezing ISIS's positions in the Euphrates River valley from the north and the south. At a minimum, MacFarland calculated, the fighters should be able to grab a foothold in southern Syria by seizing the Al-Tanf garrison and turning it into a base that stood astride the highway from Baghdad to Damascus. That would hamper ISIS's movement from eastern Syria to western Iraq, and that initiative could be supplemented by operations in western Anbar province by the Sunni tribes, should the United States succeed in mobilizing them. The mission to train the fighters was given to Colonel Kevin Leahy's 5th Special Forces Group, the same unit that sent A-teams to Baghdad in 2013 to try to help the CTS improve its game. An operation like this would require MacFarland to go to Amman to meet with Abdullah II, the king of Jordan, but the Jordanians had already made clear that they were open to the Americans' initiatives as long as they did not receive much publicity.

Across the border in Iraq, MacFarland was putting together a parallel series of steps to set the stage for the battle to reclaim Mosul. Given the capacity for training at Iraqi bases, the limited number of Iraqi trainees, and the substantial infrastructure that would need to be captured or built to launch the battle, he projected Iraqi and Peshmerga troops would position themselves near Mosul by late 2016 and take it by the summer of 2017.

After two long years at CENTCOM and multiple tours in Iraq, Lloyd Austin prepared to retire from the military in the spring of 2016 and turn over his mission to Joe Votel, the head of the Special Operations Command who had led the parachute assault into the Afghan desert that helped kick off the U.S. war there a few weeks after 9/11. As he was nearing the end of his tour, Austin flew to CENTCOM's regional headquarters in Qatar, where he had arranged for MacFarland to present his Mosul plan to him, Votel, and a group of other U.S. government officials and see what the command might do to accelerate it. After long months of trying to nudge his "marbled" partners to advance, and with decisions yet unmade in Washington about allowing U.S. advisors to accompany Iraqi frontline units on the battlefield, MacFarland believed he had made headway in setting the table for the climactic Mosul battle, and he laid out his timeline.

"Are you kidding me?" Austin shot back. MacFarland's timeline was a lot longer than Austin had expected and did not come close to meeting Ash Carter's hope of taking Mosul and Raqqa before the end of Obama's presidency.

After the session, Terry Ferrell, Austin's chief of staff, buttonholed MacFarland and said that his briefing had put the outgoing CENTCOM command in a tough position. CENTCOM's expectations and MacFarland's task force's planning were out of sync, and a roomful of people had just witnessed the disconnect firsthand. Months later, Austin dressed down MacFarland in private in their last one-on-one meeting. The two generals had different command styles and personalities, and in the end somewhat divergent missions: while Austin was trying to navigate

Washington's expectations, MacFarland was struggling with the realities in Syria and Iraq.

Obama asked Carter to provide a "top ten" list of upcoming military operations, and the request trickled down to MacFarland. Under the NSC's protocol, MacFarland had never been included in its meetings, but the president wanted a clearer sense of what the C-ISIL campaign would accomplish during the final six to twelve months of his presidency.

MacFarland made a PowerPoint map with circles, arrows, and blobs in the margin that described the situation and gave a general idea of what was planned, with the caveat being that the plan could be upset by a change in attitude on the ground or in any number of regional capitals. In military circles, the hoary saying "The enemy gets a vote" is intended to convey that even the best-laid plans can be upended by the adversary's actions. In this case, the United States' putative allies had a vote, too. MacFarland was trying to coordinate operations in two countries, which each had its own politics.

On February 19, 2016, Carter presented Obama with a brief titled "C-ISIL Coalition Military Campaign Plan Strategic Concept," which spelled out a list of objectives, some geographic and some thematic, in Iraq and Syria. The list read as follows:

1. Al-Shaddadi
2. Kisik Junction
3. Kara Soar
4. Hit
5. Rutbah
6. Secure the Tigris River Crossing at Qayyarah
7. Seize the Qayyarah Airfield West
8. Grow Anbar stabilization efforts
9. Recommence improved training and equipping
10. Develop southern Syria efforts

The Al-Shaddadi operation, at the top of the list, would deprive ISIS of a major hub in northeastern Syria that it had used to move on Mosul in 2014 and continued to draw on in shifting forces across the Iraqi border and back. To prepare the move, Brett McGurk had traveled to Kobani the previous month and told Mazloum and his team that they needed to continue their offensive against ISIS if they wanted to continue to benefit from U.S. air strikes and the fifty-man Delta Force team that was advising them. When Mazloum demanded a seat at the table at the Geneva peace talks the United States was supporting on the Syria conflict as a condition of moving on Al-Shaddadi, a condition that was sure to be blocked by the Turks, McGurk demurred. Instead, McGurk argued that the future of Syria would be decided on the ground, not in Geneva. It was the actions the SDF was taking and the territory it controlled that would give it valuable leverage in any wheeling and dealing over Syria's future. A success in Al-Shaddadi and the nearby villages would set the stage for Raqqa, which would figure prominently on a future list of "next ten plays."

Several of the other items on the list—Kisik Junction, Kara Soar, and Qayyarah Airfield West—were important preparatory steps for the long-awaited push to Mosul.

IN APRIL, EVENTS illustrated the sort of variables the U.S. commanders had to grapple with. Thousands of Iraqis had taken to the streets to protest chronic electricity outages and persistent corruption. Goaded on by Muqtada al-Sadr, they had taken their protests to the Green Zone to demand that the cabinet be ousted and replaced by technocrats. Shoddy services and poor governance were problems the Americans had long stopped trying to remedy—but nothing could happen militarily if Iraq was paralyzed by a political crisis.

In an April 13 NSC meeting, Carter stressed that the crisis was another curveball for the counter-ISIS campaign. The United States, Carter said, wanted to get forces in place for the Mosul operation by Ramadan, when a month of fasting would slow any progress on the battlefield, and that was just two months away. The political crisis, the defense secretary advised, was jeopardizing those efforts. Carter noted that he had allocated $418 million through the end of the year for Peshmerga salaries and planned to ask for more contributions from coalition defense ministers and Arab Gulf states.

"Is the political crisis a speed bump or a structural inhibitor?" asked Obama, who had observed his share of Iraqi crises.

Joseph Dunford, who had done multiple tours in Iraq, said that the "military pieces will fall in place if the political crisis is resolved."

Joe Votel, who had now succeeded Lloyd Austin as CENTCOM commander, agreed but cautioned that the political issues were key at the moment.

Obama was determined to see Operation Inherent Resolve advance. While he was not about to delve into Iraqi politics, he did have a card to play—namely, the money Washington was trying to arrange for the Iraqis from the International Monetary Fund. The president thought Brett McGurk and Stu Jones should send a signal to Baghdad. "All the parties need to understand that government stability is key to us mobilizing money for them," Obama said. "If it makes sense to send signals to Iran, we should do that, too." Once more, Obama had raised the sensitive issue of whether the U.S. and Iranian efforts against ISIS should involve more than military deconfliction.

McGurk suggested to Obama that the United States did not need to reach out to Iran. "Iran's position is close to yours, and they are sending the same message," he said. Grasping for a silver lining in Iraq's political crisis, McGurk said that the political turmoil in Baghdad had brought Abadi and Barzani, the leader of the KRG, a bit closer together. The Iraqis had ignored the Americans' entreaties to avoid Fallujah and were moving to take the city. The plan, McGurk said, was to open up a humanitarian corridor as the fighting intensified to enable the civilians to get out. As for repairing the war damage afterward, McGurk mentioned that the

United States had a list of "stabilization priorities" that he hoped the Arab Gulf states would fund.

Turning to Syria, Carter stressed the importance of taking Manbij back from ISIS. That task had been made more urgent after a 2015 effort to get the Syrian opposition fighters to clear the pocket around Manbij with U.S. air support failed. The discussion soon shifted to how to make that palatable to Erdoğan. Following MacFarland's fraught efforts, Biden had flown to Istanbul in January to confer with the increasingly autocratic Turkish leader at Beylerbeyi Palace and given the Turkish government a few months to assemble a counter-ISIS force of its own, but the fighters the Turks had recruited had not accomplished much.

Dunford suggested that the Turks might not object if Arab fighters working with Mazloum took the city with the help of Manbij residents, who were a mix of Arabs, Kurds, and other minorities. Some had fled and organized their own military council. "This is the best place we have been with the Turks for months," he said.

McGurk, who favored throwing the U.S.'s weight behind the SDF and their potential allies in the city, said that he had met with the Manbij Military Council. "It's a force of about thirty-five hundred. They will fight with anybody who is fighting ISIL, and they are itching to go," he added. "They probably won't wait indefinitely."

Carter agreed. "It is in our interest to partner with and facilitate the Manbij military council going into Manbij."

Building on Dunford's recommendation, Obama suggested that the United States might be able to navigate the tangled politics of northern Syria by restraining Mazloum's Kurdish fighters to mollify Ankara while encouraging the Syrian Arab members of the contingent to move on the city to achieve one of the campaign's key objectives. "I could envision the SAC going in earlier if we sent a message for the YPG to stand down," Obama said. If the United States showed it was prepared to address some of Turkey's concerns, it did not have to make Ankara 100 percent comfortable, the president added hopefully.

As the weeks went by, however, the Turks would not budge. They insisted that if any force moved in to clear the area in and around Manbij, it should be the Syrian Arab fighters Turkey had recruited and trained. The Obama administration's hopes of finessing Ankara's objections seemed to be waning. But the challenge in fighting ISIS was not getting any easier. With Iraq in a state of political disarray and Turkey more concerned about Mazloum's growing movement than ISIS's continued hold on Manbij, the administration's counter-ISIS campaign was again at risk of losing momentum. There was no red arrow pointing at Raqqa, just a red splotch of Mazloum's fighters in the northeastern part of the country that Erdoğan seemed determined to contain.

The question of how to move on Manbij was taken up again at an NSC meeting the next month. Carter made the case for calling Erdoğan's bluff and going with the only capable force the United States could muster: fighters under Mazloum's command and the Manbij Military Council. The Paris attacks had spooked America's European allies, too. Europeans wanted that city in the coalition's hands even if it would increase tensions with Ankara.

"The Turks are trying to veto our only play here," complained Carter. "I just don't believe they will throw us out of Incirlik. Our European allies want us to go with Turkey."

Obama said that he had recently talked with David Cameron, the British prime minister, and he had assessed that Turkey would continue to cooperate on migration—meaning that Erdoğan would not allow more Syrian refugees to flood Europe even if he did not get his way on Manbij.

John Kerry said that the Syrian force the Turks were backing was losing ground and that ISIS was shelling Turkish territory. "We need a second front soon to tee up the Raqqa campaign," he urged. If Mazloum's fighters took on the mission, perhaps no more than 450 members of the assault force needed to be Syrian Kurds. The Arab and Kurdish fighters reporting to Mazloum could pull back as soon as the mission was done and let the Manbij Military

Council secure the town after that. "I opposed overriding Turkey earlier, but not anymore," Kerry said.

McGurk backed up his boss at State. "I worry that the campaign will stall out if we don't keep up the pressure," he said.

Dunford said that Hulusi Akar, the head of the Turkish general staff, acknowledged that having Mazloum's SDF move into the areas around Manbij was the smartest move operationally but instead had backed a plan that would be more politically acceptable to Erdoğan. Dunford had worked hard to build ties with his Turkish counterpart but did not see a way to appease him. "I agree we need to move to keep up the momentum," added Dunford.

At the end of the meeting, Obama agreed that it made sense to give Mazloum the green light and said that he would call Erdoğan to try to soften the blow. Early in his administration, Obama's calls with Erdoğan had gone well, but in recent months they had become increasingly strained, and the U.S. president did not relish making another one. "I am persuaded, even though it just cost me an hour and a half of my life," he quipped.

Confirming his understanding with the Americans, Erdoğan later made clear that Turkish intelligence would be monitoring the assault to ensure that Mazloum did not use it as an excuse to extend his domain to the west. No more than 450 members of the thousands-strong force were to be Kurdish YPG, and they would primarily be there for logistical support. It was Mazloum's Syrian Arab allies and the Manbij Military Council who were to be in the lead in an operation in which the political leanings of the fighters were as important as their fighting skills.

On June 1, the long-awaited push to Manbij began. Delta Force commandos ferried across the azure Euphrates with Mazloum's fighters in zodiac boats and makeshift barges as ISIS fired from the western bank. During the assault, an ISIS anti-tank missile smashed through the window of a Delta pickup truck, exiting out the back and destroying two YPG trucks. With the river crossing behind them, Mazloum's forces quickly liberated sixteen villages within the first few days of fighting, rescued Yazidi girls who had been stolen from Sinjar, and captured a strategic hill overlooking the city.

After several days of rapid progress, the assault force suffered a setback: Abu Layla, the leader of the Manbij Military Council and a charismatic figure who had played an important role in Kobani, was shot in the head. The Americans medevacked him to Sulaymaniyah, a level of care not available to the rank and file, but were unable to save him. The Manbij campaign had its first martyr, and the loss of Abu Layla was a portent of tough fighting. Later in the battle, Abu Layla's brother Yousif Babe Aziz was captured by ISIS, appearing in orange prison fatigues in a caliphate video.

As ISIS's resistance intensified, the U.S. scheme to rely largely on Arab fighters fell by the wayside. It was Mazloum's Kurdish fighters who had the battlefield skills, command and control abilities, and political commitment to see the battle through. That ensured Manbij would be retaken, but Obama's hope of finessing Middle East politics had been challenged. The goal now was to finish the battle and then persuade the Kurdish YPG to hand over the area to the locals and withdraw east of the Euphrates.

With its back against the wall, ISIS began to conscript the townsfolk into military service and engaged in a fierce campaign of retribution against citizens it presumed were sympathetic to the would-be liberators. By July, Mazloum's fighters had made it into the city and reported they had killed Abu Khalid al-Tunisi, the ISIS emir who controlled Manbij.

Desperate to escape, ISIS fighters assembled a line of vehicles in August, took civilian hostages with them as human shields, and drove out from the city, calculating that they would be immune to U.S. air strikes. Those civilians who remained in the town smoked openly and burned burqas in defiance of ISIS's draconian religious edicts. Mazloum had lost about five hundred fighters in the battle for Manbij and had many more wounded. When I arrived on the outskirts of Manbij a year later, the senior commander in the Manbij Military Council was wearing a yellow patch on his shoulder with a photo of Abu Layla. For years afterward, the Americans tried to assure the Turks that Mazloum's YPG Kurds and their agents had pulled out of the town after their hard-won victory—to no avail.

One objective was decidedly not on the U.S. playlist, but Iraq was determined to pursue it come what may: Fallujah. The Americans had hoped to bypass the operation, the better to speed up the push to Mosul. But it remained a high priority in Baghdad, including for Iranian-backed militias. If the United States was going to rely on the Iraqis instead of American combat troops to do the fighting on the ground, it had to accept that the Iraqis had their own priorities. In this case, the fighting was carried out not only by the CTS and Federal Police but also, MacFarland later learned, by Iranian-backed militias, some of whom donned Federal Police uniforms so they would qualify for protective U.S. air strikes and were later linked to the abuse or disappearance of hundreds of Sunni men who had been separated from the fleeing civilians. With no advisors among the Iraqis, it was not easy to tell the players apart, and the militias had learned to game the system.

While the Americans had hoped to minimize their involvement in the battle for Fallujah, the Iraqi government drew them in once signs appeared that the ISIS resistance had begun to crack. On June 29, a large convoy of ISIS vehicles began to gather near the city's Salam intersection—the Iraqis took this as a sign the militants were going to make a run for it. At 4:00 a.m. on June 30, Stu Jones was roused from sleep by an agitated call from Abadi's chief of staff. The prime minister was not only worried that ISIS was fleeing but concerned that the ISIS convoy was making a beeline to Karbala, one of the Iraqi Shia's two great religious cities and the site of the Imam Hussein Shrine. Imam Hussein, a grandson of the Prophet Muhammad, had been martyred at the battle of Karbala in AD 680. A stunning mosque had been erected around his tomb, and thousands of devout Shia made pilgrimages there. Now ISIS appeared to be rushing toward this seat of Shiite power.

Al-Qaeda's Zarqawi had nearly ignited a civil war in Iraq by bombing the Shiite shrine in Samarra, north of Baghdad. This could be far worse. At a point at which the American-led coalition was just beginning to turn the tide, the Islamic State appeared poised to mount a devastating counterblow, which could plunge the nation into sectarian violence. The Iraqi government was armed but ill equipped to do much about it. The Iraqi air force had little ability to find moving targets in the dark and to strike at night. The Iraqis had taken on Fallujah against the advice of the U.S. military, but now they needed the Americans' help.

MacFarland, who had been in Iraq as a brigade commander at the time of the 2006 Samarra bombing, was asleep in his quarters when he got a call from Jones.

"What's going on with the convoy?" the ambassador wanted to know.

MacFarland had been briefed before going to bed that civilian vehicles were massing in the southern part of Fallujah. Until then ISIS had not staged any mass evacuations, and it was not clear if they planned to use the convoy to evacuate ISIS families or fighters.

MacFarland called his staff, who had been monitoring the column using drones and surveillance planes, but they had seen no sign of hostile intent, did not know for sure who was in the vehicles, and had no idea where they were headed. Was this a diabolical blow against Iraqi Shia, a bugout with human shields, or both?

Discerning what ISIS was up to was not easy. Air Force colonel Kurt Wendt, director of intelligence, surveillance, and reconnaissance (ISR) in Iraq and Syria, recalled, "We often get tips from our Iraqi partners or we see something on TV that causes us to decide it's worth it to move our ISR assets to investigate. My first thought was the numbers we were hearing—sixty to one hundred vehicles—were exaggerated. I was in disbelief that there would actually be that many enemy vehicles headed together into the desert. At that point, it became an intensive ISR process to figure out if there were truly enemies or civilians or refugees."

As the tension built, Jones decided to go to the joint U.S. and Iraqi command center at Union III, which was across the street from the fortified embassy, to monitor the situation. The U.S. ambassador never ventured outside his diplomatic compound without his security detail. But as the minutes ticked by, Jones opted to make an exception and walked alone to Union III.

MacFarland had B-52s armed with JDAM satellite-guided bombs in the air, but the best he could do with limited information was to buy time. He instructed the air war commanders to crater the ground and slow the convoy. When the sun came up, the U.S. forces could get a better look at who was in the vehicles. After the B-52s bombed the road, the column broke into two parts and began to reorganize. After monitoring the vehicles, the Americans assessed that it did not include civilians, and the order was given to strike. All told, 213 vehicles were hit, according to the battle damage assessment. U.S. military officials eventually concluded that the convoy had never been headed to Karbala, but the scare had enabled the United States to crush the attempted escape.

The air strikes, however, had an unintended and unhelpful effect on another U.S.-backed operation in remote Syria. At Al-Tanf, the U.S.-trained MaT force had been eager to push north and reclaim Al-Bukamal, a bold move to strike ISIS when it least expected it. Operation Day of Wrath, as the fighters grandiloquently called it, started off well. The fighters were loaded into American-supplied Toyota Land Cruisers and made the run to Al-Bukamal. ISIS, not anticipating an attack, had left the city largely undefended, and the MaT quickly penetrated it. No American or other coalition forces were allowed to accompany the fighters, who were so excited by their triumph that they began to celebrate and did not set their defenses. Once the ISIS fighters recovered from the shock, several dozen of them began to mount a counterattack.

Using the last of its Hellfire missiles, a U.S. Predator blew up an ISIS suicide bomber as he barreled toward the MaT in a heavily armored *Mad Max*–style vehicle. In the rush to stop the ISIS column bolting out of Fallujah, however, a B-52 that had been on station over Al-Bukamal to support the MaT with a planeload of satellite-guided bombs had instead been tasked to stop the convoy in Iraq, leaving the group without any air cover. Shortly after, the MaT was forced to retreat to Al-Tanf and would never make a serious foray north again.

14

OBJECTIVE FISH

Sean MacFarland faced an array of complications in putting the pieces in place for the Mosul operation, not least of which was prodding the Iraqis to rethink how they went to war. Iraqi officials had been focused, first and foremost, on the protection of Baghdad since ISIS first barged into Iraq. Two years after the fall of Mosul, American military officials estimated that 60 percent of the Iraqi combat power and all of its logistics were devoted to stopping ISIS suicide car-bomb attacks in Baghdad and protecting the Green Zone from the militants and from the demonstrators Muqtada al-Sadr had whipped up. If there was a spare brigade that was not tied up in the fight, chances were that Iraqi commanders would pull it to the capital for security duties.

The Mosul operation, however, would require a fundamental shift: the bulk of Iraq's largely Shiite military would need to make its way north to liberate a largely Sunni city. Expeditionary warfare was not the Iraqis' strong suit; it would tax their creaky logistics and require a level of coordination they had yet to demonstrate. During the Fallujah fight, the synchronization of the different branches of the Iraqi forces remained "elusive," concluded an after-action assessment by the 2nd Brigade of the U.S. Army's 101st Airborne, which was supplying the Inherent Resolve task force with advisors, troops for security, and artillery.

"Ultimately," the report said, "the Fallujah attack became a race to the town center between competing ISF forces." Mosul would be far tougher than Fallujah, and just getting to the outskirts of the city would be a major challenge.

The first step would be to take Qayyarah Airfield West, a large base just west of the Tigris River and about forty miles south of Mosul—step number seven in Ash Carter's ten next plays. American soldiers had taken to calling it Q-West, which they tended to pronounce as "Key West." The complex would serve as a hub to fly in supplies, mount helicopter attacks, fire surface-to-surface rockets at the enemy to the north, and manage logistics. It would be the perfect springboard for a Mosul offensive. But just how to take the base was the key question.

Additionally, there were serious questions about the viability of the airfield. The only airfield close to Mosul that could support C-130s was Erbil. Q-West, FOB Marez, FOB Kisik, and Tal Afar were all still under ISIS control. Before the United States left northern Iraq in 2011, the airfield had recently undergone extensive repairs.

Abdul Amir Rasheed Yarallah, the Iraqi general who had been designated to oversee the Mosul campaign, had his own idea. The Iraqi commander wanted to assemble his forces at Camp Speicher, the site of the ISIS massacre of Iraqi air force cadets in June 2014, and then drive up Highway 1 to the west of the Tigris. The plan had the virtue of simplicity. The Iraqi forces would proceed northward in one large column. The drawback was that the Iraqi offensive could be stopped dead in its tracks, or at least slowed to a crawl, if ISIS managed to block the route. Beyond that, the plan appeared to reflect a hidden political agenda, so much so that MacFarland wondered if it had been influenced by Hadi al-Amiri, who was leading the Badr Corps, one of the Popular Mobilization Forces, which had been placed under the prime minister's office in 2015. Amiri's scheme would enable the Iranian-backed PMF militias operating out of Camp Speicher to tuck in behind the

Iraqi military and make their way north to Tal Afar. It looked like politics had triumphed over strategy.

MacFarland had an entirely different plan in mind. Instead of aligning all of Iraq's forces along a single axis, there would be a multipronged attack. Troops from the 15th Iraqi Army Division would assemble near Makhmur, a small town east of the Tigris from which ISIS had menaced Erbil in August 2014. The town was near Camp Swift, a small U.S. outpost and Tiger base that was manned by Navy SEALs who were acting as advisors.

The Americans would provide the tents and gravel to establish the Iraqi base, which was close to the fight but not so close that ISIS could interfere. Then the 15th Division would bridge the Tigris and head west toward Qayyarah. It would be the first opposed river crossing by an Arab army since the Egyptian army crossed the Suez Canal at the start of the 1973 Yom Kippur War, and was step number six in Carter's next ten plays. To mitigate the risk to the bridging force, a CTS task force and the 9th Iraqi Army Division, Iraq's lone tank-equipped division, would move north on a separate axis from Camp Speicher and secure the western bank of the river in a carefully synchronized operation. Instead of one axis of attack, there would be two, and the Americans would help out by positioning artillery near Makhmur to silence the ISIS mortar positions west of the river and dispense smoke to cover the emplacement of the bridge. MacFarland managed to persuade Abdul Amir. As with the offensive to retake Ramadi, the Americans were playing an important behind-the-scenes role in shaping the strategy the Iraqis were to use.

Putting that plan in place required a lot of heavy political lifting: Makhmur was on the outer fringes of territory claimed by the Kurdistan Regional Government. Masoud Barzani, the Kurdish president, had deep-seated fears that the Iraqi troops who assembled in Makhmur would claim the territory as their own and would never leave. If the counter-ISIS offensive was successful, the Kurds would no longer have ISIS on their doorstep, but Barzani did not want to avert that danger only to confront an occupation by the Iraqi Army. Only the Americans had the *wasta* (clout) to negotiate a solution and make the deal stick.

Carter had smoothed the way during his December visit to Erbil by offering funds and equipment for the Peshmerga. One last-minute impediment, however, was resolved by Kurdish politics. The U.S. military's legal officers would not approve the expenditure of American funds for building the Makhmur camp without knowing who owned the land—and with the United States opening its wallet for the Mosul offensive there was no shortage of potential claimants. For a while it appeared that the whole plan might be delayed by the U.S. contracting regulations and lawyers. Finally, Barzani acted to extract the Americans from their dilemma with his version of eminent domain: the Kurdish president would authorize the use of the territory and take care of the putative landowners later.

Life at Makhmur had its challenges, including a sea of mud that ensnared the Iraqi vehicles and made life generally miserable until the Americans contracted for a few shipments of gravel. To compound the challenges, Makhmur was being targeted by ISIS rockets. In early March, four Iraqis were killed and nearly two dozen wounded by Katyusha rockets fired by militants, prompting many of the Iraqi soldiers to disperse into the hills. MacFarland had long envisioned that the Americans would position artillery in the area to support the Iraqi drive to the Tigris. With ISIS flying drones from Qayyarah and firing rockets from nearby villages, however, the artillery had to arrive soon.

MacFarland's answer was the 26th Marine Expeditionary Unit, which was serving as a reserve force for CENTCOM, had its own artillery, and was afloat in the Persian Gulf. On the night of March 17, a company of Marines and four M777 artillery pieces were flown by helicopter to Makhmur, where they established Fire Base Bell, which was less than a mile from the Iraqis and protected by sand berms and concrete T-walls. Dubbed "Task Force Spartan," the Marine artillery swung into action the next day. ISIS's response came on March 19, 2016, when the militants fired a 122mm rocket at the modest outpost. The Marines were taking shelter in a U-shaped concrete bunker when the projectile struck a blast wall, sending fragments flying toward the shelter. Staff Sergeant Louis F. Cardin was struck in the chest by the ricocheting shrapnel and was rushed to a medical facility in Erbil, where he was pronounced dead on arrival—the second American to be killed in action since U.S. forces were sent back to Iraq. Eight other Marines were also wounded, three seriously enough that they had to be evacuated to an American military hospital in Landstuhl, Germany. The event, a public relations nightmare for the U.S. military, exposed the numbers game the United States was playing to stay within the low force cap Washington had established for Iraq. The presence of the Marine unit had not been officially announced before it was struck. And since its mission was deemed to be a deployment of four months or less, the Marines were considered to be on a temporary duty (TDY) assignment and thus were not counted against the U.S. troops cap, or "force manning level," for Iraq, which at that point officially stood at 3,870. In other words, troops were being wounded and dying, and Washington was acting as if they were not even there.

U.S. military spokesmen struggled to persuade the media that they had been preparing to announce the deployment when the Marines were attacked. Another problem was that the Marines' artillery mission and the fire they were taking ran counter to Obama's assurances that the Americans deploying to Iraq would be mere advisors and would not have a combat mission, a stipulation that had already been quietly breached by the positioning of artillery at Al-Taqaddum.

In Baghdad, Colonel Steve Warren, the chief military spokesman for the Operation Inherent Resolve command, tried to square the circle. Warren had already run afoul of the White House by acknowledging to reporters in October 2015 that the American role, limited though it was, amounted to "combat." Now Warren had to explain yet another combat episode. In a briefing for the

Pentagon press corps on March 21, Warren told the media that the United States had built "a small fire base" to protect the Iraqi troops and their coalition advisors. His attempt to level with the U.S. media, however, ran afoul of political sensitivities in Iraq. The party line in Abadi's office was that the United States did not have any bases in Iraq and was merely advising and training Iraqi forces on their installations. Now Warren was talking about a U.S. "fire base." At a weekly meeting the embassy hosted for American officials on "messaging," Stu Jones accused Warren of undermining Abadi.

"Steve, you just drove a stake through Abadi's heart," Jones exclaimed.

But misstating the facts would not work either. It was impossible to pretend that the Marines were on an Iraqi installation. Fire Base Bell was hundreds of meters away from the camp in Makhmur that the United States had built for the Iraqis. It was MacFarland's British deputy, Major General Doug Chalmers, who came up with a semantic solution. Perhaps there was no need to talk about bases at all. The area the Iraqis were in was called Kara Soar, so the Marines would be described as part of the Kara Soar Counter Fire Complex, the precise contours of a "complex" being in the mind of the beholder. With a simple press release, the clash between transparency and sovereignty was swept under the carpet. The reference to "counter fire" was intended to convey that the artillery mission was defensive. But plans had already been made for the Iraqi offensive to move beyond the Kurdish front, secure strips on the west and east sides of the Tigris, and install the float bridge—all with U.S. artillery support.

AS CARTER HAD signaled during his visit to Fort Campbell, it was the 101st Airborne that would advise and mentor the Iraqi forces in the Mosul fight. Colonel Brett Sylvia was one of the officers who would need to make it work. Sylvia had done a couple of deployments in Iraq before. A brainy West Point graduate who was trained as a combat engineer, he had served as a military assistant to Paul Wolfowitz, the deputy defense secretary, before being assigned to Paul Bremer's Coalition Provisional Authority, where he worked for the retired Army lieutenant general Keith Kellogg. Sylvia later served in Diyala province, one of the most violent areas of Iraq and an AQI stronghold, during the 2007 troop surge. Like other officers fighting ISIS, however, Sylvia had to cope with the constraints imposed by Washington.

As the commander of one of the 101st Airborne Division's most storied brigades—the 2nd Brigade Combat Team—Sylvia had a lot of assets, but he would not get to bring all of them. While Obama and his aides were pressing the military for new ideas, they still maintained an iron grip on the troop levels. Sylvia was given the same troop cap as the unit he would be replacing, which was drawn from the 1st Brigade Combat Team of the 10th Mountain Division, commanded by Colonel Scott Naumann. An Army combat brigade generally ranged in size from 3,500 troops to as many as 5,000, depending on how many additional combat and support units were attached. The "force tracking number" Naumann had to adhere to was 1,236 and not one soldier more. What made the limit particularly problematic was that the 10th Mountain soldiers had deployed to Iraq in August 2015, well before the Paris terrorist attacks shocked the Obama administration and heightened the White House's interest in speeding up the campaign. Naumann's role had been principally to advise Iraqi commanders and train their soldiers, including officers at Iraq's Ground Forces Command Center, which was located near the Baghdad airport and appeared to have an important role based on Iraqi organizational charts, but in fact had little influence over Iraqi commanders in the field. Naumann's mentoring had occurred within large Iraqi bases, with the exception of the role he played in establishing Camp Swift and the Kara Soar Complex.

Yet Sylvia's mission was more ambitious and, in theory, more troop-intensive. He needed to support the push to Mosul. To do so, MacFarland had asked Joe Votel for the authority to send advisors with Iraqi brigades. The new commander had surprised MacFarland by extending that authority to the battalion level for the drive north and the battle for Mosul itself. Adding to Sylvia's burden, instead of relying on contractors at bases in the rear, his troops would need to do most of their own maintenance. The soldiers would not be driving Humvees on bases and behind the Kurds' front lines, but operating armored vehicles—including mine-resistant, ambush-protected (MRAP) vehicles—and moving with the Iraqis toward Qayyarah Airfield West and Mosul.

Sylvia's brigade would also be assuming the artillery mission from the Marines at the Kara Soar Complex and that, too, would take personnel. Before they deployed, Sylvia's troops received some sage advice from their 10th Mountain counterparts: they would be carrying out a 2016 mission with 2003 infrastructure and 2007 expectations. In other words, they would be helping the Iraqis confront a terrorist army without all of the logistics, bases, forces, and freedom to maneuver that the United States had in Iraq during the heyday of its occupation. Yet official Washington and the American public would be looking for results that were every bit as decisive as the defeat of al-Qaeda in Iraq during the 2007 surge.

The brigade was at least given one important asset: equipment and engineers to help the Iraqis bridge the Tigris. Since the Iran-Iraq War, bridging had not been a big part of the Iraqi military's repertoire. Iraqi forces had had little need of it during their clashes with ISIS: only one small span was emplaced to cross the Euphrates during the battle for Ramadi. The Iraqis did have a bridging regiment, but none of its soldiers had been trained to emplace a float bridge under fire, and the regiment's personnel were not even in the practice of carrying weapons. They were more like civilian than military engineers, and their practice was not to deploy the span until the riverbanks had been secured by the Iraqi Army. As for the boats that would be needed to install the span, the Iraqi regiment had a dozen, which were in ill repair.

To help the Iraqis get over a surging Tigris, MacFarland had arranged for Air Force C-5 transport planes to secretly fly more than thirty bridge sections to Iraq from an Army depot in California. A fifteen-member team of Army bridging engineers, including a mechanic and a welder, were also dispatched to Iraq from Fort Knox to help train the Iraqis on the new equipment. The initial training was quietly conducted at Taji, just northwest of Baghdad. The sprawling base had notoriously poor drainage, which made it prone to flooding. For once, that liability turned out to be a blessing. The excess water was channeled into a drainage pool, which was bermed and used to create an artificial lake for training that was fifty yards wide and eighty yards long. Other training was carried out in the moats around Saddam Hussein's palaces near the Baghdad airport. The American engineers were initially surprised by how relaxed the Iraqis were about the training, until they learned that the Iraqi commanders were playing their cards close to their vests and had not informed the soldiers about their upcoming combat mission. In the Iraqi military, this sort of secrecy was far from uncommon.

By June, the bridge company had completed its training and moved up to Makhmur, along with the float bridge components and American advisors. Before the float bridge could be installed, Iraqi troops needed to control the west bank of the Tigris and a jagged area on the eastern side the Americans dubbed the "shark's fin." The operation to clear the terrain along the river and eventually capture Qayyarah Airfield West was code-named "Valley Wolf." For four months, several brigades from Iraq's 15th Division struggled to clear the villages on the east side, tangling with ISIS fighters who were defending the towns with dense minefields, deep trenches, tank ditches, and twelve-foot-tall walls. The 101st's M777 howitzers moved forward from the relative safety of Kara Soar to provide covering fire for the Iraqis, who used bulldozers to breach ISIS's defenses. The village of Nasr changed hands several times before the Iraqis finally managed to secure it, but at a cost: the commander of the Iraqi 71st Brigade was shot in the back and killed during one clearing operation.

The reports filtering back to the Americans were not encouraging. The Iraqis had taken a lot of casualties, and an operation that was supposed to take hours or days ended up taking weeks. Sylvia's brigade saw it as another indication that a stepped-up American advisory effort would be needed when the Iraqis began to confront the far more formidable challenges in and around Mosul. In the short term, it also meant that the western and eastern prongs of the offensive were no longer in sync.

While the bridging operation could still go forward, the Iraqis could no longer assume that it would do so unopposed. To support the Iraqi push, the 101st would lob rounds from its howitzers to suppress ISIS mortar teams on the far side. Smoke rounds would also be fired to shroud the operation, while smoke generators provided to the Iraqis by a U.S. National Guard unit would be used to thicken the white cloud. The code name for the site where the bridge was to be assembled was "Objective Fish."

If there was ever a time to take advantage of Votel's decision to allow U.S. advisors to accompany Iraqi battalions into the field, this would be it. The case for deploying advisors with Iraqi forces had long been clear. The Americans' remoteness from the battlefield limited their understanding of what was happening at the front—the operations officer for Sylvia's brigade figured the unit had access to only 50 percent of what the Iraqis were planning.

Americans also had to contend with the Iraqis short planning horizons. They tended to make decisions in late-night planning sessions, and unless there were American advisors with the Iraqis at multiple levels of command, the United States might receive little or no warning of what its partners were doing. Above all, advisors could make the use of airpower more effective and decrease the risk of friendly fire. Nine Iraqi soldiers from the 3rd Division were killed near Fallujah in December when they rushed ahead to take an ISIS position that had been bombed twice, without realizing that a third air strike was coming. There were many factors involved, including bad weather, but it was the sort of episode that would have been less likely had an American or allied advisor been with their Iraqi brigade.

Though Votel had given his approval for an "accompanying" mission, some of MacFarland's subordinates were careful about using the new authority. None of Sylvia's advisory teams had accompanied the 9th Armored Division as it pushed up the west bank of the Tigris from Camp Speicher. (A Navy SEAL team, which had a separate chain of command, had accompanied the CTS on its drive north.) At first, it was not clear if American advisors would assist with the river crossing, and the operation began without them.

On July 15, a small group of Sylvia's soldiers, including four American bridge engineers from Fort Knox, got into their MRAPs and drove to Kharabat Jaber, a small town about eight hundred meters from the river, to monitor the emplacement of the float bridge. Bridging the Tigris, however, soon turned into an adventure. American combat bridges are typically constructed directly across the river. One by one, trucks lug sections of the floating bridge forward so that they can be dropped into the water and fastened together until they reach the far side. But after struggling to maneuver the sections in the moving river, the Iraqis decided to assemble the entire bridge along the west bank and have boats drag it into place. The maneuver went against everything in the U.S. military manuals, but it seemed to work. Major General Najim al-Jabouri, who was overseeing the Nineveh Operations Center, and several of his officers moved across the bridge that day with the Iraqi flag held high.

The operation, however, was far from over. At the joint Iraqi-American command post near Kara Soar, Sylvia was worried that the bridge had not been properly anchored in place. The Iraqis and their American partners would be moving concrete and tons of supplies across the Tigris to refurbish Qayyarah Airfield West once it was retaken, and there was a real risk that the bridge might buckle. Now Sylvia asked for the authority to send a team of bridge advisors down to the river. Major General Gary Volesky, who was in charge of the Iraqi portion of the ground campaign and reported to MacFarland, agreed. On July 16, advisors from 1st Squadron, 75th Cavalry Regiment, a light reconnaissance squadron in Sylvia's brigade, also went to the scene. It marked the first time U.S. advisors had been allowed to accompany an Iraqi battalion.

It was one thing to put a bridge into place and another thing to defend it against a terrorist army, however. American engineers in Kuwait had designed a "bridge protection system," which was a fancy name for a bunch of barrels, plywood boards, and concertina wire that was to be strung across the river to stop any floating IEDs. Determined to blow up the bridge, ISIS prepared a suicide boat packed with explosives, which a U.S. Apache destroyed with a Hellfire missile—one of the first times that the attack helicopters were used in the fight against ISIS. The protection system, however, turned out to be an ungainly contraption that sank, and was eventually replaced by other makeshift barriers that seemed to fail as often as they succeeded. The final line of defense, it turned out, was the Iraqis themselves. The Americans advised the Iraqis to position machine guns on the riverbank so that they could blast the floating bombs, and sometimes defense was left to Iraqi soldiers on the bridge itself, who were armed with nothing more than AK-47s. On one occasion, ISIS militants packed a small refrigerator with explosives and sent it down the river. It floated right over the protective barrier without detonating, prompting the Iraqis to fire at it furiously with their AK-47s until the IED blew up just meters away from the bridge.

For all the near misses, the river crossing was a success. ISIS's commanders understood the importance of Qayyarah Airfield West to the American-led strategy, and after failing to defend the base they embarked on a scorched-earth campaign to destroy it. Eventually, the facility was seized by the CTS and three Iraqi Army brigades. By the time the Americans got their first look at the base, virtually all of the buildings had been blown up. The runway was cratered. The militants had even pulled out underground water and sewage pipes, leaving empty ditches along the road.

The base would need to be cleared of IEDs and rebuilt from scratch. A U.S. Air Force team rushed to repave the runways so that C-130s could ferry in troops and supplies. Five thousand concrete T-walls were placed around the perimeter to help secure the complex, and housing for eight hundred personnel was rapidly constructed. A joint Iraqi and coalition command center was established, filled with large monitors for watching the feeds from reconnaissance drones and plotting the positions of friendly and enemy forces.

To accommodate the crash program, the White House raised the troop cap for Sylvia's brigade to 1,722, though the new ceiling still necessitated some workarounds. Sylvia's brigade had its own medical personnel, but it was the Navy that would run the field hospital while the Air Force would handle the security for the complex. Because the Navy and Air Force deployments were considered to be temporary, they were decreed to be "BOG neutral"— that is, their personnel would not count against the limit on the number of "boots on the ground."

It was not the most efficient way to organize the force, but it enabled the military to cope with the suffocating troop cap. By the time the Iraqis were ready for their push toward Mosul, Qayyarah Airfield West was a critical hub that was home to Apache attack helicopters, French artillery units, a field hospital, and Task Force Thor, which was equipped with surface-to-surface satellite-guided rockets that could be lobbed into the heart of the city.

As the fight for Mosul drew closer, U.S. special operations forces were also being called on to play a greater role. Advising Peshmerga units was already a risky mission. In May, a team of combat advisors had been advising Peshmerga fighters in the village of Tal Askuf, which was less than five miles of ISIS-held territory north of Mosul. More than a hundred ISIS fighters, equipped with truck bombs and armored vehicles, had attacked on May 3. The report of "troops in contact" had prompted commanders to rush a "quick reaction team" to the scene and unleash air strikes by A-10 attack planes, B-52 bombers, F-15 and F-16 fighters, and drones. Petty Officer Charles Keating IV, a Navy SEAL who was part of the quick reaction force, was shot by an ISIS fighter after his gun jammed and he ran to grab another weapon and take up a sniper position. He died that morning in a military hospital in Erbil, the third U.S. soldier killed in action during Operation Inherent Resolve.

In August, a Marine special operations team that took over from the SEALs began to edge forward in a mission dubbed "Evergreen II," marking the first time that U.S. special operators were authorized to accompany a Kurdish "by, with, and through" force beyond the Kurdish defensive line. The eleven-man team of Marine Raiders, as they called themselves, were told by the U.S. commanders that they needed to stay close to the leaders of the attacking Kurdish brigade and not attach themselves to platoons or companies at the front. But at six hundred troops, a Kurdish brigade was about the size of a U.S. battalion, and their commanders were not ones to lead from the rear, so the restriction was not an obstacle to the Marines' participation in the fight.

A more frustrating restriction pertained to the Marines' rate of advance. To reduce the risk from ongoing suicide car bombs and ISIS diehards, the plan was for the Marines to stay behind the Kurds and wait until the Kurdish forces ahead of them sealed their gains by digging a tank ditch. Only then could the Raiders rush forward to catch up with the Kurdish assault. That put the hard-charging Raiders in the uncomfortable position of trailing villagers who were returning to their newly liberated homes. "Because it was the first one, we had a lot of risk-mitigation measures put on top of us," one Marine participant in the operation recalled. "We did a lot of sitting and hanging out until a ditch got built over the course of two days."

By the third day, however, it became clear that the risk-reduction measures could only do so much. The Zeravani force, an elite Peshmerga unit, had bumped up against an ISIS tunnel

President Barack Obama meets with Secretary of Defense Chuck Hagel and his top Middle East commanders in Tampa to discuss the plan for the war on ISIS. From left to right: Hagel; Obama; U.S. Army General Lloyd Austin III, commander of U.S. Central Command; U.S. Army General Joseph Votel, commander of Special Operations Command; and U.S Navy Vice Admiral Mark Fox, deputy commander of CENTCOM. (The White House)

Combined Joint Task Force–Operation Inherent Resolve commander U.S. Army Lieutenant General Sean MacFarland meets in Baghdad with Secretary of Defense Ashton Carter and Carter's wife, Stephanie. (Defense Department photograph by Army Sergeant 1st Class Clydell Kinchen)

A sign in Mosul reads, "Islamic State Nineveh Province, A caliphate based on the prophetic method." (Pat Work)

Secretary of Defense Jim Mattis meets in Baghdad with Counter-ISIS envoy Brett McGurk (left) and CJTF-OIR commander U.S. Army Lieutenant General Stephen J. Townsend. (Michael R. Gordon)

U.S. Army Major General Joseph Martin discusses Mosul operations with Iraqi security forces commander Staff Lieutenant General Abdul Amir (right) and 9th Iraqi Army Armored Division commander Lieutenant General Jassem Nazal Qassem. (U.S. Army / Staff Sergeant Jason Hull)

Iraqi Humvees sit at the base of the destroyed minaret of the famed Great Mosque of al-Nouri, once a defining feature of Mosul's skyline. (Michael R. Gordon)

Two Iraqi tanks stand parked amid the rubble of Mosul. (James Browning)

A young child walks among the dead and wounded at the base of Al-Jamhouri Hospital in Mosul. (Free Burma Rangers)

David Eubank, founder of the Free Burma Rangers, carries an injured girl away from the fighting in Mosul. (Free Burma Rangers)

CJTF-OIR commander Lieutenant General Stephen J. Townsend (center) receives an operations update from U.S. Army Colonel Pat Work on the ongoing operation in West Mosul. (CENTCOM)

General Chiya Kobani, known to U.S. advisors as "the SDF's Patton," meets with CENTCOM commander U.S. Army General Joseph Votel. (U.S. Army / Staff Sergeant Timothy R. Koster)

Iraqi Federal Police break out in spontaneous celebration as the end to its fighting in Mosul is declared. (Michael R. Gordon)

A man rides his motorcycle past one of Raqqa's ubiquitous rubbled buildings. (William Roebuck)

President Donald Trump addresses troops at Al Asad Air Base in Iraq during a surprise Christmas visit in 2018, his first to troops in a combat zone. (The White House)

Smoke rises after a strike on the tent city of Baghuz, the last stand of the caliphate. (Free Burma Rangers)

Women and children, the families of ISIS fighters, wait to leave Baghuz. (Free Burma Rangers)

Syrian Democratic Forces commander Mazloum Abdi stands with Syria envoy Ambassador William Roebuck after the battle of Baghuz. (William Roebuck)

A woman walks with her child in the al-Hol camp, where the families of ISIS fighters are detained. (Rojava Information Center)

Marine Staff Sergeant Nicholas Jones receives the Purple Heart for wounds sustained during a fierce firefight against ISIS in the mountains of northern Iraq. Two Marine Raiders were killed in that operation. (Marine Raider, 2nd Marine Raider Battalion)

complex, which they were trying to clear, and the Raiders had moved by. Soon ISIS mortar rounds began to bracket the Marines' position and were landing a mere fifty meters away, which was close enough to do real damage if the rounds had been from the Russian or American inventory—instead, as they were home-made, they mainly scattered debris in the sky. Still, the Marines could not wait to see if the ISIS fighters were getting closer. The Marines were equipped with a mine-resistant all-terrain vehicle outfitted with a remotely operated .50-caliber machine gun that could be fired from the interior safety of the vehicle. No sooner did the Marines begin to shoot back, however, than the system broke down, forcing a Raider to climb on top of the vehicle to un-latch the machine gun from the truck and blast away at the enemy until the mortar fire stopped.

After Evergreen, the Raiders continued to do twice-weekly re-connaissance missions along other portions of the Kurdish de-fense line. On August 26, the Marines were visiting a Peshmerga defensive position northwest of Tal Afar in an area they dubbed the "tear drop" when they started taking heavy fire during the late afternoon from a nearby ridge. Exposed and with the sun in their eyes, the Marines could not pinpoint where the fire was coming from. Anxious to shut down the ISIS attack, the dog handler for the Raider team jumped on a Peshmerga machine gun and began laying down fire, while a Marine gunnery sergeant grabbed his sniper rifle and began firing grenade-like explosive rounds at any sign of a muzzle flash. The Americans went through the Kurdish ammo and then started going through boxes of their own, enlist-ing the Peshmerga to lug the ammo to the front. The fusillade continued until ISIS broke contact and began to slip away.

The next day, the Raiders drove back to their base in Duhok in the rain. On September 16, they returned to the tear drop fully expecting to find the enemy but bringing mortars, recoilless rifles, and a .50-caliber machine gun. Scanning the ridge with high-powered binoculars and targeting systems, the Marines saw no sign of the enemy until a Peshmerga fighter with his naked eye identified the silhouette of an AK-47 on the hill. A Marine gunnery sergeant began to shoot with the .50-cal, the rest of the Raiders opened fire, and soon a U.S. warplane was called in to drop several five-hundred-pound bombs. It was the last time the Marines took fire in the area. It was a lesson that the line between a special operations forces advisory mission and combat was a porous one and could shift in the blink of an eye.

15

EAGLE STRIKE

During the long years of the U.S. involvement in Iraq, there had never been a battle as vexing as the one to retake Mosul. American forces had seized Baghdad in 2003 after routing Saddam Hussein's Special Republican Guard, which was charged with defending the city. There was some hard fighting in the streets of the capital, but the foe was a conventional army that soon collapsed, leaving most of the city and its residents intact. In Fallujah in 2004, U.S. troops had battled their way street by street through an insurgent-held city that most of the residents had abandoned before the assault. Baqubah was the reverse: American forces took the city back from al-Qaeda in Iraq in 2007, only to discover that most of the insurgents had slipped away. But Mosul was in a class by itself. The city was defended by thousands of ISIS fighters, many of whom seemed determined to die in place, but it was also home to more than a million civilians who had been living under the militants' iron grip for more than two years.

The city was too large to take in one gulp, particularly for a force like the Iraqi military, which had struggled to muster enough battalions for the operation. The easiest approach was to start on the east side, which was more ethnically diverse and closer to Kurdish-controlled territory. The hardest part—the densely packed streets on the western side of the city, which were closer to Tal Afar and the ratlines that linked the ISIS defenders to their comrades in Syria—would be left for last.

After huddling with Iraqi generals, the U.S. advisors with the 101st Airborne thought they had come up with a workable battle plan for East Mosul. The opening blows would be delivered by the Kurdish Peshmerga and the elite Zeravani force. Following the script that had been worked out by Sean MacFarland and Ash Carter, they would advance on Mosul from the north and east, clear the villages that ISIS had taken, and then stop at a predetermined point and wait for the Iraqi military to pass through their lines. The Iraqi government had no intention of allowing the Kurds to take ground in East Mosul, and that was fine with President Masoud Barzani in Erbil. The Kurds were prepared to do their share but had little interest in sacrificing themselves for territory that would never be incorporated into the Kurdistan Region. The politics of northern Iraq made it easy to settle the division of labor.

But then what? There was an assortment of Iraqi forces to choose from, all of whom had their own strengths and weaknesses, and who reported to different ministries in Baghdad. The CTS was the best and most battle-hardened force, but after years of combat the most it could muster for the fight in East Mosul was twelve battalions, and most of those were understrength. It had only about 5,500 soldiers. The Iraqi Army had the numbers, but its quality was uneven and it had limited experience in urban warfare. The Federal Police seemed like a good force to hold ground and mop up pockets of resistance, but it had only a handful of tanks at its disposal.

The U.S. officers proposed attacking via several axes with a composite force that would draw on the strengths of all three. The CTS would be at the head of the columns so that it could breach ISIS's defenses. The Iraqi Army would follow to sustain the momentum, and then the Federal Police would move in to hold the liberated areas. The plan seemed to be on track until Talib Shaghati al-Kenani, the Air Force general who commanded the CTS, returned from a visit to northern Virginia, where his family had moved for their safety. He objected to the plan and took his complaints to Prime Minister Abadi. Kenani had no interest in serving as a battering ram so that the Iraqi Army could minimize its losses and revel in most of the glory. When the offensive came, the CTS would have its own independent axis. This was another lesson in the realpolitik of "by, with, and through" for the Americans. There were times when the United States could work behind the scenes to shape the strategy. Ultimately, however, the best military advice would need to conform to Iraq's political realities.

The plan was quickly redrawn so that each force could get its own piece of the action. After an initial assault in the north and east by the Peshmerga that would stop short of penetrating the city, the ball would be handed to Iraqi forces who would advance through the Kurdish lines. The 16th Army Division would push down from the north, while the 9th Army Division would approach Mosul from the southwest. Two CTS forces would kick off the fight by attacking from the east. Abdul Amir defended this laissez-faire approach: "I do not want to constrain my commanders," he declared once in a meeting at the Nineveh Operations Center. "I want them to have the ability to attack."

The Americans would do their advising from the Iraqi command centers on the outskirts of the city. Brett Sylvia, who figured that it would be more of a slog than a blitzkrieg, urged that outposts for the advisors be built—the brigade called them "tactical assembly areas"—and gravel laid for a battle that seemed certain to go through a soggy and chilly winter. The request went unanswered for weeks as more senior officers debated whether such measures were needed. What if ISIS cracked at the start and the construction was for naught?

Finally, two weeks before the Mosul operation was supposed to begin, work on the outposts got underway. To provide fire support, the brigade loaded its artillery onto lowboy trailers, which were hauled by a local contractor through Erbil to the foot of Mount

Alfaf, at which point the soldiers used their own trucks to haul the guns to a position near Mar Mattai, a Christian monastery at the top of the peak. During the early months of the conflict, this area had been the frontier. I had visited the high ground early in 2016 when it was home to a virtual coalition of the willing: a frontline Peshmerga unit, a few Iranian Kurds, a couple of Turkish tank crews, and two volunteers from Scotland and Romania. Now it was what the Army called a "position area for artillery." Several guns were perched on the mountain, with a commanding view of the city, along with counter-battery radars to pinpoint the location of ISIS artillery and rocket fire. Operating on Mount Alfaf had its challenges, including gulf-stream-strength winds that swept across the top of the city and shortened the range of the artillery, and the need to keep the howitzers under camouflage netting to hide them from the prying eyes of ISIS drones. The soldiers slept in concrete bunkers that looked like an inverted "U." And the shells fired by the M777 howitzers included the Excalibur, a GPS-guided shell that, at nearly $70,000 a round, was not to be used idly.

As the battle approached, the Iraqis dropped leaflets urging Mosul's residents to take precautions. They were urged to disconnect gas pipes and to stick tape over their windows in the shape of an "X" so that the glass would not shatter. Money and jewelry were to be hidden. If children were frightened, parents were to tell them that the enormous blasts were reverberating. Young men were to take up arms against ISIS. Months later, when I asked some former residents who had fled to a camp for displaced civilians whether they had heeded the leaflets, they reported that they were too afraid to pick them up. One could lose one's hand and for what? It would have been better, some said, if the United States had dropped food and other humanitarian aid. The Iraqi government dubbed the operation "We Are Coming, Nineveh." The Americans called it "Eagle Strike."

In mid-August, Lieutenant General Steve Townsend took over from MacFarland as the Inherent Resolve task force commander. Townsend had an unusual pedigree. He was the product of a love affair between a German art student and an Afghan medical student. Adopted days after he was born by a U.S. Army sergeant and his wife who were stationed in West Germany, Townsend grew up a military brat who moved from base to base. Like his father, he joined the Army, where he served in the 82nd Airborne for the invasion of Grenada and with the Army Rangers for the invasion of Panama. During his military career, he had commanded U.S. troops in some of the toughest battles in Afghanistan and Iraq, including Arrowhead Ripper, the fight to take Baqubah back from AQI in 2007. Riding in his Stryker vehicle to the city, Townsend had joked with his soldiers about retiring from the military, buying a farm, and putting his years of combat in the past. But Townsend was a military man at heart, and in deployment after deployment he continued to rise through the ranks. As the commander of the XVIII Airborne Corps, Townsend was next in the rotation to take over the counter-ISIS mission in Iraq and Syria. It was his good fortune to arrive in Baghdad after MacFarland had put many of the pieces in place, but many of the critical details remained a challenge for the commander and his senior officers as the battle approached.

Hadi al-Amiri, the leader of the Badr Corps, argued for taking Hawija first in a move that the Shiite leader thought would remove a potential threat to the Iraqi right flank—but that would also position Shiite militias near the oil fields and the military base the Kurds had claimed in Kirkuk province. Townsend met with Amiri to persuade him that bypassing the town was the best course of action. If Amiri thought clearing Hawija was so urgent, the general argued, the Popular Mobilization Forces could do that on their own without the help of the U.S. and other Iraqi forces—an option that had little appeal for Badr. Meanwhile, there had been concerns voiced from the experts on Iraq that the Mosul operation should be delayed until there was a plan for who would govern the city after its liberation. The Americans wanted to get going without delay and sort out the political problems later.

The night before the attack was scheduled to kick off, a jolt went through Townsend's command. Abadi contacted Townsend to discuss "breaking intelligence" that Turkey was going to intervene militarily while the Iranians had crossed the border near Sulaymaniyah. Conspiracy theories ran rampant in the Middle East, but ones that reached the prime minister could not be ignored. Townsend figured that the best way to dispel Abadi's worries was to run them to ground, and that meant redirecting several U.S. aircraft and later Reaper drones from ISIS to Iraq's borders with Turkey and Iran. For hours, American reconnaissance searched in vain for Turkish and Iranian troop movements. Abadi was reassured that Iraq was not facing a new threat from outside its borders, the hiccup was never formally acknowledged, and the Mosul operation proceeded on schedule.

On October 16, the Peshmerga summoned the media to embed with their fighters at their position an hour's drive from Erbil. The American military had reversed the policy that was begun under the Bush administration of embedding reporters with U.S. forces in Iraq. This move, which was instituted without much debate, limited the scrutiny that the generals received, bolstered the White House's talking points about the limited role of American soldiers, and, no doubt, made the jobs of public affairs officers easier. The Peshmerga and the CTS, by contrast, welcomed media attention. As in Sinjar, the Peshmerga's idea of an embed was to assemble their vehicles—a collection of aging armored vehicles, SUVs, and trucks with gun mounts—and invite the media to follow along in their own vehicles, with the understanding that they would need to be self-sustaining.

As a crush of reporters gathered in a small Peshmerga compound on the eve of the attack, a television flickered in the background, showing one of the campaign debates between Donald Trump and Hillary Clinton. A Kurdish officer provided no real details, but he did tell the media that there were too many journalists in soft-skinned vehicles, and that they would be an easy target for ISIS fighters armed with RPGs, sniper rifles, and mortars. The only sensible thing, he said, was for competing news organizations to double up and travel in a smaller group. The media's trucks were loaded to the gills with food, water, sleeping bags, medical kits, and satellite phones, and there was little interest in offloading supplies to make room for competitors. Nobody budged, and the Peshmerga officer shrugged. The warning had been sounded, and the responsibility was no longer his.

The attack was set for dawn. The Peshmerga did not have night-vision goggles and were planning to rush across the Nineveh plains at first light to clear several dozen villages and set the stage for the CTS push to come. As a night chill set in, the fighters and their media entourage crawled into their vehicles or into sleeping bags in the squat, unheated concrete buildings on the compound to try to grab a few hours of shut-eye. I was dozing on a concrete floor when my cell phone rang at 2:00 a.m. My first surprise was that we somehow were in range of a functioning cell phone tower. I was even more stunned by what the voice on the other end of the line was saying: the editors in New York were demanding reports about the dramatic start of the long-awaited battle for Mosul. The battle, they said, was on. Stumbling outside, I studied the Peshmerga vehicles and looked in vain for a sign of activity. In several hours, the soldiers would be grabbing their AK-47s, climbing into their trucks, dodging IEDs, and putting their trust in fate or Allah or blind luck, but for now their staging area was a sleepy campground. Nothing was stirring save for a few artillery rounds in the background, but that was hardly unusual: the Americans had been pounding Mosul for weeks.

Soon the mystery was dispelled. In Baghdad, Abadi had donned a black CTS uniform and, flanked by Abdul Amir and other senior generals, had gone on Iraqi state television. "I announce today the start of the heroic operations to free you from the terror and the oppression of Daesh," Abadi said. "The Iraqi flag will be raised in the middle of Mosul, and in each village and corner very soon." Iraq's prime minister had hitched his political future to the counter-ISIS campaign and was not about to let the Kurds steal the glory. The Peshmerga were responsible for the first day or two of the fighting, but Abadi would put his personal stamp on the campaign. Though Mosul was one of the most widely anticipated battles in modern history, the precise hour of the attack had been a secret. Now Abadi had broadcast even that.

The cardinal rule for any embedded reporter still held: the price of inclusion was to maintain operational security and not disclose what the military called "future operations." I called my colleague Tim Arango in Erbil and we cobbled together a lede: Iraq's prime minister had proclaimed the beginning of the Mosul offensive, while holding back the details of what was about to unfold. Months later, Trump would complain that the Obama administration had telegraphed its punches against ISIS in advance, but he had overlooked that it was the Iraqi leader who was doing the signaling in the public relations war. If the Iraqis were going to take on the bulk of the fighting and the political risks, their leader would decide when to announce the battle—even if it was before it actually happened.

A column of Peshmerga vehicles began to assemble in the moonlight and then rumbled off as day broke, the armored vehicles in the lead, the SUVs following. The frontier between the Kurds and ISIS was still lined with ditches, barbed wire, combat outposts, and sand walls. Over the past year, ISIS had conducted surprise attacks in an attempt to breach the defenses. Finally, the Peshmerga were pushing back. With only a limited capability to clear IEDs, the Kurds used the same tactic the Zeravani had employed during my embed in Sinjar: they drove off-road, only this time they were not rolling down a mountain but dashing across the flat Nineveh plains. The Peshmerga and the Iraqis were marginally better fighters than the militants, but they were far superior when they fought in concert with American and allied airpower, rockets, and artillery. As the Peshmerga converged, the militants set tires on fire and ignited barrels of oil, sending clouds of smoke into the sky. The Americans had fired smoke rounds to help the Iraqis conduct their Tigris River crossing. This was ISIS's attempt to shroud their fighters from American air strikes, though the clouds hardly seemed thick enough to do the job. By the end of the day, the Peshmerga had cleared some villages and did a thunder run with their armored vehicles through some others. But ISIS fighters were still hidden in some of the hamlets, waiting for an opportune moment to strike.

Before they hunkered down for the night, the Peshmerga piled large mounds of dirt along the routes near the villages to keep the enemy from bursting out of them. Abadi had had his moment in the sun, and now it was time for Masoud Barzani to have his. With Abdul Amir at his side, Barzani held an impromptu press conference in Khazir, east of Mosul, to announce that Kurdish fighters had begun to roll back the ISIS caliphate. When the Peshmerga attacked, the only flag they flew was the Kurdish regional government's tricolor, but it was still a demonstration of how Kurdish and Iraqi leaders could work together—at least as far as fighting ISIS was concerned.

Having squeezed ISIS from the east, the Peshmerga moved three days later to press the group from the north. An American AC-130 gunship sought to soften up the resistance during the night. But as the sun rose, it was clear that ISIS had been expecting an attack. The frightened residents in Fazeliya, one of the villages the Peshmerga intended to surround and then clear, had phoned a young Peshmerga fighter who had been raised in the town and was in the looming offensive. ISIS had detained sixteen men whose relatives were serving in the Peshmerga and hauled them off to Mosul. The hostages would be killed, ISIS warned, if anybody in the village assisted the Peshmerga attack.

After making a cut in the sand berm that had served as the Kurds' fortified border with the Islamic State for the past two years, a column of Peshmerga tanks, armored vehicles, and SUVs advanced. At first, the mood was upbeat: several Kurdish soldiers took photographs of themselves on the ridge as the Kurdish flag was raised in Nawaran, the first village to be taken back. But resistance in the next town, Borima, was much stiffer, and the Kurds had to call in a thunderous artillery barrage from the Americans to try to ease the way. In the distance, a bloodier drama played out as the Peshmerga closed in on Fazeliya. Suicide car bombs bolted out of the town. The Peshmerga opened fire in an attempt to disable them, but at least one of the trucks got close enough that its explosion ripped the legs off one of the Kurdish fighters. Trucks raced back across the rutted roads with the wounded as the columns of attacking fighters continued to move forward. Desperate to get an injured comrade through the snarl of military traffic to a makeshift trauma station at the front, a Kurdish fighter fired shots into the air. Blood stained the sand around the medics. The grievously wounded were driven yet again to a stretch of highway on the road to Duhok, loaded up on medevac helicopters, and flown to hospitals in the rear.

With frustration mounting over the growing losses, one Kurdish official in Erbil called me as I was leaving the front. The Americans, he insisted, had not provided nearly as many air strikes as the Kurds expected. Under the stress of combat, the unity in the counter-ISIS coalition was under strain. The Kurds believed the Iraqis were getting more than their fair share of the air strikes. I sent an email to Colonel John L. Dorrian, the Baghdad-based spokesman for the U.S.-led military coalition, asking for comment, and he acknowledged that the American and allied warplanes were struggling to keep up. "Given the size and scope of the operation to liberate Mosul, there may be times when we are unable to fully meet the demand as quickly as forces on the ground would like."

In other areas, the United States was providing much more support. To the north, the Marine Raiders were accompanying the Kurdish troops toward another Christian town, Batnaya, which was the site of the ancient Chaldean Catholic Mar Oraha Monastery. The operation was dubbed "Phoenix Raider," the title paying homage to the significance of the phoenix in Middle East lore. After several days of pushing through ISIS resistance, the Peshmerga built a defensive berm to consolidate their position while the Raiders moved their armored vehicles along the line to shore up weak points. That night, ISIS mounted a furious counterattack.

Several dozen ISIS fighters had moved within two hundred meters of the Peshmerga's position, and a car-bomb-laden vehicle that was one thousand meters away was driving menacingly toward the front while an ISIS heavy machine gun fired wildly just over the heads of the Marines and the Peshmerga. The Peshmerga shot at the ISIS muzzle flashes, while the Marines used their night-vision goggles to direct their fire at the enemy. Stopping the rolling car bomb was another matter altogether. The Marines put a few .50-caliber rounds into the vehicle, to no effect. The vehicle, they soon discerned, was a true *Mad Max* contraption. It was an armored personnel carrier that ISIS had captured and further protected with bolted-on metal plates. If it made its way to the Kurdish frontline position and exploded, dozens of Peshmerga fighters and Marines could be injured or killed, and the Kurdish operation would be stopped in its tracks.

As the vehicle approached, Staff Sergeant Dane Osthoff grabbed a Javelin anti-tank missile launcher—its projectiles were designed to strike the top and, presumably, less heavily armored portion of an enemy vehicle. The launcher misfired, and the gunnery sergeant rushed to remove the unused Javelin projectile and place it a safe distance from the Peshmerga and Marines. He reloaded the launcher with another of the more than $75,000 missiles to fire at the suicide vehicle, which by now was just eight hundred meters away. The Javelin shot was enough to stop the rolling bomb from advancing but not to detonate its cargo. That happened later when an AC-130 gunship arrived, shot up the remaining ISIS fighters, and blew up the vehicle. When the sun rose, the Peshmerga were jubilant and slapped their combat patches on the Marines. Osthoff ultimately received a Silver Star for his actions, the third-highest award for valor in the armed forces.

The episode showed that a team of eleven Marines, armed with high-powered weapons and the ability to call in air strikes, could invigorate a local partner force that was confronting a determined enemy. The Marines did not take any casualties on that mission, but on October 20 Chief Petty Officer Jason Finan, a Navy explosive ordnance technician who was attached to a Navy SEAL unit, was killed when his own vehicle struck a roadside bomb, marking the first American death in the battle for Mosul. The sort of accompanying mission the Raiders and other special operations units were carrying out was the exception. When it came to conventional units like Sylvia's 101st brigade, the advisors were still anchored well behind the advancing "by, with, and through" forces and proscribed from direct ground combat.

Abadi was upbeat when he spoke that day via video link to a group of diplomats in Paris who were discussing the future of Mosul. The assault force was pushing toward Mosul, the prime minister insisted, "more quickly than we thought and more quickly than we had programmed in our campaign plan." In fact, ISIS was still operating out of several major complexes in East Mosul, including Al-Salam Hospital, the Mosul Hotel, and the university, which it had used to manufacture crude chemical weapons. There were five bridges over the Tigris that the militants could use to send fighters and suicide car bombs from the western side. ISIS had hundreds of fighters who had dug tunnels and ditches, hidden car bombs, and otherwise fortified the outer suburbs of the city. The progress seemed to be greater the farther one was from the battlefield. At close range, the reality was already sinking in.

THE CTS WAS the first Iraqi unit to pass through the new Kurdish cordon and slice into the east. What the CTS lacked in numbers, it made up for in audacity. The force's first objective was Bartella, an Assyrian Christian town eight miles east of Mosul that was bisected by the highway to Erbil. ISIS had defaced Mar Shmony, the town's ancient church. The crucifix had been lopped off the steeple, and the statue of Patriarch Yacoub the Third smashed. ISIS's black-and-white emblem was painted on the church walls. Businesses that were confiscated from Christian residents were spray-painted "Property of Islamic State." Some shop owners who had sought to ride out the ISIS occupation put out signs reading "Owned by a Sunni Muslim." The CTS put its armored bulldozers, MRAPs, and bomb disposal teams at the head of its column as it sought to forge a path through ISIS defenses. But like the Kurds, the Iraqis drove off the roads when they could to try to circumvent the ISIS kill zones. ISIS had anticipated the maneuver and had crisscrossed the fields with tank ditches. It would take precious minutes for the Iraqis' bulldozers to fill them in, and an immobilized adversary would be a sitting duck for ISIS mortars or car bombs.

As I was accompanying the Kurds on their northern offensive, Bryan Denton, a photographer for *The New York Times*, was with the CTS heading toward Bartella. Denton was experienced in combat situations, which was all to the good because at six foot eight he stood out on the battlefield. He had wisely taken a seat in an MRAP, the most fortified vehicle in the Iraqi convoy, only to see his precautions upended when the CTS decided that the vehicle and the explosive ordnance detachment it was also carrying should lead the assault. Sniper rounds dinged off the vehicle, leaving a spiderweb pattern of cracks in the bulletproof windshield. Three suicide car bombs with bolted-on armor approached the assault force; two of them were blown apart by the CTS's M1 tanks, and one was so top-heavy that it flipped over as it was rounding a curve and lay like a turtle on its back. Finally, the soldiers, Denton, and a handful of other journalists in the MRAP disembarked, only to discover that yet another suicide driver was bearing down on them. Denton tried to dive behind a vehicle, but a flying shard of metal struck his wrist, forcing him to be evacuated with the wounded. The next day, the CTS finished clearing and filling in the tunnels dug by the militants. For the first time in more than two years, the peal of church bells could be heard.

WHILE ALL EYES were focused on East Mosul, ISIS set its sights on Kirkuk. In the push to Mosul, the United States and the Iraqis had sidestepped Hawija, the site of the 2015 prison raid and an ISIS stronghold firmly under the militants' control. The decision had expedited the Mosul offensive, but now the Americans and the Iraqis were paying the price. ISIS's October 21 attack reflected an impressive degree of preparation. The fighters had scoped out the target, knew where to position themselves, had calculated how their adversary was likely to respond to the assault, and were poised to exploit the attack for the maximum public relations effect.

Kurdish intelligence and interrogations of captured militants indicated that more than a hundred fighters moved stealthily in the night from Hawija to the outskirts of Daquq, where they were met early in the morning by seven trucks operated by drivers who knew the streets and alleyways of Kirkuk. Others had snuck in previously and were hiding in safe houses. While the city was still asleep, ISIS fighters, equipped with GPS locators, rushed to seize several tactically advantageous spots, including the tall buildings outside the emergency police headquarters, where they used snipers to bottle up Kirkuk's security forces. Still more militants took up positions in the Snowbar Hotel, which gave them a commanding view of the heavily secured compound where Najmaldin Karim, the governor of Kirkuk province, and his aides worked.

When the first reports of the attack came in, Karim, who had dual U.S. and Iraqi citizenship, was at his residence trying to keep up with the American election campaign via cable television. The governor's first call was to Lahur Talabani, the head of the Kurdish counterterrorism unit based in nearby Sulaymaniyah. He rushed to Kirkuk with his brother Polad, their men, and a small number of Delta Force operators. ISIS fighters had expected as much, and had laid an ambush for the reinforcements, whom they targeted with RPGs. The counterterrorism unit was forced to take a roundabout route as a result. ISIS also began to run suicide car-bomb attacks at frontline Peshmerga forces so they could not be diverted to Kirkuk. "What they did to us inside Kirkuk was by far the worst we have ever seen," Polad Talabani told me when I arrived in the area a few days after the assault.

The militants' media arm was poised to exploit the attack. ISIS told its captive audience in Mosul that it had achieved a dramatic victory in Kirkuk and incorporated another famous Middle East city into the caliphate. As the firefights continued in Kirkuk, a video was posted on YouTube. A parade of honking cars took to the streets in Mosul as the success was lauded in man-on-the-street interviews. Kirkuk was a city of immense symbolic importance for the Kurds, one they had claimed as their own when the Iraqi Army dissolved after Mosul was seized in June 2014. The longer Kirkuk's fate hung in the balance, the greater ISIS's propaganda gain, one that would only steel the resolve of its Mosul-based fighters.

U.S. air strikes were not an option in the heart of a city where combatants and civilians could not be easily distinguished and the Americans had not been closely monitoring. ISIS fighters were dispersed throughout Kirkuk, including on the top floors of some buildings in the center. Lahur Talabani called on his own helicopter pilots, who took off with snipers to fire at the militants. In the streets, Kurdish residents and local volunteers mobilized. Virtually every man had a gun, and people started firing with abandon, sometimes posing a danger to themselves and their neighbors.

But no predicament was more dire than that of fourteen female students at a Christian school who had left the war zone to study in the supposed safety of Kirkuk. Abu Durayd, a local church official and a hefty middle-aged man of uncommon courage, had been trying to calm the girls by phone when he learned that an already dangerous situation had become much worse: ISIS fighters had burst into their dormitory near the Snowbar Hotel and were roaming around the structure. He urged the girls to silence their phones and to hide themselves as best they could, which in their darkened rooms meant slipping under their beds. "We were terrified," said a twenty-two-year-old student, who gave her first name as Marlin. As she struggled to stifle any sounds, an Islamic State fighter raided the kitchen and then sat on her bed to wolf down the food. "We didn't take a deep breath," Marlin recalled. "All we could do is pray." This time the prayers worked. As the battle raged, some fighters fled. Others exploded their suicide belts on the lower floors. Eventually, Abu Durayd snuck into the building to lead the students to safety.

By dawn, the city was under control and Lahur Talabani was calling for U.S. air strikes against militants who had managed to flee on the way out. The Kurds learned later that the attack had been planned by Abu Islam, which was the nom de guerre of an Iraqi Sunni named Mazan Nazhan Ahmed al-Obeidi, who had fought with AQI. He had become a willing ISIS recruit after the fall of Mosul, and his wife and daughter lived in the city. ISIS's broader political goal, Abu Islam later confessed to his Kurdish captors, had been to spur a rebellion by Sunni Arabs, many of whom had sought refuge in Kirkuk, and to take over the government center, even if the gain was temporary.

At the hospital morgue, there was a pile of eighty-four bodies identified as ISIS fighters, some horribly disfigured by their own suicide blasts. One by one, the corpses were removed from black body bags so that fingerprints and DNA could be preserved. Their cell phones were mined for photos and records of other residents who might have been in contact with them. In the span of a few days, they were transformed from jihadist warriors into a biometric database. The Kurds put out the word: if relatives did not come forward to claim the remains, the bodies would be burned, which was contrary to Islamic law and seen as a great indignity.

As we moved through Kirkuk, the police converged on the traffic circle near the government center. A gunman had fired into a police SUV and scampered away. Even after the attack had been beaten back, there remained a sense of unease. Still, Kirkuk would remain what the Americans called an "economy of force" effort. Lahur Talabani's counterterrorist units and the Peshmerga would need to do what they could to keep the city and the nearby front with Hawija under control, while the American-led coalition focused on Mosul.

In another move to throw the United States and its Iraqi allies off course, ISIS set alight the Mishraq sulfur plant in late October, releasing plumes of toxic sulfur dioxide that, depending on prevailing winds, blew in the direction of Qayyarah Airfield West for a few hours each day. The United States had sought to neutralize the ISIS chemical weapons threat by bombing a pharmaceutical complex on September 12 that it believed had been turned into a factory for making chlorine and mustard gas. The punishing air strike—which included F-15Es, A-10s, B-52s, F-16s, and F/A-18s—had destroyed the entire complex. But the industry near Mosul had provided ISIS with other options. There were other environmental problems: ISIS had lit oil wells on fire near Mosul in June, and fighting by a water treatment plant had caused a chlorine leak that sent a hundred people to the hospital. But it was the sulfur fire that overwhelmed local hospitals, including those run by relief groups: six hundred children arrived at the Qayyarah hospital within three hours, with symptoms ranging from rashes to bronchitis, while others suffocated to death. On the roadside, dead cows and sheep covered the ground and crops were damaged. The United States considered bringing in specially trained firefighters, but the Iraqis finally managed to put out the blaze. The attack was not thrown off stride, but thousands of civilians dealt with the consequences of ISIS's sabotage.

16

THE TACTICAL DIRECTIVE

With Kirkuk back in the Kurds' hands, Abu Bakr al-Baghdadi broke his silence on November 3. Iraqi officials had presented any number of reports—unconfirmed and now patently untrue—that their air strikes had killed or wounded the self-styled ISIS caliph. Now in his first audio broadcast in nearly ten months, the ISIS leader sought to rally the Mosul defenders. Those who stood their ground and fought, he claimed, would be venerated forever in the history of Islam for a struggle that evoked the Prophet Muhammad's battle to save Medina in 627. They were holy warriors in a campaign of Sunnis against apostate Shia in Iraq; in Syria they were fighting Bashar al-Assad's Alawites, had extended their reach to Libya, and would soon bring their war to Saudi Arabia and Turkey.

Other incentives had been more material. As the Mosul fight approached, the ISIS military department sent a notice to units in the field outlining the rewards for battlefield valor, according to captured documents. A fighter who downed a coalition aircraft would be given a car. The destruction of a tank with a mine or an unguided missile would be rewarded with several gold dinars. A successful sniper shot was worth one gold dinar if there was photographic evidence of the kill, but only half a dinar if there was a witness without a camera. "Sheikh Abu Bakr al-Qurayshi al-Baghdadi (may God protect him) has ordered to give payments in golden dinars to all who inflict havoc in destroying the arms and equipment of the enemies of God Almighty," the directive advised.

To inculcate the notion that ISIS was being supported by a mighty international coalition of its own, the group went to great lengths to highlight the role of foreign fighters who had sacrificed for the cause. Suicide bombings that targeted Iraqi forces in November and December, ISIS proclaimed, had been carried out by Moroccan, Uzbek, and Emirati fighters.

With two years to prepare for the coalition's push, the ISIS militants established a formidable network of defenses. They had knocked holes in the interior walls of buildings so that three- to five-man squads could race from room to room to shoot while standing back from the windows to hide their muzzle flashes. They had dug tunnels and underground shelters. They had positioned artillery under highway overpasses to shield it from U.S. air strikes. They had continued experimenting with their *Mad Max* vehicle-borne IEDs, mounting anti-armor rockets on some to increase their offensive potential. Their fighters were armed with mortars, recoilless rifles, and a seemingly unlimited supply of IEDs as well as drones, which they used to direct car bombs to their targets and to drop explosives. Their fighters were operating under a centralized command, had instructions on how many mortars they could fire and when, and were functioning like a terrorist army.

At the strike cell in Erbil, Brigadier General Scott Efflandt thought the challenge had been made all the more difficult by the deficiencies in the Iraqis' strategy and tactics. As a brigade commander south of Baghdad in 2011, Efflandt had led one of the last units to leave the country. During the ensuing months in Kuwait, his staff began to receive phone calls: some of the best Iraqi officers the unit had worked with were being detained and cashiered out of the army as Nouri al-Maliki went after his political adversaries, real and perceived. Despite all the coaching the Americans had provided since their return in 2014, Efflandt was concerned that the Iraqi offensive was starting to sputter. The Iraqi forces, he thought, had been too predictable by mounting frontal assaults and eschewing maneuver warfare. It was understood that cordoning off the city from the west was beyond the Iraqis' capability at this stage of the battle, but the result was that West Mosul was still wide open and thus ISIS forces there were able to receive reinforcements. Worse, each of the Iraqi forces appeared to be fighting its own war.

In the north, the 16th Division was barely edging forward, even though it was closest to East Mosul and was literally moving downhill. In one notorious episode, the division had pushed down from Kafruk, run into a solid wall of ISIS resistance, and made a hasty retreat. In the chaos, it committed the cardinal military sin of leaving several of its soldiers behind: their mutilated bodies were later found strapped to a pole. Major General Jassem Nazal Qassem's 9th Division, which was supposed to attack from the southeast, was also lagging behind.

The slow pace of army units had already worked to the detriment of the CTS, which was drawing more than its share of ISIS fire as a result and being whittled down. The tribulations of the CTS had burst into the news when its Salah al-Din Regional Commando Battalion, and a CNN crew that accompanied it, was ambushed and trapped for twenty-eight hours after driving two miles into East Mosul. ISIS fighters smelled blood and were closing in. As the journalist Arwa Damon and a wounded photographer took sanctuary with a terrified Iraqi family, the question was whether the reinforcements would arrive in time, or at all. American reconnaissance drones were redirected to search for the trapped media members, and a team of American and Iraqi special operations forces was alerted in case the United States needed to take over the mission. To help the U.S. military pinpoint Damon's location, CNN gave permission for commanders to use their signals intelligence capability to geolocate the Nokia phone she was carrying. Damon was also instructed to form an "X" on the roof of the building in which she had taken refuge. Near the end of the ordeal, a U.S. satellite-guided JDAM bomb slammed into the house next door: A group of ISIS fighters had taken up positions on the roof and were preparing to pounce. It was, Steve Townsend later recalled, a "ring of fire" that kept ISIS at bay at that moment until Iraqi reinforcements arrived at the scene to rescue Damon, the photographer, and the beleaguered Iraqi troops.

The bottom line, Efflandt thought, was that the Iraqi attack had turned into a grind. Contrary to initial estimates of the ISIS plan—which predicted an outer security layer with the bulk of enemy combat power reserved in the city's interior—ISIS had decided to defend Mosul by moving forward and was taking advantage of its interior lines. It was making the Iraqis pay for each meter of the city's ground, which was now marked by piles of rubble, burned-out vehicles, open sewage, and, incongruously on one street, a poster of Mickey Mouse with his face blown out that still featured his large ears and suspenders. "We knew it was going to be hard," Efflandt recalled. "We didn't think it would be this hard, starting right at the edges."

U.S. commanders talked to Abdul Amir about how to change the dynamics of the fight, in part by opening up new axes of attack. On December 6, Efflandt woke up to find that the Americans' prayers had seemingly been answered. The night before, the 36th Brigade from Qassem's 9th Division began to roll through the Wadhad neighborhood under the command of General Mustafa al-Azzawi. For once, the division's tanks and armored personnel carriers appeared to be getting the respect they deserved from the militants. The Iraqi soldiers moved through one intersection after another until they arrived at Al-Salam Hospital around noon. ISIS had taken over the hospital during its occupation, and used it both as a treatment center for its commanders and as a command post. Strategically, it was the most important target the division had taken since it helped secure Qayyarah Airfield West, and the 9th Division troops seized it with hardly a fight.

The strike cell had not been told of the plan in advance, but that was not unusual. What was unusual was the boldness of the attack. Efflandt and his team in Erbil were ecstatic. It looked like a game changer. The Iraqis were no longer advancing a hundred meters a day. They had used their premier armored force, one Efflandt himself had helped stand up during an earlier tour, to conduct maneuver warfare. Perhaps the fight for Mosul did not need to be a battle of attrition after all. Intelligence reports indicated that ISIS had been caught by surprise and was desperately ordering its fighters to move to the hospital and bring their rockets forward. "It was clear that the enemy is unhinged and vulnerable," Efflandt observed. If the CTS could link up with the soldiers, perhaps the Iraqis could really strike a blow against the ISIS defense.

That evening, the 9th Division soldiers relished their long-sought victory. They blocked off the street in front of the hospital complex with two of their armored vehicles and parked the rest of their 113 armored personnel carriers side by side inside the compound as if they were in a motor pool.

The relative peace did not last long. There was a no-holds-barred, violent counterattack. Two suicide car bombs crashed into the 9th Division vehicles in the street, the first of half a dozen that would attack that night. ISIS also began to lob RPGs, mortars, and rockets. One round struck an M113, setting it alight, and the fire soon leaped to the others parked in a row until more than a dozen had gone up in flames. That, in turn, cooked off the ammo, spraying rounds in every direction. The soldiers had pushed the pedal to the floor to take the complex but then had failed to set up a proper defense. With each Iraqi force involved in its own separate war, and none of them fully coordinating with the others to take advantage of the 9th Division's initial success, the Islamic State's fighters were free to use mobile reserves to defend against the main line of attack, which for now was being manned by the hapless soldiers at the hospital.

From Townsend on down, U.S. commanders tried to persuade the Iraqis that all was not lost. The Iraqis might still be able to hold on to the hospital if reinforcements could make their way there the next day. What had made the operation a victory earlier could still make it a success if the Iraqis took the right steps. At first, the situation appeared to be in hand: An Interior Ministry emergency response force was reported to be approaching. But then word came that the Interior Ministry force had been ambushed as it sought to push up Highway 80 and never arrived.

Efflandt was in a small conference room adjoining his strike cell, talking via a secure videoconference with military officials in Baghdad, when an Air Force officer called out: "Hey, boss, you might want to look at this." Efflandt walked into the darkened command center, in which a video feed from a U.S. drone over the hospital was playing. Part of the hospital was on fire. Machine-gun fire was raining down on the Iraqis from a nearby building in the hospital compound that ISIS fighters had managed to occupy. In their desperation to escape, some Iraqi soldiers were jumping off the roof. Efflandt was afraid the Iraqis would be overrun and that a setback could become a tragedy. The United States needed to take action, and fast.

Under the rules of engagement, the hospital was normally not to be attacked, but it lost its protected status if it was being used by the enemy to mount attacks. Efflandt ordered a five-hundred-pound bomb to be dropped on the machine gun. At each stage of the chain of command, officers had to be assured that the target was legitimate. At that point, there was only one aircraft on station at the strike cell's disposal, and as the process unfolded the aircraft had to return to a tanker to refuel.

Finally, the bomb was released, silencing the fire and taking out the two top floors of the building ISIS had occupied. That broke the ISIS attack. Soon after, the CTS began to pull the besieged 9th Division's soldiers out of the complex. It was a rescue effort that could not be allowed to fail. More than two dozen bombs were dropped while U.S. Army artillery from Mount Alfaf fired shells just tens of meters in front of the complex. "Honestly, the battle was fought seventy-five percent from the air," said Sergeant Major Hassan Ali Jalil.

Once the retreat was underway, the Americans had hoped that the 9th Division soldiers would withdraw to an intermediate point so that their lunge into East Mosul would not be for naught. But the soldiers insisted on returning to their starting point on the outskirts of the city, which meant that they had nothing to show for their efforts. Not so much as a block of territory had been gained. The Iraqis had abandoned a bonanza of equipment, which the United States now had to destroy to prevent it from falling into the militants' hands, much as they did after the fall of Ramadi.

In the meantime, ISIS reoccupied the hospital complex. That was something the American commanders would not let stand. U.S. Army rockets fired from high-mobility artillery rocket system (HIMARS) launchers at Qayyarah West sliced through the building while air strikes pounded the compound. All told, more than twenty vehicles had been lost, either to the fire or to U.S. air strikes. The next day the question was whether all personnel had been accounted for. The United States did not want to watch another ISIS beheading.

Soon more bad news emerged. In the chaotic retreat, one Iraqi lieutenant pancaked his armored personnel carrier in a crater and was left behind. In desperation, the Iraqi officer called his army buddies on his cell phone. He was trapped behind enemy lines and had no idea how he was going to get back. At Camp Swift, the U.S. base in Makhmur, Specialist Erik Salmon thought there might be a way he could help. The U.S. intelligence analyst had been monitoring drone feeds of the chaos inside the heavily fortified compound. Salmon's job was to interpret the video from the Aerosonde unmanned aerial vehicle, and he was able to find the lieutenant hiding behind some bushes. Time was running out. The lieutenant had been whispering his position into his cell phone and then hanging up and changing position, but his battery was running low. Working with Salmon, the Iraqis at the command post at Camp Swift called the lieutenant to tell him he had to make a run for it. Cell phone in hand, the lieutenant began to run while the Iraqis at Camp Swift gave him instructions about how to avoid the dangers ahead. As the lieutenant got close to his parent unit, the Iraqis at Swift instructed him to jump into a ditch and wait. Crossing from no-man's-land to Iraqi-controlled territory was not easy, and the last thing they wanted was for him to become a casualty of friendly fire. Eventually, Iraqi forces were directed to his location and he was rescued.

The saga of the Iraqi lieutenant was one bright spot in a dismal chapter. The Iraqi soldiers had made numerous mistakes: they had failed to set a proper defense, parked their vehicles in a peacetime formation, failed to thoroughly clear the hospital grounds, and made no plans to reinforce their position once they seized their objective. The cost had been high. Though the Iraqis did not release the toll, one American observer at the casualty collection point counted seventy-one army soldiers wounded and at least eleven killed. Despite the air strikes, ISIS managed to spirit away one or two of the vehicles. Sylvia's brigade history noted that the ill-fated Iraqi operation had led to "significant casualties to include the loss of an entire Iraqi armor battalion worth of vehicles." Compounding the problem, Iraq's 9th Division commander had lost credibility. Iraq had seen its only mechanized division bloodied, and, the Americans feared, the idea of mobile maneuver warfare in Mosul would now be off the table. Tanks would be distributed to other units and essentially used as assault guns. Iraq would go back to fighting a war of attrition.

The Americans later concluded that they had not done everything they could. They had not positioned enough advisors where they would be most useful and some senior U.S. officers were not even aware of the Iraqis' plans until it was too late. "Despite every asset in the Coalition available to support the ISF, the absence of forward advisors made providing that support impossible," Sylvia's brigade noted in a frank account of the episode. The setback to the 9th Division reverberated up the chain of command. The offensive was temporarily paused while the Americans took stock and the Iraqis licked their wounds.

The Iraqis' bungled operation at Al-Salam Hospital could be easily picked apart. The deeper question Steve Townsend now faced was whether the U.S. military had plunged into the Mosul battle with the right tactics of its own. The military had faced an uphill battle in getting the administration to approve the use of advisors on the battlefield. But once it was given that authority two years into the counter-ISIS fight, it had used it sparingly—the Iraqi operation to bridge the Tigris being the lone example at the battalion level. None of the U.S. advisors mentoring the Iraqi Army in the battle for Mosul were at the front. There were U.S. advisors on the periphery of the city and at Camp Swift, which was forty miles southeast of Mosul and hidden behind thick blast walls. Traveling in MRAPs and accompanied by combat engineers to sweep away the IEDs as well as platoons toting M4 carbines, the advisors ventured forward for short periods with the Iraqi commanders before returning to the rear.

Though the strategy had been dubbed "by, with, and through," the "with" portion of the mission had never been fully embraced. In practice, this meant that the United States was not always in the know when the Iraqis mounted an attack, or in a position to convince the Iraqis to change their tactics if they began to stumble. "Despite every asset in the joint force being available, there was not a U.S. presence in the vicinity who could have helped establish a defense or help the Iraqis retain the terrain they had initially captured," Sylvia and his operations officer, Lieutenant Colonel Aaron Childers, wrote of the hospital incident.

The system of mentoring at a distance also added to the time needed to call in air strikes. Throughout the campaign, the use of airpower had been tightly centralized, and at the start of the Mosul operation any strikes by American and allied warplanes or drones had to be approved by a one-star general like Scott Efflandt (or at night a colonel) at the strike cells in Erbil and Baghdad—what the military called the "target engagement authority." But there was nobody forward with the Iraqis who could directly call in air strikes, share intelligence, and generally show them that the American advisors had their backs.

With an even tougher fight looming in West Mosul, Steve Townsend made the rounds and got an earful from Army advisors and also Navy SEALs, who were frustrated by their inability to move freely. The message was that the U.S military was not keeping faith with its own doctrine: fire support needed to be controlled by ground commanders on scene, not strike cells miles away. The unstated assumption at the White House had been that operating outside the wire raised the risk that U.S. troops would be in combat and thus should only be done selectively. But that was outdated if it was ever true. The Mosul front was advancing daily, and there were plenty of places American advisors could go in the city that would not plunge them into the middle of a firefight, Townsend figured. As for calling in air strikes from the field, Townsend had done that himself as a battalion commander in Afghanistan without routing the request through a strike cell. The U.S. military and its NATO partners had joint tactical air controllers, whose mission was to be with the troops and use their GPS equipment to direct air strikes where they were needed. The U.S. military did not need to break new ground so much as revert to the way it had long operated.

The product of this realization was Tactical Directive No. 1, "Enabling Coalition Support to Partner Forces," which Townsend drafted and sent to Joe Votel, the CENTCOM commander, who said he would run interference in Washington. If the United States was going to take the fight to ISIS, it needed to push the Iraqis not only to take terrain but also to defend captured territory.

Explaining the order to Sylvia, Townsend said that the Americans should be careful not to make themselves the spearhead of the effort: if the Americans were doing the fighting, the strategy of working through local forces would be undermined. Sylvia's brigade should dispatch advisors where they were needed, but if they started to receive small arms fire, they should move back. It was clear there would be some additional risk, but it could be managed. The order did not alter the basic rules of engagement: hospitals and mosques would still have protected status unless a senior commander determined they were being used by the enemy. But air strikes could be called in by advisors near the front without first contacting the Erbil and Baghdad strike cells.

The directive was issued on December 22. Putting it into action was not so easy. Initially, Sylvia's brigade drew up plans to send as many as five teams of advisors forward. But each of the advisors required a platoon to protect them, as well as equipment that would enable them to access drone feeds—what the military called "full-motion video"—and to send and receive classified email communications. With the troop cap Washington had set, the best the brigade could manage was to deploy two advisors forward: Captains Dan Fitzgerald and Quincy Bahler. Just coming up with the MRAPs the soldiers needed to advance toward the front was a scramble. The Army had destroyed many of the $1 million-a-copy MRAPs it had brought to Afghanistan, figuring it would be cheaper than shipping them home. So U.S. commanders went on a hunt in Kuwait for MRAPs and armored SUVs. Even the Spanish soldiers who were training Iraqi troops at the Besmaya range, north of Baghdad, were asked to pony up some gear so the advisors could carry out their expanded mission. Reshuffling its own stocks, the brigade also stripped some of the equipment it was using for its advisors on the periphery of the city.

It was an extraordinary degree of ad hockery for an operation that had been in the works for years. Still, more than any step taken before, Townsend's tactical directive accelerated the pace of the campaign and expanded the use of air strikes. Donald Trump had talked volubly during his presidential campaign about ratcheting up the pressure on ISIS: the candidate vowed to take the gloves off and "bomb the hell" out of the militants. But the new tactical directive—which was implemented without announcement or fanfare during the Obama administration and with no involvement by the White House —was the most important step. Colonel Pat Work, who succeeded Sylvia and served as the principal field advisor to Abdul Amir, observed later that it "unlocked the lethal potential for the Coalition."

After the setbacks in East Mosul, the U.S.-led coalition and Iraqis had declared a two-week pause. Townsend used the time to convince Abadi of the importance of synchronizing the disparate Iraqi attacks in the east. He also secured the prime minister's permission to disable the five bridges across the Tigris that connected West and East Mosul. Hoping to avoid damaging the spans, the United States had sought to dissuade the militants from using them by cratering the roads leading to them. But ISIS fighters had kept coming anyway.

Splitting the city in two was a double-edged sword. Stanching the flow of ISIS fighters would make it easier to win the battle for East Mosul. But it would also mean there would be more militants left to fight when Iraqi forces got to the warren of stone houses on the west side of the river—not to mention adding to the Iraqi government's reconstruction bill. Still, there could not be a fight for West Mosul unless the Iraqis first took the east.

The pause also gave the Iraqis' creaky logistics system time to catch up. The M1 tanks the Americans had sold the Iraqis required substantial maintenance, and the hub for repairs was located two hundred miles south of Mosul, at the base at Taji. A larger problem was that the Iraqis lacked a proper inventory system to track the status of equipment, the delivery of spare parts, and the completion of repairs. With little confidence in their own system, Iraqi commanders had a penchant for hoarding spare parts and medical supplies instead of pushing them forward. Who could say when they would be resupplied again? And since Iraqi troops doubted that damaged vehicles would be quickly repaired, they often abandoned them on the side of the road or simply destroyed them, hoping that the Americans would provide replacements. "They were just blowing things up on the side of the road," one American officer said.

On December 26, U.S. aircraft struck the Moslawi Bridge, leaving the span intact but putting enough holes in it to block vehicles from crossing. But ISIS immediately began building a pontoon bridge, in addition to ferrying fighters across the Tigris in small boats. A U.S. AC-130 made short work of the makeshift bridge, and the Americans went after the boats as well. Undaunted, ISIS used the cadre it still retained in the east to mount an audacious attack on December 28 against the 16th Iraqi Division, which had been crawling toward the city from the north. Using some of the most potent weapons in its arsenal, four heavy equipment front-end loaders, the militants punched a hole in the Iraqis' defensive berms and then dispatched a wave of nine suicide car bombs and fighters as they poured on the fire using mortars, rockets, and truck-mounted anti-aircraft guns. U.S. advisors called in air strikes, and the attack was rebuffed. During the five-hour clash, only one Iraqi soldier was killed and two were wounded. Two coalition special operations forces members were wounded, illustrating the risks of advising near the front. The ISIS losses were much higher: eighteen dead and forty-five wounded. Though the casualty toll was lopsided, it was clear that ISIS was still trying to turn the tables and put the Iraqis on the defensive.

The Iraqis finally resumed their offensive in East Mosul on December 29 in a three-pronged attack that for once was semi-coordinated. The CTS fought its way to Mosul University and struggled for two and a half days to retake it. This was of no small significance, since ISIS had used the university as a command-and-control center, as well as a facility for making explosives and trying to develop chemical weapons. In a final, diabolical act, ISIS set fire to the university and withdrew.

A month later, Abadi proclaimed that East Mosul had been liberated in a campaign that had lasted one hundred days. ISIS continued to mount raids across the river, but it would never seriously threaten the east side of the city again. Between October 2016 and mid-February 2017, about 240 boats used by the militants were blasted by Hellfire missiles from Apache helicopters, hit by air strikes, or pounded by artillery. One American officer estimated that some three hundred ISIS fighters had perished in the bloody river fight.

The firepower that had been expended in the fight for East Mosul had been enormous. ISIS's mortars and Katyusha rockets had been accurate and persistent. From the top of Mount Alfaf, the 101st Airborne's radars pinpointed more than seventeen thousand enemy mortar and rocket launches. The U.S. response had been formidable as well. The 101st artillery fired more than 6,200 rounds, including 1,250 Excalibur rounds and other shells that were modified to hold GPS satellite guidance kits. It was the most extensive use of M777 howitzers during their decade-long history— so extensive that the brigade had to intercept parts that were intended for Afghanistan and other distant deployments to keep its guns running while drawing howitzers from the strategic reserve in Kuwait.

The Iraqi government steadfastly refused to disclose its military losses. But Votel, the CENTCOM commander, shared the Iraqi toll during a pep talk for American Air Force personnel that I attended inside a hangar at a secret air base the Americans were using in the Middle East: there had been about five hundred Iraqis killed in action and about three thousand wounded during the hundred-day battle for East Mosul. The numbers did not include those lost in Ramadi, Fallujah, Tikrit, Baiji, or the long slog to the city's outskirts. Nobody, it seemed, had a good number for civilian casualties. People had been instructed to stay in their homes until the fighting subsided, but with many civilians still trapped in the city, it was clear that casualties were bound to be high.

BY MID-JANUARY 2017, Obama had gone a long way toward putting ISIS on the path to defeat. He had not, as Ash Carter once hoped, finished the job by taking Mosul and Raqqa, but the president had also not put pressure on the military to rush those operations just so his administration could score some political points. On the plus side, the United States had resumed its training program and had Iraqi Army, Federal Police, CTS, and Kurdish Peshmerga units it could work with. After two years of holding back, the Obama administration had finally given Sean MacFarland the authority to send advisors into the field with the Iraqis and to employ Apache helicopters in combat, and Steve Townsend's Tactical Directive No. 1 allowed them to get closer to the action. Thanks to Townsend's directive, during the last full month of Obama's term the United States had finally struck an acceptable balance between caution and action. Still, the toughest fight of the campaign in Iraq—West Mosul—lay ahead.

Syria would be even more challenging. Thanks to Delta Force and the Central Command, the Americans, now 250 strong, had a partner: the Syrian Democratic Forces. With the fight looming in the distance, Obama took some steps to build up fire support. Warplanes were already dropping bombs, but now HIMARS launchers were secretly moved into northern Syria. At the request of the military, Obama also quietly approved the use in Syria of Apache attack helicopters, which carried Hellfire missiles.

As in the early days of the counter-ISIS campaign, the administration was as worried about becoming ensnared in the fighting as it was about doing too little. The White House approved Joe Votel's recommendation that three Apaches at a time could fly from Iraq to Syria and operate there for seventy-two hours before having to return across the border.

Still, Obama had yet to resolve a fundamental question: whether the United States should prepare for the battle for Raqqa by arming the Kurdish component of the SDF, which had emerged as the group's most battle-hardened contingent but was still an anathema for Turkish president Recep Tayyip Erdoğan. To assuage Turkey's anxieties that the United States was inadvertently building a separatist Kurdish army near its border, the U.S. military's plan was to provide the Kurdish fighters with enough weapons to take ISIS's self-declared capital while restricting the flow of arms and ammunition they would receive afterward. Nor would the

Kurds be permitted to sit on their conquests. They would hand Raqqa over to local Arab forces, who would police the town. Beyond that, the Turks would have the Americans' word that as long as the U.S. military was involved with the SDF and their Kurdish complement, they would make sure their energies were focused on ISIS and not on encouraging the Kurds' dreams of independence in the region.

None of that was enough to mollify Erdoğan, whose suspicions of the U.S. military had been magnified, unjustifiably, by a July 2016 coup attempt. Turkey had provided a graphic demonstration of its concerns in August 2016 after some SDF elements signaled an intention to position themselves at Jarablus, north of Manbij, after liberating the city.

With no warning to the Americans, Turkey had sent some of its forces and Syrian proxies into a shallow slice of northern Syria in an operation dubbed "Euphrates Shield." The offensive signaled to Mazloum Abdi that he should not think about trying to link up his areas in northeastern Syria with Kurdish areas in the western part of the country, around Afrin. An uneasy truce appeared to be holding.

But not for long. Just as Townsend held his first meeting with Mazloum, the SDF commander's aides started receiving a flurry of calls on their cell phones. "Turkish tanks are attacking my forces south of Jarablus," Mazloum told Townsend. "Your NATO ally is attacking us!" Though the SDF knocked out a Turkish tank with an anti-tank missile, Townsend was not sure how far the Turks were going to go. Over the next few days, however, the crisis was eased. The SDF pulled its forces back over the Euphrates, the United States sent advisors with the Turks on the theory that the best way to shape future Turkish operations was to support them, and Joe Biden flew to Turkey to try to defuse the tensions, insisting that if the Kurds established a corridor on Turkey's border they would risk their American aid. Even so, the situation was anything but stable.

During Obama's last week in office, the president convened

a meeting of his National Security Council to finally take up the long-deferred arming question. There was no doubt where Ash Carter and Joseph Dunford stood. Providing the Syrian Kurds with weapons was the only realistic way to retake Raqqa and destroy ISIS's physical caliphate. Within the State Department, Antony Blinken, who was serving as the deputy secretary of state after leaving the White House, favored arming the Kurds, as did Brett McGurk, who was concerned that the campaign would lose momentum unless the arming began fast. John Kerry had been on the fence, but by the end of the administration he had thrown in his lot in favor of sending arms. But Samantha Power, the American ambassador to the United Nations, was wary of arming Mazloum's Kurdish fighters. Power had been enthusiastic about arming Syria's rebels to put pressure on Assad to negotiate more seriously with the opposition. But she saw a connection between the YPG and the PKK, which the U.S. and Turkey had designated a terrorist organization. She was also worried that the Kurdish YPG would adopt a heavy-handed approach to governing Arabs and even some Kurds in the territory it helped to liberate, fearing it could set the stage for still more strife. Mazloum was a good partner for U.S. special operations forces, but he maintained quiet discussions with the Syrian government. In Ankara, U.S. ambassador John Bass had been sending cables warning about the Turkish reaction to an arming decision.

At the January 17, 2017, NSC meeting, Obama made clear that he had come down on the side of arming. But the president did not want to give the order to proceed unless the incoming Trump team, which would have to live with the Turks' unhappiness and its strategic consequence, was consulted. Susan Rice was instructed to speak with Mike Flynn, the retired three-star general and former Defense Intelligence Agency director under Obama, who was Trump's choice to succeed her as national security advisor. Not surprisingly, Flynn, who was sympathetic to Turkey, said that the incoming administration would make its own decision. Obama would be seeing Trump three days later on Inauguration Day and would give him his recommendation, which Obama did when he shared a limousine ride with Trump to the incoming president's swearing-in, a former Obama administration official disclosed.

As Trump sat in the inaugural reviewing stand in front of the White House that day, he turned to Jim Mattis, his choice to serve as secretary of defense, and told him the Kurds were great fighters. Mattis nodded and did not pursue the matter further. The former Marine general never understood why Trump had chosen that moment to raise the issue.

17

COUNCIL OF WAR

After Iraqi prime minister Haider al-Abadi declared victory in the east, another pause was ordered so that the Iraqi forces could move into position for what was to be the toughest part of the Mosul operation. Townsend's command ordered an intelligence, surveillance, and reconnaissance "soak." Predator drones prowled over West Mosul searching for car-bomb factories—welding torches would show up in vivid colors on the infrared detectors—and barracks for foreign fighters. The plan was to mount the offensive from the south but to maintain an element of surprise in a battle that ISIS knew was coming.

Abdul Amir Rasheed Yarallah and Steve Townsend came up with a ruse. In early February 2017, bridging equipment was lugged through the streets of East Mosul toward the riverbank to make it look as if the plan was to attack directly over the Tigris in the heart of the city. To reinforce the feint, the 101st Airborne Division's artillery situated on Mount Alfaf fired at the western bank of the supposed crossing spot while French CAESAR guns launched smoke rounds. The deception was inadvertently furthered when the CTS delayed its shift to the west to continue clearing areas of East Mosul and sort out its logistics, creating the perception that Iraq's premier force was gearing up for a bold assault across the Tigris. Intelligence later showed that ISIS diverted anti-tank weapons, car bombs, and snipers away from its positions in southwest Mosul and toward the west side of the riverbank. That provided sufficient time for the Iraqis to move to their new positions. With ISIS distracted, the 9th Division left East Mosul and crossed the Tigris south of Hammam al-Alil in a massive operation: 120 heavy trucks moved artillery and tanks across a float bridge. "The last time you saw anything like this was the Arab-Israeli War or Desert Storm," said Lieutenant Colonel James Browning, who was advising the unit.

Nobody knew how many ISIS fighters were left, but the United States estimated there were as many as 5,000 inside the city, with perhaps another 2,500 in an outer defensive ring. About 1,000 were believed to be foreign fighters—the ones who had the least chance of blending in with the population when ISIS was defeated, and the most motivation to fight to the death.

The Iraqi plan was for two divisions of Federal Police to advance along the west bank of the Tigris, clear the villages south of the Mosul airport, take control of a nearby power plant, and then secure the airfield itself before pushing into the city. Meanwhile, two CTS task forces would be attacking side by side to the west. Qassem's 9th Division, still smarting from the debacle at Al-Salam Hospital, would not be part of the urban battle, but would swing west of the city to cut off the road to Tal Afar before proceeding north to the town of Badush to ensure that the insurgents inside Mosul would not receive any reinforcements. As for the Iranian-backed militias, Townsend proposed they be sent to take Kisik Junction, west of Mosul. That would help cut off the ISIS fighters in the city and keep the Shiite militias out of the heavily Sunni city. Each force would have its separate axis of attack, and the offensive would have the coordination that the assault into East Mosul had lacked.

To help the Iraqis maintain their momentum once they kicked off the push into West Mosul, Townsend sent a memo to Abadi urging that the Iraqis move their maintenance and logistics teams up to Qayyarah Airfield West so they would be closer to the front.

Given the casualties in East Mosul, it was clear the Iraqis would need as many troops as they could get for the fight in the west, so he also urged that any Iraqi units that were not already committed on the battlefield, including units that had been roughed up, be run through another round of coalition-directed training. More holding forces were needed, and fast, and so the United States and its coalition partners would move mobile training teams to Q-West.

To boost its advisory effort, Washington lifted the force management level for the 82nd Airborne to 2,200 from the ceiling of 1,700 that was in place as its 2nd Brigade deployed under Pat Work. The modest increase allowed the deployment of two additional infantry companies, which yielded several more lieutenant colonels as well as some captains who could be sent into the field as advisors, along with a platoon of soldiers that would be needed to protect them. This enabled the United States to assign more advisors to Qassem's 9th Division and the Iraqi 16th Division—two units that had stumbled badly during the fight in East Mosul. In proxy warfare with a partner as disparate as the Iraqi Security Forces, a small increase in the number of advisors could have a disproportionately beneficial effect. That supplemented the ongoing effort by John Hawbaker, who was advising General Raed Shaker Jawdat's Federal Police. Lieutenant Colonel James Downing as well as Australian and U.S. Navy special operators accompanied the CTS.

The figure the Americans most needed to work with, however, was Abdul Amir, who was the overall Iraqi commander for the Mosul operation. A bachelor married to the Iraqi military, he had survived any number of operations. As a young soldier in Saddam Hussein's army, he had served as a frogman, swimming in the Shatt al-Arab during the bloody Iran-Iraq War. He had been wounded in 2003 by the Americans near Haditha but had remained in the military and risen in the ranks. As the commander of the 6th Division in Baghdad during the U.S. occupation, he had worked with American forces, including then-Colonel Townsend when he was commanding a Stryker Brigade in 2007, and understood the capabilities they could bring to the fight.

Formally, Abdul Amir's counterpart was 1st Infantry Division commander Major General Joe Martin, who had taken over from Gary Volesky as the overall head of the advisory effort and had helped Townsend steer the campaign. It would be Pat Work, however, who spent part of each day at the side of the Iraqi general as the U.S. military's point man in the field. As a colonel, Work could not give orders to the Iraqi general, but as a conduit for American military resources he could try to make himself indispensable and thus influence decision-making on the battlefield. Work's credo was to deposit, deposit, deposit in the hope that he could make a withdrawal someday and influence the Iraqi commander's decisions.

The position, as Work quickly learned, had its hazards. It didn't necessarily help that Abdul Amir, who never carried a weapon or wore body armor, insisted on visiting the front line to troubleshoot problems, a display of confidence or fatalism depending on how one looked at it. Work had learned all this in late February when he and his security platoon had followed Abdul Amir on a visit to a Federal Police command post as the fighting raged a mere kilometer away. On the way to Abdul Amir's next stop, the Iraqi commander and his team of U.S. advisors had come under fire. Abdul Amir's convoy raced ahead, and one of the vehicles in Work's four-MRAP column got a wheel stuck in a ditch. As the soldiers rushed to hook straps onto the stricken vehicle to haul it out of the hole, the ISIS fire picked up, bullets crashed into the engine block and windshield of Work's MRAP, and .50-caliber fire shot the antenna off another MRAP. Work's MRAP fired back, popped a smoke grenade to obscure its position, and got on the radio to alert the command with a "troops in contact" alarm. For twenty minutes, Work and his soldiers anxiously fought off the ISIS ambush while they waited for an Apache helicopter to rush to the scene. After the close call, Work bluntly warned Abdul Amir that if his soldiers ever left the Americans in the lurch again, his command would never allow advisors to accompany the Iraqi officer. That night, Abdul Amir talked with Martin, apologized for the episode, and said the American advisors should never have been put in that position.

For all the preparations, there was no good answer on how to safeguard the civilians in West Mosul. Abadi's appeal that Iraqi citizens shelter in place seemed to work in East Mosul. About 550,000 people stayed in their homes, and only 160,000 left. The fighting had been tough, yet many of the homes and streets in the east were still intact. But ISIS had been able to withdraw across the Tigris from East Mosul. In West Mosul, the Iraqis were projecting a fight to the finish, in a densely populated area in which civilians could increasingly be caught in the crossfire. In February, Abdul Amir had broached the matter in a meeting at his Nineveh operations center headquarters with Major General Rupert Jones, a senior British officer and a deputy commander of the coalition forces, and Lise Grand, the senior United Nations official in Iraq. It was truly a problem from hell. ISIS could be expected to do what it could to keep its human shields in place. Abdul Amir appeared to carry the weight of the Mosul population on his shoulders, but at this stage there was not an easy solution. Abdul Amir urged his Western contacts to press Abadi to change the messaging: instead of asking civilians to shelter in place, the Iraqi government could encourage civilians to leave if they felt they could make their way out.

The assault on West Mosul began on February 19 as General Raed Shaker Jawdat's Federal Police attacked the Mosul airfield and the adjacent Ghazlani military camp on the southern fringe of the city. The Federal Police—a paramilitary force rather than a Western-style law enforcement unit—was equipped with artillery, armored vehicles, and even a few tanks, but lacked the punch of the CTS or the 9th Armored Division. The force's general avenue of attack along the river meant that its right flank would be protected, but there was a trade-off: the two-kilometer front it covered did not give much room for maneuvering. The police would be staring straight at the teeth of ISIS's defenses with little chance to envelop or circumvent the enemy.

To slow the Iraqi advance on the airfield, ISIS militants had strewn piles of rubble and dug a massive trench six feet deep and almost as wide—a deep scar across the runways. At the same time, they reinforced their positions in several stone houses to the north and positioned snipers in the air traffic control tower. Bad weather limited the effectiveness of U.S. drones and other air assets for several days, but the Federal Police forged ahead. Dismounting from their vehicles, the policemen climbed over the ditch and raced across the tarmac under enemy fire to press the assault. "The Federal Police ran through this and took triple-digit casualties," recalled Hawbaker. "They threw themselves at it, despite all of the bloodshed that they were experiencing." After the CTS joined the fight, the airport and the Ghazlani camp fell into the Iraqis' hands. The seizure of the compound produced a brief moment of euphoria. As Iraqi troops carrying belt-fed weapons and Mk 19 grenade launchers reached the runway, some broke out in celebratory songs. "We were happy for the victory but sad for the level of destruction of such an important airport," said Captain Abdulhadi Ahmed of the CTS.

ISIS's defense stiffened as the Iraqis edged into southern Mosul, and the Federal Police had a hard time countering the fighters. Neither side had night-vision technology or proficiency at fighting after dark. The shooting would pick up in the morning, and U.S. officers in the strike cell in Erbil who watched the drone feeds would determine the location of the shifting front by pinpointing the streets that were caught in the crossfire. On March 12, a dozen car bombs were targeted on a lone Federal Police platoon. Three days later, an ISIS front-end loader that the militants had turned into a rolling bomb breached the Federal Police's perimeter and exploded in an enormous fireball, killing two police officers, wounding more than thirty, and destroying an array of vehicles, including a T-72 tank.

The police's darkest moment came on March 19, when a Federal

Police battalion commander and five of his men took a wrong turn on a rubble-filled street and headed directly into ISIS-held territory. In a matter of minutes, the battalion commander called into General Raed's command post, and the news was not good: he and his security detail were holed up in a building and surrounded by twenty ISIS fighters. Fifteen minutes later, the commander's cell phone signal went dark. American signals intelligence and drones tried to pinpoint the trapped troops. If the Americans or Iraqis could find them, perhaps the Iraqis could mount some kind of rescue mission. Raed had his spies in Mosul, and the information he was getting indicated it was too late. The policemen had been captured and brought by ISIS to a nearby mosque, and one had quickly been beheaded. Raed sized up the situation. There were no prisoner exchanges in this war. His troops would be interrogated, tortured, and killed. There was nothing left to do, he reasoned, but end their suffering and take out as many of their captors as possible by ordering his own artillerymen to attack the mosque. A deliberate attack on captured prisoners was well outside the U.S. rules of engagement, but the Iraqis were doing the hard fighting on the ground and Raed was calling the shots.

For the next several weeks, Raed's troops dug in, erected berms, and concentrated on holding their turf. Major General Joseph Martin, the 1st Infantry Division commander, who was now leading the advisory mission, implored Raed to resume the march. The only thing worse than grinding their way forward was hunkering down and making the Federal Police a magnet for ISIS's mortars, rockets, and artillery. But Raed would not budge. His troops had burst through the crust of ISIS's outer defense but were now stalled on the outskirts of Mosul's Old City. They were on the defensive now.

To the west, the CTS was running into trouble, too. It had never stopped advancing, though its progress was sometimes measured in the tens of meters. The counterterrorism force had an advantage over other Iraqi units: a select cadre of its troops had been trained as forward air controllers. They could not directly summon an American air strike: only an American or allied officer could do that. But they were skilled at providing the coordinates in clear English to American officers in the field or to the Erbil strike cell—and because the CTS was still moving forward, they were drawing ISIS fighters into the battle and giving the air war commanders something to shoot at. As the battle for West Mosul raged, one American officer in the Erbil strike cell estimated that the CTS was getting nine times as many air strikes as the Federal Police. With the Federal Police fixed in place and Qassem's 9th Division swinging wide of the city, however, the CTS was not getting much support and was taking the full brunt of ISIS's attacks. ISIS's mortar fire alone was enormous: on February 26, the U.S. military counted two hundred mortar attacks directed at the CTS. American intelligence had observed a huge influx of ISIS fighters moving toward the front line—perhaps seventy-five to one hundred a day.

Early on the morning of March 17, the CTS learned that the air support it received could be a double-edged sword. A CTS task force led by the chain-smoking Lieutenant General Abdul Wahab al-Saadi—who eschewed body armor and never wore a helmet—was taking fire from two ISIS snipers on the second floor of a large building when it asked for air support from the Erbil strike cell. Brigadier General John Richardson, who was temporarily filling in for Efflandt, approved a strike, which was just the second of the day: the Americans responded with a five-hundred-pound bomb with a delayed fuse that was intended to penetrate the roof and dispose of the snipers but otherwise leave the building largely intact. Cloud cover made it hard to assess the target, but when it cleared, Richardson was shocked: the entire structure had collapsed. Worse, unknown to the CTS or to the United States, civilians had taken shelter in the building. Townsend's command later assessed that 105 civilians had been killed, all but four of them in the building that was struck. Thirty-six civilians who had been in the area were missing, and the destruction would surely be a boon for ISIS propaganda, which accused the United States of striking mosques and killing hundreds of civilians.

Until now, the United States thought it understood ISIS's modus operandi. The militants would shoo the civilians to the rear so that they could not escape or get in the way, then take over empty buildings and wait for Iraqi forces to engage. The U.S. military pointed the finger at ISIS after its investigation concluded that the group had hidden explosive materials in the structure and lured the United States into striking it with the calculation that it would cause the deaths of innocents and spark outrage that would, at a minimum, curtail the air attacks. The episode had nothing to do with the more streamlined process established by Tactical Directive No. 1 or Donald Trump. The bombing had been approved by the Erbil strike cell and had been done by the book. Still, Townsend later told Richardson that it had been vital to keep up the momentum but added that the United States could not afford a repeat.

On March 29, the Americans thought that ISIS might have laid another trap. ISIS militants were defending a building, and U.S. officials observing the scene through a drone observed a line of men, women, and children being let inside. When one civilian resisted being herded into the structure, he was summarily shot. A large tank—nobody could say what it was filled with—was perched on the roof. Richardson was convinced he was witnessing an ISIS ruse and denied the Iraqi military's request for an air strike. The Americans continued to strike Mosul but tried to use smaller bombs—what the military called "low-collateral-damage weapons." But as the Iraqi advance continued in the Old City, the problem of minimizing harm to civilians would only become harder.

One tactic that ISIS began to employ with increasing frequency in the fight for West Mosul was bomb-carrying drones. Hovering in swarms of three to ten, the drones were simply hobby-shop-like devices that militants had constructed themselves, but they spooked the Iraqi troops. ISIS considered their drones important enough to meticulously document their use, tracking the number of Iraqi forces killed or wounded and vehicles destroyed, then releasing the numbers through their media arms. Throughout the campaign, the U.S.-led coalition had controlled the skies and had never been concerned about air defense. But now ISIS was presenting an air threat below two thousand feet for which neither the Americans nor the Iraqis had an easy remedy. In a city full of buried bombs, snipers, and exploding cars, this danger was having an intimidating effect on the Americans' partners at a time when they could least afford it.

It was a young captain and a sergeant first class from the 82nd Airborne who improvised a response to the unexpected drone threat. To guard against the danger to the makeshift bases U.S. advisors were using outside the city, the Army had purchased several commercial jamming systems that were used to protect football stadiums and outdoor events from unmanned aerial vehicle (UAV)—that is, drone—attacks by neutralizing their frequencies. The innovation was to make the technology mobile by strapping the jamming device on the back of an armored truck that would drive behind the CTS task forces along with a separate vehicle that was packed full of equipment necessary to operate the device. The army's name for the system it used to defend bases was the Anti-UAV Defense System, so the mobile jerry-built contraption was dubbed "AUDS on a truck." It was generally effective in encouraging ISIS to steer its drones away from the CTS or caused the drones to stall in flight, allowing the Iraqis to shoot them down. Drones that crashed could be recovered by Iraqi troops who, at considerable risk to themselves, could sprint across the urban battlefield to seize the militants' air war system. U.S. military intelligence could then reconstruct the flight paths, mapping waypoints back to a point of origin, which was generally an ISIS command center. Turning the tables on its adversary, U.S. airpower could then target that command center, transforming Daesh's drone capability into a liability. ISIS caught on to the coalition's new capability and its chat rooms buzzed with messages hypothesizing that more powerful transmitters could resist the Army's jammers, but ultimately the suggestions amounted to little. The adaptation left the Army's bases uncovered, but that was a calculated risk to keep the Iraqis on the march. Top officers like Tony Thomas, by then the head of the Special Operations Command, ventured to the front to see the new system, which like so many other improvements in war had come from the bottom up.

In early April, Jared Kushner, serving as a senior advisor to his recently inaugurated father-in-law, President Trump, and Marine General Joe Dunford, the chairman of the Joint Chiefs of Staff, made a lightning visit to the military compound at Hammam al-Alil, which was about sixteen miles south of Mosul. Before ISIS swept across northern Iraq, Hammam al-Alil had been a sleepy town along the Tigris that was celebrated for its sulfur-laden waters. In better times, Iraqis would soak in its geothermal pools and slather on the mineral-rich mud, which was said to be a balm for any number of ailments. The town's cement plant, which had been used for the construction of Mosul Dam, was repurposed to churn out mortars and rockets for the caliphate, which were no less deadly for being improvised.

As the Iraqi forces advanced, ISIS had stripped that factory of its generators and turned its ire against the town's long-suffering residents. Iraqi troops picked up the stench of rotting corpses as soon as they stormed the town: the field near the local agricultural college had been turned into a dumping ground for ISIS's victims. Many of the bodies were headless, and the word on the street was that many of the executed were former policemen and soldiers whom the militants feared might rise up when the hour of the town's liberation was at hand. The Emergency Response Division, from Iraq's Interior Ministry, unearthed the remains of more than 370 people before halting the search because the bodies were in too advanced a state of decay.

Raed had used the base to organize the Federal Police's push into West Mosul. It included a small airfield and a modest building, whose basement was filled with communications gear and used as a command center by Raed and his American advisors. U.S. Army M109 Paladin howitzers were positioned in the reeds just outside the facility and lobbed shells at targets in and around Mosul. That

ISIS understood the military significance of the compound was made abundantly clear in late February when the militants sent a 122mm mortar streaking toward it—the same system the militants had used with deadly effect at Fire Base Bell in March 2016. The airburst killed one Federal Police officer, wounded several others, and surprised Raed, who had been meeting with Lieutenant Colonel John Hawbaker at the time. ISIS later dispatched a team of suicide bombers to assault the base, but they were uncovered by the Federal Police as they sought to sneak through the reeds along the perimeter.

By the spring, the base was secure enough for the short visit by Kushner, Dunford, and Tom Bossert, the senior homeland security official on the NSC. The trip marked the first time that officials from Trump's White House had ventured to Iraq, and its timing was not an accident. With a White House review of the counter-ISIS campaign underway, Dunford was calculating that inviting Kushner and Bossert on his travels in Iraq would provide them with "situational awareness" about the strategy, which the Pentagon still hoped to shape but which Trump would ultimately choose. Wearing ill-fitting body armor over his blue blazer, Kushner was briefed by Pat Work, who minced no words about the hard fighting that lay ahead, and then climbed inside a Paladin and addressed Iraqi troops. "I hope that the victory that you have in Mosul in the near future will not just be a victory for the American and Iraqi troops, but it will be a victory for the world," Kushner told a room full of Iraqi senior officers.

The way the campaign was unfolding, however, the Iraqis were not about to get to Mosul's old quarter anytime soon. By April, the offensive was essentially stalled. Raed's decision to halt his advance had enabled ISIS to concentrate on the two CTS task forces that were still inching their way north. Abandoned cars had been used to plug the side streets and prevent ISIS's suicide drivers from plowing into the CTS's flanks. But at the front ISIS was going after the CTS troops with mortars, including some filled with a low-grade mustard agent the militants had cooked up at

Mosul University; they were also using car bombs, machine guns, snipers, and drones—the insurgents' version of combined arms. ISIS fighters had even managed to take down an Iraqi Mi-28 helicopter with a Soviet-era Strela rocket launcher. The Iraqis had tanks, but they were not in the city.

The 9th Division was the only armored division in the Iraqi Army. Formed after the Yom Kippur War, it had suffered serious losses during Saddam Hussein's disastrous war with Iran before being disbanded in 1982. Reestablished when the Americans sought to stand up a new Iraqi Army during their occupation, the division had principally been what the military called a "force provider" during the campaign against ISIS, meaning some of its tanks had been hived off and assigned to other units. The U.S. Army had demonstrated it could take an armored force into Baghdad during the invasion of Iraq, but the Iraqis had no such experience. After the episode at Al-Salam Hospital, the 9th Division was determined to keep its distance from urban warfare and was sweeping west of Mosul in a bid to cut off ISIS routes to and from the city.

Despite their feint in East Mosul, the Iraqis were fighting pretty much how the Islamic State had expected them to fight. Most of ISIS's fighting positions, barricades, and defenses were oriented to the south, which was precisely where the Iraqis were mounting their main attack. About 445 Iraqi troops had been killed and another 3,020 wounded during the first several weeks of the push into West Mosul. Buildings were being destroyed, the streets were filled with burned-out vehicles and piles of rubble, hundreds of thousands of civilians were still trapped, and yet the offensive was going nowhere fast. Townsend had instituted Tactical Directive No. 1 after problems emerged in East Mosul. Another strategy shift was needed now as well.

Townsend and Martin had developed a plan to get the attack moving again: the Iraqis needed to open up a northern front. Experience had shown that ISIS could be taken apart if it had to contend with multiple threats. The coalition's grand strategy had been based on this premise: it would put pressure on ISIS defenders near Raqqa even as it moved to liberate Mosul, the two red arrows Ash Carter had flashed on-screen during his trip to Fort Leavenworth. The same principle applied to West Mosul. The CTS and the Federal Police could make headway in the south only if a separate Iraqi force made ISIS look north—a force like General Jassem Nazal Qassem's 9th Armored Division. The northern thrust would be the hammer, and the Iraqi forces in the south would be the anvil. ISIS would be forced to fight in two directions and to defend an ever-shrinking patch of territory.

On April 19, Townsend choppered to Hammam al-Alil to huddle with Raed and some of the other Iraqi commanders. Erected outside Raed's headquarters was a vast tent that featured a large map of northern Iraq and an enormous conference table about thirty yards long. The walls were lined with photos of Federal Police officers in their blue uniforms: martyrs who had died at the hands of ISIS in an operation that had yet to reach its most difficult phase. As Townsend prepared for the meeting, the general learned that the prime minister himself was traveling in the area with Abdul Amir and was headed toward Hammam al-Alil. Townsend's battlefield visit was about to become a full-blown Iraqi council of war.

As Iraq's prime minister, Abadi also served as commander in chief. He had no military experience, was short and pudgy, and looked nothing like a soldier. But he relished his commander-in-chief role and had taken to visiting the field wearing the black combat fatigues of the CTS. After arriving at the base, Abadi took his position at the head of the table. I had accompanied Townsend to Hammam al-Alil on the assumption that he was going to huddle with some Iraqi officers, but I pushed my way into the conference along with the prime minister's entourage. Now I had become a fly on the wall for the Iraqis' top-level debate over strategy. I had interviewed Abadi before and was concerned he would pick me out, but I was just one more American in a crowded room packed with Iraqi military officers and coalition officials, and the Iraqis had bigger things on their minds. As I was wearing a collared shirt and sitting two seats behind Townsend, my guess was the Iraqis pegged me for just another U.S. embassy official. Evincing confidence, Abadi told his commanders that the end of the operation was in sight and the hardest part was over. There had been dark days during the Fallujah fight, and then the resistance had melted away. ISIS was trying to drag out the fight, but Iraqi forces needed to finish it.

Abadi's optimism did nothing to soothe Raed's anxieties. Raed had a soft side and was devoted to his teenage son, who was blind but determined to pursue a career in the Federal Police like his father. But Raed was also a firm commander who relieved subordinates when he believed they had fallen short and sometimes even had them arrested. The police commander had been stewing for weeks about the operation in West Mosul: his men were taking horrendous casualties—sometimes forty killed in action in a day. Raed rattled off his accomplishments. His men had been fighting for 116 consecutive days against an enemy that had been preparing for months. Civilians were everywhere, and ISIS was using them as human shields. Car bombs and snipers were taking a toll. But now that the police had a toehold in the city, the Iraqi Army was nowhere to be seen and, Raed complained, was not pulling its weight.

Qassem took umbrage at the complaint and defended his division, which he argued was contributing to the effort by maneuvering through the desert to cut off the western approaches to the city. Abadi was still haunted by the 9th Division's disastrous encounter with ISIS at Al-Salam Hospital in East Mosul. During Saddam Hussein's costly eight-year war with Iran, the Iraqi Army had thirty-four armored divisions. Now it was down to one, and Abadi had no intention of risking his nation's only armored division in the western half of the city. He was quick to accept Qassem's argument that the place for tank divisions was in open terrain, not dense urban combat. "We tried and did not succeed," Abadi said. "I don't want to do it again."

Still the question lingered: The campaign was stalled, and something needed to be done to get it moving again. If another front was opened, who would fight on it? The CTS was usually the prime minister's weapon of choice, and it had done the lion's share of the fighting during the long campaign against ISIS, but two of its task forces were already engaged in southern Mosul. The Emergency Response Division, which was fighting alongside the Federal Police, was another possibility. But it could hardly spearhead a northern attack on its own. Another possibility was to use the 9th Division after all but reinforce it with other units, such as a brigade from the 16th Division, which was occupying East Mosul, or even the al-Abbas Combat Division, a Shiite militia that had been established to guard the shrines in Najaf and Karbala. As a general rule, the use of the Popular Mobilization Forces was a red flag for the U.S. commanders, who threatened to withhold air strikes to any Iraqi Security Forces that made common cause with the Shiite militia groups. But the fact was that the Shiite militias ran the gamut from Iranian-backed fighters who were virulently anti-American to more nationalist groups whose primary allegiance was to Ayatollah Sistani in the holy city of Najaf. A decision to employ the "loyal" PMF, as some American officers dubbed them, was not objectionable to the United States, as long as it was a necessary expedient to support Qassem's push.

Drawing the discussion to a close, Abadi said that each of Iraq's forces had its special role. They were all sons of Iraq. But the prime minister was still wary about sending the 9th and 16th Divisions into the West Mosul maelstrom. It had been an extraordinary session. The Federal Police and the Iraqi Army had accused each other of sitting out the fight. The need for a new front had been identified, but the meeting had broken up with no consensus on how that might be accomplished. For all that, it had ended without rancor. One officer had complained that Abadi was partial to the CTS, since he had donned their fatigues, but the prime minister took the criticism in stride. Abadi's commanders had not held back from squabbling in front of him, but it was clear that they also respected his authority and never challenged the notion that he should be the one to decide.

On his way out, Abadi remarked to Townsend that he had been unusually quiet. But the American commander knew better than to cajole the prime minister in front of his commanders. The Iraqis could not be ordered or even pressured to embrace the Americans' strategy. Townsend and his officers would need to plant the seed, make their arguments in private, and try to bring Abadi and his top military men around. If there was to be a northern front, a real northern front in which the Iraqi Army fought, it would need to be seen as the prime minister's idea. After Abadi left, Townsend shared his impressions with Work as I hovered in the background. The Iraqis, Townsend thought, could fight in the cities and the Americans should do what they could to back them up. They also needed to do what they could to buck up Raed and the Federal Police: They had drawn the short straw by being positioned by the river with little room to maneuver and were under stress. Time also mattered, Townsend added. The Iraqis could not afford to drag this one out. Work endorsed his commander's assessment and added one point. The Americans needed to keep the Iraqis focused on logistics and help them when they could. If the Iraqis began a push from the north, their need for ammunition would skyrocket. They could not be allowed to run short. To give the Iraqis some additional help, Townsend told Work to get the Army's TOW anti-tank weapons out of storage so U.S. soldiers could support the Iraqis' advance from a distance. Even though the 9th Division would be part of the attacks, Iraqi M-1 tanks struggled to hit targets if they were more than a few hundred yards away.

For several weeks, the Americans quietly repeated their message at all levels of the Iraqi chain of command. Their own experience had proved that armored forces could play a role in urban warfare. The Americans, however, could not dictate the strategy. That had been clear since the planning for Eagle Strike, when the Iraqis rebuffed the idea for combined CTS, Iraqi Army, and Federal Police columns. They did, still, have an important card that was yet to be played: intelligence about ISIS's forces inside Mosul. Dubbed by Colonel Work as the "Intel Oracle," Major Kevin Ryan, an intelligence officer from the 82nd Airborne Division, was considered by Abdul Amir to be a highly skilled analyst. Ryan told the Iraqi general that a northern offensive would likely divert one out of every four ISIS fighters away from the group's southern defenses—and that, Ryan said, could reduce Iraqi casualties by 25 percent, no small concern for a force that was taking enormous losses and having trouble coming up with replacements. The prime minister's fears, Ryan demonstrated, were misplaced. Far from leading to another Al-Salam Hospital fiasco, a northern thrust would reduce the already mounting casualty toll. Everyone from Joe Votel to Mark Milley, who was then serving as the army chief of staff, to Work pursued this line of argument with the Iraqis. Within a few weeks, the lobbying paid dividends: there would be a northern front, and Qassem's 9th Division would be part of it.

18

THE FINAL DAYS

Jassem Nazal Qassem had been known for his battlefield exploits as a young soldier. After being wounded during the Iran-Iraq War, he had made his way back through Iraq's southern marshes to friendly lines. But his experience with armored units had not prepared him for urban warfare. His 9th Division had often provided M1 tanks to buck up the firepower of other units but had rarely operated independently on the battlefield. A wealthy man, Qassem contracted for the U.S. advisors' meals so they did not have to exist off a diet of meals ready to eat (MREs). During lulls in the fighting, he shared his philosophy of combat, which despite his push to Al-Salam Hospital emphasized deliberate movement and firepower over audacity. It was always possible to seize an objective more quickly, Qassem confided, if one wanted to pay a higher price.

The 9th Division's swing around West Mosul had been supported by the coalition's firepower, including a French artillery unit, which was not initially allowed by its government to fire explosive rounds into the city and was eager to get into the fight. In a matter of weeks, Qassem's division had cut the east–west route that ran from Tal Afar to Mosul—which the Americans code-named "Santa Fe." It was an important move that was intended to cut off the potential flow of reinforcements but also ensured that the ISIS militants in Mosul would fight with their backs against the wall.

By May, Qassem had made it to the ridgeline overlooking Badush, a town that included the notorious prison where al-Qaeda in Iraq had sprung hundreds of militants during its Breaking the Walls campaign and where ISIS used to punish anyone it suspected of disloyalty. Local informants told Qassem's troops that the Cubs of the Caliphate, ISIS's version of the Boy Scouts, had been led into the jail and ordered to shoot some of the prisoners as a kind of rite of passage. One sixteen-year-old ISIS fighter the Iraqis captured and interrogated turned out to be in charge of the town's defense. In Badush, the Iraqi troops found still more evidence of the sophistication of the enemy they were to fight: a room-sized sand table that ISIS used to plan its actions on the battlefield. The 9th Division had already had 120 soldiers killed in action before it was agreed it would push into Mosul and open a northern front.

To support Qassem's push into the city on May 4, 2017, Abdul Amir provided the division with one of his intelligence teams: Iraqi officers who had taken a page out of ISIS's book and had a fleet of their own quadcopters to carry out reconnaissance over the city. The Iraqis also received some more help from the French. One of the missions of the French troops, whose ranks included French soldiers of Arab descent, was to identify and by some accounts in some way ensure that French jihadists never returned home after their days of fighting for the caliphate were over. Officially, the French were not advising Qassem, but they arranged for their own drone video to be fed into a forward command post his division was using, which was also receiving Iraqi and U.S. reconnaissance transmissions, broadening the view of the urban battlefield. To beef up the northern thrust, the Emergency Response Division would also attack, while the 16th Division troops would move on its left flank. ISIS had detected signs that the Iraqis were preparing to strike from the north. This was no blitzkrieg, and in the days that it had taken the division to haul its tanks into position, the Iraqis had telegraphed their strategy. Nonetheless, the entire battlefield had shifted: ISIS would have to defend against attacks from the north, west, and south. Surrounded on three sides and with its back to the Tigris, the ISIS defenders would finally be cornered.

Ties between Qassem and the American advisors he had been assigned for the fight in East Mosul had been strained, marked by mutual recrimination after the debacle at Al-Salam Hospital. Lieutenant Colonel James Browning, an 82nd Airborne Division battalion commander with previous deployments in Iraq and Afghanistan, made an effort to restore trust. He joined Qassem's soldiers in their Ramadan fast, abstaining from food and water during daylight, during the division's push into West Mosul. Like other advisors, he addressed the Iraqi general as *sa'eedi*, the Arabic equivalent of "sir." Qassem and his soldiers called Browning "Abu Ella," honoring him as the father of his oldest daughter. The cultural sensitivity gave him a way to try to influence Qassem when the going got tough, but so did his ability to marshal U.S. airpower and artillery strikes if the 9th Division moved forward or to withhold them if the Iraqis tarried. "This was about understanding the physical demands and out of respect so that when those challenging moments came, I could look at him and say, 'I am in this moment with you in every respect, but we must move forward,'" Browning said.

As anxious as Iraqi commanders were about the fight ahead, rumors swirling through the ranks provided them with additional incentive to advance. Many of the ISIS leaders had arranged for their families to reside in the 17 Tammuz neighborhood, an affluent area of marble and stone homes in the northwestern part of Mosul. Iraqi CTS, Federal Police, and Iraqi Army officials were widely convinced that cash, gold, and other valuables were located in the quarter, and that those rewards would go to whichever Iraqi unit made it there first—a fantasy that led small squads to detour to the neighborhood, despite the danger, in quest of a treasure that was never found.

Qassem's division and the other Iraqi troops charged with opening up the northern front, however, had a major obstacle in their path: the Al-Jamhouri hospital complex, which ISIS had repurposed as a command post and a communications link to the caliphate beyond, even as it continued to provide medical care to ISIS fighters. Pat Work had taken to calling it ISIS's Pentagon. The installation featured a thirteen-story building that was the highest piece of ground in West Mosul, as well as a network of tunnels and stocks of weapons. The complex could not be bypassed, and somebody would need to take it. At the end of May, Qassem was told that it was his mission to do just that.

To help the push from the north, including the all-important logistics, Abdul Amir sent the 16th Division and ordered an Iraqi engineering unit to lay a bridge over the Tigris north of the city. That was one Iraqi initiative that was taken without any prodding by the Americans, who welcomed it when they found out.

The Al-Jamhouri complex was well defended. The militants had ingeniously mounted a ZSU anti-aircraft gun on rails within the structure and moved it to blast away at Iraqi forces through hospital windows. With the Iraqi forces stymied, Browning thought the solution was to call in an air strike to take out the top four floors of the main building and silence the ISIS fighters who were lodged there. That, however, was no simple task. Abadi had signaled that he did not want to destroy another hospital, even one that had legally lost its protected status after ISIS turned it into a fighting position.

In deference to the Iraqi prime minister, U.S. commanders had drawn a big goose egg around the structure on their maps: everything inside the egg was off-limits from the air. To document the danger the ZSU presented to the Iraqi soldiers and the U.S. advisors with them, the Iraqis flew several of their camera-carrying quadcopters near the structure. Browning transmitted iPhone photos of the imagery back to the Iraqi headquarters before ISIS militants blew the quadcopters out of the sky. The photos were sent to Scott Efflandt at the Erbil strike cell, but permission to bomb the Al-Jamhouri complex still did not come.

As frustrations mounted, one of Qassem's brigade commanders decided to take matters into his own hands and led a raiding party into the hospital building. But ten Iraqi troops were killed almost immediately, and for days the fighting was too fierce to recover the bodies. Several bloody attempts by Qassem's troops were made to storm the complex, including a raid in which more Iraqi soldiers were killed and left unrecovered amid the ISIS fire. The goose egg was shrunk, which gave the Erbil strike cell a little more elbow room in calling in aircraft and drones. To help the 9th Division get over the hump in West Mosul without losing too many more Iraqi troops, Townsend gave the go-ahead for the Americans who accompanied the Iraqis to shoot at ISIS positions directly with their own TOW missiles as well as Barrett .50-caliber sniper rifles and Javelin missiles.

The difference between firing Hellfire missiles from an Apache helicopter and shooting an anti-tank missile from the ground was almost theological, and U.S. special operations forces near Mosul had already engaged in ground combat. But the advisors who were drawn from conventional Army units had sought to honor Townsend's enjoinder that they were not to conduct the main effort and should respect the policy in Washington that it was the Iraqis who were supposed to be engaging in ground combat. Now, operating under the expanded rules of engagement, Browning put his snipers to work while Work arranged for U.S. soldiers on the east bank of the river to fire at the hospital complex with sniper rifles and anti-tank weapons. The mission was not risk-free, as the United States discovered when one American soldier who was providing fire support from East Mosul was wounded while moving into position. As the U.S. military's policy was to publicly identify its dead but not its wounded, that episode was never disclosed.

Even with U.S. support for the Iraqis, ISIS held firm. So Qassem's division maneuvered around the hospital complex and then attacked from the west with the adjoining Emergency Response Division. Qassem's new angle of attack forced the U.S. team to halt its sniper and anti-tank missile support. So many holes had been punched in the main building that it had been hollowed out. Some of the TOW missiles U.S. troops fired from East Mosul had entered one floor of the structure, only to have the thin guide wires severed by debris, sending the missiles streaking unguided out the other side toward the Iraqi forces.

The battle for the hospital had become so intense that it was threatening to tie down Qassem's entire division and divert it from its broader mission of pushing into the neighborhood known as the Old City. In the end, Qassem's division opted to bypass the hospital complex and push toward the Old City, leaving the task of seizing the structure to the Emergency Response Division, which began to advance. Sensing that ISIS would lose its grip on the hospital installation, civilians near the complex began to run for their lives. Enough ISIS fighters remained, however, to make that a deadly gamble. The militants calculated that once the civilians were gone, it would be easier for the coalition to pour on the firepower—so they began shooting at individual men, women, and children to try to keep the bulk of the people from running. That meant that not only was the hospital still in ISIS's hands, but it was fast becoming the scene of a humanitarian catastrophe.

ONE OF THE more unusual figures on the battlefield was a former U.S. Army Special Forces officer turned Christian missionary who had been working in Myanmar but had rushed to northern Iraq to provide medical assistance to civilians. He had brought along his wife and three children, as well as ethnic Burmese and international members of his Free Burma Rangers team, which included several other U.S. veterans. David Eubank not only carried a weapon but also had engaged in combat in May 2015 with ISIS in the operation to liberate Sinjar, which made him a different kind of evangelist. Eubank had been wounded in the left arm at point-blank range when he joined a 9th Division lieutenant in house-to-house fighting to clear the 17th of July neighborhood, and had provided first aid to the lieutenant, who was shot in the chest, but was fighting the next day.

Throughout the Mosul operation, Eubank had phoned journalists to fill them in on the plight of civilians in the neighborhoods and newly liberated villages. More important, Eubank had provided useful information to the Erbil strike cell that filled in some of the blanks in their intelligence reports, including the all-important geographic coordinates of key events on the battlefield. U.S. military officers would not strike targets based on Eubank's calls alone, but they could move drones or aircraft overhead to take a second look, and given his military training, his information was unfailingly accurate.

As the fighting intensified, Eubank was calling about the civilians at the hospital complex and wanted the U.S. troops to help rescue them. Efflandt came up with a plan. U.S. artillery would lob smoke rounds near the hospital complex so that Eubank and his team could rush in with the Iraqis to pull out the civilians. The problem was that the U.S. Army had not brought many smoke rounds to Iraq, figuring they would be of little use in an urban fight. What rounds it did have were white phosphorus, which were good for generating smoke but could cause horrible injuries if they struck civilians; their use as an incendiary was therefore limited by the laws of war. To make the plan work, the military identified an empty lot upwind where the rounds could fall without igniting the nearby neighborhood, and an Army artillery battery worked around the clock to adjust the software: only two guns would be needed, and they would lob shells from different directions. The idea was to fire early in the morning to obscure the battlefield before the baking summer heat caused the vapor to dissipate.

When the plan was implemented, scores of civilians escaped, but the next day, June 2, Eubank was calling on his cell phone again. More civilians had been shot trying to escape and had died just outside the compound's walls. In the mound of bodies lying in the hot sun was a small child still very much alive and nestled in the arms of her dead mother. Eubank was determined to make another try to get her out. To shield himself from ISIS gunfire, Eubank crept behind a 9th Division M1 tank along with Ephraim Mattos, a former Navy SEAL, and other members of his team. The gas turbine engine on the tank was so hot that it singed the hair on Mattos's arms, but following at a distance was not an option: that was a recipe for getting shot. As they arrived at the complex, Mattos and a teammate jumped into the open to provide covering fire while Eubank raced to the pile of corpses, snagged the child, and then scampered back behind the tank. The adventure, however, was not over yet. The Iraqi tank crew was so eager to get away from the battle zone that it began backing up fast, forcing Eubank, Mattos, and the others to run ahead in the open. Mattos took an ISIS bullet to his calf, was temporarily knocked off his feet, but then got back up, blood dripping down his leg. As he hobbled to safety, he stumbled over the corpse of another child that was surrounded by flies. For every innocent who was saved, several seemed to have perished.

The opening of a northern front had had the desired effect of forcing ISIS to fight in two directions, but the militants still had their abundant supply of car bombs, mortars, and grenade-dropping drones, and they had experimented with unconventional weapons, too. In April, ISIS had fired mortar rounds that contained a variety of chemical agents, including chlorine and a substance the militants had concocted from pesticide. The rounds had caused forty casualties among the Iraqi Security Forces, including burns and respiratory ailments, as well as one fatality. Nobody was sure what new tactics ISIS might employ as the Iraqis closed in. The insurgents had been pushed into a five-square-mile patch that extended from the Tigris and Mosul's Old City to the Al-Jamhouri hospital complex, allowing them to dig in.

A 9th Division patrol base was set up just west of the Old City, which would be the scene of the climactic phase of the battle. If the northern front was going to be the hammer that it was supposed to be, Qassem was going to need a lot more help. The fresh reinforcements were a mixed blessing, as the new division was accompanied by a troublesome Popular Mobilization Forces unit that, according to reports from the street, had taken the law into its own hands by throwing suspected ISIS fighters off a cliff and brazenly taking a video of the execution.

Keeping the Shiite militias out of the city had been imperative from the start of the operation. The problem had largely been sidestepped when Abdul Amir had the militia leadership take on the mission of securing the Tal Afar airport and clearing ISIS out of Arab villages near Iraq's western border—operations that kept them away from Mosul, even if they also allowed them to establish a corridor to Iranian-backed forces in Syria. The need for manpower on the northern front had been so substantial that some careful exceptions had been made: militia forces that had been directly established by Ayatollah Sistani to protect the Shiite shrines in Najaf and Karbala, and which were not deemed to be loyal to Iran, were allowed to hold territory in the north so that the Iraqi troops could move forward. But James Browning saw that this militia was cut from a different cloth. Jumping into an MRAP, he delivered the word to the 16th Division officers and to the militia itself: the PMF unit had to go before it did any more damage and before ISIS used the episode to its advantage. Fighting ISIS was tough enough without turning the battle for Mosul into a civil war.

The new two-front strategy was taking shape, but two confrontations just north of the Old City offered a taste of the maelstrom that lay ahead. As the 9th Division was crawling forward, a small group of Qassem's soldiers scampered into a building that ISIS had abandoned and rushed to the roof so that they could survey the defenses below. In a battlefield in which there were often no clear front lines, a group of militants reoccupied the first floor of the building, isolating the Iraqi soldiers. As the hours went by, the plight of the rooftop vanguard became increasingly desperate: parched by the baking sun and taking fire from inside the structure, most of the trapped men were soon wounded. To sustain the beleaguered force, the Iraqis on the ground heaved plastic bottles of water to the rooftop, but it was clear the men would not be able to hold out for long. Retaking the first floor was too heavy a lift: one gutsy soldier who raced across the street to try to help was shot dead. With friendlies and the enemy in the same structure, an air strike seemed to be out of the question, but the situation had become so dire that it appeared to be the only hope. Browning's plan was to have a drone shoot a Hellfire missile into the first floor and then attempt a rescue on the rooftop. This sort of "danger close" strike meant that the U.S. commander on the ground had to provide his initials to the strike cell in Erbil to take ownership of the situation in case it turned into an ugly instance of friendly fire.

The strike went ahead. With a giant *whoosh*, the Hellfire smashed into the first floor of the building, which to the surprise of the Iraqi troops pancaked on top of itself. Walid Khalifah, the one-star deputy commander of the division, ran to the semi-collapsed structure, put a ladder against the wall, climbed up to the roof, and began retrieving the wounded soldiers. His comrades below hauled them to safety across the street. One was dead, but the remaining three, including the senior officer, were still alive. It was, a U.S. officer later recalled, a Medal of Honor moment, but it was nothing that would be officially recognized in the annals of the war.

After the soldiers pulled back, Browning gave the order to level all of the buildings on the far side of the street. The Iraqi soldiers would move forward again, yard by yard. As the soldiers advanced along the river, they saw a tangled mound of civilian bodies near the bank. Many appeared to be dead, but a young child was lodged in the arms of her mother. This rescue would be trickier than the one performed earlier by David Eubank, since the Iraqi soldiers would need to climb over mounds of the dead and wounded to reach the child. As soon as they began to do so, an ISIS fighter lying among the civilians detonated a suicide vest, which set off several others, killing everybody in the vicinity. Others might have been rescued, but the casualty toll for the Iraqi Army was already enormous and the battle was far from over. The division's senior officers directed the Iraqi troops away from the river so they could resume their slog toward the Old City.

WITH THEIR BACKS against the Tigris, ISIS fighters were preparing a counterattack. The old streets in Mosul had been turned into an obstacle course by the dozens of air strikes the U.S. forces mounted to keep the Iraqis moving forward and by the car bombs ISIS had detonated to retard the advance. To turn the tables, ISIS mounted a three-pronged counterattack on June 10. Suicide car-bomb attacks were used to pin down Raed's Federal Police at the end of the Old City. Then at least 150 ISIS fighters slipped into the river at night, floating down the Tigris on inner tubes while their caches of AK-47s and other weapons followed in inflatable boats. After drifting for a mile and a half in the water, the militants crawled ashore near a water treatment plant, hoping to attack the Federal Police from the rear and help the hundreds of militants still in the Old City break out of the tightening noose. They were joined by groups of other ISIS fighters who had infiltrated south through Mosul's sewer system.

Of all the Iraqi forces impinging on the ISIS enclave, Raed's police were operating in some of the most complex terrain. Rushing to avoid a break in his lines, Raed sent a brigade of his toughest policemen south from the Al-Jamhouri hospital complex on an hourlong drive through a war zone to shore up his frontline positions. U.S. advisors accompanying Raed's brigade, meanwhile, passed on targeting information to John Hawbaker at Hammam al-Alil, and U.S. HIMARS launchers and artillery responded with more than two dozen strikes. The vicious six-hour fight came at a high cost—the Federal Police had about twenty killed and more than seventy wounded—but Raed's troops did not crack. Iraqi forces later counted more than eighty ISIS bodies, many shot by

Raed's troops at close quarters rather than killed by U.S. air or missile strikes.

Toward the end of June, another breakout was attempted. About two hundred fighters from the ISIS stronghold in Tal Afar coalesced in small platoon-size units, moving first to Talal al-Atshana, a high ridge on the western outskirts of Mosul, led by a teenager who knew the city and its streets like the back of his hand. After the militants split into two groups, one sought to infiltrate from the west while the other maneuvered around the city and then made its way down the river. The plan was to move at night, rest at safe houses during the day, attack targets of opportunity, and create enough chaos that fellow militants trapped in the Old City could flee. The fighters, including the youthful shepherd, were corralled within days, but they remained unintimidated. When brought before a group of Iraqi officers, the teenager was asked if he knew who their leader was. "Yes," the detainee shot back matter-of-factly. "You're Abdul Amir."

Having frustrated the ISIS breakouts, the Iraqi commanders moved to eliminate the trouble that remained in their rear. After taking over the bitter fight for the Al-Jamhouri complex, the Emergency Response Division struggled to move forward, only to be confronted by volleys of RPGs and machine-gun fire from ISIS fighters who were determined to hold on to the structure at all costs and who were also using a network of tunnels to reinforce their position and get supplies.

The stalemate put Abadi on the horns of a dilemma. The prime minister had ruled out leveling the hospital, which would have added millions of dollars to the already soaring tab of rebuilding Iraq's second-largest city and would have symbolized the government's failure to preserve its most important infrastructure. But the battle for Mosul had already been grinding on for months, with tens of thousands of the city's residents still trapped in a clash that was fast becoming a humanitarian catastrophe. To keep the offensive moving, Martin and Work decided to state the obvious: the complex was no longer a hospital but a half-destroyed enemy compound that civilians had already fled.

Townsend finally received Abadi's approval to bomb within the goose egg he had drawn around the installation, and air strikes pummeled the ISIS command center on June 30. Then the Iraqi forces moved forward, literally rolling over ISIS diehards with armored bulldozers—a battlefield improvisation so effective that a U.S. Army report would later describe it as an essential element of the Iraqis' combined arms formation. Two days later, on July 2, Iraqi troops finally hoisted their flag over the Ibn Sina hospital, the largest building in the complex. The final battle, however, was yet to come.

AS THE CTS crept within fifty yards of the Great Mosque of Al-Nouri on June 21, ISIS blew up the structure, toppling its twelfth-century minaret. The very structure from which Abu Bakr al-Baghdadi had delivered his sermon proclaiming a caliphate had collapsed, leaving only its iconic green dome intact. ISIS charged that the Americans had bombed the mosque—a piece of propaganda designed to mobilize Islamic sentiment against the U.S.-led coalition and force a hiatus in the air campaign. The allegation was brushed aside, and the battle entered its most desperate phase. Perched on a rooftop near the ruined mosque, Lieutenant General Abdul Wahab al-Saadi sketched out the endgame. ISIS, he figured, was down to perhaps 150 fighters, who were maneuvering across an urban wasteland. While the eastern side of Mosul was largely intact, the streets and alleyways on the west side of the river had been blasted and churned to the point that much of the Old City had become unrecognizable and U.S. surveillance imagery constantly needed to be refreshed. To protect themselves from American air strikes, ISIS fighters had taken refuge in the basements of partially collapsed buildings. U.S. B-52s had been dropping satellite-guided bombs to break the concrete at the top so that yet another bomb could burrow down and kill the militants. Trying to advance, ISIS fighters snuck behind fleeing civilians and donned uniforms stripped off of dead Iraqi soldiers. "They can't drive car bombs at us anymore, so they hide bombs in abandoned vehicles or just try to run up to us and blow themselves up," Saadi told me matter-of-factly.

Facing the dilemma of being shot by ISIS fighters or waiting to see if they might be crushed by concrete as a result of American air strikes, waves of famished civilians began to trudge out of the Old City. As the 16th Division moved south, an ISIS fighter called one of the Iraqi officers on his cell phone and said that the militants were prepared to surrender. But ISIS communication was broken off after the Iraqis refused a demand by the foreign fighters among the ISIS militants that they be allowed to keep their AK-47s. Small squads of ISIS fighters tried to sneak in among the crowds walking out. The Iraqi Army set up hasty checkpoints, ordering men and boys to remove their shirts and even strip to their underwear before they could pass. Calculating that women would not be carefully searched, ISIS instructed female suicide bombers to join the exodus. A battlefield report noted that one woman holding a baby and wearing a long-sleeved robe had blown herself up as she approached an Iraqi soldier.

Trauma stations had been set up inside some battered storefronts a short drive from the front by a handful of valiant aid workers from international nongovernmental organizations (NGOs). With ISIS fighters hiding among the anguished civilians streaming out of the city, medical care near the front was a dangerous business. It could not be provided without proper security, and the Iraqi forces were the only ones capable of providing it, which meant that some of the battlefield NGOs would have to operate under the protection of the CTS or the Iraqi Army. The UN's World Health Organization understood the reality of the situation and was funneling medical supplies to aid workers. There was no place for neutrals near a front where suicide bombers roamed freely.

At one center I visited that was run by the Iraqi Army and

CADUS, a humanitarian organization based in Germany, an Iraqi Humvee rushed up, straight from battle in the Old City. Anxious Iraqi soldiers unloaded a comrade wrapped in a thick, blood-soaked blanket. A gaping bullet hole was in the back of the soldier's head, the work of an ISIS sniper. The doctors quickly pronounced the soldier dead, and he was lifted into a black body bag. His name and unit were inscribed on a strip of paper that was taped to the outside. A small bag containing his possessions and athletic shoes was placed alongside his body. He was soon taken away, and a small pool of blood was wiped from the floor.

Many of the casualties, however, were civilians. At an aid station run by Global Response Management, a U.S.-based NGO, a nurse explained to me in early July that she could gauge the progress of the battle by the number of casualties that arrived. A surge in Iraqi soldiers with gunshot wounds signaled that the army was making another push. Civilians with limbs and torsos crushed by debris were an indication that the Americans had been conducting air strikes. Severe burns and missing limbs were indications of suicide vest attacks. The casualties arriving from the bombings in recent days had been "half civilians, half Iraqi military," said Pete Reed, an emergency medical technician who founded the organization. "The majority of suicide vest attacks in the past few days have been by females," he added.

On Sunday, July 9, a tweet from the prime minister's office disclosed that Abadi was coming to Mosul to proclaim the city's liberation. He soon arrived at the Mosul airport wearing the same black CTS uniform and cap he had donned three months earlier at Hammam al-Alil. The catch was that the battle was not over quite yet. Abadi had jumped the gun at the start of the offensive, but this time he saw the risk of being shown up by ISIS, and his victory announcement would need to wait.

In the days before the prime minister's arrival, the drone feeds at the forward headquarters of the 9th Division showed that ISIS had arranged for a cluster of men, women, and children to march in circles in its shrunken bastion near the Tigris, a tactic to fend off air strikes. It was becoming increasingly difficult to drop bombs at all since so many of the blasts were "danger close." Again the bulldozers had swung into action, moving from the north and south. The earth movers sustained damage from grenades, machine guns, and suicide vests worn by fighters who blew themselves up under the dozers' tracks. In the final days, virtually all the remaining ISIS fighters seemed to be wearing suicide vests.

The mission to seize the final fifty meters of territory was undertaken by a special ranger unit, created by Abdul Amir, that maneuvered from hole to hole, house to house, dropping between sixty and seventy grenades on enemy positions as it accompanied a bulldozer driven by an intrepid Iraqi soldier who buried ISIS fighters in their holes—most of them dead, but some who were alive. "I have been with the Iraqi Army for 40 years," said Major General Sami al-Aradi of the CTS. "I have participated in all of the battles of Iraq, but I've never seen anything like the battle for the Old City." He continued: "We have been fighting for each meter. And when I say we have been fighting for each meter, I mean it literally."

Abadi called Townsend and explained that he wanted to make his victory announcement but wanted to be sure the U.S.-led coalition would not contradict it. Townsend assured him that for all intents and purposes the city had been liberated and that what remained could be described as mopping up. Reassured, Abadi formally declared victory on July 10 in an address broadcast on Iraqi state television from the CTS forward headquarters. "I announce from here the end and the failure and the collapse of the terrorist state," the prime minister said as he hoisted the Iraqi flag. Even so, skirmishing in the city continued. By the morning of July 16, the Iraqis figured that ISIS was pinned down in a forty-by-forty-meter area. The next day, the United States dropped its last bomb on Mosul. There was every likelihood that some ISIS fighters were still hiding in the city or trying to sneak out. If there were still bands of ISIS fighters skulking around, however, the Iraqi military and the ISIS fighters were at such close quarters that air support was no longer a feasible option in the Old City.

The "by, with, and through" strategy had yielded a victory. But as had been apparent from the Mosul Dam operation in 2014, the Iraqis were heavily dependent on air strikes to advance, and when the strategy was applied in an urban environment it came at a great cost. Street after street was covered in soaring piles of rubble, with rebar poking out of shattered masonry. In a church used as a weapons-making factory by the Islamic State, mortars were lying on the ground next to a pink backpack decorated with a picture of a kitten. When troops unzipped the backpack, they found plastic sachets of a white explosive powder, which they identified as C4. Of the fifty-four neighborhoods in West Mosul, fifteen were heavily damaged, according to data provided by the United Nations; those fifteen neighborhoods encompassed thirty-two thousand houses. An additional twenty-three neighborhoods were moderately damaged. The cost of the near-term repairs and the more substantial reconstruction needed in Mosul stood at more than $700 million.

Before the battle began, the worst-case estimate by the United Nations was that 750,000 people—in a city of around 1.4 million—would be displaced. By early July, 920,000 had left, including the remnants of ISIS's forces. Stabilizing the city would be as complicated as the battle itself.

Raed had established his forward headquarters in an abandoned marble building. When his forces heard the battle was over, an uproarious celebration broke out in the foyer. The policemen were chanting, parading the Federal Police banner, and recording the moment on their smartphones. Over steaming cups of sugary tea, Raed and Work met to discuss the Federal Police's next steps. Raed made clear that he was not impressed by what the politicians were doing to take care of their newly liberated and famished constituents and win the battle of hearts and minds. "The people are suffering, and we are handing out food and water, but neither the governor, not the provincial council nor the minister are here," he said. Then Raed delivered another message. Abdul Amir had asked him to keep four Federal Police brigades in Mosul to maintain order while committing his remaining brigade to the looming fight for Tal Afar to the west. But the Federal Police commander had no intention of honoring that request. There were too many people in Mosul who had long memories of how the Iraqi government had mistreated Sunnis, and securing the trust of the population would therefore be all but impossible. "We have sacrificed our blood, but mismanagement during earlier history of the Federal Police had affected their mentality," Raed said. Beyond that, Raed was not prepared to split up his force or play second fiddle to the CTS or the Iraqi Army. The prime minister, the defense minister, and ranking officials all flocked to visit the CTS, but none of the VIPs came to see the Federal Police. Nor had the delivery of much-needed supplies—including tires, rifles, and ammunition—been arranged, Raed complained. "You can't just go to a map on a wall and start drawing arrows with pens and pencils," Raed said in a dig at Abdul Amir's planning. "Any mission I am given, we must go in with full force." Work was powerless to rewrite Abdul Amir's orders but listened respectfully: "I heard what you said, *sa'eedi*." It was an example of how decisions could be made and unmade in Iraq's decentralized command structure and of the limits of the U.S. advisory mission.

The final casualty toll was enormous. In the final weeks, 610 Iraqi soldiers were killed in action and 3,100 wounded. ISIS had detonated 10 bombs, while 87 had been found and destroyed before they could be activated. There were 7,542 ISIS mortar attacks—what the military called "indirect fire." The declassified statistics for the entire Mosul battle were even more staggering. Among the Iraqi Security Forces, 1,320 service members had been killed and 6,880 wounded. The Peshmerga had lost another 60 soldiers in battle, with 200 wounded. No fewer than 191 car bombs had gone off, while 452 had been destroyed by the coalition. There had been some 12,432 enemy mortar or artillery attacks, which had led to 1,488 U.S. and allied counterattacks. By and large, the Iraqi forces had conducted themselves like an army and not like vigilantes out for revenge. But Townsend sent Abadi a confidential list of Iraqi personnel who had been accused of violating the laws of armed combat in 2016 and 2017—a list that remains classified to this day.

A massive challenge lay ahead in restoring electricity and other essential services to the city, as well as providing housing and schools. Hundreds of millions of dollars in aid had been funneled through the United Nations Development Programme. Those monies would be administered by Nineveh's governor, Nawfel Akoub, who had taken the reins with Masoud Barzani's support after Atheel al-Nujaifi, the previous governor, fled. For weeks, the Americans waited for the funds to be turned into programs, only to conclude that Akoub was sitting on the funds until he could steer some of the contracts to his inner circle. Finally, the authority for spending the money was given to the Iraqi government, which assigned a technocrat to get the aid projects underway. Six months later, West Mosul was still identified as one of five areas in Iraq and Syria where millions more would need to be spent to win proverbial hearts and minds and ward off ISIS sympathies.

Nobody was under any illusion that the larger campaign was over, and the Iraqis still needed to consolidate their gains. "It's going to continue to be hard every day," Work said as we rolled through the streets in his MRAP. "ISIS will challenge this."

A sign that ISIS was not quite vanquished soon emerged at Imam Gharbi, a modest village of stone houses on the west bank of the Tigris. Armed with machine guns and mortars, ISIS fighters who had been bypassed in Hawija on the Iraqi Army's march to Mosul crossed the river, infiltrated the town, and executed two Iraqi journalists who had rushed to cover the development. ISIS had captured an Iraqi T-55 tank and a Humvee, and human intelligence reports indicated that fighters had captured some antiaircraft artillery that they might use to fire at planes landing at and taking off from Qayyarah Airfield West.

At a minimum, the episode provided a small taste of how ISIS would try to create havoc as it reverted to its guerrilla roots. With

Iraq's commanders still preoccupied with Mosul, Work figured out a response. Rushing south on July 17, he brought in Juma Inad Saadoun al-Jabouri, a staff lieutenant general from the Salah al-Din Command who had once been Abdul Amir's instructor at Iraq's military academy, and who would later be named Iraq's defense minister. Juma added some tribal forces and an Interior Ministry SWAT team. Major Steve Ackerson, an executive officer from a U.S. artillery detachment who could call in coalition air strikes, was assigned as Juma's advisor. Two days later, the town was retaken.

Following the difficult days in Imam Gharbi, Tal Afar was one fight that turned out to be easier than expected. Subjected to constant air strikes, ISIS defenses in the city were attacked by columns of Iraqi Army units and the CTS, as well as Raed's Federal Police and Emergency Response Division. Some of the ISIS fighters bled into the hills north of the city, but after twelve days of fighting, Tal Afar was in Iraqi hands by September. ISIS still held Hawija and was active in western Iraq, but for ISIS and the United States, the main fighting in Iraq was now over and the action was shifting to Syria.

19

WRATH OF THE EUPHRATES

On July 11, 2017, the day after Haider al-Abadi proclaimed that Mosul was back in Iraqi hands, President Donald Trump sat down in the Oval Office to congratulate the prime minister on his victory. ISIS diehards were still roaming the battlefield in northern Iraq. Much of the city lay in ruins. Iraq's casualty toll, military and civilian, had been enormous, and hundreds of thousands of residents had fled to tent cities the United Nations had rushed to stand up in the region. Raqqa, Syria, the militants' capital, had yet to be taken, but at least one of the large arrows Ash Carter had drawn in 2015 had hit its mark. As with any presidential call, Trump's talking points had been prepared in advance by a team of NSC aides, but this president could not be scripted. After Trump hailed the Mosul triumph, Abadi explained that the job was not over: there was still fighting to be done to reclaim Hawija and other ISIS strongholds before anybody could say that ISIS had been routed from Iraq. Concerned that more help would still be needed from Washington, Trump shot back that there was something he wanted in return.

"I want the oil," Trump blurted out. For good measure, the president also accused Iraq of smuggling oil exports to Iran. The White House's official readout of the call, issued later that day, presented the message the president was supposed to have delivered but nary a word about the president's actual spoken demand. "The President praised the heroism of the Iraqi and American soldiers and underscored his commitment to the total defeat of ISIS," the White House said in its press release. "He stressed the need to consolidate gains to prevent ISIS or any other terrorist group from returning to liberated areas."

As word of the conversation spread behind closed doors in Baghdad, Abadi and his senior aides were distressed. Iraq had suffered tens of billions of dollars in war damage. The Iraqi street was restive. Now the U.S. president was insisting that Iraq hand over much of its only remunerable resource—a demand that did not have a prayer of a chance of being accepted by an increasingly nationalistic Iraq, but raised questions about the durability of the United States' commitment to Baghdad's security. Trump had mused during the campaign about taking the oil. Republicans had dismissed that as rhetorical excess, mere posturing for his base. But this time Trump had put the proposition squarely on the table with the head of Iraq's government. The United States still needed the Iraqi government as a partner, both to finish the job in Iraq and as a platform for operations in Syria. The ongoing fight against terrorism and the hope of rolling back Iran's influence in the Middle East was subordinated to the president's transactional instinct to secure a business advantage for the United States.

After the July 11 call to Abadi, H. R. McMaster, who had been named national security advisor in February, accompanied Trump to the president's golf resort at Bedminster, New Jersey, where he devised a plan to smooth things over. On the face of it, Trump's demand did not make much sense. Little of the Sunni-dominated Iraqi territory the American forces had helped liberate from ISIS actually had oil fields, nor did the United States have a state-owned oil company on whose behalf McMaster could demand concessions. In his new post, McMaster consulted periodically with Henry Kissinger, and as he drove to see the former national security advisor and secretary of state, he called Abadi on a secure telephone line and sought to translate Trump's impulse into terms that both sides could accept. The United States and Iraq had a strong security relationship, McMaster told Abadi, and now they should have a strong economic relationship, one that would benefit American companies and help Iraq's economy grow. McMaster had defused the diplomatic contretemps, but Trump's phone call pointed to deeper and still unsettled questions about the White House's patience to see the counter-ISIS campaign through.

The immediate question before the administration, however, was what should be done about Operation Inherent Resolve. Obama had flown to Tampa on December 6, 2016, to deliver his final national security address and to defend his record on counterterrorism. The president challenged the idea that keeping troops in Iraq after 2011 would have impeded ISIS's gains. A continued troop presence, he argued, would not have curbed Nouri al-Maliki's sectarian actions or averted the civil war in Syria, which provided a boost to ISIS's ambitions. Nor would it have prevented the hollowing-out of Iraq's security forces that led to their collapse in Mosul. The failure of the SOFA talks, he insisted, was all Maliki's fault. In contrast, his "by, with, and through" campaign had been conditioned on the installation of a new Iraqi government, had the support of an international coalition, and relied on local forces to do the fighting. "Instead of pushing all of the burden onto American ground troops, instead of trying to mount invasions whenever terrorists appear," Obama pointed out, "we've built a network of partners."

The U.S. government's most experienced Iraq hands believed that the strategy Obama had put in place did show results, especially after the constraints the president and his aides initially imposed on the presence of advisors on the battlefield were removed and the troop ceilings the White House leveled on the military were raised. But many officials also acknowledged that the presence of an American force in Iraq after 2011 would have given Washington a window into the erosion of Iraq's military forces, an earlier heads-up on ISIS's capabilities, and more influence in Baghdad to try to counter Maliki's sectarian policies.

Trump's campaign speeches had not pointed the way to a new policy. Pressed on what he would do differently, Trump vowed to "bomb the shit" out of ISIS and kill the militants' families—and then he added that he had a plan to achieve "total victory" that he dared not disclose, lest it tip off Abu Bakr al-Baghdadi. Once he occupied the White House, however, Trump would be put to the test and his strategy could stay secret no more.

Eight days after his inauguration, as the battle for Mosul still raged, Trump issued National Security Presidential Memorandum No. 3, directing his administration "to develop a comprehensive plan to defeat ISIS." The memorandum called for a draft plan within thirty days on how to defeat the militants, including mechanisms to cut off ISIS's financial support as well as "cyber strategies"—all of which had also been components of Obama's "by, with, and through" strategy. The directive ordered officials to identify new coalition partners, which opened the door in theory to a possible role for Turkey or perhaps even Russia. The memorandum made no mention of the still-unresolved question of whether the United States should arm the Kurdish elements of the Syrian Democratic Forces, the issue that the Obama administration had debated extensively but eventually left for its successor, though it did allude generally to the need to "empower coalition partners." It sought to make good on Trump's rhetoric by opening the door to relaxing the rules of engagement intended to reduce civilian casualties—or, as the order put it, officials were to recommend changes to policy restrictions "that exceed the requirements of international law regarding the use of force against ISIS."

There were some major differences between the two administrations on Syria. The missile strikes Trump authorized in 2017 and 2018 in response to Bashar al-Assad's chemical weapons attacks marked an abrupt departure from Obama's reluctance to enforce his red line. Another policy distinction emerged when Trump canceled the covert program of CIA assistance to the anti-Assad opposition, a decision Trump confirmed in a tweet. But the twenty-four days in January and February 2017 that Mike Flynn spent as national security advisor before being shown the door did not yield any adjustments to the strategy Trump had inherited from Obama.

As Trump began to search for Flynn's replacement, word began to circulate among the cadre of former U.S. Army officers on Capitol Hill that this might be just the role for Lieutenant General H. R. McMaster. McMaster had had an impressive military career, including a Silver Star from the 1991 Gulf War and command of counterinsurgency operations in Tal Afar in 2005 that were deemed so successful they were included in the Army's counterinsurgency manual. A freethinker in a service that tended to reward get-along, go-along officers, McMaster had written *Dereliction of Duty*, a 1997 book that criticized the Joint Chiefs of Staff for sticking with a losing strategy in the Vietnam War, and he had spearheaded the strategy review for David Petraeus when Petraeus was the commander in Iraq. Under General Ray Odierno, McMaster had risen to three stars and emerged as the senior officer in charge of figuring out how the Army should fight in the future. McMaster was edging toward retirement when he was invited to Mar-a-Lago for an audience with Trump himself. With Flynn ousted and the White House in seeming disarray, McMaster wondered aloud about the wisdom of rushing into a burning building. Nevertheless, he yielded to his sense of duty and made the trip. McMaster got a sense of who some of the other contenders were when he ran into John Bolton in a bathroom at Trump's estate, but this time McMaster won the competition and was selected.

McMaster's first inkling of the difficulties he might face came when he paid a courtesy call to Jim Mattis. The Pentagon chief advised him to retire from the military. As national security advisor, Mattis said, McMaster would be dealing with four-star generals, and it would be awkward to interact with commanders in the rank-conscious military as a mere three-star. McMaster was taken aback by the suggestion. He intended to hit the ground running without the distraction of going through the process of retiring and finding a place to live off-post.

The bigger problem was that the episode reflected a deeper disagreement over the national security process and who should be calling the shots. To shape policy, Mattis made common cause with a person he figured would emerge as a powerful ally. Before they took office, Mattis had invited the new secretary of state and former CEO of ExxonMobil, Rex Tillerson, to a Georgetown restaurant where he asserted that the Pentagon and State Department had been at odds for too long, that foreign policy had become too militarized, and that the two future secretaries should work together. The former oilman had reached across the table to shake on the understanding.

As McMaster saw it, he would run the process, give the principals an opportunity to debate, tee up the options for the president, and then let Trump decide. For Mattis, the national security advisor was not a maestro but a high-level staff officer whose role was to coordinate policies developed primarily by the State and Defense Departments for a president with little background in foreign policy. At the NSC, Mattis and Tillerson were dubbed "the Club of Two." There was a lot of chatter outside the administration about Trump's reliance on the generals: Would the new president become too dependent on the brass, and would his reliance on their input moderate his decisions or make him too quick to pull the trigger? But the real problem was that the retired and active-duty generals who were thrust into new policymaking roles were at odds with themselves.

The tensions within the administration spilled over into deliberations about ISIS. While serving at the Army's training command, McMaster had drawn on his deployments in Iraq and Afghanistan in drafting the Army's Operating Concept, which outlined how the service was to handle future conflicts. The goal, it held, was not merely to win on the battlefield; rather, it was to lay the groundwork for achieving a "sustainable political outcome." McMaster had some ideas of his own about how to make the gains stick. If Mazloum Abdi's Syrian Democratic Forces could quickly defeat ISIS, establish control of northeastern Syria, and put in place a new government acceptable in the region, that might not only inhibit a return by the militant group but also limit Iranian and Russian influence. If and when there were diplomatic negotiations over Syria's future, the SDF would have more leverage, as would its Washington patrons—or so the theory went.

Taking charge of the ISIS review, McMaster posed three questions: To what extent was control of territory, population, and resources necessary to achieve a sustainable political outcome in Syria and Iraq? How important was the speed of the campaign given the military operations that the Assad regime, Iran, and Russia were also undertaking in Syria? And to what extent were U.S. interests congruent with those of the SDF? The answers could point the way to one possible plan for cementing the peace after the eventual defeat of ISIS.

Mattis favored a diplomatic solution for Syria but doubted that Trump had the patience to see the effort through. For every statement Trump made vowing to stick it to ISIS, he also made remarks, in public as well as in private, saying that he wanted to put the Middle East in the rearview mirror. McMaster's "sustainable political outcome" entailed a modest but open-ended U.S. military presence, which was not something Mattis believed Trump would easily stomach. Efforts to make the anti-ISIS campaign more robust by expanding the U.S. role got even less traction. The Middle East team on Trump's NSC staff did a classified analysis of how the campaign might be accelerated by deploying an armored brigade or a brigade of the 82nd Airborne to fight with the SDF, perhaps including Jordanian or Saudi National Guard troops in the mix. The U.S. military had endorsed the "by, with, and through" strategy, but what if the "with" was expanded to expedite and seal ISIS's defeat in Raqqa and the Euphrates River valley in Syria? Small U.S. conventional combat forces might increase U.S. leverage in any potential diplomatic resolution of the conflict. Like Obama, however, Trump was not looking to put more American forces in a ground combat role or accept the risk of additional casualties, and the idea never made it very far.

One change McMaster did make, and which bolstered the U.S. effort, was to remove the 503-person force manning level the Obama administration had established for Syria and to stop the Obama-era practice of having the NSC discuss and debate the deployment of additional forces. That gave Mattis the freedom to send more forces, which he did by deploying Army Rangers to northern Syria to show the flag and tamp down tensions between Mazloum's Kurdish forces and Turkish-backed militias, and by dispatching a Marine artillery battalion to boost firepower for the fight ahead for Raqqa.

The idea of deploying the Marine artillery had been quietly explored during the waning weeks of the Obama administration. Several artillery pieces could cover an area and suppress enemy movement in a way five-hundred-pound bombs could not, and could also be effective in bad weather, which inhibited air strikes. The force would need to protect itself and sustain itself logistically in an environment in which there was virtually no infrastructure. Directed to quietly scope out the option, Lieutenant Colonel Matthew Lundgren and a small group of planners from the 11th Marine Expeditionary Unit disembarked in Djibouti from their amphibious ships, donned civilian clothes, caught a commercial flight to Erbil, and then traveled in December 2016 to northeastern Syria so they could get the lay of the land. By March 2017, the troop caps had been thrown aside and some four hundred Marines were driven south to a small outpost Army engineers built for them twenty miles north of Raqqa.

The Marines had studied the lessons of the 2016 deployment at Fire Base Bell, where Staff Sergeant Louis F. Cardin had been killed, and sought to do what they could to lower their profile. Marines were instructed not to bring any cell phones or electronic devices that would emit a telltale signature. There would not be any Facebook posts, and for the first month or so, no family members were to know where they were. That did nothing, however, to reduce the risk from ISIS militants who could plainly see the Marines from their defensive positions north of Raqqa and who began to fire rockets and artillery at the Americans until Army Apache helicopters silenced them. "We built our base in plain view of ISIS," recalled one Marine. "We didn't take any casualties. We were very lucky."

With the decision on arming Mazloum's Kurdish fighters yet unmade, Steve Townsend and Mazloum focused on another way to maintain the momentum on the battlefield. They would mount an assault on Tabqa, thirty-five miles west of Raqqa and on the south side of the Euphrates River. Mazloum had felt that the task was too much to take on when Sean MacFarland suggested it in 2016, but he was ready for it now. ISIS had taken the city in 2014 in a battle led by one of its most important field commanders, the Chechen known as Abu Omar al-Shishani, who had been killed in July 2016 in the Iraqi city of Shirqat as Iraqi forces were advancing toward Mosul. Seizing Tabqa would enable the SDF to control the western flank of their Raqqa offensive and open up an additional axis for the eventual move on the self-styled capital of the ISIS caliphate. Taking Tabqa would also enable the SDF to control a nearby air base and, importantly, a fifteen-story-tall hydroelectric dam on Lake Assad that generated much of the electricity in the region and whose destruction could send floodwater racing to Raqqa and beyond. The SDF knew the city well, as one of its commanders had lived there. ISIS's positions to the north of Raqqa were strongly defended, so the SDF would bypass them as it waited for heavy weapons to arrive.

Mazloum's initial plan was to put his force on barges and cross Lake Assad, which was to the town's west, an eight-kilometer maneuver that even Townsend thought would have been extraordinarily ambitious. After lots of discussion, the American special operations advisors to the SDF proposed that SDF fighters be flown to a peninsula on the far side of the lake and to let them maneuver toward Tabqa from there. Even that posed some challenges. A few members of Lahur Talabani's Counter Terrorism Group and some four hundred SDF fighters, including many who had never flown on an aircraft before, would be put aboard helicopters and Osprey tilt-rotor aircraft at night and deposited south of Lake Assad behind enemy lines. They would establish a lodgment, receive supplies, and wait for reinforcements who would come over on barges and boats. They would then take the airfield and seize the town and dam—preferably intact.

The plan, which was dubbed "Operation Wrath of the Euphrates," was sent to Steve Townsend, who approved and forwarded it to Joe Votel at CENTCOM. He then had the SDF fighters practice what the military called "static load training": getting on and off helicopters and Ospreys in a combat zone. The plan was one of the boldest operations of the entire Inherent Resolve campaign. It was quickly approved, and preparations began—a stark contrast to the weeks and sometimes months of scrutiny the Obama White House was known to give when briefed on concept of operations (CONOPS) in Iraq. "I did not go back to the SECDEF and ask him for permission," Votel recalled, referring to his relationship with Jim Mattis. "I kept the SECDEF informed but did not have the CONOP approved in Washington. We took on a lot of risk." Later, Mattis himself expressed surprise to the CENTCOM commander at the scale of the operation.

The operation that began on the night of March 21, 2017, was the first major air assault in the war, marking a new milestone in the "by, with, and through" campaign. The United States did not leave advisors with the SDF fighters it ferried to the south side of Lake Assad. That advising would be done remotely. But it had helped 428 SDF troops get to the fight; brought in mechanics to help them get their boats working; and joined the battle with Marine howitzers, Army attack helicopters, HIMARS surface-to-surface rockets, and U.S. airpower. Townsend expected a strong ISIS counterattack, which did not come. The SDF cut the road out of Tabqa to protect its toehold on the peninsula, and then took the airfield on March 27, which opened up another way to bring in supplies. The fighting stiffened, however, as the SDF moved toward the city and the dam, which was fast becoming a serious worry.

With rain and melting snows in the north, the water in Lake

Assad was rising. As fighting raged near the dam, fears began to mount that it might suffer a break. To try to hold back the rising water, the SDF arranged for engineers to dam tributaries that fed into Lake Assad and use a crane to open a jammed floodgate in the main dam itself.

As the battle intensified, Mazloum let Townsend know that he was interested in striking a deal with ISIS that would allow the militants to withdraw to Raqqa unmolested while leaving Tabqa intact. Townsend urged Mazloum to stay the course. Mazloum appeared to yield, and by early May few major pockets of resistance remained. One was defended by fifty or so ISIS militants in heavily fortified apartments, and the other consisted of about twenty militants inside the massive dam. This time, Mazloum cut the deal allowing ISIS safe passage out of the city with their arms if they left peacefully, disarmed their IEDs, and did not damage the dam. When Townsend learned belatedly about the arrangement, he made it clear that he would not be bound by it. The United States tried to scramble its reconnaissance drones and aircraft, but the ISIS convoy soon scattered to avoid being targeted.

The surrender deal reflected a deep divide between the mindsets of the U.S. proxies in Syria and their American backers. Once the fate of battle had been determined, the SDF saw every reason to work out an arrangement in which it captured its objective, spared the infrastructure further damage, and minimized the risk to civilians—no small consideration, as the SDF commander for the Tabqa fight was an Arab who hailed from the city. It was a trade-off that allowed some ISIS militants to survive to fight another day, but it blunted the damage to those who would inhabit the newly liberated ground, whose reconstruction was far from certain. The arrangement also limited the losses to the SDF, which still needed to preserve its strength for the bigger battle ahead in Raqqa.

When I arrived at the dam in late June, I saw that ISIS had sprayed the control panels inside the structure with bullets. Years later, *The New York Times* reported that it had been hit with at least one two-thousand-pound bomb, which failed to detonate. "SDF agreed to this arrangement in accordance with local warfighting customs in order to reduce civilian casualties and property damage, protect the Tabqa Dam, preserve combat forces and accelerate the isolation of Raqqa," Townsend's command noted in its official internal history. "CJTF-OIR [Combined Joint Task Force–Operation Inherent Resolve] was unable to mass sufficient airpower to reduce the convoy upon its departure from the city limits."

Now that Raqqa was isolated from the west, the question on the table was how the U.S.-led coalition planned to move on the city itself. Nearly 200,000 people had lived in the Euphrates River city before the Syrian war—Sunni Arabs but also a smattering of Alawites, Armenians, and Maronite Christians. Jabhat al-Nusra and other anti-Assad groups had taken control of the city in the spring of 2013, only to have ISIS dislodge them in January 2014—the same month the militants established control over Fallujah. By the fall of 2016, American intelligence estimated that there were nearly 2,000 fighters in the city—with another 900 to 1,600 in the surrounding towns—who could be expected to fall back to Raqqa as the U.S.-led coalition advanced.

While the issue of arming the Kurdish portions of the SDF still percolated within the Trump administration, the military found ways to drive home the case. In February 2017, Joe Votel climbed into an Osprey in Erbil and flew to a Syrian training range outside Manbij with me, CBS's David Martin, the author Linda Robinson, and Paul McLeary of the digital publication *Breaking Defense* in tow, the better to publicize the fighters who had taken back that city and whom the U.S. military was counting on to control northeastern Syria after ISIS had been routed—if only Washington would properly arm them. Townsend's private counsel to the White House, which Votel endorsed, was unequivocal. If the weapons were not provided, not only would the timeline for taking Raqqa slip but the entire "by, with, and through" concept might be in question. The U.S. military had identified no other partner capable of capturing the ISIS capital.

Erdoğan had arranged for a referendum on April 16 on whether to expand his powers, and the Americans did not want the Turkish autocrat to have more political ammunition. So McMaster arranged for the decision on whether to arm the Syrian Kurds to be put off until after that date. Trump presided over a classified videoconference when it was time to make the call. Speaking to Trump from a trip to Norway, Mattis and McGurk made the strongest case they could: If the United States armed the Syrian Kurds, they could take Raqqa with no additional U.S. forces. If the president yielded to Erdoğan's complaints, the other option would be to rely on the Turkish military and ten thousand American troops. That was an easy choice for the "America First" Trump, who wanted no part of Middle East entanglements. Trump said that the military should arm Mazloum's Kurdish fighters, take Raqqa, and then "get the hell out."

Still, nothing could be taken for granted. Erdoğan was scheduled to make a state visit to Washington, and when he and Trump got together, anything might happen. On May 9, McMaster hosted a high-level Turkish delegation that had come to lay the groundwork for the meeting and informed them that the decision to arm the Kurds had already been made. The final piece had been put into place: the Kurdish element of the YPG would finally get heavy machine guns, armored vehicles, and mortars for the Raqqa operation.

Ten days later, Trump directed Mattis to convene a rare press conference at the Pentagon with Joe Dunford and Brett McGurk to tout the progress being made in the still-incomplete campaign. Like McMaster, Mattis had been pulled to Washington from the twilight of his career by Trump's unexpected victory. He had cultivated the image of a cerebral warrior who had a library of thousands of books but did not own a television. Trump had taken to calling the Pentagon chief "Mad Dog Mattis," a moniker that Mattis hated and that was not in fact his nickname: his radio call sign during the invasion of Iraq was "Chaos."

In the main, though, Mattis was careful about the use of force: He had initially advised against an all-out assault on Fallujah after insurgents ambushed four Blackwater contractors in 2004, killed them, and hung their bodies on a bridge over the Euphrates. It was better, he argued, to take the time to gather intelligence and do targeted raids instead. He valued NATO and Asian allies, was skeptical of Russia, supported the 2015 nuclear accord with Iran, and opposed the use of torture against terrorists—all positions that were at odds with Trump's "America First" instincts. Mattis was also famously discreet. In the age of Wikileaks, he chose not to take notes at CENTCOM to reassure Arab leaders that nothing would leak out, and he had a penchant for deleting his emails. Mattis figured he could make the Pentagon job work by managing his messaging and staying under the radar. Knowing that Trump got most of his information from television, Mattis turned down requests to go on *Fox & Friends* and suspended the time-honored practice of holding formal news conferences at the Pentagon, turning instead to impromptu gatherings in the correspondent work spaces, which were on the record but away from the television cameras.

Trump's request that he hold a news conference, however, was one Mattis could not refuse. He had recently returned from a meeting with NATO allies, who were worried that homegrown militants who had joined the caliphate might now flee back to their own countries and carry out massacres like the one on November 13, 2015, in Paris. So the defense secretary used the May 19, 2017, news conference to send a message. Thanks to President Trump's leadership and the coalition, Mattis told the press, more than 55 percent of ISIS's caliphate had been taken back and the campaign was now focused on surrounding the enemy in its strongholds and eliminating it. "The foreign fighters are the strategic threat should they return home to Tunis, to Kuala Lumpur, to Paris, to Detroit, wherever," Mattis said. "By taking the time to deconflict, to surround and then attack, we carry out the annihilation campaign so we don't simply transplant this problem from one location to another." The outcome in Tabqa, at the SDF's insistence, had been the very antithesis of an annihilation campaign, but it went unmentioned. McGurk, who had praised Trump's leadership during a visit to Tabqa, picked up the theme. All of the relevant U.S.

agencies, he said, were involved in "an anaconda-like approach to suffocate ISIS of its territory, finances, propaganda, and ability to move foreign fighters."

For all of his bombast, however, Trump had not altered Obama's "by, with, and through" strategy or rewritten the rules of engagement. Trump's management style carried some benefits: by ceding tactical decisions to the commanders on troop levels, the number of helicopters deployed, and operations, he allowed the military campaign to proceed without the halting pauses that sometimes delayed action under Obama. It could be said that he was executing Obama's strategy more efficiently than the former president had himself, simply by staying out of it. The approach carried some risks, which would come back to haunt Trump: if the president delegated too many decisions, he risked losing touch with how things were evolving on the ground and with the logic of the campaign itself. Soon after I wrote an article about this shift in command styles, Dunford stopped me in a Pentagon corridor and said that he was determined to keep Trump fully briefed so that he would have ownership of the operations.

WITH THE CLIMACTIC battle for Raqqa looming, the Assad regime and its Russian and Iranian backers began to cast their eyes on eastern Syria and the territory they hoped to control once the caliphate collapsed. Mazloum was well aware of the jockeying. After taking Raqqa, the plan was for the SDF to pursue the remnants of the caliphate and its leaders in Deir al-Zour, the oil-rich Syrian province that sat astride the Euphrates. The region was known by the U.S. military as the MERV, which stood for "Middle Euphrates River Valley"; it was also home to an array of towns that were under ISIS's thumb, such as Madan, Al-Mayadin, and Al-Bukamal, and a sanctuary for the group's leadership. The dilemma Mazloum faced was that the SDF did not have enough forces to take on Raqqa and Deir al-Zour at the same time. In meetings with Townsend, it was determined that Raqqa had to come first and that the SDF, along with its American backers, would have to hope that Assad's forces and their Russian and Iranian enablers did not beat Mazloum to the punch.

Initially, that seemed like a safe bet. When the weight of the American effort was on retaking Mosul, deconflicting the U.S.-backed efforts in Syria from those of Bashar al-Assad and his allies had been relatively simple. The Americans and the Russians agreed that the Euphrates River would serve as a rough dividing line. U.S. airpower and the SDF would generally stay east of the Euphrates, while the Russians, the Iranians, and the Assad regime operated to the west of the river. To minimize the risk of an inadvertent confrontation, the U.S. and Russian militaries had improvised an arrangement: a humble commercial phone line linked the air war command at Al-Udeid to the Russian military headquarters in Syria. The Russian interlocutors ranged from a first lieutenant to a major general, depending on the calls, which often happened several times a day. As it was quickly determined that the U.S. Air Force linguists were better at speaking Russian than the Russian officers were at speaking English, the Americans bulked up their team of Russian speakers. To ensure that the Russian deconfliction line was not engaged on extraneous business at a moment when urgent communication was needed, a label was taped to the receiver that read "Do Not Use. RDC Only," and the channel was backed up by an unclassified Gmail account. A similar phone line was later installed at Townsend's command centers in Baghdad and Kuwait so he could sort out issues with his Russian counterpart, Colonel General Sergey Surovikin.

The push to roll back ISIS's caliphate, however, had introduced some potential areas of friction. After Syrian troops and their Russian advisors captured Palmyra, an important way station for any push to the MERV, Russian commanders declared a fifty-five-kilometer zone around the city and warned the Americans and their allies to stay away. Soon Townsend had returned the favor: a fifty-five-kilometer zone was declared for the Al-Tanf garrison at the intersection of the Syrian, Jordanian, and Iraqi borders. If Syrian or Russian forces were chasing ISIS in the area, the Americans would give them the green light to proceed. Otherwise, they should stay out. Now that ISIS's days appeared to be numbered and a scramble for the MERV was brewing, however, the deconfliction arrangements were coming under challenge.

At the start of the counter-ISIS campaign, the use of airpower had been tightly controlled, and coalition pilots had a tendency to look to the U.S. air war command at Al-Udeid for instructions before pulling the trigger. With tensions heating up in eastern Syria, Lieutenant General Jeffrey Harrigian, who had taken over from Charles Q. Brown as the air war commander, thought that events were moving too fast for that degree of centralization. During a visit to the aircraft carrier USS *George H.W. Bush* in the Mediterranean, the British air base in Cyprus, and other coalition airfields, Harrigian told the pilots that they needed to be prepared to operate within the rules of engagement but without asking permission from the air war command. Events came to a head on June 18. As part of the Tabqa operation, Mazloum's fighters had been lifted south of the Euphrates and were moving on a village called Ja'Din. The Russians had been alerted through the deconfliction phone line that the United States and its SDF allies would be operating temporarily south of the Euphrates for Wrath of the Euphrates. But the U.S. military had no similar deconfliction line with the Assad regime, and relied on the Russians to pass on the word to the Syrian authorities on its operations there.

Earlier in the day, pro-Assad militiamen had tangled with the SDF fighters, whom Damascus appeared to think did not belong on that side of the river, as it was looking at extending its authority to Deir al-Zour. F/A-18s from the *George H.W. Bush* had been sent to shoo the Syrians away. Lieutenant Commander Michael Tremel flew his F/A-18 over a Syrian Su-22 and fired flares—a tactic known as a "headbutt." But that did nothing to deter the Syrian plane, which proceeded to unleash two bombs on the SDF fighters. Tremel flipped the switch to arm a Sidewinder heat-seeking missile and fired, only to miss. The Navy pilot had been so close to his target that he was not sure the Sidewinder had even fused in time. Making another try, Tremel fired an advanced medium-range air-to-air missile (AMRAAM) from half a mile away into the rear of the Syrian plane and swung left to avoid the debris. Nobody could say for sure if the Syrians fully understood where the boundaries were being drawn in the skies or exactly whom they had bombed. If the Syrians had not understood before, however, they had to understand now. For the United States, the unexpected turn of events was a military milestone: the first American air-to-air kill in eighteen years. A Russian Su-35 had been in the vicinity of the engagement and never intervened.

The episode did not put an end to the confrontations. In June, the Iranians and the Assad regime began to ratchet up the pressure on the Al-Tanf garrison. The outpost had been manned by American, British, and Norwegian commandos, the latter of whom took up positions at the garrison before the Obama administration allowed U.S. Special Forces to stay there, and who had been using it to train the Jaysh Maghawir al-Thawra, the anti-ISIS militia dubbed "the MaT." In theory, they all shared a common enemy in the Islamic State. But the Al-Tanf garrison was key terrain that was located near a major route from Iraq to Damascus, which Iran and the Shiite militias it backed fancied. The Assad regime and its partners wanted the Americans out. In May, they came to set up a small outpost outside the Al-Tanf garrison's fifty-five-kilometer deconfliction zone as they moved east toward Deir al-Zour. Soon they moved inside the zone itself. On May 18, the United States bombed a tank and a bulldozer that ventured within the zone, a strike it was compelled to repeat when a similar encroachment occurred three weeks later.

The episodes seemed more a matter of harassment than a serious challenge. But two days later relations grew tense when Colonel General Vladimir Zarudnitsky, who was filling in for Surovikin, faxed a threatening message to Townsend over the two sides' hotline. Townsend's first call was to Harrigian to alert him that the U.S. forces at Al-Tanf might need help, and fast. He next called Votel and then the Russian commander. Sprouting a shock of white hair, Zarudnitsky had led a reconnaissance company in East Germany as a young officer and had climbed the ladder up the ranks of the Russian army, acquiring a reputation as a loyal but not particularly innovative or subtle officer. Now Zarudnitsky was demanding in the June 7 call that the Al-Tanf garrison be vacated in two hours or face attack. For a few tense minutes, it was unclear if the Russian general was merely engaging in brinkmanship or was actually warning of military action.

"Are you threatening my forces?" asked Townsend, speaking from his command center in Baghdad. "Are we going to talk or are we going to fight? Because if we are going to fight, this call is over."

After a long pause, Zarudnitsky replied that the two sides would talk. The Russian commander observed that the two generals seemed to be like two boxers in the ring. The U.S. F-15s in Jordan were put on alert, but no forces were dispatched, and the tensions eventually eased. It was one thing to blast an Iranian drone or pound some of the Shiite militia fighters backed by Iran. It was something else for the two nuclear powers to come to blows over a remote part of Syria.

Tensions appeared to ease with the Russians after the call, but the Iranian harassment continued. On June 8, an Iranian Shaheed-129 drone ventured into southeastern Syria, dropped a bomb near MaT fighters, and was shot out of the sky by an F-15 with a radar-guided AMRAAM. Then, on June 20, an F-15 Strike Eagle shot down an Iranian drone heading toward Bowling Green, a small combat position the MaT had established near the Al-Tanf garrison. Notwithstanding the distractions at Al-Tanf, Raqqa was the next objective for the U.S.-led coalition, and after that Deir al-Zour. It was clear that Mazloum was not the only one eyeing that terrain.

20

ECLIPSE

Surrounded by flat farmland, Raqqa was a forbidding objective for Mazloum Abdi's fighters. Nestled on the north bank of the Euphrates along a timeworn trade route, Raqqa had begun as the Greek city of Nikephorion, and over the centuries had been claimed by Rome, Persia, the Byzantine Empire, and the Muslim conquerors, to mention a few. With Syria's catastrophic civil war, Raqqa had once more become caught up in a violent tug-of-war. The city had been embroiled in the uprising against Bashar al-Assad and taken in 2013 by the anti-Assad opposition. But the city had totemic significance for Abu Bakr al-Baghdadi as the storied center of the Umayyad Caliphate in the sixth and seventh centuries.

In January 2014, Baghdadi's fighters, their black flags flying, routed other opposition groups to claim Raqqa as the Islamic State's capital after a tit-for-tat campaign of harassment and assassinations. Local residents dubbed ISIS "Al-Tanzeem" (The Organization), as it sought to control every aspect of the city. Accounts of life within the heart of the Islamic State had filtered out from a trickle of defectors who managed to escape. Beheadings and other harsh punishments for transgressions, real or perceived, were common. An all-female morality police, the Khansaa Brigade, confronted women who wore makeup or form-fitting abayas. The hospital was open, but ISIS fighters were given priority. Smoking was banned, and the economy sagged as shops had difficulty buying goods and customers became wary of venturing out on the streets. But however demoralized some residents might have felt about ISIS's rule, there was not going to be a revolution from within. The Islamic State ruled with an iron hand.

With the battle telegraphed long in advance, several thousand ISIS diehards had improvised a defense intended to slow down the SDF and turn the urban landscape into a vast killing zone. On the outskirts of the city, the militants had dammed the tributaries feeding into the Euphrates to create two sizable lakes, the better to channel the SDF into belts of IEDs that would be covered by sniper and machine-gun fire, but the dams also had the unfortunate effect of flooding some of the city's neighborhoods with fetid water. Inside the city, ISIS had draped hundreds of tarps over the city's narrow streets and alleys, shielding thoroughfares from the prying eyes of American reconnaissance.

Like Mosul, Raqqa had an Old City, which in the case of the ISIS capital was defined by an ancient 2,500-meter wall that Daesh had fortified and mined, and that the SDF would need to breach at its peril. Underground, ISIS had dug a labyrinthine network of tunnels, which would enable fighters to pop up where the SDF least expected, including behind Mazloum's lines. Unlike Mosul, Raqqa also featured tall apartment buildings, which provided an excellent line of sight for snipers and would be difficult to take back. If ISIS fighters sought to escape, it looked likely that they would try to use the ferry crossings over the Euphrates, which ran just south of the city. Many ISIS officials, including those responsible for implementing plots abroad and running the caliphate's media operations, had already slipped out of the city and left for Deir al-Zour, Madan, Al-Bukamal, or other places deep in the MERV, according to U.S. intelligence. Baghdadi himself was nowhere to be found. But the city had to be taken back. The U.S. military estimated that there were anywhere from 2,900 to 5,600 ISIS fighters before the battle, and many of those who remained were determined to make a final stand. The code name for the U.S.-backed operation was "Eclipse."

Raqqa presented U.S. commanders with some unique challenges. In Mosul, the Americans had enjoyed uncontested control of the skies, save for a nettlesome low-altitude ISIS drone threat. In eastern Syria, U.S. and coalition planes would be operating within the range of Russian and Syrian air defenses and sharing the skies with Russian and Syrian aircraft, which it hoped would not interfere despite the June 18 shootdown of the Syrian Su-22 at Ja'Din. To beef up its airpower, U.S. F-15Es were secretly based at Muwaffaq Salti Air Base in Jordan, obviating the need for the coalition to fly combat aircraft from bases in the Persian Gulf, some six hours away. The Muwaffaq base was also home to American drones, Patriot batteries, and HIMARS launchers, and later underwent a multimillion-dollar expansion, courtesy of the Army Corps of Engineers. From Muwaffaq, U.S. warplanes could be on station in southern Syria in twenty minutes.

Still, the potential threat from Russian or Syrian fighters meant that some of the U.S. warplanes that carried out air-to-ground strikes had to be guarded by F-22s or F-15s equipped with air-to-air missiles, and their time on station had to be limited when Russian aircraft were in the area. Nor could the United States assume that its drones could loiter indefinitely over Raqqa with impunity. Some allied air forces took greater precautions. While British warplanes and Reaper drones joined the Raqqa fight, the Australian air force largely avoided the area following the Ja'Din episode. With the exception of a lone air strike in the MERV, the Australians restricted their operations to Iraqi airspace throughout the Raqqa battle, according to Australian defense documents.

As with previous operations in Syria, the advisory effort was entirely in the hands of U.S. special operations forces. Even with the armored vehicles, mortars, and machine guns Mazloum's Kurdish fighters had been given, the SDF was little more than light infantry and did not have anywhere near the punch of the Iraqi military, which was equipped with its own artillery and tanks. In addition to the airpower, the United States relied heavily on the Marines' M777 artillery and on HIMARS launchers. So intense was the artillery fire they unleashed that the Marines burned out the barrels of two of their howitzers.

On June 5, 2017, the SDF began its attack, moving on multiple axes, capturing the thousand-year-old Harqalah fortress on the western edge of the city and pushing into the district of Al-Meshleb in the east. As with Tabqa, SDF commanders wanted to leave a back door from which ISIS could flee so as to mitigate their losses and limit the destruction. But the Americans were adamant that the city had to be encircled so ISIS fighters could not escape to fight another day.

Within a few weeks the SDF had succeeded in surrounding the city, only to see its push from the west lose momentum as Mazloum's fighters ran into belts of IEDs. On July 3, in an effort to turn the tables, U.S. F-15Es blasted two holes in the southeast portion of the ancient wall in the Old City so that SDF fighters could mount a surprise attack. Rushing through the rubbled openings, the SDF established a foothold three hundred meters into the city, which featured narrow streets framed by multistory stone residences with walled courtyards. The urban landscape soon became a battleground as ISIS fought back furiously and used its tunnel system to pop up behind the SDF lines.

On August 14, ISIS mounted a general counterattack. Using car bombs, grenade-dropping drones, and mortar fire, the ISIS fighters cut through the SDF's lines. U.S. air strikes helped put an end to that.

After fighting their way through the Old City, the SDF soldiers finally advanced to a warren of high-rise structures in the northern part of the city. ISIS fighters were making a final stand there at a city hospital and at the Al-Naim roundabout, where they had carried out so many executions that Mazloum's fighters had dubbed it "the circle of hell."

The United States estimated that ISIS had sustained enormous casualties, but the SDF had suffered serious losses, too, including

Adnan Abu Amjad, the head of the Manbij Military Council, whom I had met during my visit to northeastern Syria with Joe Votel. The SDF had excelled in maneuvering in the open, conducting pincer movements to cut off ISIS and prompting it to flee. Now they were involved in house-to-house fighting, and some of those houses had been rigged with so many IEDs that they had been transformed in effect into one large explosive. There were more than 260,000 civilians in Raqqa in April 2017, the vast majority of whom had fled as the fighting ground on. The United States dropped leaflets encouraging the residents to flee and outlining instructions to identify themselves to the SDF. By October, however, at least several thousand had fled into the interior of the city, where they were trapped or were being held by Daesh as human shields. ISIS snipers positioned throughout the city shot many of those civilians who sought to escape. The United States decreased its air and artillery strikes that month, but the fighters and civilians were compressed in such a small area that the number of incidents in which civilians were harmed increased, according to a study of the harm to civilians in the battle that was prepared for the Pentagon by the RAND Corporation.

In mid-October, Mazloum approached Colonel Jeff VanAntwerp, the new commander of the Delta Force, and said that it was time to change course. The two commanders had been carrying on a steady dialogue about the plight of the civilians, and it had become clear that their hope that ISIS would loosen its grip on the population as the battle reached its climax had been dashed.

The SDF was going to need to secure the city it had liberated, which meant that it would need the help of Arab fighters it had recruited who had relatives in the city, including family members who might have been forcibly married to ISIS fighters. To drive the point home, Mazloum said that he had just met with two dozen Arab sheikhs in Ayn Issa, a town around thirty miles north of Raqqa. VanAntwerp, Mazloum said, should hear their pleas himself. Mattis had declared that the United States was determined to annihilate ISIS on the battlefield and was not content to simply push the militants from one town to another. In line with the U.S. strategy, the SDF had encircled Raqqa at the start of the battle and blocked any escape south over the Euphrates. But the larger goal was to liberate the caliphate's unhappy subjects and somehow help the region recover.

What VanAntwerp heard was impossible to ignore. Through tears, the sheikhs told him that if the Americans continued with the Raqqa operation, there would be massive civilian casualties and they would have blood on their hands. The ISIS fighters were not about to surrender, and would die in place and take the city's surviving men, women, and children with them. What kind of army, they asked, encircled an entire city and left the enemy with no way to get out? The United States was forcing ISIS to fight on. The only answer was for the Americans to allow the ISIS fighters to leave Raqqa for their sanctuaries in the Euphrates River valley. The sheikhs would take responsibility for any deal they struck and ensure that the militants held up their end.

The entreaty recalled the contrasting ideas approach the SDF and the United States had taken in Tabqa and raised an urgent issue for the United States' "by, with, and through" strategy. The more the SDF pushed into the MERV, the more it would need the help of the Arab tribes. VanAntwerp was also convinced that the assault could not continue grinding on block by block without an exponential increase in civilian casualties and trouble between Raqqa's residents and its SDF liberators. VanAntwerp went to Major General James Jarrard, the the overall commander of coalition special operations troops in Iraq and Syria, and explained the situation. Two days later, Jarrard met with the group of tribal leaders, who were just as passionate as before.

The Americans agreed to halt the fight, and on October 15 a deal was reached. The ISIS fighters who left would need to have their fingerprints and other biometric data taken by the SDF on their way out. They would not be allowed to leave with any heavy weapons. Eighteen-wheel tractor trailers, buses, and dozens of other battered vehicles drove into the battered city to pick up the ISIS fighters. The scheme, however, became all but impossible to enforce. U.S. officers had estimated that 300 fighters and perhaps 1,500 of their family members were holed up in Raqqa. As the exodus began, however, some 2,000 fighters and more than twice as many family members jammed into the trucks and buses. Many of them were wearing suicide belts or carrying weapons, and many refused to be fingerprinted. Under the terms of the safe passage agreement, the trucks did not fly the black ISIS flag. The United States monitored the convoy from the air but, unlike in Tabqa, did not try to interfere. The vehicles snaked their way across the desert, stopping along the way at roadside shops where ISIS fighters and their relatives cleaned out the provisions. They harassed the shop owners for selling cigarettes, proscribed under Sharia law, but they paid for the food they took. The U.S. military said little publicly about the convoy at the time but acknowledged it in its internal accounts. "The SDF offered a surrender agreement to the remaining ISIS fighters 15 OCT and allowed them to withdraw with their families," noted a still-unpublished report by the U.S. Army's Asymmetric Warfare Group on the lessons from Raqqa. It was another by-product of the "by, with, and through" strategy. If the Americans were going to rely on the locals to serve as proxy fighters, those people would get the say on when the battle was going to end. As for Mattis, he later observed that meeting the locals' concerns was within the purview of U.S. commanders.

At least 1,400 ISIS fighters were estimated to have been killed or wounded in Raqqa. The SDF reported that 655 of its fighters had died in the battle to capture the city. In the end, the U.S. military documented 178 civilians killed and 62 wounded as a result of actions by the U.S.-led coalition. Estimates that came from outside the government were far higher. According to a detailed study by Airwars, a London-based organization that assesses civilian casualties, and Amnesty International, the number of civilians who were likely killed by the American-led coalition were at least 744, with 30 wounded. The actual number, the group asserted, might be as high as 1,600. "The victory proved costly," the Army's lessons-learned report continued. "Much of Raqqa was destroyed as a result of the fighting." Among the destroyed buildings were eight hospitals, twenty-nine mosques, and more than forty schools. Raqqa, the RAND Corporation later observed, had a population that was one-fifth the size of Mosul before the battles in those cities, but there were nearly two thousand more structures damaged in Raqqa than in Mosul.

William Roebuck, the State Department's representative to the SDF, was shocked by the scale of the damage when he rode through Raqqa a few months after its liberation. For blocks on end, it was impossible to find a building that had not been damaged in the fighting. Some thirty to forty thousand homes—65 percent of the total—had been leveled or were battered to the point that they could not be fixed. "I had never seen anything like it," Roebuck later wrote in *The Foreign Service Journal*. "It reminded me of World War II photographs of the destruction of Dresden." There were still signs of ISIS's occupation, too, including rows of prepared graves, that ISIS had used to intimidate the population and defiant graffiti: "We Remain." For years afterward, Raqqa would stand as a symbol of the punishing force that could be brought to bear through the "by, with, and through" strategy and also of the need to be mindful of its consequences for civilians.

AS ISIS FIGHTERS were fleeing deep into the Euphrates River valley, H. R. McMaster was moving to flesh out his plan for the aftermath. McMaster's years in Iraq had taught him that it was not enough to take a stick to the enemy: the United States needed to prevent the insurgency from regenerating itself the way that al-Qaeda in Iraq had morphed into the Islamic State. Jim Mattis's vow to annihilate ISIS did not mean much to McMaster. All the firepower in the world could not obliterate the threat unless the United States had a way to stop ISIS from recruiting more supporters. The key, McMaster thought, was not Mattis's annihilation tactic, but a policy to stabilize the region afterward and get at the root causes that had allowed ISIS to gain traction in the first place. McMaster envisioned a Syria policy that would give the United States a way to cement the defeat of ISIS, build leverage for the quest for a diplomatic solution to the Syrian civil war, and blunt Tehran's efforts to establish a land corridor to ship arms via Iraq to Lebanese Hezbollah and other militias in Syria. The scheme involved taking Mazloum's SDF—the "by, with, and through" force the Americans had nurtured to demolish the caliphate—and turning it into a postwar ally.

To sustain an American-backed proto-state in the wake of the caliphate and build up clout in future negotiations with Bashar al-Assad and his foreign backers, McMaster figured, the SDF should secure the one resource northeastern Syria offered: oil. During the summer of 2017, McMaster discussed with Trump that the United States should encourage the SDF to keep the oil fields in Deir al-Zour out of its adversaries' hands. Trump thought that was a fine idea, so McMaster sent a memo to the Pentagon asking for proposals on how to carry out the White House idea. The Defense Department, however, thought the idea smacked of mission creep, a diversion from the main objective of destroying ISIS— and slow-rolled it. One Joint Staff officer went so far as to describe the effort to secure the oil as unseemly.

One principal who supported McMaster's hope of fashioning a modicum of order out of chaos in Syria was Rex Tillerson, Trump's first secretary of state. The former CEO of ExxonMobil was obsessed with bringing his sense of corporate efficiency to Foggy Bottom and dispensing with anything that hinted at duplication. Whiteboards had been set up in Tillerson's wood-paneled seventh-floor suite so that the secretary and his inner circle could brainstorm about their new wiring diagrams for running foreign policy, which mainly succeeded in depleting the agency's ranks and lowering morale. Tillerson, however, had some respect for the

SDF. Brett McGurk had arranged a secret meeting on December 6, 2017, between Tillerson and Mazloum at the U.S. Air Force base in Ramstein, Germany. The stated purpose of Tillerson's stop at Ramstein was to confer with senior military officers at the U.S. Africa Command, which was headquartered at the base, in advance of a long-planned trip to the continent.

The face-to-face meeting between the chief U.S. diplomat and Mazloum took place at an out-of-the-way weapons bunker on the base. Tillerson was concerned that the fact that the U.S. chief diplomat had secretly met with the Kurdish paramilitary leader would leak. In a demonstration of Mazloum's trustworthiness, however, it never did. Tillerson asked his Pentagon partner for some time to give the strategy a chance to work. To enable the diplomatic effort, Mattis was prepared to cut his ally at the State Department some slack.

On December 7, Trump was briefed on his administration's new approach. Having helped the SDF retake Raqqa, U.S. special operations troops would stay in Syria for now, but there would be periodic reviews of whether the deployment should be continued and how well the strategy was faring. In the meantime, the State Department would try to negotiate a de-escalation zone with the Russians in a stretch of southern Syria, which would move Iranian operatives and proxies away from the Israeli border. Befitting a major policy pronouncement, the strategy would be unveiled the next month in a major speech titled "The Way Forward in Syria," which Tillerson would deliver in the friendly confines of Stanford University, where he would be hosted by former secretary of state Condoleezza Rice, who had recommended Tillerson for his position at Foggy Bottom in the first place. Tillerson's life in a corporate bubble hardly equipped him for the messaging the secretary of state was traditionally required to engage in on foreign policy. As he had done so many times before, Tillerson dispensed with the blue-and-white Boeing 757 that John Kerry had taken around the world, opting instead for an executive jet with little, if any, room for the media, who would doggedly book commercial flights to catch up with the itinerant secretary.

Laying out the new policy, Tillerson said that the U.S. military presence in Syria would be "conditions-based"—military-speak for the notion that U.S. forces would stay as long as needed to ensure that ISIS could not make a comeback. "We understand that some Americans are skeptical of continued involvement in Syria and question the benefits of maintaining a presence in such a troubled country," Tillerson added. "However, it is vital for the United States to remain engaged in Syria for several reasons: Ungoverned spaces, especially in conflict zones, are breeding grounds for ISIS and other terrorist organizations." If finishing off ISIS was not reason enough to stay in Syria, Tillerson stressed that taking on al-Qaeda elements who had sought sanctuary in Idlib and safeguarding Israel were also reasons to stay.

Finally, Tillerson argued that the United States could use its leverage to usher in a new Syrian government that would no longer be a "client state of Iran." In the meantime, the Americans would work with the Russians to de-escalate the fighting in the country. It was an ambitious strategy for a commander in chief with a deep aversion to prolonging Middle East wars, but it also sounded themes designed to appeal to war-weary Americans: fighting terrorism, including the very organization that had carried out the 9/11 attacks in New York and Washington; pushing back on Iran; and safeguarding Israel. Though Tillerson did not mention it, U.S. losses had also been minimal and there had been no major protests at home urging the Americans to leave.

Though the building blocks of a postwar strategy had been put in place, there was still a big piece missing as far as Trump was concerned: the cost. Iraqi prime minister Abadi had responded with disbelief when the president had broached the subject of taking Iraq's oil. The most the United States might muster for its efforts in Iraq would be some new multibillion-dollar contracts to revamp the country's energy infrastructure. Syria, a collapsed state that was in the midst of a disastrous civil war, did not offer the hope of even that.

The cost of the fight against ISIS was nothing like the trillion-dollar expense the United States had borne in Afghanistan, but it was not negligible. By July 2017, it had run to $14.3 billion for operations in Iraq and Syria—or some $13.6 million a day. Then there would be the price of the modest "stabilization" effort—removing IEDs from population centers, getting electricity up and running, and providing enough basic services so that people would come back. Fundamentally, the United States was pursuing its own interests by moving to finish off ISIS and blocking Iran from filling the vacuum, but Trump chafed at the notion that the nation's Arab allies were not sharing the burden, all the more so since his first foreign trip had been to Saudi Arabia. If the United States' partners were benefiting from the operation, he thought, they should open their wallets and pay for it. Working with the State Department's Bureau of Near Eastern Affairs, McMaster came up with a specific cost estimate for the U.S. military operations in Syria and the stabilization effort that was to follow: $4 billion. Just as he had done with Abadi after the retaking of Mosul, Trump rattled the tin cup in a December 20 phone call with King Salman, the Saudi monarch who served as the titular head of the kingdom but was long past his prime. The call was initiated by the Saudis to stress the importance of the United States remaining in Syria. Trump left the conversation convinced he had secured a commitment from Salman for the $4 billion. For the transactional president, however, the deal was done, and it was time to collect.

Serving as Trump's bill collector was no easy task. Trump wanted the secretary of state to go right away to nail down the contribution, but Tillerson's greater priority was to try to resolve Saudi Arabia and the United Arab Emirates' dispute against Qatar; accusing the Qataris of supporting fundamentalist Islamist groups, they had placed the country under an economic blockade. A political war among Gulf nations that hosted U.S. forces was not in Washington's interest, and the secretary of state wanted to make progress on that question before hitting up the allies for money for Syria. McMaster, however, knew that patience was not one of Trump's strengths. In meetings with McMaster in Washington, Tahnoun bin Zayed, the national security advisor for the United Arab Emirates, and his Saudi counterpart, Dr. Musaad al-Aiban, appeared open to shouldering some of the Syria burden, and McMaster also made an appeal to Gulf state ambassadors.

While McMaster and Tillerson found themselves on the same side on Syria policy, the national security advisor's efforts still did not sit well with the secretary of state, who was used to running things from the top of a steep corporate pyramid. Tillerson complained to the White House chief of staff, John Kelly, the former Marine general, that McMaster was straying out of his lane, and Kelly upbraided the national security advisor. Trump had been criticized for appointing too many active-duty and retired generals. But Kelly, McMaster, and Mattis were hardly a unified bloc. It would be left to Tillerson and Wilbur Ross, the billionaire investor turned commerce secretary, to take on the uphill struggle to collect the tab, which Trump still expected to be delivered fast.

21

JAZEERA STORM

Mazloum Abdi had taken to calling the campaign he planned in the Euphrates River valley "Operation Jazeera Storm." The name evoked the fast-paced mobile warfare his commanders welcomed after the grinding combat in the streets of Raqqa. Even before the victory in Raqqa had been sealed, Mazloum and his commanders gathered in Al-Hasakah, in northern Syria, in September 2017 to plan what was to be a lightning offensive to the south. The objectives included the Al-Omar and Al-Tanak oil fields as well as the Tabiyah gas field. From there, the SDF hoped to continue its push to Al-Mayadin and then the villages near Al-Bukamal: the southernmost points in Deir al-Zour province.

Mazloum and his special operations allies had planned to wait until the battle for Raqqa was over before beginning the push south. But there were abundant signs that the Assad regime and especially its Russian allies wanted to get to the Deir al-Zour region and oil resources first. That same month, regime forces had moved through the mountainous terrain north of al-Suknah in order to move west more quickly. Mazloum calculated that control of the region would boost his leverage in future discussions with the regime over how much autonomy the Syrian Kurds might negotiate. The U.S. military, for its part, was convinced that Assad and the Russians would not deliver the coup de grâce to ISIS but would merely push them to other areas in Syria and take the oil and gas reserves. The race was on. U.S. special operations had established an outpost in 2018 at the Tabiyah Gas Plant, which it dubbed "Conoco." As the SDF rushed south, U.S. special operators also set up a headquarters near the Al-Omar oil field about twenty-five miles to the southwest, which was located among stretches of scrubland and incongruously dubbed "Green Village." The makeshift base included offices and dormitory-style accommodations under the Assad regime but had been looted and left in a state of utter disrepair during Syria's civil war. ISIS had briefly occupied the installation until Delta Force cornered Abu Sayyaf, the militants' oil minister, and killed him there in a 2015 raid.

Green Village would now serve as a hub for logistics and as a refueling point for the U.S. Army's helicopters. Notably, it would also include a military surgical team to attend to the coalition and SDF wounded. In Iraq, the United States had sought to medevac its casualties to a combat hospital within sixty minutes, the "golden hour" that maximized the chances of survival. The distances and terrain in Syria posed a challenge for that standard, so combat surgeons were pushed to Green Village, as they had been to command posts outside Raqqa, to care for the wounded until they could be moved to field hospitals in the rear. The plan was for a series of small U.S. advisory teams to establish austere outposts south of Green Village as the SDF juggernaut moved south—what the military called "mission support sites." But Green Village would anchor the offensive.

Almost from the start, the tensions with the Russians began to heat up. Mazloum's force had beaten the Russians to the MERV and were sitting on the north side of the city of Deir al-Zour when Russian aircraft began to fly sorties east of the Euphrates to drop bombs that the Russian military claimed had been aimed at ISIS but which landed near SDF positions. The air operations were a violation of the understanding between the two sides that the Euphrates River would serve as a dividing line between Russian and U.S. air operations, except in exceptional circumstances. U.S.

and Russian military officers met in Amman that month to discuss ways to avoid an inadvertent clash. But as the two sides met, Assad regime forces crossed the river on floating bridges and occupied a small piece of ground east of Deir al-Zour. The Russians claimed that they had no control over the forces and the United States took no action to stop the move. The Americans called the regime's foothold the Deir al-Zour "Slice." Anxious to avoid a confrontation, both sides accepted the arrangement, though its occupiers pressed the envelope by adding new checkpoints and occasionally taking potshots at the SDF.

Soon it became clear that the MERV was about to become more crowded. A substantial force that was not in uniform began to assemble artillery, armored vehicles, and pontoon barges on the west side of the Euphrates. The mysterious mobilization occurred close enough to U.S. and SDF positions near the Tabiyah oil field to cause concern. The U.S. did not want to be drawn into an unnecessary melee that would sidetrack Operation Jazeera Storm. If it was a provocation intended to draw the U.S.-backed offensive west instead of south, it was best ignored. Whoever it was, though, the Americans could not afford to let the force cross the river and plow its way east. Such a result could outflank the Americans and the SDF, and interfere with the final stages of the MERV campaign. "We saw a buildup on the other side of the river, and the indications and warning that they were planning for something," one official recalled. The United States reinforced the small advisory team at the mission support site near the Tabiyah field, instructed it to dig in, and pressed the SDF to beef up its force in the region. U.S. airpower, artillery batteries, HIMARS launcher units, and more special operations commandos—who could be whisked to the battlefield in less than an hour in V-22 Ospreys—were alerted that they should be ready to respond. Another response force was a thirty-minute drive from Al-Shaddadi.

In early February 2018, more than two dozen unflagged vehicles were ferried across the river to beef up that small enclave, including tanks and tracked vehicles with mounted machine guns. On February 7, several of the artillery from across the river began to fire, bracketing the U.S. positions. There was nothing stealthy about the operation. It was a muscular show of force that appeared to be designed to send a signal that it was time for the SDF and anyone with them to pull back from the area.

U.S. commanders in Baghdad and at Al-Udeid got on the deconfliction line with the Russian command in Syria. The Russian brass insisted they did not know the identity of the force heading across the river and were certainly not taking ownership of the operation. If a clash erupted, the Americans could be involved in a confrontation with international implications, and nobody was sure yet what those might be.

The U.S. military followed its "escalation of force" procedures, which were intended to deter an attack and, if that failed, to respond proportionately: "Shout, show and then shoot to kill." U.S. air strikes struck the enemy guns, which was justified as a straightforward matter of self-defense. Then the Americans fired a warning shot in front of the lead vehicle in the mysterious formation. It was a signal for the adversary to turn around and cut its losses, but one that was ignored. The assault force kept coming and began to lob tank rounds. U.S. forces declared "troops in contact," and the gloves were off. For the next several hours the attackers were pummeled by F-15Es from the Jordan base, Reaper drones, B-52s carrying satellite-guided bombs, AC-130 gunships, and Apache helicopters firing Hellfire missiles and conducting strafing runs while the Marines fired rocket artillery.

Intelligence had picked up that the aggressors were speaking Russian, confirming the U.S. commanders' suspicions. As the battle wound down Russian commanders—without identifying who the attackers were or acknowledging that they were firing on the Americans—called and asked for a pause so that they could pick up the wounded and dead. What was left of the assault force was allowed to retreat back across the Euphrates.

The enemy was later determined to be fighters from the Wagner Group, a mercenary organization that was Russia's answer to the Blackwater-style contractors the United States used in Iraq, with the important difference that Moscow used it to carry out offensive operations from Ukraine to Africa at the behest of the Russian authorities and not merely for training militaries or for lesser security operations.

The goal of the operation in Syria, which was the Wagner Group's first and only assault against a U.S. position, had been to lay claim to the Conoco facility and presumably the neighboring Al-Omar oil field. H. R. McMaster, it seemed, was not the only one who thought control of Syria's resources would be useful in shaping the country's future, though the Wagner Group also believed there was profit to be had. Beyond that, the attack appeared to be designed to throw a monkey wrench in the U.S. efforts to work with the SDF in the Euphrates River valley. It was clear that the Russians and the Assad regime wanted the oil-rich region for themselves. The Syrian militias the Russians used to retrieve the Wagner Group bodies on the east side of the Euphrates did not give up the Slice, and actually moved their outpost another kilometer to the east. Even in defeat, Russia and its allies gained a little ground.

The extent of the Russian losses was not openly acknowledged by U.S. officials until the spring, when the Trump administration confirmed that a couple of hundred Russians had been killed, which reflected the U.S. military's battle damage assessment. Not a single U.S. or coalition troop had been harmed. The Kremlin, for its part, insisted that it had nothing to do with the attack. When McMaster met with his Russian counterpart, Nikolai Patrushev, several weeks later, neither man mentioned the clash. Russia's version of "by, with, and through" included forces that were disposable and whose role in furthering Moscow's foreign policy and economic objectives could be denied. The bloodiest direct clash between American and Russian combatants in decades was off the table for diplomatic discussion. In an odd way, the episode lent support to the strategy McMaster and Tillerson had put forth. If Moscow wanted the oil fields that badly, that was probably a good reason to hold on to them or at least trade them for something lasting.

AT THE WHITE HOUSE, Trump's patience with the strategy was wearing thin. The president had touted the seizure of Raqqa as a "critical breakthrough" in the campaign and long delegated the details on how to wrap it up to the Pentagon.

In March 2018, a Delta Force commando and a British SAS trooper were killed near Manbij. Initially, it was thought they had hit an IED, but it later emerged that the munitions in their vehicle had accidentally detonated. That blew the lid off the supposedly covert British deployment in Syria and raised the number of Americans who had lost their lives in the country to four. McMaster sensed that Trump was becoming uneasy with the United States' Syria policy, not least because the billions he had expected the Saudis and other Arab states to contribute had not been collected by the State Department and the casualties were trickling in. McMaster thought this might be a good time to review that strategy with the president, including what had yet to be accomplished, but the White House chief of staff, John Kelly, was reluctant to schedule another top-level Syria meeting. With Trump, the outcome was unpredictable, and if Syria was brought to his attention it might prompt the president to reopen the internal debate on whether to keep troops in the country at all. As it happened, Trump used a rally in Ohio to challenge his own strategy. "We're knocking the hell out of ISIS," he said. "We'll be coming out of Syria like very soon. Let other people take care of it now."

On March 29, Trump ordered the State Department to freeze $200 million in funds for stabilizing Syria after reading a newspaper article about the unglamorous but essential efforts to demine battered cities and restore electricity to its long-suffering citizens. The U.S. program to achieve a sustainable outcome had survived the Russian attack, but less than three months after it had been unveiled, Trump had turned against it. The military pleaded for more time to finish off the caliphate, and Brett McGurk mounted an intensive effort to raise funds for stabilization from Saudi leadership, which belatedly made good on an earlier pledge to provide $100 million. The United Arab Emirates donated $50 million. No deadline for vacating the country was set; Trump was still prepared to strike Assad for his chemical weapons attack. But when it came to lingering after the defeat of ISIS, the writing was on the wall. "The president is done with Syria," Joe Dunford told McGurk after one White House session.

That same month, Tillerson learned after returning from his first and only trip to Africa that he had been fired. The news had been broken via a tweet from the president. The former oil company executive had never clicked with Trump, and had never been forgiven for using an obscene epithet to criticize the president behind closed doors after Trump engaged in a tirade against the military leaders and their prosecution of endless wars—comments that Tillerson refused to discuss publicly but never denied. A week later, McMaster was dispatched as well. The three-star general had been respectful of the office of the presidency—so much so that he eschewed the temptation to write a tell-all book after his firing, and instead delivered a tome on foreign policy. But his public criticism of Russia's intervention in the 2016 election, his hawkishness on North Korea, and his support for the U.S. mission in Afghanistan were decidedly non-Trumpian. The Trump administration was no team of rivals: the president looked for validation, not independent judgment, in his aides and kept shuffling the deck until he had the loyalty—obsequiousness in the eyes of critics—that he prized. Personalities, however, often determined the policy. Not only was the Syria strategy in question, but its principal architects were gone.

With his interventionist credentials and a trademark walrus mustache that Trump reputedly found unbecoming, John Bolton was an unusual choice to replace McMaster. But he was a presence on Fox News and had been the runner-up to McMaster in 2017. As the new national security advisor, Bolton installed a gold-framed painting that depicted President George H. W. Bush at his Oval Office desk, surrounded by the vice president, the national security advisor, and the secretaries of state and defense, who had settled on the policy to liberate Kuwait in 1991. The message, which he often shared with visitors, was that the way to get things done was through high-level, small-group decision-making—not the NSC-driven policy reviews and frequent interagency meetings that McMaster favored. Not all the principals were enamored of this style. After weeks went by without a meeting on the major foreign policy crises roiling the administration, Jim Mattis compiled a list of the issues that needed to be discussed and shared it with Mike Pompeo, who had been named to replace Tillerson after a stint as director of the CIA. He made a few edits before Mattis submitted it to Bolton.

Bolton did not hesitate to leave his imprint on the administration's Syria policy. His concern was the role that Syria played in the U.S. face-off with the Iranian regime. Bolton said that he did not care about Assad and his fight with Syrian rebels. "I care about Iran," he told McGurk, Pompeo, and David Satterfield, the top official in the State Department's Bureau of Near Eastern Affairs, in one meeting. It was more than bombast. In line with the State Department plan for stabilizing Syria, McGurk and Satterfield had been negotiating with the Russians to establish a series of de-escalation zones in southern Syria. Iranian operatives and proxies would pull to a point eighty kilometers from the Israeli border while the opposition would remain, the theory being that this would bolster Israeli security and enable Jordan to open its border with Syria to trade. The discussions between the U.S. and Russian officials had been memorialized in what diplomats called an aide-memoire, which recorded the substance of the exchanges. Russia's foreign minister, Sergei Lavrov, presented the document to Bolton when he visited Moscow in October 2018, but the national security advisor rebuffed him. What McGurk and Satterfield had discussed was not the approved White House policy. The U.S. goal was not to get the Iranians off Israel's border but to get them to leave Syria altogether.

This was a bold declaration, but unsurprising coming from a national security advisor who had framed a copy of Trump's memorandum declaring his decision to withdraw from the 2015 nuclear accord with Iran that the Obama administration had negotiated. It did, however, raise the question of how the United States was to oust Iran from the country now that it had stepped back from its long-shot goal of ushering in a new Syrian government.

The U.S. intelligence community, for one, did not think the Russians had the influence or even the desire to pressure their Iranian partners to leave Syria. There was an unstated division of labor in which Moscow supplied the airpower to keep Assad in power, along with some Russian special forces and advisors, and Tehran provided the troops to augment the Assad regime's forces on the ground under the direction of Iranian Quds Force operatives. The Russian intervention had been successful at propping up Assad at modest cost to Moscow in terms of lives and treasure, but U.S. intelligence assessed that supporting Assad was not a burden Russia wanted to assume all by itself. "There are a lot of hot spots there," Dan Coats, Trump's director of national intelligence, observed. "Russia would need to make significantly greater commitments from a military standpoint, from an economic standpoint. We don't assess that they are keen to do that."

One way the Trump administration was able to chip away at the Iranians was to support Israel's approach to the problem. Syria had once been Israel's quietest frontier—so much so that in the early Obama years Fred Hof, a State Department envoy who later resigned in 2012 over the administration's reluctance to devise a regime-change strategy for Syria, sought to broker a settlement that would have returned the Golan Heights to Syria in exchange for peace and its reorientation away from Tehran until civil war turned Syria inside out.

With Qassem Soleimani backing Bashar al-Assad and Lebanese Hezbollah also in Syria, the Israelis had taken matters into their own hands. Starting in 2013, they began carrying out air strikes to prevent advanced Iranian weapons from making their way to

Hezbollah. By lobbing missiles from outside Syria's airspace at weapons warehouses near Damascus, Israel could avoid any claim of responsibility. The Israeli strikes were a double-edged sword for the Americans: they kept Iran at bay, but there was a risk that the Syrians, Iranians, and Russians might think that some of the attacks were being carried out by Washington, signaling a U.S. escalation. That could confound U.S. efforts to deconflict operations in the skies over Syria.

The problem was all the more pressing when the Israelis began to overfly the Al-Tanf garrison on their way to their targets in Syria, taking a route the Israeli air force favored to circumvent Syrian air defenses. To mitigate the risk, a secret procedure was established under which the Israeli military would inform the Americans of air strikes in advance. The Israeli strike plans were submitted through the U.S. military chain and reviewed at CENTCOM, usually days in advance of the strike; the strike plans outlined the purpose of the mission, the number of warplanes that would carry out the attack, and when it would occur. They also spelled out the routes the Israeli planes would take and the coordinates of the target that would be struck. CENTCOM would examine the request, which would also be shared with the U.S. defense secretary, who would have the final say. "It was a well-developed and deliberate process," one former official said of the secret arrangement. On rare occasions, the Americans vetoed a strike, but most were approved. Publicly, the Pentagon insisted it had nothing to do with the attacks. Privately, the United States was a silent partner.

Trying to shield itself from Israeli strikes, Iran and its Shiite militia proxies began making greater use of Iraqi territory, calculating that the Israelis would be reluctant to strike inside Iraq for fear of creating problems for the Americans, who still wanted to keep troops there. While some of the initial Israeli strikes took place along Iraq's border with Syria, by the next year, the Israelis were occasionally going after targets well inside the country, including a base north of Baghdad. So sensitive were the attacks that the Israelis relied on covert channels to keep the Americans in the loop. When the Pentagon asked why it had not been informed of one Israeli strike in Iraq, it was told that Mossad had carried out the strike using an armed drone and had provided advance notice only to the CIA.

The strikes drew objections in Baghdad, and the Americans were at pains to indicate that they had not been involved. In an August 26, 2019, statement, the Pentagon spokesman insisted that the United States supported Iraqi sovereignty and spoke out against "any potential actions by external actors inciting violence in Iraq." The carefully worded statement avoided pointing the finger of blame at Israel and instead repeated U.S. talking points about the role of Iranian-backed militias in Iraq. Israel never publicized its strikes in Iraq, and the United States never formally acknowledged them.

One massive headache for Bolton was Trump's repeated insistence that his aides make good on Tillerson's failure to collect the $4 billion he believed he had been promised by the Saudi monarch. To defray the cost of staying in Syria, the president instructed Bolton to see if Egypt and other Arab nations would contribute some of their own forces to holding the line in the northeast of the country; doing so would fill a vacuum that Iran and the regime could exploit if American troops were to leave. Bolton dutifully made the call to Abbas Kamel, Egypt's acting intelligence chief, but got nowhere. Egypt had its hands full trying to cope with terrorists in the Sinai and, if anything, had tilted toward Assad. Many of the Gulf states talked a big game about Syria, but in fact did very little. Saudi Arabia and the United Arab Emirates were focused on fighting Iranian-supported Houthis in Yemen, and any Arab forces that joined the battle against ISIS would expect American help. There was nobody to hand off the baton to in northeastern Syria beyond the SDF, whose utility depended heavily on its cooperation with U.S. troops and their airpower.

Frustrated with his assignment, Bolton told Pompeo that Trump had given him a task that was really the province of the

State Department. Predictably, Pompeo rushed to protect his turf by taking on the mission. Bolton felt like Tom Sawyer: he had found a cabinet member to whitewash his fence.

IT WAS TURKEY that threw Operation Jazeera Storm off course by taking action hundreds of miles away. In a major political meeting in January 2018, Turkish president Recep Tayyip Erdoğan lashed out at Trump's decision to arm the Kurdish wing of the SDF. Even as the United States claimed that Turkey was an ally, it also sent truckloads of weapons to Mazloum Abdi's YPG, he complained. "You do not listen to us; you listen to their leaders," added Erdoğan, who had already demonstrated a penchant for mounting air and ground operations against Syrian Kurds without consulting Washington. Turkey had previously sent special forces and Syrian militias into northern Syria in August 2016 in Euphrates Shield to create a wedge between the two heavily Kurdish areas in the region and ensure they could not link up. Now Erdoğan ordered Turkish forces to move on Afrin, the heavily Kurdish city in western Syria. The goal, he said, was to strangle any Kurdish aspirations at their birth.

The United States did not have any advisors in western Syria. But the Turkish attack, which carried the Orwellian name "Olive Branch," was facilitated by the sudden withdrawal of Russian troops in the area. The operation, which relied heavily on Turkish airpower and Turkish-backed Syrian and Turkmen militias, killed hundreds of Kurds and displaced thousands more. Fearful that Erdoğan's next targets would be Manbij, Kobani, and other population centers in the SDF's enclave, many of Mazloum's best commanders and some 1,500 of his fighters left the battlefield to head north to protect their families in case the Turks pressed their offensive to the east.

It was a difficult time for the SDF: the sister of Mazloum's chief of staff was killed by a Turkish air strike, and U.S. officers attended the funeral. In terms of Kurdish politics, the Turkish offensive also put Mazloum in an awkward position: How could he justify an offensive to reclaim largely Arab areas in the MERV at a time when his fellow Kurds in the north were in danger? The situation was a demonstration of how international politics could present more formidable challenges than ISIS itself could; now the particular challenge the Americans faced was getting the SDF to focus on completing the mission against the caliphate.

After a two-month pause, the Americans succeeded in jump-starting the ISIS campaign in May, and the next month Mazloum's fighters moved near the town of Dashisha. To try to regain the momentum, the Iraqis and U.S. Marines set up a temporary artillery position in far western Iraq and fired across the border toward Al-Bukamal. ISIS, however, had used the lull to step up its attacks and dig in. The SDF's progress was fitful, and soon the U.S. and Turkish differences surfaced again.

At an event hosted by *The Washington Post* on December 6, 2018, the Joint Chiefs of Staff chairman, Joe Dunford, said that the United States hoped to train up to forty thousand locals as a constabulary force to keep order in Syria after ISIS was defeated, and that 20 percent of them had been trained already. Most of the recruited fighters would be Arabs, though there was little doubt that the Kurdish-led SDF would do the vetting. What the United States saw as a "stabilization" program to prevent the return of ISIS, the Turks saw as the beginning of a permanent Kurdish enclave with a U.S.-trained army. This was not a "well-intended approach," the spokesman for Erdoğan's party said darkly, but a move that would strengthen "terror elements in Syria."

To keep Erdoğan at bay and dissuade him from expanding Olive Branch, a presidential call had been arranged for December 14. The talking points that Bolton's team prepared stipulated that Trump urge Erdoğan not to intervene. The Turkish president, however, was adept at playing to Trump's concerns, which was why McMaster had rammed through the decision to arm the SDF before Erdoğan came to town. As the call got underway, it soon went off script. Erdoğan asked why the United States was still in Syria if ISIS's caliphate had been reduced to a sliver, as Trump had repeatedly claimed, and offered his word that his forces would finish off the militants—catnip for the "America First" president. To the surprise of Bolton, who was listening in, Trump agreed. "We have won against ISIS," Trump said in a video that he later posted on Twitter. "Our boys, our young women, our men— they're all coming back, and they're coming back now." At a critical moment in the long campaign, the coup de grâce against ISIS was to be subcontracted to a neighboring army that was deeply hostile to America's most reliable ally in the area—and that had no experience operating deep in the Euphrates River valley and little intelligence about the situation on the ground.

At the Pentagon, Mattis had for months been experiencing a growing feeling that his relationship with Trump had changed. The defense secretary had avoided television appearances to stay off the president's radar when it came to sensitive subjects on which the two men might disagree. Once, Mattis had been "Mad Dog," the nickname he hated but that Trump used to rev up his base. Now he was beginning to discover that he was being left out of the loop on decisions of enormous consequence for the armed forces.

Mattis favored making David Goldfein, the cerebral Air Force chief of staff and a former F-16 pilot, the next chairman of the Joint Chiefs of Staff. Before settling on Goldfein, Mattis had asked Jack Keane, the former vice chief of staff of the Army, to take a look at the available candidates. Keane had also settled on Goldfein, and Mattis asked him to relay that recommendation to Trump. At six feet three inches tall, the New York–born Keane had his own relationship with the president and had even been Trump's initial choice for secretary of defense—an idea Keane had dismissed due to the recent passing of his wife. When Keane called Trump in December 2018 and broached the subject of the chairman position, Trump blurted out that the choice was already made: Mark Milley, the Army chief of staff.

Milley had not hidden the fact that he was available for the post. During a breakfast with John Bolton at his Fort Myer residence he made it clear that he did not want the NATO commander position that Mattis had in mind for him and was open to bigger things. Defense secretaries did not always get their pick, but it was unheard of for one to be chosen without a serious consultation with the leadership of the Pentagon. Yet the decision had been made nine months before the post was to be filled. When Keane informed Mattis that Trump had made up his mind without so much as a heads-up to the secretary of defense, Mattis was stunned.

Trump's Syria decision rubbed more salt in Mattis's wounds. Mattis had just returned from a NATO meeting in Canada where he had praised the allies for their contributions and assured them that the United States was not about to abandon the counter-ISIS fight. But Trump saw the allies as partners who were not pulling their weight, and his own statements made it clear in foreign capitals that his Pentagon chief no longer spoke for the administration. Worse, Mattis was convinced that Erdoğan could not make good on his promise to finish off ISIS in the MERV. The SDF was signaling that if the Turks attacked, they would rush to the sound of guns and might even abandon the prisons they had been guarding, which would loose thousands of ISIS fighters onto the battlefield. Overnight, the hard-won gains against ISIS could turn into a strategic defeat.

On December 21, I spied Mattis and a towering military aide leaving the State Department as I was entering the building. I did not know it at the time, but the secretary of defense had come to inform Mike Pompeo that he intended to make a last push to get Trump to change his mind on Syria, after which he expected he would resign. In the one-on-one meeting with Trump that followed, Mattis made his case, and after forty-five minutes of discussion handed the president a resignation letter, which appeared to catch Trump by surprise.

Mattis had planned to stay through February to assist with the transition, but Trump did not like the optics of being rejected by the Pentagon chief he had once celebrated, and told Mattis to leave by the end of the year. Trump's decision also accelerated the exit of Brett McGurk, the ultimate survivor, who had risen to become the Trump administration's point man for the coalition fighting the Islamic State and had been considered by Mattis as a top Pentagon official for the Middle East. With Bolton's accession to the national security post, McGurk had already made plans to move to Stanford when the news broke that Trump was ready to hand the Syria project over to Erdoğan. At the time, he had just finished briefing the State Department press corps on why it was important for the United States to carry out its efforts to stabilize northeastern Syria and how it would be "reckless" to take U.S. troops out before ISIS was defeated. Not only would Trump's decision leave the job undone, but it seemed likely to set the stage for a new war between Turkey and the SDF. Instead of finishing off the caliphate, a U.S. NATO ally and its battlefield partners would be bloodying each other while ISIS benefited from the spectacle. Denouncing Trump's decision as a "shock and a complete reversal of policy," McGurk also handed in his resignation.

The generals who were pressing the fight were also shocked by Trump's decision. Joe Votel had visited Joe Dunford's Pentagon office in mid-December, and nary a word had been said about leaving. But on December 18, Votel received a call from the Joint Chiefs of Staff chairman notifying him that Trump had given the order that U.S. troops were to leave Syria right away. Votel did not know how much time he had, but the talk in Washington was that it might need to be done in as little as thirty days, an extraordinarily brief period for reversing a deployment that had been underway for several years.

Getting out was trickier than it seemed. The modest American force had been reliant on Mazloum's fighters to secure the roads in northeastern Syria, but if the United States was abandoning the SDF, it certainly could not count on the force to protect American forces as they left. The American military had about 2,500 troops in Syria, and more would have to be sent in to help them get out safely. The U.S. presence would have to get bigger in order to get smaller. If the decision was to rush to the exits, CENTCOM planners figured that the U.S. deployment would first have to increase to 3,200 troops so that the force could draw down under adequate protection while fighting was still going on in the MERV—assuming the SDF was even willing to keep fighting ISIS on its own. Step by step, the force in northeastern Syria would pull back to Kobani and to the northern landing zone in the eastern part of the country. It was unclear what to do about the Al-Tanf garrison, where a couple hundred U.S. and allied advisors were still based.

Before Mattis resigned, the U.S commanders had been expecting a visit from the secretary of defense to review their plan for withdrawing under pressure—military-speak for removing troops while the fighting was still raging and before the job was done. Now word spread within the U.S. military command that a new VIP was coming.

On December 26, Air Force One, its cabin lights darkened, flew to Al-Asad in Iraq's western Anbar province. Trump was making his first visit to a war zone just as he had ordered the campaign brought to a close. It was a backward way of doing things: the commander in chief would finally get a formal military briefing on the consequences of the U.S. departure from Syria—but only after his decision had been made. Upon landing, Trump and his wife, Melania, were greeted by Lieutenant General Paul LaCamera, the new Operation Inherent Resolve commander, and Brigadier General John Daniel "Raisin" Caine, a special operations officer, and went to the gym to greet the troops.

Afterward, Major Anthony Aguilar, one of LaCamera's planners, walked the president through the military's mission. The caliphate had once been the size of Great Britain and was now smaller than Fayetteville, North Carolina, the home of Fort Bragg. ISIS had been pushed into Baghuz, a hamlet so modest that virtually nobody had ever heard of it, but the job was not yet done, the briefer explained. Trump wanted to know how long it would take to finish the campaign and was taken aback when Aguilar reported it would take until the first of April, which was no surprise to the military. The fighting would be at close quarters, and there were civilians on the battlefield. As in West Mosul, the more the battlefield shrank, the tougher and more complex the fighting became.

Much as some feared, Trump's tendency to delegate the commander-in-chief responsibilities had left him somewhat distant from the pace of operations on the Middle East battlefields. The PowerPoint maps the president had seen that showed an ever-shrinking caliphate disguised the fact that the final stage could be one of the hardest. There was another complicating factor that the businessman turned president could not easily disregard. If the U.S. forces left immediately, the American military would be abandoning radars, rockets, artillery, vehicles, and prefabricated housing units. The cost of all the weapons and war matériel that would need to be abandoned ran into the billions of dollars, Aguilar said. Every additional month that the United States stayed in Syria was another month that the fight could be waged against ISIS and another month in which the military would be able to haul equipment out of the country. The logisticians had looked at the numbers: it would take until May to get all of the equipment out by ground transportation and C-17s. The bottom line was that the mission needed to run several more months to continue the fight while removing the gear. Trump looked at LaCamera, who signaled that he agreed. Continuing the mission until then would be a "big win," LaCamera added, using a term that the president relished. "It would be good for America."

Afterward Trump addressed the troops. The president said that he had just met with some of the soldiers' "representatives" and had some ideas about next steps. "Do we like to win? We are going to win," he said. "There will be a strong, deliberate, and orderly withdrawal of U.S. forces." He then added that American troops would stay in Iraq "to watch over Iran." Trump had little interest in meeting with the new Iraqi prime minister, Adil Abd al-Mahdi, so it was arranged for the president to talk with him on the phone. There would be some cleaning up to do for Doug Silliman, the U.S. ambassador in Baghdad: the Americans had been invited in to help the Iraqis fight ISIS, but Trump had demonstrated no interest in coming to Baghdad to meet with the Iraqi leadership.

The briefing Trump received appeared to buy the military some time, but how much? In Baghdad, the planners continued to add details. The idea was to map out a glide path that would turn the current force in Syria of some 2,500 troops into a lean deployment half that size. That would make the continuing presence of U.S. forces less of a bitter pill for Trump to swallow and also make it easier to withdraw quickly if the president decided he had finally had enough of Syria.

In January 2019, Votel, LaCamera, and other senior planners reviewed the planning at Union III, the forward headquarters for Operation Inherent Resolve across from the embassy. Votel cautioned that slashing the numbers to 1,000 troops might not be enough and that a plan that brought the American troop levels in Syria down to the hundreds might be easier to sell to Joe Dunford and the White House. One planner determined that removing a mortuary affairs officer from the Lafarge cement plant would get the number down to 999. Few American or coalition troops were being killed, and if any were, a mortuary affairs officer could be flown in.

That seemed too clever by half to Major General Eric Kurilla, who was serving as the chief of staff of Votel's Central Command. So it was decided to also remove the two technicians who kept the heat and ventilation running at the Lafarge cement plant to get the number down to 997 troops, who would be deployed at nine bases. Once the major equipment was out, a residual force of 997 could be out of Syria in forty-eight hours if Trump so commanded. If Trump did not order an immediate departure, the gradual winding-down of the deployment could continue, bringing U.S. troop levels to 683 at the six-month mark and to fewer than 300 after a year.

There was more than a little irony in the planning. The Trump administration was now going through all the bean-counting that for years had typified the Obama administration's planning in Iraq and Syria—and that Trump officials had roundly deplored. McMaster had thrown out the force management level for Syria, and now a political troop cap had been restored. Left unclear were the questions of how Washington would prevent ISIS from trying to mount a comeback and how it would pressure the Iranians to leave Syria. Because the drawdown would be occurring as the U.S. was continuing the fight against ISIS, the plan was known within the military as "Continuing Resolve."

22

CONTINUING RESOLVE

For the 5th Special Forces Group, Trump's gyrations on Syria came at the worst possible time. The unit had sent the first Green Beret teams into Afghanistan after 9/11. Its soldiers had ridden on horseback alongside fighters from the Northern Alliance as they toppled the Taliban. They had then fought in all phases of the eight-year war in Iraq, typically carrying out six-month deployments before returning to Fort Campbell, Kentucky, just long enough to prepare to deploy again. Gabe LaMois's A-team had deployed from Fort Campbell in 2013 to help the Iraqi CTS, and the 5th Special Forces had helped stand up the Al-Tanf garrison. The campaign in northeastern Syria against ISIS had become another occasion for the unit's services. While Delta Force had been the first to work with Mazloum Abdi, it had a limited number of commandos at its disposal, which meant that the 5th Special Forces had been brought in to help with training and with the advisory mission. In the military's vernacular, Delta Force, with its penchant for clandestine activities, was dubbed the "black SOF," while the 5th Special Forces was known as the "white SOF." And whereas the heavily classified Delta Force soldiers in Syria were known as Task Force 9, the soldiers from the 5th Special Forces were dubbed Task Force 9.5. It was unusual for Delta Force to control such a diverse array of units from outside JSOC, which also included Marine artillery as well as the Fort Campbell Green Berets. The Special Operations Joint Task Forces for OIR even had its own Twitter account.

As the next rotation of 5th Special Forces soldiers at Fort Campbell got ready for their upcoming deployment, the early word was that they might be gone for no more than 120 days. That would provide time to put pressure on ISIS in the Middle Euphrates River Valley and begin the process of shutting down outposts elsewhere in the country and removing equipment through the spare airfield at Kobani and the border crossing into Iraq. Nobody could say precisely how long the deployment might last, but it looked like it could be a "hello-I-must-be-going" mission. There was a paradox at the heart of the enterprise, which could be managed but never really resolved: as the U.S. military footprint shrank and its capabilities diminished, the risk to the security of U.S. forces in Syria could mount. There was some safety in numbers—a point some civilians who favored troop caps sometimes forgot.

The mission the soldiers encountered when they arrived in January 2019 was still a frighteningly difficult one. The town of Baghuz, in which most of the ISIS fighters had taken refuge, seemed like an unlikely place for the Islamic State's last stand. Mosul, where Abu Bakr al-Baghdadi had proclaimed his caliphate, was a symbolically important city, as was ISIS's self-proclaimed capital in Raqqa. Baghuz was little more than a parched encampment adjacent to a range of steep cliffs riddled with caves. A field of tents in the valley below covered a system of tunnels, heavy-machine-gun emplacements, and famished diehards and their families. Though Baghuz did not offer ISIS much in the way of defensible terrain, capturing it presented some challenges for the Syrian Democratic Forces. The village was located on the Syrian side of the border, between the cities of Al-Bukamal on the Syrian side and Al-Qaim on the Iraqi side. To get there, the SDF and its coalition advisors would need to fight their way down the length of the MERV and then come up with a plan to ensure that some ISIS fighters and their families would be able to slink out the back door and into neighboring Iraq. The Americans had studied imagery of the area and estimated that it contained no more than five thousand fighters and civilians. That estimate, however, had underestimated ISIS's strength in Raqqa.

The SDF field commander for the push into the MERV was General Chiya Kobani, a stocky officer known affectionately by U.S. advisors as "the SDF's Patton." Chiya's first plan for finishing off ISIS was to deliver a roundhouse punch: SDF fighters would maneuver well east of the Euphrates River valley, swing south of Baghuz to envelop the town, and then press north. There were two reasons for Chiya's plan, which Mazloum supported. Chiya worried that ISIS had used the time when the campaign had been stalled due to the Turkish incursion to seed the approach from the north with IEDs. Another concern was to secure the area south of Baghuz to preempt Iranian-backed Shiite militias at Al-Qaim, who were offering to help, from crossing the border and establishing a foothold.

U.S. commanders were concerned that this strategy would leave the SDF with challenging logistics and a vulnerable western flank. The small SDF outposts that would be set up to protect the push south would be spread out over a long stretch of desert and could be assaulted by ISIS raiding parties, especially when bad weather rolled in and U.S. reconnaissance and air support were limited. But in the end it was the SDF that was going to do the fighting and dying, and Jeff VanAntwerp agreed to give Chiya's approach a try. One lesson of the "by, with, and through" approach was that there were times when the United States had to let its local partners pick the tactics and strategy.

To support the offensive, the U.S. 5th Special Forces Group had established pop-up mission support sites several kilometers behind the SDF's advancing lines, close enough to help but not so close that the Americans would become the main line of defense. Twelve-man A-teams would rotate through makeshift bases for several days at a time and would be augmented by medical specialists and perhaps a dozen additional Marines or Army soldiers for security.

After years of fighting against the SDF and its American allies, ISIS had a healthy respect for U.S. technology but had also become aware of its limitations. When bad weather rolled in one day in November 2018, hampering reconnaissance drones and strike aircraft, about 150 ISIS militants had attacked the SDF using a mix of vehicles they had stolen off the battlefield, including armored Humvees and Toyota trucks with .50-caliber guns mounted in the back. From the rear, ISIS mortar teams and snipers provided supporting fire.

Stung by the assault and with their logistical abilities stretched, the SDF pulled back, retreating so quickly that a U.S. A-team at Mission Support Site Munson was left isolated and at risk—even more so when pinpoint ISIS fire took out the system that had enabled the Americans to remotely fire a vehicle-mounted gun without exposing themselves. One of the biggest risks a small U.S. force faced was the danger of being cut off by fanatical ISIS fighters and killed or captured, which—given ISIS's record—essentially amounted to the same thing. For two days, the Americans withdrew to their sanctuary in the town of Hajin. It was a nail-biting moment for U.S. commanders and an episode that might have led to significant losses. It was never made public, however, as there were no embedded reporters with the U.S. forces in Syria and the Pentagon had little interest in advertising its close calls.

With ISIS pushing back, the SDF consolidated its position at Hajin, constructed a long tank ditch that stretched to the border with Iraq to keep the car bombs at bay, and reworked its plan. After huddling at the Lafarge cement factory with Joe Votel and Mazloum, Chiya settled on a new strategy. Mazloum sent in more Kurdish fighters, the Arab members of the SDF were retrained and then sent back to the front, and the idea of an envelopment from the south was shelved. The SDF would fight its way down the MERV with the backing of coalition airpower and U.S. special operators.

As the SDF advanced, ISIS sought to stir up trouble elsewhere to distract the U.S.-led coalition. In Raqqa, sleeper cells were activated for a series of assassinations carried out by motorcycle-riding hitmen—causing the SDF to ban the use of motorcycles in the city, to the disgruntlement of some residents, who couldn't drive cars through the rubble-strewn streets. ISIS struck closer to home in January 2019 when a fighter wearing a suicide vest observed a small group of U.S. military personnel and officials near the Palace of the Princes restaurant in Manbij, a favored venue for international personnel and VIPs. The group had parked in front of the restaurant and gone on a patrol in the town with a civil affairs unit. A suicide bomber lay in wait and then detonated himself when they returned to their vehicles, creating an enormous fireball that spilled out into the street. The blast killed the four-member party, which included a 5th Special Forces sergeant, a Defense Intelligence Agency civilian, and a Navy cryptologic technician, Chief Petty Officer Shannon Kent, who was the first female service member to be killed in Inherent Resolve. Soon after, a car bomb targeted a joint U.S. and SDF patrol near Al-Shaddadi but missed.

By February, Mazloum's fighters only had fifteen kilometers to go to reach Baghuz, and with each advance the ISIS fighters and their families were being pushed closer together, making the potential civilian casualty problem all the more complex. The United States bombed the bridge from Baghuz to Al-Bukamal and fired Hellfires and other precision munitions at any boat reckless enough to try to cross the Euphrates. The 5th Iraqi Army Division had taken up positions on the other side of the border and was offering to help, even by crossing the border into Syria. The Americans found an empty stretch of desert for the Iraqis to shell from their side of the border. The battle was hard enough without trying to integrate Iraq's blunderbuss artillery into the fight.

The SDF had suffered a heavy toll during the Raqqa fight and was taking casualties again now: the fight for Hajin between

September and December alone had killed 539 of Mazloum's fighters. To try to minimize its losses, the SDF started attacking at night, which carried with it the risk that fighters would stumble on an IED or barge into a booby-trapped house. ISIS had been unforgiving with the SDF fighters it had captured, beheading or gutting them and leaving their corpses behind as a gruesome warning to Mazloum's cadres. When SDF fighters got hit by a car bomb or some other ISIS counterblow, truckloads of the wounded would race to Green Village, where the battered troops, sometimes as many as fifty at a time, would be brought into the gym, which was turned into a giant mass casualty treatment area. Brave as its soldiers were, the SDF was not eager to jump into another meat grinder just as the campaign appeared to be coming to an end. At least five thousand SDF fighters had been killed during the campaign against ISIS, and Mazloum asserted that the total was more than double that. As the noose tightened around ISIS, the friction between Chiya and the Special Forces began to increase. Pounding the table, Chiya wanted U.S. air and artillery strikes to support his men, but with ISIS fighters and civilians pressed together, that was becoming all but impossible.

A March 18 air strike dramatized the risks. After SDF fighters came under attack, 5th Special Forces Group soldiers called in an air strike, which inadvertently killed a group of civilians. An internal investigation later established that the soldier had been relying on a drone that had limited reconnaissance capabilities and that a separate high-definition drone that was flying at the time offered a more accurate picture. More concerning, the episode was not acknowledged publicly by CENTCOM until it was ferreted out more than two years later by *The New York Times*.

As in Tabqa and Raqqa, ISIS was looking to negotiate a way out. As the battle neared its climax, ISIS proclaimed that it had thirteen hostages—Arab tribal fighters who had been part of the SDF coalition—and promptly posted a video showing the execution of one of them to demonstrate what would happen if its demands were not met. ISIS insisted that its families be granted safe passage to Al-Hol, 240 miles to the north, where thousands of displaced Syrian men, women, and children were already gathered in a refugee camp with loose security. ISIS was calculating that if it could get its families and fighters to Al-Hol, it could retain its faithful, usher in a new generation there, and eventually make its way to other ungoverned spaces in Syria. Even if they were detained at Al-Hol, the ISIS members might be sprung in some version of Baghdadi's 2012–2013 Breaking the Walls campaign.

The demand put Mazloum and Chiya in a difficult position. The Kurdish leaders of the SDF did not want to give the impression that they did not care about the Arab members of their force, whose support they needed to finish the fight in the MERV and ultimately govern the newly liberated towns in the aftermath—and perhaps sustain the SDF's goal of establishing their own preserve within Syria with oil and natural gas resources. The Americans, however, made it clear that they had had enough of negotiated retreats. If some sort of exit was arranged, it would need to be a surrender and not an arrangement that would allow ISIS to carry on the fight.

As a first step, ISIS released three hostages while the SDF sent trucks down the cliffs to pick up a group of women and children and then drive them to Al-Hol. As the U.S. side monitored the proceedings with drones, alarm bells went off: the SDF was so anxious to wrap up the battle that none of the women were being searched, which meant they could lug all sorts of contraband to Al-Hol. When the next group of women were finally searched by the Yekîneyên Parastina Jin (YPJ), the female Kurdish complement of the YPG, they were found to be carrying bars of gold, shanks, weapon components, SIM cards, and wads of cash totaling thousands of dollars.

With prodding from the United States, a system was established to take retina scans and other biometric information from all the women who were not born in Syria or Iraq. Even so, ISIS tried to game the system. Accepting the fact that the trucks were the only way out, ISIS tried to flood the zone, hoping that some of the men would somehow evade the screening and get to Al-Hol or beyond. "It would start off vanilla," one Special Forces non-commissioned officer recalled. Women and children would arrive, but as night fell and it became dark and cold, more contraband would be found. Then among the mix appeared fighters, many of whom had suffered grievous injuries exacerbated by a lack of medical care. "They would be fighters who had legs pinned together with rebar, hands sewn to their stomach or no hands at all," the officer said. The men, the Americans decreed, would be going not to Al-Hol but to pop-up prisons in northeastern Syria, which were sometimes nothing more than a dilapidated school that had been fenced off with makeshift barriers and barbed wire. As soon as word got back to ISIS that it did not look like its fighters would be headed to Al-Hol, the hostage talks were broken off and the insurgents executed more prisoners.

In fits and starts, the SDF and the United States continued the offensive to shrink the ISIS perimeter around Baghuz. Trapped in the open and bereft of supplies, the caliphate was starving and surviving on cattle feed and grass. The SDF put out the word that anybody who wanted to leave would receive medical care, food, and water. By March, the SDF convoy was down to its final truck-load: a group of women, some with children, who were wearing suicide vests. Once they got to the vetting site, a few of the women refused to remove the vests or allow themselves to be searched. A decision was made to cut a circle of security guards around them and to hold them overnight. The next day, several still balked at being screened. One handed her baby to a member of the YPJ, and then detonated her belt, killing herself, her child, and the YPJ guard. The gruesome episode recalled the final days of the battle for Mosul when female suicide bombers, some with infants in hand, had prowled the streets. The SDF and the coalition were on the verge of getting the "snake out of the hole," Mazloum said.

With the exodus complete, the SDF moved in to clear out the caves, which still included scores of ISIS militants determined to fight to the death. As Mazloum's fighters worked their way through the encampment below, some of the tents caught fire and the flames spread, turning the tent city to ash. An enormous yellow SDF flag was unfurled on top of a bullet-scarred building that was still standing in the village. All told, about fifty thousand people had been removed from Baghuz—ten times the initial U.S. estimate. More than ten thousand were ISIS fighters, including about nine hundred foreign fighters, who were put in the pop-up prisons. More than three thousand ISIS fighters, the U.S. estimated, had been killed. Of the thirteen Arab tribesmen who had been held as hostages, about half were freed; the rest were casualties of ISIS's endgame strategy.

In a March 23 ceremony at Green Village, William Roebuck gave an address commemorating the victory. The State Department's man in northeastern Syria and a former ambassador to Bahrain, Roebuck hailed the end of the caliphate and then assured the SDF that the United States was determined to help the victors consolidate their gains as ISIS returned to its guerrilla roots. "We still have much work to do to achieve an enduring defeat of ISIS," Roebuck said, adding that Trump and Pompeo fully understood the campaign was not over. The next month, Baghdadi acknowledged in an audio recording that ISIS had lost Baghuz but would now carry out a war of attrition. "The battle for Baghuz is over," Baghdadi said. "There will be more to come after this battle."

In Ankara, Erdoğan was more concerned with the SDF's gain than with the mopping up that needed to be done with ISIS. The Turkish president asked to meet with Trump in September 2019 on the margins of the United Nations General Assembly session but was not granted a meeting. Once more, he began to rattle the saber. Following the Turkish intervention in Afrin, the U.S. military proposed an improvisation to try to dissuade Turkey from repeating its intervention in northeastern Syria: U.S.-manned outposts were set up in November 2018 near the Syrian-Turkish frontier. The ostensible reason was to stop ISIS from threatening Turkey, but the unstated reason was to function as a trip wire and dissuade the NATO ally from coming south. While Jim Mattis and

Brett McGurk had backed the idea before they left government, the top envoy for Syrian issues, Jim Jeffrey, had been opposed, fearing that the Turks would see the outposts as an American scheme to bolster Mazloum's longer-term aspirations to control a swath of northeastern Syria and to deter Turkey. To minimize any affront to Turkey, the military's contingency plans to build half a dozen outposts had been pared down to three positions, at Ras al-Ayn, Tal Tamir, and Kobani.

When Roebuck visited them, he saw that some were so rustic that the U.S. Special Forces or Marine units rotating through them used sheets of plastic to replace the shattered windows. While no U.S. flags were displayed there, U.S. military personnel driving to the positions used U.S. military vehicles and not civilian SUVs to make clear to the Turks that Americans were present. No SDF were allowed near the outposts, which rarely figured in the news. Now, however, Erdoğan was talking about setting up a Turkish-controlled thirty-kilometer buffer zone in an operation he dubbed "Peace Spring." The obscure outposts and the several dozen U.S. troops who manned them were squarely in the way.

On October 6, 2019, Trump talked with Erdoğan, who made clear his intentions. Later that day, the Pentagon ordered the troops in the outposts to pull back. Three days later, Trump sent Erdoğan a blunt letter proposing that the two leaders work out a deal that would ease Turkey's security concerns without upending the counter-ISIS campaign in Syria; the letter threatened economic sanctions if they failed. "You don't want to be responsible for slaughtering thousands of people, and I don't want to be responsible for destroying the Turkish economy," Trump wrote the Turkish leader.

For all that, the American president's patience for staying in Syria had been exhausted. The caliphate had been destroyed and, with it, the U.S. reason for staying, said Trump, who made it clear he felt no lingering obligation to the SDF for their sacrifices against ISIS. "They didn't help us in the Second World War, they didn't help us with Normandy," he told reporters. As he had almost a year earlier, Trump was prepared to wash his hands of the situation and let Turkey and the SDF sort it out—or fight it out, if need be. On October 14, the Pentagon ordered all of the U.S. troops to leave Syria and take their equipment with them.

Roebuck was not responsible for the decision, but as the mixed messages emanated from the White House, he struggled to salvage the situation. Speaking from the Lafarge cement factory, Roebuck explained the plan in a videoconference with Mazloum's headquarters in Al-Hasakah. Mazloum got right to the point: the Turks were mounting air strikes and firing artillery, and the attacks were going beyond the thirty-kilometer zone they said they would control. The Turkish military had not yet crossed the border, but "sleeper cells" of Turkish-backed Syrian militias had seized two villages south of Ras al-Ayn.

Roebuck said that Washington did expect Turkey to extend its offensive farther than thirty kilometers, but he added hopefully that there might yet be a chance for the Erdoğan government and the Syrian Kurds to sort out their political differences. In response, Mazloum insisted that he was not seeking a "statelet," as Ankara alleged, and was prepared for his fighters to come under the authority of the Syrian state. That was why, he insisted, the SDF had long sought to become part of the United Nations talks on Syria. "All I want is for Turkey not to attack Syria. We want an agreement with them," Mazloum said. "We do not want autonomy."

Mazloum continued: "Let me make sure I understand, the United States of America wants Turkey to occupy this land? You are leaving us to be slaughtered." Issuing a rare threat, he warned that if the Americans turned their back on his forces, he would turn to Moscow. "There are two forces in Syria that can stop this massacre. The United States and Russia," he said. "If you do not want to do this, then we will ask them. I am watching my sons, my brothers, and my families being killed. I have to go elsewhere."

After all the efforts to keep the Russians from venturing east of the Euphrates, the last thing Roebuck wanted was to see the territory handed over to the Russian military. Playing for time, he asked that Mazloum give Jim Jeffrey forty-eight hours to work on the diplomacy. Mazloum said he would give Jeffrey twelve hours. Developments on the battlefield were moving fast, and the United States had no answers. As the Turks and the Turkish-backed Syrian militias crossed the border, a report came in that the Kurdish human rights activist Hevrin Khalaf had been pulled from her car and executed. Soon the shooting began to get close to Roebuck as well: reports from the Lafarge cement factory indicated that the leading edge of the Turkish offensive was just a few kilometers away.

Roebuck was in his makeshift living quarters when a massive explosion shook the compound and drove him to his knees. At first, he thought the Turks were shelling the compound, but then U.S. Special Forces told him that the SDF was blowing up all of their stores of ammunition so that Turkish forces could not seize them. Mazloum's fighters were so angry at what they thought was an American betrayal that they had not bothered to tell their U.S. partner about the demolitions. Later that evening a Chinook helicopter arrived to fly Roebuck and the other U.S. personnel at the factory to Kobani, and soon after that to Erbil. Days later, as the U.S. forces left Syria, the Americans joined in the destruction: two F-15Es bombed the factory so that it would be of no use to the Russians, Turks, or whatever force might now occupy the area.

It was the nadir of the "by, with, and through" campaign. The Americans had destroyed their main headquarters in Syria in a shambolic retreat that threatened to plunge the area into chaos and give ISIS a new lease on life. If the confrontation between Turkey and the SDF escalated, there was a risk that Mazloum's fighters would be diverted from guard duty at Al-Hol and the pop-up prisons where nine thousand ISIS militants—two thousand of them foreign fighters—were detained. Thousands of ISIS combatants could be unleashed onto the battlefield, and the Baghuz operation would be for naught.

Roebuck later caught a flight to Al-Hasakah, where Mazloum

was based, and sent a series of cables to the State Department warning that Islamist groups armed by Turkey—what the U.S. military dubbed "the Turkish-supported opposition"—were engaging in ethnic cleansing in the Kurdish heartland along the border. At the Al-Hasakah base, Roebuck did not have access to the equipment U.S. officials relied on for classified communications, so Roebuck typed the cables on his BlackBerry using an unclassified email account. As he saw it, time was running out, and he described the risk of an even greater catastrophe in a cable bluntly titled "Present at the Catastrophe: Standing By as Turks Cleanse Kurds in Northern Syria and De-Stabilize Our D-ISIS Platform in the Northeast":

> As more news emerges from northeast Syria of Turkish/ Turkish supported groups/organizations (TSO) atrocities and expulsion of citizens, the reputational risks to the US and criticism of our decisions will rise. To protect our interests, we need to speak out more forcefully, publicly and privately, to reduce the blame placed on the US and to highlight the Turkish responsibilities for civilian wellbeing. By acting now, we have a chance to minimize the damage for us and hopefully correct some of the impact of Turkey's current policies, as we seek to implement the President's guidance for our presence in northeastern Syria.

In Washington, some of Trump's political allies were on the same page as Roebuck. Senator Lindsey Graham had gotten a heads-up from his contacts in the Pentagon and the State Department that Trump had all but green-lighted Erdoğan's intervention and thought it was a political and strategic calamity. The South Carolina Republican, who had in recent years withdrawn his once-harsh criticism of Trump, asked the president why he had not talked to him before making such a fateful decision, which Graham was convinced would work to the benefit of ISIS and hurt the Americans and their allies. Trump replied unconvincingly that he hadn't been able to get hold of Graham, but then went on to say that he had made a campaign promise to bring the troops home and his supporters wanted out.

This was only partly true. Christian conservatives like Franklin Graham and Pat Robertson of the Christian Broadcasting Network liked the SDF for its commitment to protect Syrian Christians and saw Erdoğan as little better than the Iranian ayatollahs. It was important, however, to talk to Trump in transactional terms he could understand. Lindsey Graham and his ally Jack Keane, the former vice chief of staff of the Army, went to the White House on October 14 to urge a course correction.

No sooner did Graham and Keane arrive than they were ushered into the Oval Office. It was a packed house. Trump was seated at his desk with his top aides around him in a semicircle: National Security Advisor Robert O'Brien, who had replaced John Bolton; Treasury Secretary Steve Mnuchin; Deputy National Security Advisor Matt Pottinger; National Security Advisor to the Vice President Keith Kellogg; and others. Greeting Trump, Keane said to the president that he knew that Trump did not agree with him on the importance of staying in Syria, but he hoped he had some room to talk about it. But first Trump had to manage the crisis at hand.

A call had been scheduled between Trump and Mazloum. The president listened over a speakerphone as the Kurdish commander argued that a Turkish invasion would put thousands at risk. Trump had yet another call with Erdoğan shortly thereafter. The Turkish leader was upset about the sanctions Trump had threatened in a letter he had sent on October 9 and began listing them one by one. Trump had no talking points in front of him, and when he hit the mute button the Oval Office attendees began to offer some, including asking for an immediate cease-fire as a prelude to negotiations. Erdoğan shot back that he would not negotiate with a terrorist, meaning Mazloum. Again, Trump pushed mute. Keane said that Trump should tell him that he would be negotiating with the United States, not with Mazloum. Erdoğan asked for Trump to come to Ankara; Trump said he would send Mike Pence.

As the meeting wound down, the discussion shifted to oil. Keane had come equipped with a map depicting the oil fields in northeastern Syria, which he had picked up from the Institute for the Study of War, a Washington think tank. Syria was no Saudi Arabia, and its oil reserves were relatively meager, but there was no more potent symbol for Trump of the American stake in the region than its natural resources. Putting the map in front of Trump, Keane explained that U.S. forces, the SDF, and their British and French allies controlled the air and ground east of the Euphrates, where much of the oil was concentrated. The Iranians were massing their proxies on the western side of the river and would move in and take control of the oil with Russian airpower. Iran would repair the facilities, pocket the oil, and use the funds to blunt the effect of Trump's economic sanctions, which the president had imposed to compel Tehran to abandon its nuclear program. There was no sense turning the oil fields over to them when the Syrian people could be the beneficiaries. It was a simplistic message, but it worked. Graham sought to reinforce Keane's argument. "Everybody who supports you listens to this man on TV," Graham said, referring to Keane, who was a regular analyst on Fox News. Trump leaned back in his chair and, with resignation in his voice, said, "I got it. I got it."

Days later, Trump reversed course and ordered U.S. forces back into Syria to secure Conoco and much of the adjoining oil fields. In Baghdad, the U.S. military had drawn up a plan to create a buffer zone of its own after leaving Syria. If chaos was about to unfold in northern Syria as the Turks and SDF clashed, and ISIS prisoners potentially managed to get free, the military would set up a security zone along the northern portion of the Syrian-Iraqi border to prevent the threats from spilling into Iraq. Now that the White House had decided that U.S. troops would return, the plan was modified: a new Eastern Syria Security Area was declared—a new phase for the operation Continuing Resolve. The U.S. had forfeited its presence in Raqqa and Tabqa. But the U.S. patrol bases near Manbij had been relinquished to the Russians, who also swooped in to take control of the airstrip and base the Americans had set up at Kobani, where they raised the Russian flag, flew in helicopters and planes, and filmed the muscle-flexing for Russian television.

The resolution of Turkey's incursion, however, was a matter that went beyond Trump. During marathon negotiations in Sochi, Russian and Turkish officials would come to agree on a memorandum of understanding that affirmed the thirty-kilometer zone Turkey had conquered but dictated that Russian and Syrian soldiers would have responsibility for patrolling the other side of the zone as a buffer between Turkey and the SDF.

Though the U.S. foothold was now smaller, it was enough to preserve the alliance with Mazloum for the time being. "People said to me, 'Why are you staying in Syria,'" Trump claimed, explaining his about-face. "Because I kept the oil, which frankly we should have done in Iraq." The boast was a convenient myth the president invented to placate his base, lest it think he was shifting away from his "America First" theme. Jim Jeffrey patiently explained to anyone who would listen that in fact the United States was bringing in Delta Crescent, an American-run company, so that the local authority in northeast Syria might develop and export the oil to boost its own revenue.

With the Turkish and Russian forces moving into the northernmost tier of Syria, the battlefield was getting more crowded. The Russians began to pressure Mazloum to give their firms access to the oil fields he controlled. Near the site of the confrontation with the Wagner Group, the Russians began to reinforce an old bridge over the Euphrates so that they could potentially move some of their armor across. That prompted the United States to rush in mechanized Bradley fighting vehicles from a U.S. National Guard unit in Kuwait, a move that was left unexplained at the time. To reduce the risk of another confrontation, Lieutenant General Robert P. "Pat" White, who succeeded Paul LaCamera as the Operation Inherent Resolve commander, held a workmanlike meeting in

Jordan with his Russian counterpart and worked out a three-page agreement intended to deconflict the two sides' operations.

On October 27, the strained relationship between the two countries was again put to the test. After years of searching, the United States had pinpointed Abu Bakr al-Baghdadi's location in a compound in Barisha, a town in Syria's Idlib province. As the SDF had moved through the MERV, ISIS's caliph and other leaders had sought refuge in the northwestern corner of the country. Mazloum later said that some of the critical intelligence that led to the discovery of Baghdadi's whereabouts, including the layout of his refuge, was provided by one of the SDF's informants, whose relatives had suffered under ISIS and who wanted revenge. The operation would be named in honor of Kayla Mueller, the aid worker who in 2014 had been taken hostage and, after Delta Force was unable to rescue her, killed by ISIS.

As Delta Force commandos flew to the compound, Brigadier General Scott Naumann, now the senior operations officer for the Inherent Resolve task force, used the deconfliction line to call his Russian counterpart and let him know the Americans would be flying through Russian-controlled airspace. The U.S. military, he said, was not a threat to Russian or Syrian government forces. But it would be taking action against a terrorist who had to be destroyed— and it had no intentions of staying long in Idlib. The Russian officer refused to give the U.S. forces permission to operate in the Russian zone. "We categorically oppose these strikes," he said.

Nevertheless, the United States continued with its mission, but not everything went according to plan. Noticing a van speeding down the road away from the direction of Baghdadi's compound, it blasted the vehicle with a Hellfire missile. The van was later described by NPR to have been carrying three civilians, two of whom were killed and one severely wounded.

Unaware of the mistake at the time, the Deltas moved on to their ultimate objective. With warplanes circling overhead, they landed, blew a hole in the walled compound, and engaged in a firefight in which five residents were killed and two captured. Wearing a suicide vest, Baghdadi grabbed two of his children and crawled into a tunnel as a Delta Force dog gave pursuit. Baghdadi ended his ordeal by detonating his vest.

Like Osama bin Laden, Baghdadi was buried at sea so that his grave would not become a militant shrine. ISIS named a new caliph, Abu Ibrahim al-Hashimi al-Qurayshi, a relative unknown in the West who lacked Baghdadi's talent for theater and who had a $10 million bounty put on his head by the United States.

With ISIS reeling, the tussle for influence in Iraq between the United States and Iran began to heat up. The Shiite paramilitary group Kataib Hezbollah had grudgingly shared Al-Taqaddum Air Base with the Americans when Ramadi was up for grabs. In December, however, the Iranian-backed militia fired more than thirty rockets at an Iraqi base near Kirkuk. It was the eleventh such attack in two months, but this time it crossed an American red line by killing a U.S. contractor and wounding four troops. Two days later, the United States attacked three of the militia's bases in Iraq and Syria. After an angry mob approached the U.S. embassy in Baghdad, Apache helicopters hovered overhead as a show of force and Marines from Kuwait were brought in to bulk up the embassy's security.

At the White House, Trump and his advisors considered the rising tensions. For years, Qassem Soleimani had moved easily in and out of Iraq as he carried out his duties as the Quds Force commander and a central node managing Iran's network of influence in the Middle East. Convinced that Soleimani was planning even more attacks against U.S. forces and diplomatic outposts, Trump ordered that the Iranian commander be killed by a U.S. drone soon after he arrived at Baghdad's international airport on January 3, 2020. The gruesome strike, ordered without consulting the Iraqis, ripped apart Soleimani's body; his severed hand, bearing his outsized red ring, was deposited on the road. Also killed was Abu Mahdi al-Muhandis, who oversaw the Popular

Mobilization Forces. Four days later, Iran struck Al-Asad Air Base with eleven missiles. Iran was not hiding behind an Iraqi militia this time. There was nothing deniable about this strike. U.S. spy satellites had detected the Iranian preparations, and the death of U.S. personnel was avoided only by evacuating many of them, along with the aircraft, before the attack was carried out. Even so, more than one hundred soldiers suffered traumatic brain injuries in the attack.

The assassination of Soleimani produced a backlash in the Iraqi parliament, which passed a nonbinding resolution demanding that U.S. troops leave. Continuing Washington's topsy-turvy relationship with Baghdad, Trump rebuffed the vote and threatened to impose sanctions if the United States was forced out. The Obama administration had once refused to keep troops in Iraq unless the parliament endorsed a new status of forces agreement. Now the White House was insisting that U.S. troops would stay no matter what the parliament wanted. Over the next several months, cooler heads prevailed. General White, the Inherent Resolve commander, developed a plan to withdraw from the majority of Iraqi bases, staying only at Al-Asad and Erbil. NATO troops would be brought in to give the mission less of an American coloration. Later, Trump himself drove the number of troops down from 5,200 to 2,500, and U.S. advisors limited their advising to Iraqi division headquarters and stopped going outside the wire.

ISIS had been active in the region even as the United States was jousting with Iran. By March 2020, the Americans were looking to step up the pressure again. The target this time was a group of ISIS fighters who had sought refuge in a complex of caves in the Qarachogh Mountains just south of the Kurdish-controlled areas in Iraq. Iraq's CTS would take on the foe accompanied by French special operations forces and fourteen members of an elite team of Marine Raiders.

On March 8, U.S. warplanes plastered the complex with five-hundred- and two-thousand-pound bombs before an assault force arrived. Then U.S. helicopters flew the assault force to the battle zone from a staging area near Mosul Dam. With the CTS leading the raid, the Marine Raiders and French troops moved down the steep terrain until they reached an enormous rock face, which the Americans dubbed the Witch's Hat. Moving into the first cave, Staff Sergeant Nicholas Jones spied the body of an ISIS militant at its mouth: he had been killed by a bomb blast but was resting against a rock with an AK-47 in his hand as if he were still in the fight. Other ISIS fighters, however, had survived the bombardment and were very much alive. Jones peeked around the cave, uncovering a cache of light machine guns, thousands of rounds of ammunition, and enough bomb-making material to run an insurgency right along the fault lines of Iraqi society. Noticing an increasing volume of gunfire behind him, Jones received the words over the radio no operator wants to hear: "Eagle down." The code word signified that a U.S. special operator had become a casualty.

In the melee that erupted, there were no front lines or safe areas for the advisors. Sprinting to the sound of gunfire, Jones threw off his rucksack, rushed to the ravine where the ambush had occurred, and among the rocks spotted a wounded French commando, whom he pulled to safety as he fired into a nearby cave to suppress the enemy fire. Jones then called his command to confirm that he had identified two Raiders killed in action a short distance away. Jones was now trapped behind a wall of rock with bullets exploding all around, but one of the other Raiders threw a smoke grenade to cover his escape.

Climbing above the cave to direct artillery strikes, Jones finally saw who the downed Raiders were: Chief Gunnery Sergeant Diego Pongo and Captain Moises Navas. The loss of the two Marines who had been deployed as advisors came as such a shock that when Jones called to report their deaths, his command asked how he was sure. "I can see their fucking faces," he answered.

Unwilling to leave the bodies behind, Jones attacked the cave solo over and over again, getting driven off each time. Apache helicopters fired Hellfire missiles and 30mm rounds to try to silence the ISIS diehards so that the bodies could be retrieved, but the resistance continued. Jones grabbed some grenades, ammo, and water and with some fellow Raiders set out again, until a bullet ripped through his leg. Unable to go on, he was medevacked to safety, and the Raiders withdrew.

The next day, after a fierce firefight, Delta Force finally retrieved the bodies of Pongo and Navas. Jones later received the Navy Cross and was medically retired from the military after undergoing six surgeries on his leg. Though the operation continues at a low ebb, as of this writing Pongo and Navas were the last Americans to die at the hands of ISIS during Operation Inherent Resolve.

EPILOGUE

In his September 21, 2021, speech to the United Nations General Assembly, President Joe Biden declared, "I stand here today, for the first time in 20 years, with the United States not at war. We've turned the page." It was a bold claim, intended to highlight a sudden end to the U.S. military involvement in Afghanistan. As the United States was closing a "period of relentless war," Biden said earlier in his speech, it was now opening "a new era of relentless diplomacy."

Yet earlier in the year, Biden's administration had reaffirmed its support for Operation Inherent Resolve. At the time of his speech, there were still 2,500 U.S. troops in Iraq training and advising Iraqi forces. Another 900 U.S. soldiers were working with the SDF in northeastern Syria, while 200 U.S. Special Forces and regular Army troops were based at the Al-Tanf garrison, where they continued to train the MaT.

Nor was the fighting over. More than forty-eight air strikes were carried out by the U.S.-led coalition against ISIS targets in Iraq and Syria during Biden's first seven months in office, killing more than sixty fighters.

The shadow war between Washington and Tehran went on as well. With Iranian-backed militias continuing to launch drone strikes against U.S. troops, the United States responded with two air raids, which were devised to minimize the risk of enemy casualties. The militias exercised no such restraint and responded by firing thirty-four rockets at U.S. forces near Green Village, though to no effect.

A more formidable challenge came on October 20, when Iran directed five drones at the Al-Tanf garrison, two of which struck the sleeping quarters for U.S. troops there. The Iranians made clear in a confidential message that the attack was in retaliation for an Israeli air strike that had killed two Iranian officers in Syria, hoping it would induce Washington to constrain its Middle East ally.

For days, Biden and his top aides deliberated about how to calibrate the U.S. response. American casualties had been averted because commanders had withdrawn troops based on intelligence about an impending attack. Though the president was initially inclined to strike back, the White House sought to avoid an escalation by sending Lloyd Austin, Biden's secretary of defense, written guidance that the Pentagon needed to ensure that any air raid would not result in any civilian or enemy casualties. The search for casualty-free targets led the Pentagon to consider a location that had been bombed before and a militia training area. In the end, the administration settled for sanctioning individuals and companies involved with Iran's drone program and sending a message to Iran through Mustafa al-Kadhimi, who had been confirmed as Iraq's prime minister in May 2020, that Washington reserved the right to take action at a place and time of its choosing.

Biden's strategy to handle the politics at home and in Iraq over the U.S.'s continued military involvement in the region also required rebranding the ongoing fight against ISIS. No longer a war to destroy a major terrorist threat to the West, it was now described as a military training effort in an unsettled region. Biden hosted Kadhimi at the White House in July 2021 and announced that the American combat mission in Iraq would be over by year's end. The announcement, which Brett McGurk had negotiated in advance during a visit to Baghdad, was largely semantic: While it would help the Iraqi prime minister handle political pressures at home, it did not actually presage a reduction in U.S. troops or an end to U.S. air strikes against ISIS.

A tougher test for Biden came in January 2022 when the militants took a page out of the "Breaking the Walls" campaign and plotted a prison breakout in al-Hasakah, where about 3,500 ISIS fighters and more than 700 minors were being held at the time. For days, the SDF sought to regain control, backed up by American Apache helicopters, RQ-9 drones, F-16s, an AC-130 gunship, U.S. troops in Bradley fighting vehicles, and U.S., British, and French special operations forces. In the end, more than 150 SDF fighters were wounded or killed, including some prison guards who were beheaded. More than 200 ISIS fighters and prisoners died. Some ISIS operatives, however, managed to escape.

It was Biden who struck the next blow. Over months of intelligence gathering, the U.S. had pinpointed the location of Baghdadi's successor: Abu Ibrahim al-Hashimi al-Qurayshi, who was hiding in northwest Syria near the Turkish border. The U.S. had targeted al-Qurayshi before. The ISIS operative had survived a 2015 air strike near Mosul while losing a leg. This time the mission was more complex. Al-Qurayshi was holed up on the top floor of a three-story building. A family was living on the first floor, serving as unwitting human shields.

In a February 2 raid, a Delta Force team, backed up by Apache helicopters and RQ-9 drones, swooped in. The family was rescued. But al-Qurayshi had arranged for the third floor to be rigged with explosives so as not to be taken alive; as the attack began, they detonated in a massive explosion that blew the ISIS leader and his family out of the structure. An ISIS lieutenant, his wife, and a child on the second floor were also killed. Delta commandos rushed to identify al-Qurayshi's remains. Mark Milley later told Biden, who watched the episode in the White House Situation Room, that they had a "visual I.D. jackpot." A DNA sample of the caliph was taken to be sure.

After a day or two of congratulations, however, the spotlight shifted. At the Pentagon, the focus was on what the generals called "great-power competition": the Chinese and Russian military threats that would, far more than counterinsurgency, shape the American defense budget for decades to come. Even before the Qurayshi raid, CENTCOM announced that the Operation Inherent Resolve commander would no longer be a three-star general. A two-star officer would suffice.

Yet the ongoing Inherent Resolve campaign deserves a fuller accounting, both because of the prodigious effort and sacrifice involved and because it will likely serve as a template for future conflicts against extremist groups. In an age in which effective counterinsurgency operations have been hard to come by, the U.S.-led campaign could be largely counted a success. The ISIS caliphate, which controlled forty-one thousand square miles in Iraq and Syria and ruled more than eight million people, was systematically dismantled. Mosul and Raqqa were liberated in tough street-to-street fighting. Many of the forty thousand foreign fighters who joined ISIS were killed, as were many of the twenty-five thousand recruited from inside Iraq and Syria. Others fled to remote regions in Iraq and Syria. The risk of ISIS terrorist attacks abroad was substantially reduced.

The victories did not come easily. By any measure, the firepower expended during the campaign had been enormous. U.S. and allied air and artillery strikes in Iraq numbered more than 13,500, and in Syria exceeded 19,300. By the standards of Middle East wars, however, American casualties had been extraordinarily light. Between the return of U.S. troops to Iraq in August 2014 and Biden's UN speech in September 2021, 20 American service personnel died as a result of hostile action and 270 were wounded. Though Americans played the pivotal role, a large international coalition was assembled. The decision to work through local proxies also relieved the United States of the need to take on burdensome and costly occupation duties.

Still, while the air, rocket, and artillery strikes carried out by the U.S.-led coalition enabled the SDF, Iraqi forces, and Peshmerga to advance, U.S. partners suffered many casualties. SDF officials put the number of their dead at more than 5,000. The Iraqis would not publicize their losses, but they were estimated to have been enormous. Worst of all, the war was much harder on civilians. According to the conservative CENTCOM calculations, more than 1,400 civilians were inadvertently killed by the U.S-led coalition. Some nongovernmental organizations estimated the toll to be at least 8,300.

The numbers also pointed to some of the challenges ahead. At the end of 2021, more than 59,000 people languished at the Al-Hol camp, some of them committed ISIS followers, in conditions so violent that 60 were killed at the hands of fellow detainees in the first half of 2021. The violence prompted an SDF operation to root out ISIS fighters that netted 70 prisoners, but nobody thought the operation was complete. Another 10,000 hardened ISIS fighters were being held at other SDF facilities in Syria. Approximately 2,000 of these prisoners hailed from countries other than Iraq and Syria—a situation that, Secretary of State Antony Blinken told his fellow foreign ministers in June 2021, was "untenable."

Though ISIS's caliphate had collapsed, what was left of it remained a danger. It was still a cohesive organization, in the view of the U.S. Defense Intelligence Agency; it was raising money through extortion and kidnapping; and it had a leader: After the raid that killed al-Qurayshi, ISIS announced yet another caliph. In Iraq, it operated from rural areas where there were few Iraqi forces, as well as from sanctuaries in the Hamrin Mountains near Kirkuk and desert areas in Anbar province. It still launched guerrilla-style attacks against Iraqi Security Forces and tribes aligned with the Iraqi government, claiming responsibility for attacks on cell phone towers and a power plant. Some of its boldest attacks were a series of bombings in Baghdad's Sadr City in July.

In Syria, ISIS conducted hit-and-run attacks against the SDF and Arab tribal leaders who worked with the group. It also stepped up activities in desert areas nominally under the control of President Bashar al-Assad and his Iranian and Russian allies, including a June attack that killed two members of the Iranian Revolutionary Guard Corps. Nurturing hopes of a resurgence, ISIS continued its recruiting, particularly in camps for displaced civilians. It sought to smuggle prospective fighters to training areas in the Syrian desert, where it believed they would be beyond the reach of U.S. warplanes. The Syrian desert also remained a useful way station, linking the ISIS presence in western Iraq to Syria's Idlib province, the region where Baghdadi was killed by Delta Force and where other ISIS leaders still took shelter.

Though the threat from ISIS was greatly diminished, Iraqi forces were still a work in progress. They depended heavily on U.S. reconnaissance and had only a limited capability to secure their country's border with Syria. Meanwhile, the fate of the Syrian Kurdish enclave and Mazloum Abdi's forces was still uncertain, given the vicissitudes of Syrian politics and Turkish behavior. "The U.S. government continued to make incremental progress toward its goal of preventing ISIS from regenerating in Iraq and Syria," the Pentagon's inspector general said in a July report. "However, Coalition partners in Iraq and Syria continued to rely on Coalition support to conduct operations, and ISIS remained entrenched as a low-level insurgency."

Even with the caliphate's collapse, the ISIS brand was resilient, prompting military action that was smaller in scale than Inherent Resolve but still significant. In Libya, the United States had carried out hundreds of air strikes to help local fighters retake the city of Sirte from ISIS in 2016. In the Philippines, the United States provided reconnaissance for the government's offensive against Abu Sayyaf, an Islamic insurgent group that had pledged allegiance to the caliphate that same year.

In Afghanistan, an outfit known as the Islamic State–Khorasan Province (referred to by the U.S. military as ISIS-K) famously became a lethal threat to Afghans and American soldiers, too. Inspired by Baghdadi's proclamation of a caliphate, ISIS-K first emerged in late 2014. By 2021, it was estimated to have 1,500 to 2,200 fighters in Afghanistan's eastern Kunar and Nangar-har provinces, including many who broke with the Taliban after it agreed to talks with the West. Though it has maintained communications with ISIS leaders in Iraq and Syria, the core of the organization is made up of Afghan and Pakistani nationals, as well as some Tajiks and Uzbeks. During its time in Afghanistan, the United States sent Special Operations Forces on raids with Afghan troops against ISIS-K and quietly used drone strikes to pick off the ISIS-K militants after they revealed their positions in clashes with the Taliban. The group's attack on the Kabul airport on August 26, 2021, killed thirteen Americans and hundreds of others, and intensified the chaos surrounding the U.S. withdrawal from the country. Since then, ISIS-K has carried out attacks on Afghanistan's Shiite minority and made it clear it will continue to stir up trouble for the new Taliban government.

The idea of coupling a small number of U.S. forces with a larger proxy force that would be protected by American airpower predated the counter-ISIS campaign. The concept of "by, with, and through" emerged decades ago, principally in the doctrine for special operations forces. A 2003 publication on the doctrine of joint operations defined the concept as calling for lengthy operations carried out by local forces who were trained, equipped, and supported by the United States. Elements of the approach have been applied over the years. During the 2001 U.S. intervention in Afghanistan to topple the Taliban, small numbers of U.S. special operators and CIA operatives aligned themselves with the Northern Alliance and Pashtun warlords as U.S. airpower punished the foe. Seven years later in Sadr City, a U.S. Army brigade and Iraqi troops took on Shiite militants while American commanders drew on an array of missile-firing drones, Apache attack helicopters, and reconnaissance aircraft in a battle that showed the potential of using a network of air war capabilities in urban warfare.

The "by, with, and through" approach employed in Inherent Resolve expanded greatly on these missions. It involved mounting a robust training mission, fielding a substantial corps of advisors, and then lashing them to an air armada, including around-the-clock reconnaissance as well as rocket and artillery fire. The strategy evolved throughout the campaign and was applied not just to a lone battle or a phase of the campaign but to the entire war.

Though the Pentagon has never formalized them, some lessons were already clear to current and former commanders. "By, with, and through" cannot be done effectively from a distance. The Obama administration's hesitance to let advisors accompany Iraqi and Peshmerga forces into the field, and its strict caps on the number of Special Operations Forces in Syria, sapped momentum during a critical phase of Inherent Resolve. The restrictions were relaxed over time but were not fully eased until Steve Townsend promulgated Tactical Directive No. 1 in the wake of the 9th Division's setback at Al-Salam Hospital in East Mosul, little more than a month before President Obama left office.

The "accompanying authorities," as they were called, were not only essential for allowing U.S. and allied service personnel to call in air strikes and gather better intelligence in a timely manner. They also enabled U.S. officers to better understand the plans, capabilities, and strategies of their partners, which sometimes changed by the hour, and thus gain their trust. This, in turn, gave the United States influence over important decisions, such as whether to open a northern front in West Mosul. It also gave partners more confidence to advance when the going got tough, as with the bridging operation over the Tigris that enabled Iraqi forces to advance to Qayyarah. Even when U.S. forces do not participate in the main combat on the ground, there is a benefit in sharing the battlefield, and at least some of the risks, with U.S. allies. Those insights are in danger of being lost as the Biden administration talks optimistically, and unrealistically, about how it hopes to keep terrorist dangers in Afghanistan in check through "over the horizon" air strikes.

Another lesson was that the United States does best when its partner is credible and principled, at least by the prevailing local standards, all the more so as it is American regional allies who are charged with the main burden of governing liberated areas. The United States found such partners, at least temporarily, with the SDF in Syria, and with the Iraqi and Peshmerga forces in Iraq. It would not have had such an alliance had it thrown in its lot with Turkish-backed Syrian fighters as Erdoğan urged, or with Russia's Syrian allies or many of the Shiite militias in Iraq.

The U.S. experience in Inherent Resolve also points to the need to formulate a better strategy for reducing harm to civilians. This means reducing civilian casualties as military operations proceed and also mitigating the longer-term risk to innocents when their infrastructure is destroyed, populations are displaced, and the international community is not always available to help them rebuild. The imperative is important not only for humanitarian reasons but also to avoid handing a propaganda victory to the enemy.

From the start, the "by, with, and through" strategy presented commanders with imperatives that were difficult to reconcile. Terrorists who were capable of exporting their violence to Western cities and prompting copycat attacks were to be destroyed before they could do more harm. American military casualties were to be held to the absolute minimum—preferably zero. Finally, no civilians were to be hurt. Reconciling these goals was all the more challenging in a campaign that involved urban warfare against a fanatical enemy that had had years to dig in and who often sought to prevent civilians from fleeing.

The military has techniques to limit "collateral damage," its antiseptic term for the unintended deaths of civilians and damage to their infrastructure. High-tech reconnaissance was conducted of potential targets, small munitions with special fusing were often employed to limit the scope of the blasts, and calculations were made of the "the noncombatant casualty cutoff value"—the number of innocents who were in danger of being killed in the vicinity of an authorized target. In Mosul, the U.S.-led coalition sought to disable the bridges that linked East and West Mosul in a way that would allow for their repair after the battle was won.

Technology, however, is far from a panacea. The adversary has its own tactics to counter U.S. reconnaissance. In Mosul, ISIS fighters knocked out interior walls so they could shift their firing positions without exposing themselves, while in Raqqa they covered streets with long canopies. The repeated use of what the military calls "precision" fires can itself produce a trail of destruction if the adversary repurposes hospitals as command centers and moves its fighters from one civilian structure to another. In Raqqa, 60 to 80 percent of the city was deemed to be uninhabitable after the battle. In a paradox that the U.S. military had not imagined when it began introducing laser- and satellite-guided bombs decades earlier, the city had been left in ruins not by carpet-bombing of the sort Donald Trump argued for on the campaign trail, but by precision air strikes—so many of them that they precisely destroyed one structure after another.

The U.S. use of proxy forces itself also carried risks because of the enormous firepower that was employed to keep the SDF, Iraqi forces, and Peshmerga moving forward. The air strikes and artillery fire often went beyond what would have been needed to facilitate operations by more proficient U.S. military units on the battlefield, and the local troops passing along strike requests sometimes were less exacting than U.S. infantry commanders more schooled in the laws of war. In effect, the United States held down its own military casualties by employing a strategy under which proxy forces—and by extension civilians—assumed more of the risks.

There are ways to adjust the "by, with, and through'" to diminish the danger of civilian harm, though some come with trade-offs that decision makers would need to embrace. Deploying more U.S. troops and allowing U.S. advisors to operate at the front instead of moving slightly behind its partner forces, as was generally the practice in fighting ISIS, could improve intelligence on the rapidly changing urban battlefields, notes a report by the RAND Corporation on reducing "civilian harm" in future conflicts that was prepared at the request of the Pentagon. The price would be a risk of greater U.S. casualties.

Eschewing the sort of encirclement strategy the United States used in Raqqa, and the "annihilation tactics" that Jim Mattis touted in the Pentagon briefing room, could make it easier to avoid a situation in which civilians were trapped in the interior of a city with terrorists who were prepared to die in place. Leaving a way out for civilians, however, could keep open an escape route for militants, too, and potentially lengthen a campaign, an outcome leaders would need to accept. In the case of Raqqa, it was Mazloum who urged the United States to suspend the assault and agree on an exit corridor for civilians and ISIS fighters to avoid a situation in which the campaign's larger objective of winning the peace would be overwhelmed. But that was an improvisation later in the battle.

A more efficient and better resourced system for fielding reports of collateral damage, investigating them on the ground once territory is retaken, and quickly making course corrections while a fight is still underway would also help. No measures, however, can turn the difficult business of digging a terrorist army out of foreign cities into an antiseptic enterprise. An awareness of the inevitable risks of urban combat should make officials in Washington and their foreign partners think twice before allowing the emergence of power vacuums that militants can exploit—as happened in Iraq following the U.S. military withdrawal from the country in 2011.

Finally, officials in Washington should avoid bold promises they cannot keep, such as "turning the page" on an era of "forever wars." The concept is misleading in an age in which the actions of terrorist groups cannot easily be foreseen; militant insurgencies are long-lasting; and the military actions Washington orders in response are carried out principally by local forces, backed up by U.S. advisors and airpower, and take time.

The military's efforts to identify the lessons of its counter-ISIS fight have been surprisingly scattershot for such a pivotal campaign. They included two brief Army studies of the Mosul and Raqqa battles, a declassified history by Lieutenant General Steve

Townsend's command, an oral history by Lieutenant General Pat White, several articles by some of the military's advisors in defense journals, and a detailed history of air operations by the RAND Corporation prepared at the Air Force's request. The Pentagon has not undertaken a systematic review to divine the lessons of the Inherent Resolve campaign. It is a common axiom that the military tends to fight the last war—that is, to assemble forces and carry out training to deal with familiar foes instead of preparing for the dangers on the horizon. There is also a risk, however, in doubling down on assumptions about the next war and assuming that the old days of messy counterterrorism campaigns will never come again. Even as the Pentagon pivots to Chinese and Russian threats, it is noteworthy that it has a model for hedging against terrorist dangers in distant regions that does not require large troop deployments; exploits U.S. strengths in intelligence, logistics, and precision firepower; and relies on local partners to do the bulk of the fighting. The strategy came about by trial and error, evolved over several years, was adapted to local conditions, involved breakthroughs as well as setbacks, still calls for more study, and had an ungainly name: Inherent Resolve.

DRAMATIS PERSONAE

THE AMERICANS

The Presidents

Barack Obama
President, 2009–2017

Donald Trump
President, 2017–2021

Joe Biden
Vice President, 2009–2017; President, 2021–

The Cabinet

Mike Pence
Vice President, 2017–2021

Chuck Hagel
Secretary of Defense, 2013–2015

Ashton Carter
Secretary of Defense, 2015–2017

James Mattis
Commander, U.S. Central Command, 2010–2013; Secretary of Defense, 2017–2019

Hillary Clinton
Secretary of State, 2009–2013

John Kerry
Secretary of State, 2013–2017

Rex Tillerson
Secretary of State, 2017–2018

Mike Pompeo
Director of the Central Intelligence Agency, 2017–2018; Secretary of State, 2018–2021

Antony Blinken
National Security Advisor to the Vice President, 2009–2013; Deputy National Security Advisor, 2013–2015; Deputy Secretary of State, 2015–2017; Secretary of State, 2021–

Tom Donilon
National Security Advisor, 2010–2013

Susan Rice
National Security Advisor, 2013–2017

H. R. McMaster
National Security Advisor, 2017–2018

John Bolton
National Security Advisor, 2018–2019

Denis McDonough
Deputy National Security Advisor, 2010–2013; White House Chief of Staff, 2013–2017

David Petraeus
Director of the Central Intelligence Agency, 2011–2012

The Diplomats

John R. Allen
Special Presidential Envoy for the Global Coalition to Counter the Islamic State in Iraq and the Levant, 2014–2015

Brett McGurk
Deputy Assistant Secretary of State for Iraq and Iran, 2014–2016; Special Presidential Envoy for the Global Coalition to Counter the Islamic State in Iraq and the Levant, 2015–2018; National Security Council Coordinator for the Middle East and North Africa, 2021–

James Jeffrey
Ambassador to Iraq, 2010–2012; Special Representative for Syria Engagement, 2018–2020; Special Presidential Envoy for the Global Coalition to Counter the Islamic State in Iraq and the Levant, 2019–2020

Robert Stephen Beecroft
Ambassador to Iraq, 2012–2014

Stu Jones
Ambassador to Iraq, 2014–2016

Doug Silliman
Ambassador to Iraq, 2016–2019

William Roebuck
Ambassador to Bahrain, 2015–2017; Representative to the Syrian Democratic

Forces and Deputy Special Envoy to the Global Coalition to Defeat ISIS, 2017–2020

Robert Ford
Ambassador to Syria, 2011–2014

The Generals

General Martin Dempsey
Chairman of the Joint Chiefs of Staff, 2011–2015

General Joseph Dunford
Chairman of the Joint Chiefs of Staff, 2015–2019

General Mark Milley
Chief of Staff of the Army, 2015–2019; Chairman of the Joint Chiefs of Staff, 2019–

Lieutenant General John Hesterman
Commander, U.S. Air Force Central Command and Combined Forces Air Component Command, Al-Udeid Air Base, 2013–2015

Lieutenant General Charles Q. Brown
Commander, U.S. Air Force Central Command and Combined Forces Air Component Command, Al-Udeid Air Base, 2015–2016

Lieutenant General Jeffrey Harrigian
Commander, U.S. Air Force Central Command and Combined Forces Air Component Command, Al-Udeid Air Base, 2016–2018

General Lloyd Austin
Commander, U.S. Central Command, 2013–2016; Secretary of Defense, 2021–

General Joseph Votel
Commander, U.S. Special Operations Command, 2014–2016; Commander, U.S. Central Command, 2016–2019

General Frank McKenzie
Commander, Combined Joint Task Force–Operation Inherent Resolve, 2019–2021; Commander, U.S. Central Command, 2019–

Lieutenant General James Terry
Commander, Combined Joint Task Force–Operation Inherent Resolve, 2014–2015; U.S. Army Central, 2013–2015

Lieutenant General Sean MacFarland
Commander, III Corps and Combined Joint Task Force–Operation Inherent Resolve, 2015–2016

Lieutenant General Steve Townsend
Commander, XVIII Airborne Corps and Combined Joint Task Force–Operation Inherent Resolve, 2016–2017

Lieutenant General Paul Funk
Commander, XVIII Airborne Corps and Combined Joint Task Force–Inherent Resolve, 2017–2018

Lieutenant General Paul LaCamera
Commander, XVIII Airborne Corps and Combined Joint Task Force–
Operation Inherent Resolve, 2018–2019

Lieutenant General Robert P. "Pat" White
Commander, III Corps and Combined Joint Task Force–Operation Inherent
Resolve, 2019–2020

Major General Mike Nagata
Commander, Special Operations Command Central, 2013–2015

Colonel Chris Donahue
Commander, 1st Special Forces Operational Detachment–Delta (Delta
Force), 2013–2014

Colonel Brett Sylvia
Commander, 2nd Brigade, 101st Airborne Division, 2016

Colonel Pat Work
Commander, 2nd Brigade, 82nd Airborne Division, 2017

THE SYRIANS

Mazloum Abdi
Commander, Syrian Democratic Forces (SDF)

General Chiya Kobani
Syrian Democratic Forces Field Commander, Middle Euphrates River
Valley operation

Bashar al-Assad
President, 2000–

THE IRAQIS

The Prime Ministers

Nouri al-Maliki
Prime Minister, 2006–2014

Haider al-Abadi
Prime Minister, 2014–2018

Adil Abdul Mahdi
Prime Minister, 2018–2020

Mustafa al-Kadhimi
Prime Minister, 2020–

The Generals

Lieutenant General Abdul Amir Rasheed Yarallah
Iraqi Security Forces (ISF) Commander, Mosul operation

General Talib Shaghati al-Kenani
Director, Counter Terrorism Service (CTS), 2006–2020

Lieutenant General Abdul Wahab al-Saadi
Deputy Commander of the Counterterrorism Command; Director, Counter Terrorism Service (CTS), 2020–

General Raed Shaker Jawdat
Commander, Federal Police

Major General Jassem Nazal Qassem
9th Armored Division Commander, Iraqi Army

Major General Najim al-Jabouri
Commander, Nineveh Operations Center

THE KURDS

Masoud Barzani
President of the Kurdistan Region of Iraq, 2005–2017

Masrour Barzani
Chancellor, Kurdistan Regional Security Council, 2011–; Prime Minister of the Kurdistan Region of Iraq, 2019–

Fuad Hussein
Chief of Staff to Masoud Barzani, 2005–2017; Foreign Minister of Iraq, 2020–

Lahur Talabani
Head, Counterterrorism Group

THE MILITIAS

Hadi al-Amiri
President of the Badr Organization, 2009–

Abu Mahdi al-Muhandis
Commander, Popular Mobilization Forces, 2014–2020; Secretary General of Kataib Hezbollah, 2003–2020

Muqtada al-Sadr
Leader of the Sadrist Movement, 2003–

ISIS

Abu Bakr al-Baghdadi
Leader of the Islamic State in Iraq, 2010–2013; leader of the Islamic State in Iraq and al-Sham, 2014–2019

Abu Ibrahim al-Hashimi al-Qurayshi
Leader of the Islamic State in Iraq and al-Sham, 2019–2022

Abu Omar al-Shishani
Senior commander and war minister of the Islamic State in Iraq and
al-Sham, 2013–2016

Abu Muhammad al-Adnani
Senior commander and spokesperson of the Islamic State in Iraq and
al-Sham, 2013–2016

OTHERS

Recep Tayyip Erdoğan
President of Turkey, 2014–

Lieutenant General Qassem Soleimani
Commander, Quds Force, Islamic Revolutionary Guard Corps, 1998–2020

King Abdullah
King and Prime Minister of Saudi Arabia, 2005–2015

King Salman
King and Prime Minister of Saudi Arabia, 2015–

Muhammad bin Zayed
Crown Prince of Abu Dhabi, 2004–

King Abdullah II
King of Jordan, 1999–

NOTES

INTRODUCTION

3 *the Islamic State*: The full name of the Islamic State in Iraq and al-Sham initially led to confusion over what it should be called in English. The coalition first called it ISIL, for Islamic State in Iraq and the Levant, since al-Sham is an Arabic word similar to the area known as the Levant. Others surmised the last S in ISIS should be translated as Syria. For this book, the group is referred to throughout as ISIS, short for the Islamic State in Iraq and al-Sham.

4 *"degrade and ultimately destroy"*: Barack Obama, "Remarks from the President on ISIL" (Washington, DC, September 10, 2014), The White House, https:// obamawhitehouse.archives.gov/the-press-office/2014/09/10/statement-president -isil-1.

6 *without my friend*: Richard Goldstein, "Bernard E. Trainor, 89, General Turned Military Analyst, Is Dead," *The New York Times*, June 4, 2018, https://www .nytimes.com/2018/06/04/obituaries/bernard-e-trainor-dead.html.

1. IMPALA RIDER

7 *A-team at Fort Lewis*: The A-Teams are the common name for the standard unit of Army Special Forces, known formally as Operational Detachments-Alpha.

7 *up-and-coming colonel*: On the day of the September 11, 2001, terrorist attacks, Chris Donahue, then a young Army captain, was serving as an aide to General Richard Myers, the chairman of the Joint Chiefs of Staff. General Ralph Eberhart, the commander of the North American Aerospace Command, called Donahue on the morning of 9/11 to get to his boss. Several planes had been hijacked. Richard B. Myers and Malcolm McConnell, *Eyes on the Horizon: Serving on the Front Lines of National Security* (New York: Threshold, 2009), 9.

8 *After stints with*: Davis Winkie, "Last Soldier Out of Afghanistan Was This Former Delta Force 2-Star," *Army Times*, August 31, 2021, https://www.armytimes.com /news/2021/08/31/last-soldier-out-of-afghanistan-was-this-former-delta-force-2 -star/.

8 *"The tide of war"*: "Moving America Forward," 2012 Democratic Party Platform (Charlotte, NC: Democratic National Committee, 2012).

8 *brazen jail breaks*: Following a jail break at Tikrit in 2012, ISIS, commonly called al-Qaeda in Iraq, launched a complicated assault complete with mortars and

small arms against the infamous Abu Ghraib prison and the Taji prison, claiming to have freed at least five hundred mujahideen. Michael R. Gordon and Duraid Adnan, "Brazen Attacks at Prisons Raise Worries of Al Qaeda's Strength in Iraq," *The New York Times*, July 23, 2013, https://www.nytimes.com/2013/07/24/world/middleeast/al-qaeda-asserts-responsibility-for-iraqi-prison-breaks.html?searchResultPosition=2.

11   *"I will say it very bluntly"*: Author interview with Mike Nagata.

12   *called a responsible end*: Barack Obama, "Bringing the War in Afghanistan to a Responsible End" (remarks, Washington, DC, May 27, 2014), The White House, https://obamawhitehouse.archives.gov/blog/2014/05/27/bringing-war-afghanistan-responsible-end.

12   *"The defense of freedom requires"*: President George W. Bush delivered this line in a speech at the National Defense University, Washington, DC. "Transcript of Bush Speech on Terrorism," *CNN*, March 8, 2005, http://www.cnn.com/2005/ALLPOLITICS/03/08/bush.transcript/.

12   *in his Chicago office*: Michael R. Gordon and Jeff Zeleny, "Interview with Barack Obama," *The New York Times*, November 1, 2007, https://www.nytimes.com/2007/11/01/us/politics/02obama-transcript.html.

12   *(AQI)–the Sunni jihadist*: Al-Qaeda in Iraq, led by Zarqawi and joined by Ansar al-Sunna veteran Abu Ali al-Anbari, who later became a top deputy to ISIS leader Abu Bakr Al-Baghdadi, was formally created in 2004 after Zarqawi pledged allegiance to Osama bin Laden. It was composed of jihadists, including veterans of the Iraq Army who renounced Baathism and secular nationalism. Aymenn Jawad al-Tamimi, "The Biography of Abu Ali al-Anbari: Full Translation and Analysis," aymennjawad.org, December 17, 2018, https://www.aymennjawad.org/21877/the-biography-of-abu-ali-al-anbari-full.

13   *Barbero recalled*: Author interview with Mike Barbero. Also see Contemporary Operations Study Team, Combat Studies Institute, "Interview with Lieutenant General Michael Barbero."

14   *During a swing through*: On the trip, U.S. partners in Israel and the Gulf expressed concern about U.S. staying power after a perceived abandonment of Hosni Mubarak to Islamists. Robert M. Gates, *Duty: Memoirs of a Secretary at War* (New York: Alfred A. Knopf, 2014), 507, 535, 536.

15   *down to sixteen thousand troops*: Michael R. Gordon, "In U.S. Exit from Iraq, Failed Efforts and Challenges," *The New York Times*, September 22, 2012, https://www.nytimes.com/2012/09/23/world/middleeast/failed-efforts-of-americas-last-months-in-iraq.html?searchResultPosition=2.

15   *distressed by Mullen's letter*: Gordon, "In U.S. Exit from Iraq, Failed Efforts and Challenges."

16   *negotiated the Bush-era SOFA*: "Unofficial Translation of U.S.-Iraq Troop Agreement from the Arabic Text," *McClatchy*, November 18, 2008, https://www.mcclatchydc.com/news/nation-world/world/article24511081.html.

16   *the diplomacy had ground*: Tim Arango and Michael Schmidt, "Despite Difficult Talks, U.S. and Iraq Had Expected Some American Troops to Stay," *The New York Times*, October 21, 2011, https://www.nytimes.com/2011/10/22/world/middleeast/united-states-and-iraq-had-not-expected-troops-would-have-to-leave.html?searchResultPosition=3.

17   *"A war is ending"*: "Remarks by President Barack Obama and Prime Minister al-Maliki of Iraq in a Joint Press Conference" (press conference, Washington, DC, December 12, 2011), The White House, https://obamawhitehouse.archives.gov/the-press-office/2011/12/12/remarks-president-obama-and-prime-minister-al-maliki-iraq-joint-press-co.

2. PLAN B

18   *Obama had rebuffed*: While Petraeus was Gates's preferred choice for chairman of the Joint Chiefs of Staff, Gates went into his last meeting with President Obama to discuss succession at the Pentagon knowing the White House would not accept the general for the post. Gates instead recommended Petraeus for CIA director; Leon Panetta, then CIA director, for secretary of defense; and General Martin Dempsey, then Army chief of staff, for chairman of the Joint Chiefs of Staff. Robert M. Gates, *Duty: Memoirs of a Secretary at War* (New York: Alfred A. Knopf, 2014), 546–547.

20   *Maliki told me*: Author interview with Nouri al-Maliki.

20   *his own vice presidency*: Owning the Iraq portfolio, Biden chaired a videoconference on the way forward for Iraq. Topics included who, if anyone, should succeed Maliki as prime minister. Michael R. Gordon and Bernard E. Trainor, *The Endgame: The Inside Story of the Struggle for Iraq, from George W. Bush to Barack Obama* (London: Atlantic Books, 2012), 643.

21   *warned that Maliki was moving*: Dan Morse, "Iraq Issues Arrest Warrant for Vice President on Terrorism Charges," *The Washington Post*, December 19, 2011, https://www.washingtonpost.com/world/middle_east/iraqi-government-issues -arrest-warrant-for-vice-president-on-terrorism-charges/2011/12/19/gIQA7bb D5O_story.html.

22   *On December 22*: A series of car bombings on December 22, 2011, killed at least 63 people and injured 185. The deadliest came when an ambulance filled with explosives detonated outside Iraq's Integrity Commission, initially killing 23 people, destroying the building and nearby apartments, and shattering windows ten blocks away. Jack Healy, "Blasts Rock Baghdad as Political Crisis in Iraq Deepens," *The New York Times*, December 22, 2011, https://www.nytimes.com /2011/12/23/world/middleeast/explosions-rock-baghdad-amid-iraqi-political -crisis.html?searchResultPosition=2.

26   *shuttering the Baghdad Police Academy*: Spencer Ackerman, "U.S. Quietly Ends Iraqi Police Training, Its Last Major Baghdad Project," *Wired*, March 18, 2013, https://www.wired.com/2013/03/iraqi-police/.

29   *A major setback*: A background paper from the Iraqi Ministry of the Interior (MOI) on how to treat disabled Iraqi police proposed a pilot program to provide care at a U.S. Defense Department facility and a weeklong visit to Walter Reed and the Brooke Army Medical Center in San Antonio, Texas, which has a special unit for treating burns. The MOI severely lacked the capacity to care for its wounded veterans, having only five physicians and fifty staff to care for between 800,000 and 900,000 police officers. The Federal Police itself only had two doctors among six divisions. The government of Iraq was willing to pay all expenses for travel and lodging to treat 20 MOI officers in the pilot program, which could eventually expand to more depending on its success. "Background Paper on Support to the Ministry of the Interior Health Care Initiatives."

29   *Caslen had sent a November 11*: Recognizing that the request wasn't necessarily the norm in terms of security cooperation, Caslen nonetheless gave his endorsement to Marrogi's proposal, noting that "this may present a unique opportunity to both strengthen and deepen our ties with Iraq." Robert L. Caslen to Robert Stephen Beecroft, November 11, 2012, Office of Security Cooperation, Iraq.

29   *once planned to capture*: Plans to detain Muqtada al-Sadr were devised as early as 2003. In a dissenting email from Lieutenant General Ricardo Sanchez, then commander of coalition ground forces in Iraq, to General John Abizaid, the CENTCOM commander at the time, Sanchez opposed any operation to detain

Sadr, arguing it would only make him a martyr and be cause for "open season" on the coalition. Ricardo Sanchez, email to John Abizaid, August 20, 2003, declassified by CENTCOM, 2015.

After members of Sadr's movement occupied the Shrine of Ali in Najaf, one of the holiest sites in Shia Islam, a memo from the Coalition Provisional Authority to the secretary of defense, secretary of state, and National Security Council characterized the episode as the "last straw" and argued that the coalition had multiple causes to arrest Sadr and should act on existing sealed warrants. Coalition Provisional Authority to Secretary of Defense, Secretary of State, and National Security Council, January 18, 2004, "The Last Straw: Muqtada Sadr's Supporters Make a Grab for Holiest Shia Shrine," declassified by CENTCOM, 2015.

The plan to kill or capture Sadr, named "Operation Stuart," aimed to capture Sadr in mid-February 2004 at the earliest. The plan called for extensive intelligence preparation before capturing Sadr at his home and transporting him to a prison at Camp Golf and eventually to Baghdad International Airport. In a PowerPoint outlining the operation, the coalition indicated that it knew Sadr's movement patterns, the number of women and children in his home, the number of guards surrounding him, and which car he was driven in. The operation was never carried out. "Operation Stuart," PowerPoint, Iraq, 2004, declassified by CENTCOM, 2015.

3. AN APPEAL FROM BAGHDAD

32   *had been finished off*: Waleed Ibrahim, "Al Qaeda's Two Top Iraq Leaders Killed in Raid," *Reuters*, April 19, 2010, https://www.reuters.com/article /us-iraq-violence-alqaeda/al-qaedas-two-top-iraq-leaders-killed-in-raid -idUSTRE63I3CL20100419.

33   *straightforward news article*: According to Brigadier General Kevin Bergner, the voice on the tapes purported to be that of Abu Omar al-Baghdadi was actually that of a man named Abu Abdullah al-Naima. The United States believed Baghdadi to be an invention created by the Egyptian-born AQI leader Abu Ayyub al-Masri to give the group an Iraqi face. The group's media emir, Khalid Abdul Fatah Daoud Mahmud al-Mashadani, who was captured by coalition forces, claimed Baghdadi was imaginary, although some terrorism experts cautioned that Mashadani could be lying to conceal the identity of Baghdadi if he were to exist. The military later discovered he did. Michael R. Gordon, "U.S. Says Insurgent Leader It Couldn't Find Never Was," *The New York Times*, July 19, 2007, https://www.nytimes.com/2007/07/19/world/middleeast/19baghdadi.html.

33   *Islamic State in Iraq*: Brian Fishman, *The Master Plan: ISIS, Al-Qaeda, and the Jihadi Strategy for Final Victory* (New Haven: Yale University Press, 2016), 112–16.

33   *the leadership post*: Haroro J. Ingram and Craig Whiteside, "Don't Kill the Caliph! The Islamic State and the Pitfalls of Leadership Decapitation," *War on the Rocks*, June 2, 2016, https://warontherocks.com/2016/06/dont-kill-the-caliph-the -islamic-state-and-the-pitfalls-of-leadership-decapitation/.

34   *the militants' pamphlets*: Fishman, *The Master Plan*.

34   *wrote one fighter*: Conflict Records Research Center (CRRC) AQ-MCOP-D-001-773, "A Hand Written Diary Belonging to an Insurgent," circa 2007 or 2008. Previously housed at the National Defense University, the CRRC contained digital copies of records captured from jihadist groups during the War on Terror, as well as from Saddam Hussein's regime. At the time of the center's closing due to budget cuts in June 2015, it was in the process of releasing more

AQI and early Islamic State records. Michael R. Gordon, "Archive of Captured Enemy Documents Closes," *The New York Times*, June 21, 2015, https://www .nytimes.com/2015/06/22/world/middleeast/archive-of-captured-terrorist -qaeda-hussein-documents-shuts-down.html.

34 *Islamic studies and jurisprudence*: William McCants, "The Believer," Brookings Institution, September 1, 2015, http://csweb.brookings.edu/content/research /essays/2015/thebeliever.html.

35 *"Fallujah Memorandum"*: Chapter 5 in Haroro J. Ingram, Craig Whiteside, and Charlie Winter (eds.), *The ISIS Reader: Milestone Texts of the Islamic State Movement* (New York: Oxford University Press, 2020), 107–45.

36 *a range of options*: Acknowledging that 65 to 75 percent of all foreign fighters in Iraq came from Syria, U.S. military officials prepared a confidential memo that outlined a variety of steps to force Damascus to rein in foreign fighter flows. Those steps ranged from demonstrative actions such as shows of force or psychological operations against Syrian leaders, to nonkinetic attacks such as cyberattacks or drone flights over Syria, and finally to military actions that would include cratering the runways at the Damascus airport. CENTCOM CCJ3 Info Paper, August 3, 2005, declassified by Michael Garrett, 2015.

36 *Myers told me years later*: Author interview with Richard Myers.

37 *a cross-border raid*: Abu Ghadiya had been under surveillance for months, and David Petraeus repeatedly asked for permission to eliminate him, only to be denied by President Bush. When Bush finally gave the go-ahead, a Predator strike was canceled when Ghadiya moved locations, so a direct raid was cleared to capture or kill him. Michael R. Gordon and Wesley Morgan, "The General's Gambit," *Foreign Policy*, October 1, 2012, https://foreignpolicy.com/2012/10/01 /the-generals-gambit/.

38 *its Arabic acronym, Daesh*: In Arabic, the name for the Islamic State in Iraq and al-Sham (a term for the Levant) was al-Dawlah al-Islamiyyah fi al-Iraq wa al-Sham, which became acronymized as Daesh.

38 *instead pledged fealty*: Mona Alami, "Syrian Rebels Pledge Loyalty to Al-Qaeda," *USA Today*, April 11, 2013, https://www.usatoday.com/story/news/world/2013 /04/11/syria-al-qaeda-connection/2075323/.

38 *delivered a major policy speech*: Antony Blinken, "Toward a New Partnership with Iraq" (speech, Washington, DC, March 16, 2012), The American Presidency Project, https://www.presidency.ucsb.edu/documents/remarks-deputy-assistant -the-president-and-national-security-advisor-the-vice-president.

39 *When Tim Arango*: Tim Arango, "Dozens Killed in Rising Iraqi Violence, Including at Least 40 by Truck Bomb," *The New York Times*, July 3, 2012, https:// www.nytimes.com/2012/07/04/world/middleeast/scores-killed-in-iraq-by-truck -bombs-explosives-and-gunfire.html?searchResultPosition=4.

39 *Blinken challenged the analysis*: Antony Blinken, letter to the editor, *The New York Times*, July 11, 2012, https://www.nytimes.com/2012/07/12/opinion/measuring -violence-in-iraq-a-biden-advisers-view.html?searchResultPosition=4.

43 *the right side of history*: Macon Phillips, "President Obama: 'The Future of Syria Must Be Determined by Its People, but President Bashar al-Assad Is Standing in Their Way'" (Washington, DC, August 18, 2011), The White House, https:// obamawhitehouse.archives.gov/blog/2011/08/18/president-obama-future-syria -must-be-determined-its-people-president-bashar-al-assad.

43 *"the magic words"*: Hannah Allam, "The 'Magic Words': How a Simple Phrase Enmeshed the U.S. in Syria's Crisis," *McClatchy*, August 15, 2015, https://www .mcclatchydc.com/news/nation-world/world/article31016274.html.

45 *went far over the line*: "Syria Chemical Attack: What We Know," *BBC*, September 24, 2013, https://www.bbc.com/news/world-middle-east-23927399.

46 *plan was abandoned after*: The imaginary attack route would parallel the route taken when Israeli aircraft mounted their September 2007 strike on Syria's Al-Kibar facility, which North Korea was helping to construct.

46 *The rethink began when*: "Syria Crisis: Cameron Loses Commons Vote on Syria Action," *BBC*, August 30, 2013, https://www.bbc.com/news/uk-politics -23892783.

46 *the Russians urged*: Michael R. Gordon and Steven Lee Myers, "Obama Calls Russia Offer on Syria Possible 'Breakthrough,'" *The New York Times*, September 9, 2013, https://www.nytimes.com/2013/09/10/world/middleeast/kerry-says -syria-should-hand-over-all-chemical-arms.html?searchResultPosition=19.

47 *trip to London*: Peter Baker and Michael R. Gordon, "An Unlikely Evolution, from Casual Proposal to Possible Resolution," *The New York Times*, September 10, 2013, https://www.nytimes.com/2013/09/11/world/middleeast/Syria-An -Unlikely-Evolution.html.

4. MAKE OR BREAK

49 *LaMois and his soldiers*: Author interview with Gabe LaMois.

50 *a lot of work to do*: The history of the CTS is detailed in a Brookings Institution paper by Colonel David Witty, a U.S. Army Special Forces officer in Baghdad who served as an advisor to the organization. In December 2003, the United States moved to establish an Iraqi counterterrorism force that would be multiethnic and multisectarian. Its members were trained by U.S. and Jordanian special forces. By May 2004, it was composed of two Iraq Special Operations Forces (ISOF) brigades. U.S. Special Forces advisors "lived at ISOF bases and were collocated with ISOF down to the company level," Witty wrote. David M. Witty, *The Iraqi Counter Terrorism Service* (Washington, DC: Brookings Institution, 2015), 6–7, 10, https://www.brookings.edu/wp-content/uploads/2016/06/David-Witty -Paper_Final_Web.pdf.

50 *add a third brigade*: Witty, *The Iraqi Counter Terrorism Service*, 26.

51 *had been dispensed with*: Some CTS courses would have graduation rates of 100 percent. Witty, *The Iraqi Counter Terrorism Service*, 26.

52 *during a visit to Rutbah*: Michael R. Gordon and Eric Schmitt, "U.S. Sends Arms to Aid Iraq Fight with Extremists," *The New York Times*, December 25, 2013, https://www.nytimes.com/2013/12/26/world/middleeast/us-sends-arms -to-aid-iraq-fight-with-extremists.html?searchResultPosition=1.

52 *Anbar province had camped out*: Patrick Markey and Suadad al-Salhy, "UPDATE 1-Tens of Thousands of Sunni Iraqis Rally Against Maliki," *Reuters*, January 11, 2013,https://www.reuters.com/article/iraq-protests-idCNL5E9CB6U620130111.

52 *to attack Fallujah and Ramadi*: ISIS had engaged in a gradual encirclement of Ramadi as early as 2013, with attacks in the city reaching forty-four a month by April 2014. While fighting for Ramadi, ISIS had by October captured Al-Qaim, Haditha, and Hit, cutting off the highway between Ramadi and Syria. By February, it had taken Al-Baghdadi close to Al-Asad Air Base. Surging from villages under their control, ISIS swiftly captured Al-Hawz, Al-Mala'ab, Fursan, and Al-Hay Dhubat. Controlling areas within and around Ramadi, ISIS had effectively fixed the Iraqi Army in place and was able to keep up its assault on the city center, eventually taking the government complex, the Iraqi Army's Anbar Operations Command Center, and Camp Ramadi, home to the 8th Brigade. Rick Burns, "The Fall of Ramadi: ISIS on the March," *Red Diamond*, November 2015.

53 *cemented their victory*: Yasir Ghazi and Tim Arango, "Iraq Fighters, Qaeda Allies, Claim Falluja as New State," *The New York Times*, January 3, 2014, https://www.nytimes.com/2014/01/04/world/middleeast/fighting-in-falluja-and -ramadi.html?searchResultPosition=4.

55 *Witty told me years later*: Author interview with David M. Witty.

56 *United Nations estimated*: Luke Harding, "Iraq Suffers Its Deadliest Year Since 2008," *The Guardian*, January 1, 2014, https://www.theguardian.com/world /2014/jan/01/iraq-2013-deadliest-year-since-2008.

57 *When Obama was asked*: David Remnick, "Going the Distance," *The New Yorker*, January 19, 2014, https://www.newyorker.com/magazine/2014/01/27/going-the -distance-david-remnick.

60 *As a stopgap*: Gordon and Schmitt, "U.S. Sends Arms to Aid Iraq Fight with Extremists."

60 *in a confidential letter*: The letter called broadly for more training for the CTS and the Iraqi Army and border guards; additional intelligence, target acqui- sition, surveillance, and reconnaissance for the border and desert between Nineveh and Karbala; improvements for Iraq's border defenses; the deployment of counterterrorism experts to Iraq; bunker-busting missiles that could pen- etrate ISIS structures but avoid harming civilians; and direct air support for Iraqi forces to control the border regions pursuant to the Strategic Framework Agreement. Lukman Faily to Jake Sullivan and Brett McGurk, Embassy of the Republic of Iraq, May 21, 2014.

61 *delivered from the Rose Garden*: Barack Obama, "Bringing the War in Afghan- istan to a Responsible End" (remarks, Washington, DC, May 27, 2014), The White House, https://obamawhitehouse.archives.gov/blog/2014/05/27/bringing -war-afghanistan-responsible-end.

5. ALL FALL DOWN

65 *Obeidi told me*: Author interview with Khalid al-Obeidi.

66 *reached the outskirts*: Rod Norland, "Extremists in Iraq Attack Shiite Shrine, Kill- ing 6," *The New York Times*, June 30, 2014, https://www.nytimes.com/2014/07 /01/world/middleeast/sunni-extremists-in-iraq-fire-mortars-into-shiite-shrine .html?searchResultPosition=1.

67 *sectarian militia engaged in*: Solomon Moore, "Brutality, Corruption Pervade Iraqi Police Force," *The Baltimore Sun*, July 9, 2006, https://www.baltimoresun .com/news/bs-xpm-2006-07-09-0607090150-story.html.

69 *in a series of texts*: Author interview with Atheel al-Nujaifi.

71 *had secretly stored*: Michael R. Gordon and Bernard E. Trainor, *The Endgame: The Inside Story of the Struggle for Iraq, from George W. Bush to Barack Obama* (Lon- don: Atlantic Books, 2012), 640.

71 *almost come to blows*: In an offensive aiming to push Sunni insurgents from Di- yala, Iraqi forces also confronted the Peshmerga in several disputed settlements. The stalemate eased after Army Staff Sergeant Dave Schlicher kept leaders on both sides in the mayor's office for more than five hours, earning him the nickname "General Schlicher." Scott Peterson, "US Referees Iraq's Troubled Kurdish-Arab Fault Line," *The Christian Science Monitor*, October 21, 2008, https://www.csmonitor.com/World/Middle-East/2008/1021/p01s04-wome .html.

73 *notorious Badush prison*: On June 10, 2014, ISIS also carried out a large massa- cre at the prison, systematically separating Sunnis from Shia and executing six hundred of the latter after lining them up in front of a ravine. There were only fifteen Shiite survivors. "Iraq: ISIS Executed Hundreds of Prison Inmates,"

Human Rights Watch, October 30, 2014, https://www.hrw.org/news/2014/10/30
/iraq-isis-executed-hundreds-prison-inmates#.

74 *read the headline*: The words "Big City" appeared in an early edition of the article,
but in the archived version they were changed to "Mosul." Suadad Al-Salhy and
Tim Arango, "Sunni Militants Drive Iraqi Army Out of Mosul," *The New York
Times*, June 10, 2014, https://www.nytimes.com/2014/06/11/world/middleeast
/militants-in-mosul.html?searchResultPosition=3.

74 *Tikrit gave way*: "Iraq Crisis: Militants 'Seize Tikrit' After Taking Mosul," *BBC*,
June 11, 2014, https://www.bbc.com/news/world-middle-east-27800319.

75 *Hundreds of cadets*: Tim Arango, "Escaping Death in Northern Iraq," *The New
York Times*, September 3, 2014, https://www.nytimes.com/2014/09/04/world
/middleeast/surviving-isis-massacre-iraq-video.html.

75 *died in a U.S. air strike*: Peter Cook, "Statement from Pentagon Press Secretary
Peter Cook on Nov. 13 Airstrike in Libya," press release, U.S. Department of
Defense, December 7, 2015, https://www.defense.gov/News/Releases/Release
/Article/633221/statement-from-pentagon-press-secretary-peter-cook-on-nov
-13-airstrike-in-libya/source/GovDelivery/.

76 *Maliki told me*: Author interview with Nouri al-Maliki.

76 *henceforth be known*: "Isis Rebels Declare 'Islamic State' in Iraq and Syria,"
BBC, June 30, 2014, https://www.bbc.com/news/world-middle-east-28082962.

77 *The most dramatic gesture*: Alissa J. Rubin, "Militant Leader in Rare Appearance
in Iraq," *The New York Times*, July 5, 2014, https://www.nytimes.com/2014/07
/06/world/asia/iraq-abu-bakr-al-baghdadi-sermon-video.html.

6. BACK TO THE FUTURE

78 *leaving by charter aircraft*: Tim Arango and Michael R. Gordon, "U.S. Plans to
Evacuate Many Embassy Workers," *The New York Times*, June 15, 2014, https://
www.nytimes.com/2014/06/16/world/middleeast/embassy.html.

84 *issued a fatwa*: Alissa J. Rubin, Suadad Al-Salhy, and Rick Gladstone, "Iraqi Shiite Cleric Issues Call to Arms," *The New York Times*, June 13, 2014, https://www
.nytimes.com/2014/06/14/world/middleeast/iraq.html?searchResultPosition=1.

84 *Sistani hailed from*: Michael R. Gordon and Bernard E. Trainor, *The Endgame:
The Inside Story of the Struggle for Iraq, from George W. Bush to Barack Obama*
(London: Atlantic Books, 2012), 40.

84 *Sistani was in the room*: Gordon and Trainor, *The Endgame*, 42.

85 *twice-daily flights*: Michael R. Gordon and Eric Schmitt, "Iran Secretly Sending
Drones and Supplies into Iraq, U.S. Officials Say," *The New York Times*, June
25, 2014, https://www.nytimes.com/2014/06/26/world/middleeast/iran-iraq.html
?searchResultPosition=3.

86 *military equipment to Damascus*: Michael R. Gordon, "Iran Supplying Syrian Military via Iraqi Airspace," *The New York Times*, September 4, 2012, https://www
.nytimes.com/2012/09/05/world/middleeast/iran-supplying-syrian-military-via
-iraq-airspace.html?searchResultPosition=6.

90 *readily acquiesced to*: Gordon and Trainor, *The Endgame*, 639.

93 *airtight promise*: Peter Baker, "Diplomatic Note Promises Immunity from Iraqi
Law for U.S. Advisory Troops," *The New York Times*, June 23, 2014, https://www
.nytimes.com/2014/06/24/world/middleeast/us-advisory-troops-get-immunity
-from-iraqi-law.html?searchResultPosition=25.

93 *leadership of the Islamic Dawa*: Islamic Dawa Party to Ali al-Husseini al-Sistani,
June 25, 2014.

94 *Sistani responded in a letter*: Ali al-Husseini al-Sistani to Islamic Dawa Party, July
9, 2014.

7. IRAQ FIRST

100 *Austin directed the*: To get ahead of the quickly collapsing situation in Iraq, Austin directed three lines of effort: 1) an ISR surge and preparation for deliberate strikes and RPA strikes; 2) a plan to embed Special Forces advisors, stand up a joint intelligence fusion cell, and initiate info ops; and 3) the refinement of plans for an orderly embassy departure.

100 *became more complicated*: Michael R. Gordon and Eric Schmitt, "Iran Sends 3 Attack Planes to Iraqi Government," *The New York Times*, July 8, 2014, https://www.nytimes.com/2014/07/09/world/middleeast/iran-sends-3-attack-planes-to-iraqi-government.html?searchResultPosition=3.

102 *Nearly 800 Yazidis*: Damien Cave and James Glanz, "Toll in Iraq Bombings Is Raised to More Than 500," *The New York Times*, August 22, 2007, https://www.nytimes.com/2007/08/22/world/middleeast/22iraq-top.html; Felice D. Gaer et al., *Report of the United States Commission on Religious Freedom in Iraq* (Washington, DC: U.S. Commission on International Religious Freedom, 2008), 2, https://www.uscirf.gov/sites/default/files/resources/iraq%20report%20final.pdf#page=20.

102 *fled the ISIS onslaught*: An informal understanding existed between the Yazidis of Sinjar and Masoud Barzani's Kurdistan Democratic Party (KDP), in which the Peshmerga defended Sinjar in return for Sinjaris' votes for the KDP. Despite the arrangement, most Peshmerga fled the approaching ISIS fighters. Christine Van Den Toorn, "How the U.S.-Favored Kurds Abandoned the Yazidis When ISIS Attacked," *The Daily Beast*, August 17, 2014, https://www.thedailybeast.com/how-the-us-favored-kurds-abandoned-the-yazidis-when-isis-attacked.

102 *slaughtered thousands of*: During the capture of Sinjar and ongoing massacre of Yazidi males, ISIS also captured the critical dam north of Mosul. Tim Arango, "Jihadists Rout Kurds in North and Seize Strategic Iraqi Dam," *The New York Times*, August 7, 2014, https://www.nytimes.com/2014/08/08/world/middleeast/isis-forces-in-iraq.html?_r=0.

102 *forced Yazidi women*: According to one report, there was disagreement within the Islamic State's leadership on whether or not to enslave the Yazidis. Salem al-Jabouri, an aide to Abu Bakr al-Baghdadi, told the BBC that one faction, led by Abu Ali al-Anbari, opposed oppressing the Yazidis because they were Iraqi and it could lead to retribution. They also opposed the enslavement of Christian women. But Baghdadi's eventual successor, Abu Ibrahim al-Hashimi al-Qurayshi, believed that enslaving the Yazidis was justified under Islamic law. Feras Kilani, "A Caliph Without a Caliphate: The Biography of ISIS's New Leader," *Newlines Magazine*, April 15, 2021, https://newlinesmag.com/reportage/a-caliph-without-a-caliphate-the-biography-of-isiss-new-leader/.

102 *into sexual slavery*: ISIS would abduct more than five thousand Yazidi women and girls and subject many of them to sexual slavery, arguing that the Koran obligated believers to rape nonbelievers. Rukmini Callimachi, "ISIS Enshrines a Theology of Rape," *The New York Times*, August 13, 2015, https://www.nytimes.com/2015/08/14/world/middleeast/isis-enshrines-a-theology-of-rape.html.

102 *trudged up rugged mountain*: Alissa J. Rubin, "For Refugees on Mountain, 'No Water, Nothing,'" *The New York Times*, August 9, 2014, https://www.nytimes.com/2014/08/10/world/middleeast/chased-onto-iraqi-mountain-there-is-no-water-nothing.html?searchResultPosition=4.

103 *Yazidi American community made*: Dina Al-Shibeeb, "'Abandoned' Yazidis Seek U.S. Action from White House Trip," *Al Arabiya*, November 17, 2014, https://english.alarabiya.net/perspective/features/2014/11/17/-Abandoned-Yazidis-seek-U-S-action-from-White-House-trip-1193.

103 *Bashur Airfield*: The base was well known to the U.S. Special Operations community: during the invasion of Iraq, nearly one thousand troops from the 173rd Airborne Brigade had parachuted into the airfield to set up operations for the northern front directed against Saddam Hussein.

104 *The air drop began*: Helene Cooper, Mark Landler, and Alissa J. Rubin, "Obama Allows Limited Airstrikes on ISIS," *The New York Times*, August 7, 2014, https://www.nytimes.com/2014/08/08/world/middleeast/obama-weighs-military -strikes-to-aid-trapped-iraqis-officials-say.html?searchResultPosition=5.

104 *dropped more than*: Jennifer Hlad, "Breaking the Siege on Sinjar," *Air Force Magazine*, September 28, 2015, https://www.airforcemag.com/article/breaking-the -siege-on-sinjar

104 *launched air strikes*: Alissa J. Rubin, Tim Arango, and Helene Cooper, "U.S. Jets and Drones Attack Militants in Iraq, Hoping to Stop Advance," *The New York Times*, August 8, 2014, https://www.nytimes.com/2014/08/09/world/middleeast /iraq.html?searchResultPosition=6.

104 *reports that the Yekîneyên Parastina Gel*: Tracey Shelton, "'If It Wasn't for the Kurdish Fighters, We Would Have Died Up There,'" *Global Post*, August 29, 2014, https://www.pri.org/stories/2014-08-29/if-it-wasn-t-kurdish-fighters-we -would-have-died-there.

105 *flew to Mount Sinjar*: The commandos were also accompanied by U.S. Marines. Helene Cooper and Michael Shear, "Militants' Siege on Mountain in Iraq Is Over, Pentagon Says," *The New York Times*, August 13, 2014, https://www .nytimes.com/2014/08/14/world/middleeast/iraq-yazidi-refugees.html?_r=0.

105 *the operation had worked*: Shortly after the relief operation on Mount Sinjar, the United States would conduct another humanitarian airdrop. ISIS had surrounded the predominantly Turkmen town of Amirli in June, and for the next several months the Iraqi Security Forces attempted to lift the siege with the assistance of the United States, France, Australia, and the United Kingdom. The United States airlifted humanitarian supplies, and the Iraqis broke the siege by the end of August. Helene Cooper, "U.S. Strikes Militants Besieging Turkmen in Iraq," *The New York Times*, August 30, 2014, https://www.nytimes .com/2014/08/31/world/middleeast/us-strikes-militants-besieging-turkmen-in -iraq.html?searchResultPosition=5; Katharine Lackey and Tom Vanden Brook, "Iraqi Forces Break Militant Siege After U.S. Airstrikes," *USA Today*, August 31, 2014, https://www.usatoday.com/story/news/world/2014/08/31/iraq-military -us-airstrikes-amirli/14897741/.

105 *from the State Dining Room*: Barack Obama, "Statement by the President" (Washington, DC, August 7, 2014), The White House, https://obamawhitehouse .archives.gov/the-press-office/2014/08/07/statement-president.

107 *as the militants moved*: Becca Wasser et al., *The Air War Against the Islamic State: The Role of Airpower in Operation Inherent Resolve* (Santa Monica, CA: RAND Corporation, 2021), 22, https://www.rand.org/pubs/research_reports/RRA388-1.html.

109 *which ISIS had seized*: A threat report issued by the U.S. Army's Training and Doctrine Command detailed the battlefield tactics that had allowed ISIS to seize and defend territory as effectively as it had. For Mosul Dam, ISIS had prepared an area defense integrating various buildings and civilian hostages into "complex battle positions." ISIS put various obstacles and IEDs around the dam, not to destroy the Iraqi soldiers' eventual assault but to slow them down and corral them effectively into kill zones. ISIS particularly maintained tactical flexibility: it was able to shift forces to reach locations quickly and launch small counterattacks with small arms, rocket-propelled grenades, and technical support while utilizing camouflage, cover, concealment, and deception. TRADOC

G-2 Intelligence Support Activity, "Threat Tactics Report: Islamic State of Iraq and the Levant," November 2014.

109 *Joe Biden had called*: Dexter Filkins, "A Bigger Problem Than ISIS," *The New Yorker*, January 2, 2017. https://www.newyorker.com/magazine/2017/01/02/a -bigger-problem-than-isis?utm_source=NYR_REG_GATE. Also noted in Wasser et al., *The Air War Against the Islamic State*, p. 135.

111 *use of punishing airpower*: Wasser et al., *The Air War Against the Islamic State*, 136.

111 *the dam and several*: Helene Cooper, Mark Landler, and Azam Ahmed, "Troops in Iraq Rout Sunni Militants from a Key Dam," *The New York Times*, August 18, 2014, https://www.nytimes.com/2014/08/19/world/middleeast/iraq-mosul -dam.html?searchResultPosition=39.

111 *eighty-five air strikes*: Wasser et al., *The Air War Against the Islamic State*, 136.

112 *beginning to take shape*: Kareem Fahim and Azam Ahmed, "Lawmakers Approve Cabinet in Iraq, but 2 Posts Are Empty," *The New York Times*, September 8, 2014, https://www.nytimes.com/2014/09/09/world/middleeast/iraq.html ?searchResultPosition=8.

112 *The new president*: "Kurdish Politician Elected Iraq's New President," Radio Free Europe/Radio Liberty, July 24, 2014, https://www.rferl.org/a/iraq-kurd -new-president/25468998.html.

112 *As for the speaker*: Alissa J. Rubin and Suadad Al-Salhy, "Iraqi Parliament Elects Speaker in Effort to Form New Government," *The New York Times*, July 15, 2014, https://www.nytimes.com/2014/07/16/world/middleeast/iraq.html.

112 *unveiled his new strategy*: Barack Obama, "Remarks from the President on ISIL" (Washington, DC, September 10, 2014), The White House, https://obamawhite house.archives.gov/the-press-office/2014/09/10/statement-president-isil-1.

8. TALON ANVIL

117 *had clashed violently*: Michael M. Gunter, "The KDP-PUK Conflict in Northern Iraq," *Middle East Journal* 50, no. 2 (Spring 1996): 224–241, http://www .jstor.org/stable/4328927.

117 *individual Peshmerga units*: The competing institutions of the PUK and the KDP resulted in a dual-governance structure within the Kurdistan Region of Iraq. Both parties controlled not only their own military forces but also their own intelligence services, media arms, and other civil society institutions.

118 *dubbed "Viking Hammer"*: Kenneth Finlayson, "Operation Viking Hammer: 3/10 SFG Against the Ansar Al-Islam," *Veritas* 1, no. 1 (2005), https://arsof -history.org/articles/v1n1_op_viking_hammer_page_1.html.

118 *Lahur Talabani recalled*: Author interview with Lahur Talabani.

119 *described as political work*: Born in the town of Kobani in Syria, Mazloum was involved in the PKK at an early age. PKK founder Abdullah Öcalan made Kobani his refuge during his years of exile from Turkey. Mazloum was based in Europe between 1997 and 2003 to build the PKK brand. Can Acun and Bünyamin Keskin, *The PKK's Branch in Northern Syria: PYD-YPG*, SETA Publications 82 (Ankara, Turkey: SETA, 2017), 74, https://www.setav.org/en/the-pkks-branch -in-northern-syria-pyd-ypg.

In interviews, Mazloum vaguely referred to his time in Europe as "political work." Ben Hubbard and Eric Schmitt, "Mazlum Kobani Called the U.S. 'Comrades in Arms' Against ISIS. Now the U.S. Is Eyeing the Exit," *The New York Times*, May 12, 2019, https://www.nytimes.com/2019/05/12/world /middleeast/syria-sdf-us-islamic-state.html. In one interview, Mazloum claimed to have been imprisoned five times by the Syrian government. Robin Wright, "America's Ally in Syria Warns of Ethnic Cleansing by Turkey," *The New Yorker*,

October 20, 2019, https://www.newyorker.com/news/q-and-a/americas-ally-in
-syria-warns-of-ethnic-cleansing-by-turkey.

Later he was alleged to have overseen the special forces of the Kurdish
Yekîneyên Parastina Gel (YPG). Acun and Keskin, *The PKK's Branch in Northern Syria*, 74.

119 *The Turks knew him*: Turkish sources allege that Mazloum operated in Turkey
as a PKK commander between 1991 and 1996 under the nom de guerre Sahin
Cilo. Yeter Ada Şeko, "Mazloum Kobani Is Becoming Another Thorn in US-
Turkey Relations," *Politics Today*, November 22, 2019, https://politicstoday.org
/mazloum-kobani-is-becoming-another-thorn-in-us-turkey-relations/; Acun and
Keskin, *The PKK's Branch in Northern Syria*, 74.

During Mazloum's time in Europe, BBC Turkey reported that Abdullah
Öcalan had mentioned him in a court statement, claiming that a cease-fire pro-
posal between the PKK and Turkey was passed through Mazloum, then known
as Ferhat Abdi Sahin. "Mazlum Kobani Kimdir: Trump'ın Teşekkür Ettiği,
Erdoğan'ın 'Bize Teslim Edin' Dediği SDG Komutanı," BBC News–Türkçe,
October 25, 2019, https://www.bbc.com/turkce/haberler-dunya-50179867.

120 *met earlier that day*: Robin Wright, "How Trump Betrayed the General Who Defeated ISIS," *The New Yorker*, April 4, 2019, https://www.newyorker.com/news
/dispatch/how-trump-betrayed-the-general-who-defeated-isis.

121 *Ankara saw as a*: The United States had fully understood Turkey's animus toward the PKK during its occupation of Iraq. When he commanded the U.S.
and allied forces in Iraq, David Petraeus had even made a secret arrangement
so that Turkish warplanes could fly into Iraqi airspace to bomb PKK operatives
who were using northern Iraq as a sanctuary, a move that he calculated would
forestall a broader Turkish intervention. Gordon and Trainor, *The Endgame*,
449–55.

122 *A setback came*: Ben Hubbard, "ISIS Militants Capture Jordanian Fighter Pilot
in Syria," *The New York Times*, December 24, 2014, https://www.nytimes.com
/2014/12/25/world/middleeast/isissyria.html?searchResultPosition=42.

122 *set on fire by*: "ISIS Burns Hostage Alive," Fox News, February 3, 2015, https://
video.foxnews.com/v/4030583977001#sp=show-clips.

122 *and the partners*: In the immediate aftermath of the Jordanian pilot shootdown,
the United Arab Emirates suspended its air strikes until the United States agreed
to place V-22 Ospreys in northern Iraq instead of Kuwait for enhanced search
and rescue. Helene Cooper, "United Arab Emirates, Key U.S. Ally in ISIS Effort, Disengaged in December," *The New York Times*, February 3, 2015, https://
www.nytimes.com/2015/02/04/world/middleeast/united-arab-emirates-key-us
-ally-in-isis-effort-disengaged-in-december.html?searchResultPosition=11.

123 *more than fifty thousand*: Some 60,000 refugees from Kobani and some 130,000
refugees from elsewhere in northern Syria fled to Turkey to escape ISIS. Daren
Butler, "Turkey Struggles with Spillover as Syrian Kurds Battle Islamic State,"
Euronews, September 22, 2014, https://web.archive.org/web/20140922220715
/http://www.euronews.com/newswires/2699412-turkish-deputy-pm-says
-45000-syrian-kurds-enter-turkey-fleeing-islamic-state-advance.

124 *"highly possible"*: Lloyd Austin, "Department of Defense Press Briefing by General Austin in the Pentagon Briefing Room," U.S. Department of Defense, October 17, 2014, https://www.defense.gov/News/Transcripts/Transcript/Article
/606948/department-of-defense-press-briefing-by-general-austin-in-the
-pentagon-briefing/.

124 *ISIS had an estimated four thousand*: Becca Wasser et al., *The Air War Against
the Islamic State: The Role of Airpower in Operation Inherent Resolve* (Santa Mon-

ica, CA: RAND Corporation, 2021), 142, https://www.rand.org/pubs/research
_reports/RRA388-1.html.

124   *The first big airdrop*: Eric Schmitt, "U.S. Airdrops Weapons and Supplies to
Kurds Fighting in Kobani," *The New York Times*, October 20, 2014, https://www
.nytimes.com/2014/10/20/world/middleeast/us-airdrops-weapons-and-supplies
-to-kurds-fighting-in-kobani.html?searchResultPosition=1.

125   *one shipment of rocket-propelled grenades*: The misdirected shipment was destroyed by a coalition air strike before it could be captured by ISIS. Wasser
et al., *The Air War Against the Islamic State*, 149.

125   *"People sitting at home"*: Author interview with Fuad Hussein.

126   *the Peshmerga relief column*: Kareem Fahim and Karam Shoumali, "Turkey to
Let Iraqi Kurds Cross to Syria to Fight ISIS," *The New York Times*, October
20, 2014, https://www.nytimes.com/2014/10/21/world/middleeast/kobani-turkey
-kurdish-fighters-syria.html?searchResultPosition=3.

127   *Mazloum's own house*: The YPG and ISIS traded control of Mazloum's house
three times. On the third time, Mazloum gave the United States its GPS coordinates and asked them to bomb it. Luke Mogelson, "America's Abandonment of
Syria," *The New Yorker*, April 27, 2020, https://www.newyorker.com/magazine
/2020/04/27/americas-abandonment-of-syria.

127   *According to U.S. calculations*: The United States expended an extraordinary
amount of airpower throughout the battle, conducting 663 total strikes, with
this particular battle comprising just shy of 40 percent of all coalition air strikes
during the time frame of the battle, and 80 percent of strikes in Syria. Notably,
the battle was also the first instance in which the U.S. military used the F-22
Raptor in a combat role. Wasser et al., *The Air War Against the Islamic State*,
144–147.

127   *unusual joint operation*: Orhan Coskun, "Turkish Military Enters Syria to Evacuate Soldiers, Relocate Tomb," *Reuters*, February 22, 2015, https://www.reuters
.com/article/us-syria-crisis-turkey-idUSKBN0LQ03U20150222.

127   *A few months later*: Cale Salih, "Is Tal Abyad a Turning Point for Syria's Kurds?,"
BBC, June 16, 2015, https://www.bbc.com/news/world-middle-east-33146515;
Tom Perry and Laila Bassam, "Syria Kurds Seize Town from Islamic State
Near Its 'Capital,'" *Reuters*, June 23, 2015, https://www.reuters.com/article
/us-mideast-crisis-syria/syria-kurds-seize-town-from-islamic-state-near-its
-capital-idUSKBN0P316F20150623.

129   *written an impassioned article*: John R. Allen, "Destroy the Islamic State Now,"
Defense One, August 20, 2014, https://www.defenseone.com/ideas/2014/08/gen
-allen-destroy-islamic-state-now/92012/.

130   *but for a different position*: Thom Shanker, "To Lead Afghan War, Obama
Chooses Marine Known for Swaying Sunnis in Iraq," *The New York Times*,
April 28, 2011, https://www.nytimes.com/2011/04/29/world/asia/29allen.html.

130   *"Multilateralism regulates hubris"*: Jeffrey Goldberg, "The Obama Doctrine,"
The Atlantic, April 2016, https://www.theatlantic.com/magazine/archive/2016
/04/the-obama-doctrine/471525/.

134   *only to stumble*: Rod Norland and Helene Cooper, "U.S. Airstrikes on ISIS in
Tikrit Prompt Boycott by Shiite Fighters," *The New York Times*, March 26,
2015, https://www.nytimes.com/2015/03/27/world/middleeast/iraq-us-air-raids
-islamic-state-isis.html?searchResultPosition=36.

9. THE DARKEST HOUR

136   *Chuck Hagel handed over*: Helene Cooper, "Hagel Resigns Under Pressure as
Global Crises Test Pentagon," *The New York Times*, November 24, 2014, https://

www.nytimes.com/2014/11/25/us/hagel-said-to-be-stepping-down-as-defense
-chief-under-pressure.html.

136 *Ashton Carter*: Barack Obama, "Remarks by the President in Nominating Ashton Carter as Secretary of Defense" (Washington, DC, December 5, 2014), The White House, https://obamawhitehouse.archives.gov/the-press-office/2014/12/05 /remarks-president-nominating-ashton-carter-secretary-defense.

136 *had accompanied him in*: Michael R. Gordon and Bernard E. Trainor, *The End-game: The Inside Story of the Struggle for Iraq, from George W. Bush to Barack Obama* (London: Atlantic Books, 2012), 533.

136 *the wonkish Carter had coauthored*: Carter authored the book alongside President Bill Clinton's second secretary of defense, William Perry. Ashton B. Carter and William J. Perry, *Preventive Defense: A New Security Strategy for America* (Washington, DC: Brookings Institution, 1999).

137 *"Team America"*: Ashton Carter, *A Lasting Defeat: The Campaign to Destroy ISIS* (Cambridge, MA: Belfer Center for Science and International Affairs, 2017), 5.

139 *Allen's proposal to*: This was not a new idea. Doug Lute, an Army lieutenant general, had run a similar "cell" in Iraq for George W. Bush when his administration was trying to carry out the "surge." The White House could not fight a war by holding a meeting every time a decision had to be made.

139 *bird and animal feces*: U.S. Marine Corps History Division, interview with Katherine Scoffield.

140 *"a Valley Forge scenario"*: U.S. Marine Corps History Division, interview with Sean Hankard.

140 *for perhaps a hundred miles*: U.S. Marine Corps History Division, interview with Samuel McGrury.

140 *a ten-man ISIS squad*: In later oral history interviews with the Marines present, Lieutenant Colonel Sean Hankard would recall the attack on Al-Asad. Already dealing with low morale among the Iraqis on the base, Hankard was going about his day when he heard others discussing gunfire from that morning. Hankard realized the base was under attack, but the Marines were unsure whether the attack was restricted to the Iraqi part of the base or whether ISIS was disguised as Iraqi soldiers. One or two of the attackers got within fifty meters of the division headquarters wearing Iraqi Army uniforms, and all had suicide vests. All the attackers—eight who came into the base and two who stayed outside—were killed. U.S. Marine Corps History Division, interview with Sean Hankard.

141 *sought to inoculate*: Jon Harper, "Dempsey: Embattled Ramadi Not as Important as Oil Center Beiji," *Stars and Stripes*, April 16, 2015, https://www.stripes .com/theaters/middle_east/dempsey-embattled-ramadi-not-as-important-as -oil-center-beiji-1.340605.

142 *provoked a scorching response*: Lindsey Graham and John McCain, "Statement by Senators Graham and McCain on General Dempsey Diminishing Possible Fall of Ramadi to ISIL," April 17, 2015, https://www.lgraham.senate.gov/public /index.cfm/2015/4/statement-by-senators-graham-and-mccain-on-general -dempsey-diminishing-possible-fall-of-ramadi-to-isil.

142 *why was its security*: Dempsey's comments betrayed a misunderstanding of the Islamic State's history. When the group unfurled its black banner in 2006, it declared Ramadi to be its capital, its third at the time after being chased from Fallujah and Al-Qaim by the United States. Gordon and Trainor, *The Endgame*, 229.

142 *adjusted the message*: Thomas Weidley, "Department of Defense Press Briefing with General Weidley via Teleconference from Southwest Asia," U.S. Department of Defense, May 15, 2015, https://www.defense.gov/News/Transcripts

/Transcript/Article/607050/department-of-defense-press-briefing-with-general
-weidley-via-teleconference-fr/.

144 *Abadi had a change of heart*: Kristina Wong, "Coalition Airstrikes Destroying
Abandoned Vehicles in Ramadi," *The Hill*, May 22, 2015, https://thehill.com
/policy/defense/242956-coalition-airstrikes-destroying-abandoned-vehicles-in
-iraq.

151 *direct combat mission*: It was not a new idea. James Jeffrey had developed a similar
Plan B when he served as the U.S. ambassador in Baghdad.

151 *Obama went to the Pentagon briefing*: Barack Obama, "Remarks by the President
on Progress in the Fight Against ISIL" (Washington, DC, July 6, 2015), The
White House, https://obamawhitehouse.archives.gov/the-press-office/2015/07/06
/remarks-president-progress-fight-against-isil.

10. COMBAT

152 *Risha himself was assassinated*: "Top Sunni Sheik Killed in IED Attack," ABC
News, February 12, 2009, https://abcnews.go.com/Politics/story?id=3596631.

152 *"I am more convinced"*: Sean MacFarland, personal diary.

153 *"Rather than three"*: Marcus Weisgerber and Patrick Tucker, "Meet the New
Army General in Charge of the ISIS War," *Defense One*, October 23, 2015,
https://www.defenseone.com/business/2015/10/meet-new-army-general-charge
-isis-war/123105/.

154 *Joseph Dunford took over*: Leo Shane III, "Senate Confirms Dunford as Next Joint
Chiefs Chairman," *Military Times*, July 29, 2015, https://www.militarytimes.com
/news/your-military/2015/07/29/senate-confirms-dunford-as-next-joint-chiefs
-chairman/.

154 *But after his plane*: Richard Sisk, "Iraqis Try to Divert Top US Military General's Plane," *Military.com*, October 20, 2015, https://www.military.com/daily
-news/2015/10/20/iraqis-try-to-divert-top-us-military-generals-plane.html.

159 *John Allen resigned*: Karen DeYoung, "Obama Administration's Envoy to Anti-
Islamic State Coalition to Resign," *The Washington Post*, September 22, 2015, https://
www.washingtonpost.com/world/national-security/obama-administrations-envoy
-to-anti-islamic-state-coalition-to-resign/2015/09/22/601ae71c-6152-11e5-b38e
-06883aacba64_story.html; Michael R. Gordon, "Obama's Anti-ISIS Point Man
Leaving as Russia Steps In," *The New York Times*, October 23, 2015, https://www
.nytimes.com/2015/10/24/world/middleeast/general-john-allen-obama-isis.html;
"Obama Names Brett McGurk as Envoy to Coalition Fighting Islamic State,"
Reuters, October 23, 2015, https://www.reuters.com/article/us-mideast-crisis
-whitehouse-mcgurk-idUSKCN0SH1XT20151023.

160 *hideout near Raqqa*: In a raid on an oil refinery in northern Syria, Delta Force
operators failed to find any hostages, and one operator was slightly wounded. Michael Shear and Eric Schmitt, "In Raid to Save Foley and Other Hostages, U.S.
Found None," *The New York Times*, August 20, 2014, https://www.nytimes.com
/2014/08/21/world/middleeast/us-commandos-tried-to-rescue-foley-and-other
-hostages.html.

160 *to capture Abu Sayyaf*: Helene Cooper and Eric Schmitt, "ISIS Official Killed in
U.S. Raid in Syria, Pentagon Says," *The New York Times*, May 16, 2015, https://
www.nytimes.com/2015/05/17/world/middleeast/abu-sayyaf-isis-commander
-killed-by-us-forces-pentagon-says.html.

161 *Time appeared to be*: Carter approved Delta Force's participation in the operation.
Michael R. Gordon and Eric Schmitt, "U.S. Soldier Dies in Raid to Free Prisoners of ISIS in Iraq," *The New York Times*, October 22, 2015, https://www
.nytimes.com/2015/10/23/world/middleeast/us-commandos-iraq-isis.html.

162 *Master Sergeant Joshua Wheeler*: Master Sergeant Wheeler was posthumously awarded the Silver Star, the third-highest medal for valor, for his actions. Paul Szoldra, "We Got a Copy of the Silver Star Award for Joshua Wheeler, the Delta Force Hero Killed Fighting ISIS," *Insider,* August 10, 2017, https://www .businessinsider.com/silver-star-award-master-sgt-joshua-wheeler-2017-8.

162 *Instead they found*: Gordon and Schmitt, "U.S. Soldier Dies in Raid to Free Prisoners of ISIS in Iraq."

163 *a Canadian soldier had*: Sergeant Andrew Doiron, a member of the Canadian Special Operations Regiment, was killed in a friendly-fire incident in March 2015. Three Canadian commandos were wounded. "Sgt. Andrew Doiron's Death Blamed on 'Mistaken Identity' in Report," *CBC,* May 12, 2015, https://www.cbc .ca/news/politics/sgt-andrew-doiron-s-death-blamed-on-mistaken-identity-in -report-1.3071198.

164 *ISIS had run Hawija*: Michael R. Gordon, "ISIS Captives Say They Faced Blade as Rescue Came," *The New York Times,* October 27, 2015, https://www.nytimes .com/2015/10/28/world/middleeast/freed-prisoners-of-isis-tell-of-beatings-and -torture.html.

165 *As I prepared to leave*: Gordon, "ISIS Captives Say They Faced Blade as Rescue Came."

166 *The day the president*: "Daily Press Briefing by the Press Secretary Josh Earnest 10/30/15," The White House, Office of the Press Secretary, October 30, 2015, https://obamawhitehouse.archives.gov/the-press-office/2015/10/30/daily-press -briefing-press-secretary-josh-earnest-103015.

166 *"We're in combat"*: "Department of Defense Press Briefing by Colonel Warren via Teleconference in the Pentagon Briefing Room from Baghdad," U.S. Department of Defense, October 28, 2015, https://www.defense.gov/News/Transcripts /Transcript/Article/626351/department-of-defense-press-briefing-by-colonel -warren-via-teleconference-in-th/.

11. DWELLER

170 *Ba'aj to the south*: When H. R. McMaster's Third Armored Cavalry Regiment was fighting in northern Iraq in 2005, it soon learned that it had less than forty-five minutes to set up concrete T-walls around a new position before al-Qaeda began to send suicide bombers its way.

171 *Protection Force of Sinjar*: In Kurdish, Hêza Parastina Şingal (HPS).

172 *arrested and thrown into a jail*: Christine Van Den Toorn, "The Hero Yazidis Hope Will Save Them," *The Daily Beast,* May 10, 2015, https://www.thedailybeast .com/the-hero-yazidis-hope-will-save-them?ref=scroll.

175 *with a walrus mustache*: Michael R. Gordon and Rukmini Callimachi, "Kurdish Fighters Retake Iraqi City of Sinjar from ISIS," *The New York Times,* November 13, 2015, https://www.nytimes.com/2015/11/14/world/middleeast/sinjar-iraq -islamic-state.html.

175 *Mass graves of ISIS victims*: Shortly after Sinjar's liberation, the Peshmerga were alerted to the presence of several potential mass graves. Local officials also told the Peshmerga that ISIS had executed Yazidi women ages forty to eighty, seeing them as too old to take as sex slaves. Michael R. Gordon, "Kurds Investigate Reports of Mass Grave of Yazidis in Sinjar," *The New York Times,* November 14, 2015, https://www.nytimes.com/2015/11/15/world/middleeast/iraq-sinjar-kurds -mass-graves-yazidis.html.

175 *formally incorporated into*: Gordon and Callimachi, "Kurdish Fighters Retake Iraqi City of Sinjar from ISIS."

175 *outlast Sinjar's liberation*: With Sinjar in dispute between federal Iraq and the Kurdistan Regional Government, Baghdad and Erbil signed the Sinjar Agreement on October 9, 2020, with the blessing of the United Nations Assistance Mission for Iraq. It called for all nonfederal armed groups to leave Sinjar, for both sides to agree on the selection of a mayor for the town, and other security measures. Few of the measures have been implemented. Hanar Marouf, "The Sinjar Agreement Has Good Ideas, but Is It a Dead End?," Atlantic Council, May 18, 2021, https://www.atlanticcouncil.org/blogs/menasource/the-sinjar -agreement-has-good-ideas-but-is-it-a-dead-end/.

177 *at an Ankara train station*: "Ankara Explosions Leave Almost 100 Dead—Officials," *BBC*, October 10, 2015, https://www.bbc.com/news/world-europe-34495161.

179 *During the summer of 2015*: Lieutenant General Charles Q. Brown discovered that 90 percent of Operation Inherent Resolve strikes were dynamic when he was made commander of the Combined Forces Air Component Command. Becca Wasser et al., *The Air War Against the Islamic State: The Role of Airpower in Operation Inherent Resolve* (Santa Monica, CA: RAND Corporation, 2021), 67–68, https://www.rand.org/pubs/research_reports/RRA388-1.html.

180 *thanks to the CTS*: "Iraqi and Kurdish Forces Recapture Mosul Dam from ISIS," *The Guardian*, August 18, 2014, https://www.theguardian.com/world/2014/aug /18/iraqi-kurdish-forces-recapture-mosul-dam-isis.

181 *strike the targeted spans*: Zeina Karam, "US-Led Coalition Unleashes Wave of Airstrikes on Raqqa," *Associated Press*, July 5, 2015, https://apnews.com/article /a4a221cc24364bf69adddec2bb20a5d3.

182 *On the night of*: Wasser et al., *The Air War Against the Islamic State*, 208–209.

184 *the operation was approved*: The strike targeting the Mosul bank was one component of a larger operation dubbed "Point Blank" that targeted ISIS's hard currency, complementing Tidal Wave II, which was intended to target ISIS's oil revenue. For the January 2016 Mosul strike, weaponeers in the Combined Air Operations Center used information on the bank's size and structure and devised a plan to drop three GBU-39 small-diameter bombs (SDBs) on timed fuses that would successfully open a hole in each floor of the bank down to the vault in the basement. This was followed by two joint direct attack munitions (JDAMs), each two thousand pounds, that penetrated the vault and destroyed the entire stockpile, estimated at 75 percent of the total cash for fighter salaries. Similar strikes would be attempted but were not always as successful. The strike targeting the leftover cash that killed a civilian woman attempted to replicate the precision weaponeering of the January strike, but failed. Wasser et al., *The Air War Against the Islamic State*, 227, 231, 232.

12. THE WAR ROOM

188 *gunmen barged into*: "Timeline of Paris Attacks According to Public Prosecutor," *Reuters*, November 14, 2015, https://www.reuters.com/article/us-france-shooting -timeline-idUSKCN0T31BS20151114#h8KRqimXftutLeR3.97.

189 *arranged for a dozen*: Alissa J. Rubin and Anne Barnard, "France Strikes ISIS Targets in Syria in Retaliation for Attacks," *The New York Times*, November 15, 2015, https://www.nytimes.com/2015/11/16/world/europe/paris-terror-attack.html.

192 *Under David Petraeus*: The CIA operation to arm and train Syrian rebels was code-named "Timber Sycamore." CIA officers were directly involved in training rebels on small arms and anti-armor weapons, which were shipped from Jordan and frequently stolen to be sold on the black market. Mark Mazzetti and Ali Younes, "C.I.A. Arms for Syrian Rebels Supplied Black Market, Officials Say,"

The New York Times, June 26, 2016, https://www.nytimes.com/2016/06/27/world/middleeast/cia-arms-for-syrian-rebels-supplied-black-market-officials-say.html.

192 *journalist James Foley*: Chelsea Carter, "Video Shows ISIS Beheading U.S. Journalist James Foley," *CNN*, August 20, 2014, https://www.cnn.com/2014/08/19/world/meast/isis-james-foley/index.html.

193 *RAND Corporation study*: Robert W. Komer, *Bureaucracy Does Its Thing: Institutional Constraints on U.S.-GVN Performance in Vietnam* (Santa Monica, CA: RAND Corporation, 1972), https://www.rand.org/pubs/reports/R967.html.

194 *Spooked by their first*: "U.S.-Trained Syrian Rebels Gave Equipment to Nusra: U.S. Military," *Reuters*, September 26, 2015, https://www.reuters.com/article/us-mideast-crisis-usa-equipment/u-s-trained-syrian-rebels-gave-equipment-to-nusra-u-s-military-idUSKCN0RP2HO20150926.

195 *"The administration knew"*: "Press Briefing by Press Secretary Josh Earnest," The American Presidency Project, September 16, 2015, https://www.presidency.ucsb.edu/documents/press-briefing-press-secretary-josh-earnest-148.

195 *the White House formally suspended*: Michael Shear, Helene Cooper, and Eric Schmitt, "Obama Administration Ends Effort to Train Syrians to Combat ISIS," *The New York Times*, October 9, 2015, https://www.nytimes.com/2015/10/10/world/middleeast/pentagon-program-islamic-state-syria.html.

195 *The program had not been*: Later, U.S. Marine Raiders deployed to Iraq in support of operations to liberate Mosul would have the secondary task of standing up an armed Sunni tribal force in Rabia. The resistance force was repeatedly sidelined, as the Kurdistan Regional Government was loath to let armed Arabi Sunnis move through their territory and the Shia factions in the Iraqi parliament were equally loath to let a Sunni tribal militia have any credit for liberating Mosul. The Rabia force was specifically requested by coalition special forces to hold liberated territory in Mosul, but the force remained benched. Author interview with Marine Raiders.

196 *Kerry flew to Sochi*: Michael R. Gordon, "Kerry Arrives in Russia for Talks with Vladimir Putin on Cooperation," *The New York Times*, May 12, 2015, https://www.nytimes.com/2015/05/13/world/europe/vladimir-putin-john-kerry-russia-sochi-ukraine-syria.html.

196 *meeting with Vladimir Putin*: The encounter brought an end to White House talk of isolating Russia after its invasion of the Crimean Peninsula and intervention in eastern Ukraine.

196 *unannounced trip to Moscow*: U.S. officials said that Soleimani's trip violated UN sanctions imposed as a result of Iran's nuclear program, which barred travel by senior Iranian officials. Michael R. Gordon, "U.S. Says Iranian Military Figure's Visit to Russia Violates U.N. Ban," *The New York Times*, August 12, 2015, https://www.nytimes.com/2015/08/13/world/middleeast/us-says-iranian-military-figures-visit-to-russia-violates-un-ban.html.

196 *initially flew over*: Michael R. Gordon and Eric Schmitt, "U.S. Moves to Block Russian Military Buildup in Syria," *The New York Times*, September 8, 2015, https://www.nytimes.com/2015/09/09/world/europe/us-moves-to-block-russian-military-buildup-in-syria.html.

197 *the State Department announced*: "Kerry Expresses US Concerns About Russian Moves in Syria," *VOA News*, September 5, 2015, https://www.voanews.com/a/kerry-expresses-united-states-concerns-russian-moves-syria/2949320.html.

197 *White House news conference*: Alistair Bell and Tom Perry, "Obama Warns Russia's Putin of 'Quagmire' in Syria," *Reuters*, October 2, 2015, https://www.reuters.com/article/us-mideast-crisis-syria-airstrikes/obama-warns-russias-putin-of-quagmire-in-syria-idUSKCN0RW0W220151003.

198 *op-ed that*: Vladimir V. Putin, "A Plea for Caution from Russia," *The New York Times*, September 11, 2013, https://www.nytimes.com/2013/09/12/opinion/putin-plea-for-caution-from-russia-on-syria.html.

198 *Another surprise*: Iraqi defense minister Khalid al-Obeidi visited Moscow on August 31, signing an arms deal and several security agreements during his trip. Mustafa al-Kadhimi, "Can Iraq Meet US, Russia Halfway?," *Al-Monitor*, October 21, 2015, https://www.al-monitor.com/originals/2015/10/iraq-abadi-intervene-russia-us-islamic-state.html.

198 *joint operations command*: Imran Khan, "Iraq, Russia, Iran and Syria Coordinate Against ISIL," *Al Jazeera*, September 27, 2015, https://www.aljazeera.com/news/2015/9/27/iraq-russia-iran-and-syria-coordinate-against-isil.

199 *they targeted the CIA-backed*: Dion Nissenbaum et al., "Russian Airstrike in Syria Targeted CIA-Backed Rebels, U.S. Officials Say," *The Wall Street Journal*, September 30, 2015, https://www.wsj.com/articles/russian-airstrike-in-syria-targeted-cia-backed-rebels-u-s-officials-say-1443663993.

199 *two Blackjack bombers*: John Barnett, "The Costs of Russia's Air Expeditionary Campaign," Washington Institute for Near East Policy, December 11, 2015, https://www.washingtoninstitute.org/policy-analysis/costs-russias-air-expeditionary-campaign.

199 *In August 2016*: The publicizing of the strikes led to criticism by Iran, with Iranian defense minister Hossein Deghan calling it "show-off" behavior. The fighters based at Hamedan were returned to Russia. "Russia 'Showed-Off' over Use of Iran Airbase for Syria Strikes," *BBC*, August 22, 2016, https://www.bbc.com/news/world-middle-east-37154043.

200 *After a flare-up*: On November 24, two Russian Su-24 fighter jets entered Turkish airspace after receiving multiple warnings to change course. Turkish F-16s on a combat air patrol fired at the Russian jets, with one crashing in Syria. The plane crash-landed in an area that Turkey claimed had recently been bombed by Russian jets, and local Turkmen fighters began shooting at the Russian crew as they ejected from their jet, killing the pilot, Lieutenant Colonel Oleg Peshkov. In a failed rescue attempt, a Russian marine was killed when his Mi-8 helicopter came under fire. The navigator for the fighter, Captain Konstantin Murakhtin, was eventually rescued and taken to Syrian government lines. "Turkey's Downing of Russian Warplane—What We Know," *BBC*, December 1, 2015, https://www.bbc.com/news/world-middle-east-34912581.

200 *deployed an advanced S-400*: Judah Ari Gross, "Russia Deploys S-400 Missile Battery in Syria, State Media Says," *The Times of Israel*, November 26, 2015, https://www.timesofisrael.com/russia-deploys-s-400-missile-battery-in-syria-state-media-says/.

200 *mass shooting at*: Adam Nagourney, Ian Lovett, and Richard Pérez-Peña, "San Bernardino Shooting Kills at Least 14; Two Suspects Are Dead," *The New York Times*, December 2, 2015, https://www.nytimes.com/2015/12/03/us/san-bernardino-shooting.html.

200 *Donald Trump exploited*: Jenna Johnson, "Trump Calls for 'Total and Complete Shutdown of Muslims Entering the United States,'" *The Washington Post*, December 7, 2015, https://www.washingtonpost.com/news/post-politics/wp/2015/12/07/donald-trump-calls-for-total-and-complete-shutdown-of-muslims-entering-the-united-states/.

205 *who had coauthored*: William Mullen and Daniel Green, *Fallujah Redux: The Anbar Awakening and the Struggle with al-Qaeda* (Annapolis, MD: Naval Institute Press, 2014).

206 *declared the city to be*: Falih Hassan, Sewell Chan, and Helene Cooper, "Celebrating

Victory over ISIS, Iraqi Leader Looks to Next Battles," *The New York Times*, December 29, 2015, https://www.nytimes.com/2015/12/30/world/middleeast /haider-al-abadi-iraq-ramadi-isis.html?searchResultPosition=13.

207 *directed at the Iraqi Army bases*: U.S. officials estimated that 180 ISIS fighters were killed by coalition air strikes during the attack. Michael R. Gordon, "ISIS Carries Out First 'Serious' Attack in Northern Iraq in Months, U.S. Says," *The New York Times*, December 17, 2015, https://www.nytimes.com/2015/12 /18/world/middleeast/isis-carries-out-first-serious-attack-in-northern-iraq-in -months-us-says.html.

208 *holding on to the equipment*: Gordon, "ISIS Carries Out First 'Serious' Attack in Northern Iraq in Months, U.S. Says."

209 *Carter used his address*: "Text of Secretary Carter's Speech to 101st Airborne Division in Fort Campbell" (Fort Campbell, KY, January 13, 2016), *Stars and Stripes*, https://www.stripes.com/migration/text-of-secretary-carter-s-speech -to-101st-airborne-division-in-fort-campbell-1.388591.

13. THE NEXT TEN PLAYS

210 *charged by French prosecutors*: During the investigation into Lafarge, famous for building both the Suez Canal and the coastal fortifications for the Nazis in France that Hitler called the Atlantic Wall, it was revealed the company had funneled at least $15 million through intermediaries to ISIS and other groups to allow its business to keep operating. French courts allowed prosecution on counts of financing terrorism, violating the European Union's embargo on Syria, and endangering the lives of others. While the courts initially dropped the charge of crimes against humanity, as of 2021 that charge was reinstated on appeal. Liz Alderman, Elian Peltier, and Hwaida Saad, "'ISIS Is Coming!' How a French Company Pushed the Limits in War-Torn Syria," *The New York Times*, March 10, 2018, https://www.nytimes.com/2018/03/10/business/isis-is-coming -how-a-french-company-pushed-the-limits-in-war-torn-syria.html; "France: Lafarge Loses Ruling in Syria Crime Against Humanity Case," *Al Jazeera*, September 7, 2021, https://www.aljazeera.com/news/2021/9/7/frances-lafarge-loses -ruling-in-syria-crimes-against-humanity.

211 *Syrian Democratic Forces*: Until this point, the main fighting force for the Kurds had been the Yekîneyên Parastina Gel (YPG). The SDF—which combined existing Kurdish (largely YPG), Arab, Turkmen, and Christian militias—became the official defense force for the Administration of North Syria, also known as Rojava (meaning "west" in Kurdish), in December 2016. Harriet Allsopp and Wladimir van Wilgenburg, *The Kurds of Northern Syria: Governance, Diversity and Conflicts* (London: I. B. Tauris, 2019), 66–67.

215 *to the Green Zone*: Tim Arango, "Days of Chaos in Baghdad: Protest or Meltdown?," *The New York Times*, May 2, 2016, https://www.nytimes.com/2016/05 /03/world/middleeast/baghdad-iraq-green-zone-protests.html.

217 *Biden had flown*: Biden was accompanied by Colin Kahl, who was then the vice president's national security advisor, for meetings with Erdoğan and Turkish prime minister Ahmet Davutoğlu. The Biden-Davutoğlu and Biden-Erdoğan meetings could not have been more different, and Erdoğan was far more recalcitrant in his attitude toward the Syrian Kurds. "Readout of Vice President Biden's Meeting with President Recep Tayyip Erdogan of Turkey," The White House, Office of the Vice President, January 24, 2016, https://obamawhitehouse .archives.gov/the-press-office/2016/01/24/readout-vice-president-bidens -meeting-president-recep-tayyip-erdogan; Colin Kahl, "The United States and Turkey Are on a Collision Course in Syria," *Foreign Policy*, May 12, 2017,

https://foreignpolicy.com/2017/05/12/the-united-states-and-turkey-are-on-a
-collision-course-in-syria-trump/.

217 *organized their own military council*: The SDF announced the official formation
of the Manbij Military Council on April 4, 2016. This was followed by the announcement of a civilian council to govern Manbij after its liberation on April
6. Wladimir van Wilgenburg, "US Seeks to Close ISIS Major Pocket Northern
Syria, Supports Kurds to Retake Manbij," *ARA News*, April 5, 2016, http://
aranews.net/files/2016/04/us-seeks-close-isis-major-pocket-northern-syria
-supports-kurds-retake-manbij/; Wladimir van Wilgenburg, "Kurds Set Up
New Civilian Council for Recapturing Syria's Manbij from ISIS," *ARA News*,
April 6, 2016, http://aranews.net/files/2016/04/kurds-set-new-civilian-council
-recapturing-syrias-manbij-isis/.

217 *"I could envision the SAC"*: Syrian Arab Coalition, a loose coalition of militias in
northern Syria.

219 *Erdoğan later made clear*: At a press conference, Erdoğan acknowledged that
450 Kurdish fighters would participate in the Manbij liberation, but that the
whole operation would be watched closely by Turkish intelligence. "Turkish Intel 'Closely Watching' Anti-ISIL Operation Near Its Border: Erdoğan," *Hürri-
yet Daily News*, June 2, 2016, https://www.hurriyetdailynews.com/turkish-intel
-closely-watching-anti-isil-operation-near-its-border-erdogan-100016.

219 *through the window of*: Jack Murphy, "The 75th Ranger Regiment Hits the
Ground in Syria for Raqqa Offensive," SOFREP, March 6, 2017, https://sofrep
.com/news/75th-ranger-regiment-hits-ground-syria-raqqa-offensive/.

219 *Mazloum's forces quickly liberated*: The SDF liberated six villages after the river
crossing as well as the strategic Seraj Hill, and another ten villages by June
4. On June 5, fifteen Yazidi girls enslaved by ISIS were discovered and rescued. Hisham Arafat, "Kurdish-Led Forces Approach Manbij, Liberate Several Villages," *Kurdistan24*, June 3, 2016, https://www.kurdistan24.net/en/story
/6909-Kurdish-led-forces-approach-Manbij,-liberate-several-villages; Ahmed
Shiwesh, "US-Backed Syrian Democratic Forces Advance Against ISIS Near
Manbij, Liberate Eight Villages," *ARA News*, June 4, 2016, https://web.archive
.org/web/20160909232732/http://aranews.net/2016/06/us-backed-sdf-advances
-isis-near-manbij/; Hisham Arafat, "Kurdish Forces Release Ezidis in Manbij,
Raqqa," *Kurdistan24*, June 4, 2016, https://www.kurdistan24.net/en/story/6913
-Kurdish-forces-release-Ezidis-in-Manbij,-Raqqa.

220 *suffered a setback*: Abu Layla, reputed as a symbol of the Syrian resistance, led
the Northern Sun Battalion and had been injured in previous campaigns against
ISIS. In his honor, the SDF christened the Manbij offensive "the Martyr Abu
Layla Operation." Wladimir van Wilgenburg, "Leading FSA Commander
Heavily Injured in Manbij Operation, Moved to Iraqi Kurdistan for Treatment," *ARA News*, June 4, 2016, https://web.archive.org/web/20160606064520
/http://aranews.net/2016/06/leading-fsa-commander-heavily-injured-manbij
-operation/; Frida Ghitis, "Why Abu Layla Will Be Missed," *CNN*, June 11,
2016, https://edition.cnn.com/2016/06/10/opinions/abu-layla-inspirational-leader
-ghitis/; Hisham Arafat, "Syrian Kurdish FSA Commander Died in Manbij,"
Kurdistan24, June 6, 2016, https://www.kurdistan24.net/en/story/6915-Syrian
-Kurdish-FSA-commander-died-in-Manbij.

220 *Later in the battle*: Zhelwan Z. Wali, "Brother of Abu Layla Captured by ISIS,"
Rudaw, July 5, 2016, https://www.rudaw.net/english/kurdistan/050720163.

220 *ISIS began to conscript*: According to the London-based war monitor Syrian Observatory for Human Rights, ISIS had forcibly conscripted two hundred men as
their numbers dwindled. In a tactic they would repeat in many battles, ISIS kid-

napped seven hundred civilians in and around Manbij for use as human shields. "IS Plants Houses in Menbej Countryside and Arrests 200 Young Men," Syrian Observatory for Human Rights, June 19, 2016, https://www.syriahr.com /en/47861/; Siman Ciwan, "ISIS Arrests 700 Civilians North Syria, Mostly Kurds," *ARA News*, June 21, 2016, http://aranews.net/files/2016/06/isis-arrests -700-civilians-north-syria-mostly-kurds/.

220 *By July, Mazloum's fighters*: The SDF had captured 70 percent of the city by July 11 and advanced to within three hundred meters of the city center. Hisham Arafat, "Kurdish-Led Forces Control Nearly 70% of Manbij, Northern Syria," *Kurdistan24*, July 11, 2016, https://www.kurdistan24.net/en/news/d8ff2656-c6e1 -4954-a138-580f3d42fe9d.

220 *Abu Khalid al-Tunisi*: Helin Saeed, "ISIS Emir Killed Under SDF Fire North Syria," *ARA News*, July 10, 2016, https://web.archive.org/web/20160713063334 /http://aranews.net/2016/07/isis-emir-killed-sdf-fire-north-syria/.

220 *Desperate to escape*: After repeated offers of amnesty if ISIS released its civilian hostages, ISIS freed its last two thousand civilian human shields on August 12, but kidnapped another two thousand in Jarablus to avoid being targeted by coalition aircraft. Jubilant civilians welcomed ISIS's departure by defying their rules openly, including burning burqas, dancing, and smoking. Suleiman Al-Khalidi and Lisa Barrington, "U.S.-Backed Forces Wrest Control of Syria's Manbij from Islamic State," *Reuters*, August 12, 2016, https://www .reuters.com/article/us-mideast-crisis-syria-islamic-state-idUSKCN10N178; "'Islamic State' Abducts 2,000 Civilians in Northern Syria," *Deutsche Welle*, August 12, 2016, https://www.dw.com/en/islamic-state-abducts-2000-civilians -in-northern-syria/a-19471640; Tess Owen, "US-Backed Syrian Fighters Take Manbij City, Islamic State's Gateway to Europe," *Vice*, August 13, 2016, https:// www.vice.com/en/article/mbnz38/us-backed-syrian-fighters-take-manbij-city -islamic-states-gateways-to-europe.

220 *Mazloum had lost*: During the encirclement of Manbij, the SDF had lost approximately 150 fighters, and another 480–550 during the fighting for the city itself. Michael Knights and Wladimir van Wilgenburg, *Accidental Allies: The US–Syrian Democratic Forces Partnership Against the Islamic State* (London: I. B. Tauris, 2021), 168, https://www.washingtoninstitute.org/policy-analysis/accidental-allies -us-syrian-democratic-forces-partnership-against-islamic-state.

221 *the Americans tried*: The SDF withdrew from Manbij on August 19 as promised and handed over control to the Manbij Civil Council, then established a defense at the Sajur River to block an ISIS counteroffensive from Jarablus. The announcement of a military council for Jarablus would ultimately start a process that ended in Operation Euphrates Shield, the Turkish intervention that would liberate Jarablus from ISIS and push the SDF back over the Euphrates. Wladimir van Wilgenburg, "SDF Withdraws from Manbij After Liberation, Handing City Over to Local Council," *ARA News*, August 19, 2016, https://web.archive .org/web/20160821072129/http://aranews.net/2016/08/22872/; Jan Mohammed, "Syrian Democratic Forces Secure Defense Lines North Manbij to Prevent ISIS Infiltration," *ARA News*, August 21, 2016, https://web.archive.org/web /20160823072559/http://aranews.net/2016/08/syrian-democratic-forces-secure -defense-lines-north-manbij-prevent-isis-infiltration/; "The Military Council of Jarablos Declared," Hawar News Agency, August 22, 2016, https://web.archive .org/web/20160822133816/http://en.hawarnews.com/the-military-council-of -jarablos-declared/; Ahmed Deeb, "Operation 'Euphrates Shield' Ends ISIL Rule in Jarablus," *Al Jazeera*, August 25, 2016, https://www.aljazeera.com

/gallery/2016/8/25/operation-euphrates-shield-ends-isil-rule-in-jarablus/; "US-Backed Kurds Retreat in Syria; Kerry in Saudi Arabia to Gather Support for Plan," *VOA News*, August 25, 2016, https://www.voanews.com/middle-east/us-backed-kurds-retreat-syria-kerry-saudi-arabia-gather-support-plan.

221 *disappearance of hundreds*: Abdulla Hawez, "The Torturers Taking on ISIS in Fallujah," *The Daily Beast*, June 15, 2016, https://www.thedailybeast.com/the-torturers-taking-on-isis-in-fallujah.

223 *given to strike*: In an assessment of the air war, the RAND Corporation determined that coalition A-10s and AC-130s destroyed the first two-thirds of the second convoy, while Iraqi helicopters destroyed the final third—in all some 150 vehicles. Becca Wasser et al., *The Air War Against the Islamic State: The Role of Airpower in Operation Inherent Resolve* (Santa Monica, CA: RAND Corporation, 2021), 91, https://www.rand.org/pubs/research_reports/RRA388-1.html.

223 *according to the battle damage assessment*: The battle damage assessment would conclude a total of 213 vehicles, five buildings, three VBIEDs, and three heavy machine guns and rockets destroyed in nine strikes. The coalition targeted the southern convoy after it moved and broke into two elements, then the northern convoy as it fled north of Ramadi. "CJTF-OIR Macro Storyboard: Da'esh Convoys," PowerPoint, Iraq, 2016.

14. OBJECTIVE FISH

226 *American soldiers had*: Surrounded by fortified munitions bunkers, the complex had been known as Saddam Airbase during Iraq's bloody war with Iran. During the U.S. occupation, it had become FOB Endurance, an apt name considering how many years the Americans spent trying to stabilize Iraq.

226 *placed under the prime minister's*: Rod Nordland, "After Victory over ISIS in Tikrit, Next Battle Requires a New Template," *The New York Times*, April 7, 2015, https://www.nytimes.com/2015/04/08/world/middleeast/iraq-isis-anbar-sunni-shiite.html?_r=0.

227 *deep-seated fears*: Kurdish and Iraqi troops had nearly come to blows in 2008, and the Americans worked furiously to head off the confrontation, going so far as to set up a temporary system of American, Kurdish, and Iraqi checkpoints across northern Iraq to keep the two sides apart.

229 *Eight other Marines*: Matthew Schehl, "Marines Identify Staff NCO Killed in ISIS Rocket Attack in Iraq," *Marine Corps Times*, March 20, 2016, https://www.marinecorpstimes.com/news/your-marine-corps/2016/03/20/marines-identify-staff-nco-killed-in-isis-rocket-attack-in-iraq/.

229 *In a briefing*: Steve Warren, "Department of Defense Press Briefing by Colonel Warren via Teleconference in the Pentagon Briefing Room from Baghdad, Iraq," U.S. Department of Defense, March 21, 2016, https://www.defense.gov/News/Transcripts/Transcript/Article/699172/department-of-defense-press-briefing-by-colonel-warren-via-teleconference-from.

230 *Kara Soar Counter Fire Complex*: Barbara Starr, "Pentagon Quietly Renames 'Fire Base,'" *CNN*, March 30, 2016, https://www.cnn.com/2016/03/30/politics/pentagon-fire-base-name/index.html.

233 *dubbed the "shark's fin"*: The bridging operation over the "shark fin" would be the first instance of American advisors going past the established Kurdish forward line of troops and a significant step toward a new paradigm for advising and assisting the Iraqi Security Forces. Ryan Wylie, Aaron Childers, and Brett Sylvia, "Expeditionary Advising: Enabling Iraqi Operations from the Gates of Baghdad Through Eastern Mosul," *Small Wars Journal*, February 22, 2018, https://smallwarsjournal

.com/jrnl/art/expeditionary-advising-enabling-iraqi-operations-gates-baghdad
-through-eastern-mosul.

234   *Sylvia's brigade saw it*: In an article published in *Small Wars Journal,* Sylvia laid out the role of Task Force Strike in advising Iraqi forces and the trial-and-error process that eventually led to the concept of "advise, assist, accompany, and enable" (A3E). "It very quickly became clear that this paradigm for conducting advise and assist, while extremely low risk to U.S. forces, could not compel Iraqi success," Sylvia said. Wylie, Childers, and Sylvia, "Expeditionary Advising."

234   *only 50 percent*: Wylie, Childers, and Sylvia, "Expeditionary Advising."

236   *Eventually, the facility was seized*: "Iraqi Army Takes Key Base South of Mosul from ISIS," *Al Arabiya*, July 9, 2016, https://english.alarabiya.net/News/middle -east/2016/07/09/Iraqi-army-takes-key-base-south-of-Mosul-from-ISIS.

237   *More than a hundred ISIS*: Andrew Tilghman, "'Bullets Everywhere': Navy SEAL Killed by ISIS Was Sucked into a Hellish Fight," *Navy Times*, May 4, 2016, https://www.navytimes.com/news/your-navy/2016/05/04/bullets-everywhere -navy-seal-killed-by-isis-was-sucked-into-a-hellish-fight/.

238   *mission dubbed "Evergreen II"*: Author interview with Marine Raiders.

239   *Soon ISIS mortar rounds*: According to the Marines who were there, the ISIS mortar rounds had a fragmentation pattern that went up instead of out, making it unlikely that anyone would be seriously injured if a mortar landed close by. Author interview with Marine Raiders.

239   *No sooner did the Marines*: Author interview with Marine Raiders.

239   *dubbed the "tear drop"*: Alternatively called "Suicide Alley" by other coalition special forces. Author interview with Marine Raiders.

239   *Anxious to shut down*: Setting up an RQ-20 Puma surveillance drone, the Marines conducted reconnaissance throughout the valley until the sun began setting, at which point they came under withering fire. Taking fire in the open and with the sun in their eyes, the Marines were unable to pinpoint the location of the ISIS attack but returned fire furiously from their own weapons and from machine guns mounted in Peshmerga pickup trucks. The Marine dog handler, Staff Sergeant Patrick Maloney, would later earn a Bronze Star for his actions. Author interview with Marine Raiders; Hope Hedge Seck, "Special Ops Dog Handler Awarded Bronze Star for Heroism in ISIS Fight," *Military.com*, November 9, 2017, https://www.military.com/daily-news/2017/11/02/special-ops-dog -handler-awarded-bronze-star-heroism-isis-fight.html.

240   *the rest of the Raiders*: Author interview with Marine Raiders.

15. EAGLE STRIKE

243   *The Americans would do*: Sylvia notes that Task Force Strike's ability to coordinate joint fires and the forward presence of U.S. advisors providing full-motion video allowed the Iraqi Security Forces to find and eliminate ISIS positions while avoiding friendly-fire incidents: "The TF dedicated over 70% of its force structure to advise and assist support and enabling tasks, with more forces dedicated to securing advisors than actually advising. These forces did not come ad hoc but were instead part of their organic unit and they had trained together through a training center rotation before deployment." Wylie, Childers, and Sylvia, "Expeditionary Advising."

244   *the Iraqis dropped leaflets*: Ahmed Rasheed, "Iraqi Army Drops Leaflets over Mosul in Preparation for Offensive," *Reuters*, October 16, 2016, https://www .reuters.com/article/us-mideast-crisis-iraq-mosul/iraqi-army-drops-leaflets -over-mosul-in-preparation-for-offensive-idUSKBN12G0GN.

247 *Iraqi state television*: Michael R. Gordon and Tim Arango, "East of Mosul, Kurdish Troops Advance on ISIS-Held Villages," *The New York Times*, October 17, 2016, https://www.nytimes.com/2016/10/17/world/middleeast/iraq-isis -mosul-battle.html?searchResultPosition=9.

248 *As the Peshmerga converged*: Bryan Denton and Michael R. Gordon, "At the Mosul Front: Traps, Smoke Screens and Suicide Bombers," *The New York Times*, October 17, 2016, https://www.nytimes.com/2016/10/18/world/middleeast/mosul -iraq-isis-kurds.html?searchResultPosition=12.

249 *The frightened residents*: Michael R. Gordon, "Kurds, Heading into the Teeth of ISIS, Open a New Front," *The New York Times*, October 20, 2016, https://www .nytimes.com/2016/10/21/world/iraq-mosul-kurds-pesh-merga-isis-second -front.html?searchResultPosition=13.

249 *the mood was upbeat*: Gordon, "Kurds, Heading into the Teeth of ISIS, Open a New Front."

250 *Desperate to get an injured*: Gordon, "Kurds, Heading into the Teeth of ISIS, Open a New Front."

250 *toward another Christian town*: The Marine Raiders described their push to Batnaya as deliberate, with the Kurds pausing repeatedly to create defensive berms and leave behind sentries, which resulted in only seventy-five Peshmerga actually getting to Batnaya by the end and the rest manning ten kilometers of defensive berms. Taking fire from Batnaya and unable to view a drone's feed due to broken equipment, the Marines had to communicate directly with the drone operator to get an idea on what was happening. The firefight climaxed when a Norwegian Peshmerga volunteer called out a *Mad Max*–style VBIED barreling toward their position, enabling an air strike to destroy it. Author interview with Marine Raiders.

250 *ISIS mounted a furious*: A Marine major who led the MARSOC unit present during Phoenix Raider said that he awoke to the sound of gunfire at 11:00 p.m. Rushing to reorient their M-ATVs and snipers, the Raiders saw at least thirty ISIS fighters within two hundred meters of their position and a VBIED lumbering toward them. The gun mount on the major's truck malfunctioned, forcing two Marines to repair the gun in the open while under heavy fire with rounds pinging off the truck. A bomb disposal expert attached to the team suffered an injury after shrapnel from a bullet ricocheted off the truck. Author interview with Marine Raiders.

251 *the gunnery sergeant*: Author interview with Marine Raiders.

251 *The Javelin shot was enough*: Author interview with Marine Raiders.

251 *Osthoff ultimately*: Author interview with Marine Raiders; Shawn Snow, "A Marine Raider Was Awarded a Silver Star for Taking Out an Armored-Vehicle IED with a Javelin," *Marine Corps Times*, February 12, 2019, https://www .marinecorpstimes.com/news/your-marine-corps/2019/02/12/a-marine-raider -was-awarded-a-silver-star-for-taking-out-an-armored-vehicle-ied-with-a -javelin/.

251 *but on October 20*: Tara Copp, "Navy EOD Tech Died Directing SEALs, Iraqis Away from Roadside Bomb," *Stars and Stripes*, October 23, 2016, https://www .stripes.com/branches/navy-eod-tech-died-directing-seals-iraqis-away-from -roadside-bomb-1.435491.

253 *Denton tried to dive*: Bryan Denton, "ISIS Sent Four Car Bombs. The Last One Hit Me," *The New York Times*, October 26, 2016, https://www.nytimes.com /2016/10/27/world/middleeast/iraq-mosul-isis-car-bombs.html.

254 *rushed to seize*: Michael R. Gordon, "Seeking Clues to ISIS Strategy in Corpses and Cellphones Left in Kirkuk," *The New York Times*, October 29, 2016, https://

www.nytimes.com/2016/10/30/world/middleeast/isis-counterterrorism-kirkuk
-iraq.html?searchResultPosition=2; Tim Arango, "ISIS Fighters in Iraq Attack
Kirkuk, Diverting Attention from Mosul," *The New York Times*, October 21,
2016, https://www.nytimes.com/2016/10/22/world/middleeast/iraqkirkuk.html
?searchResultPosition=3.

254 *The governor's first call*: Gordon, "Seeking Clues to ISIS Strategy in Corpses and
Cellphones Left in Kirkuk."

255 *burst into their dormitory*: Gordon, "Seeking Clues to ISIS Strategy in Corpses
and Cellphones Left in Kirkuk."

256 *Mazan Nazhan Ahmed al-Obeidi*: Robin Wright, "Face to Face with the Ghost
of ISIS," *The New Yorker*, March 24, 2017, https://www.newyorker.com/news
/news-desk/face-to-face-with-the-ghost-of-isis.

256 *In another move*: The Mishraq plant had similarly been set alight in 2003, sending plumes of toxic smoke into the air as U.S. forces rushed to put it out. "Mosul
Battle: Hundreds Treated over Toxic Fumes in Iraq," *BBC*, October 22, 2016,
https://www.bbc.com/news/world-middle-east-37738667.

257 *bombing a pharmaceutical*: Barbara Starr, "US Bombs ISIS Chemical Weapons
Plant," *CNN*, September 12, 2016, https://www.cnn.com/2016/09/13/politics
/isis-chemical-weapons-plant/index.html.

257 *other environmental problems*: United Nations Environment Programme, "Iraq:
Mosul Battle Brings Environmental Damage, with Serious Impacts on Health,
Prospects of Recovery," press release, October 27, 2016, https://reliefweb.int
/report/iraq/iraq-mosul-battle-brings-environmental-damage-serious-impacts
-health-prospects-recovery.

257 *But it was the sulfur fire*: Tamer El-Ghobashy and Joby Warrick, "The Islamic
State's Toxic Farewell: Environmental Sabotage and Chronic Disease," *The
Washington Post*, February 4, 2018, https://www.washingtonpost.com/world/the
-islamic-states-toxic-farewell-environmental-sabotage-and-chronic-disease
/2018/02/04/927ff2b6-05c8-11e8-ae28-e370b74ea9a7_story.html.

16. THE TACTICAL DIRECTIVE

258 *broke his silence*: Rukmini Callimachi, "With Mosul Under Siege, ISIS Leader
Breaks Silence to Issue a Rallying Cry," *The New York Times*, November 2, 2016,
https://www.nytimes.com/2016/11/03/world/middleeast/islamic-state-leader
-baghdadi-new-recordingmosul.html.

258 *rewards for battlefield valor*: To spur fighters to action, the Islamic State's Delegated Committee published a circular on August 30, 2016, for the Diwan al-
Jund (Department of Soldiers) detailing various rewards for specific battlefield
actions. Rewards included a car worth at least ten golden dinars for the destruction of an aircraft; seven golden dinars for destroying a tank with any weapon,
with the exception of a guided missile, for which only one dinar was given; four
golden dinars for destroying armored vehicles by any means other than land
mines; two golden dinars for destroying general vehicles by means other than
land mines; one golden dinar for every sniper kill with photographic evidence,
but only half a dinar if there was a witness but no photo; one silver dirham for
any projectile that hit a target and had a witness or photographic proof; ten silver
dirhams for any chemical weapon that hit a target; ten silver dirhams for killing
an enemy by any means except sniping; and one golden dinar for capturing an
enemy. The circular also included specific instructions for reporting these deeds
and for the disbursement of the reward as well as the percentage a unit was enti-
tled to. "Circular from the Delegated Committee on Rewards for Deeds in War,"

Islamic State Archives, April 4, 2021, https://islamicstatearchives.com/2021/04
/04/circular-from-the-delegated-committee-on-rewards-for-deeds-in-war/.

259 *the role of foreign fighters*: A bombing in Mosul on December 5 that killed thirty
Iraqi soldiers and civilians was carried out by a Moroccan ISIS fighter ("IS
Claims 3 Suicide Bombings, One by Young Moroccan, Killing 30 in Mosul,"
SITE Enterprise, December 5, 2016, https://ent.siteintelgroup.com/Statements
/is-claims-3-suicide-bombings-one-by-young-moroccan-killing-30-in-mosul
.html); a bombing on November 8 that killed seventeen Iraqi soldiers was carried out by an Uzbek fighter ("IS Claims Killing over 17 Iraqi Forces in Suicide
Bombing by Uzbek Fighter, North of Mosul," SITE Enterprise, November 8,
2016, https://ent.siteintelgroup.com/Statements/is-claims-killing-over-17-iraqi
-forces-in-suicide-bombing-by-uzbek-fighter-north-of-mosul.html); and a bombing on November 6 to beat back an Iraqi assault was carried out by an Emirati
fighter ("IS Claims Suicide Bombing by Emarati [*sic*] Fighter on Iraqi Forces in
Eastern Mosul," SITE Enterprise, November 6, 2016, https://ent.siteintelgroup
.com/Statements/is-claims-suicide-bombing-by-emarati-fighter-on-iraqi
-forces-in-eastern-mosul.html).

259 *mounting anti-armor*: "'Amaq Video Shows IS' Use of New Weapon: VBIED
Equipped with Anti-Armor Rockets," SITE Enterprise, April 21, 2017, https://
ent.siteintelgroup.com/Multimedia/amaq-video-shows-is-use-of-new-weapon
-vbied-equipped-with-anti-armor-rockets.html.

260 *was ambushed and trapped*: Stephen J. Townsend, "The Coalition Military Campaign to Defeat the Islamic State in Iraq and Syria 21 AUG 2016–05 SEP 2017,"
declassified command history, September 3, 2017, 51–52.

260 *As the journalist Arwa Damon*: Hamdi Alkhshali, "Rescuing Arwa and Brice:
The Toughest 24 Hours of My Life," *CNN*, November 14, 2016, https://www
.cnn.com/2016/11/14/middleeast/rescuing-arwa-damon-producers-notebook
/index.html.

263 *Soon after, the CTS*: The CTS became pinned down two hundred meters from
the hospital. ISIS renewed its assault on the 36th Brigade, which was subject
to both a suicide-vehicle-borne IED detonation and twenty rocket-propelled
grenades. The hospital caught on fire, forcing the remaining Iraqi soldiers onto
the roof or through the back door. Eighty soldiers fought to the street and withdrew with the CTS. The 9th Armored Division would report thirteen soldiers
killed, forty-eight wounded, and thirteen BMPs and five Humvees destroyed
or abandoned. The coalition estimated that between seventy and one hundred
ISIS fighters were killed. Townsend, "The Coalition Military Campaign to Defeat the Islamic State in Iraq and Syria," 24.

264 *Specialist Erik Salmon*: Salmon, reflecting on his experience and his relationship
with the Iraqis, told Army Public Affairs, "They're people fighting for their
country, fighting for freedom for their people, so put yourself in their situation . . . These people value human life. It is important to them and to us. People are generally the same everywhere." Jason Hull, "US, Coalition Soldiers
Extract Teammate from Enemy Lines Using Drone Feed," U.S. Army, January
26, 2017, https://www.army.mil/article/180701/us_coalition_soldiers_extract
_teammate_f.

267 *Tactical Directive No. 1*: Townsend, "The Coalition Military Campaign to Defeat
the Islamic State in Iraq and Syria," 24.

268 *Colonel Pat Work*: In an article published in *Joint Forces Quarterly*, Pat Work
reflected on the evolution of the U.S. advise-and-assist paradigm. For soldiers
who could one day be called upon to do something similar, Work provided a set

of rules for how to engage with partner forces. Rule #2 was "Maintain contact." "Only by staying with key ISF commanders much of the time, and listening to them *all of the time*, did our A&A network begin to understand how our partners saw IS, the environment, and themselves," he wrote, referring to the Islamic State. Iraqi Security Force commanders were pragmatic when evaluating risk; they fought knowing that the Iraqi government might not be sending replacement troops, combat systems, or ammunition anytime soon. "This gave our relationships, no matter how cozy, a transactional quality," Work wrote. J. Patrick Work, "Fighting the Islamic State By, With, and Through: *How* Mattered as Much as *What*," *Joint Forces Quarterly* 89 (2018), https://ndupress.ndu.edu /Portals/68/Documents/jfq/jfq-89/jfq-89_56-62_Work.pdf.

269   *two-week pause*: Townsend, "The Coalition Military Campaign to Defeat the Islamic State in Iraq and Syria," 24.

269   *struck the Moslawi Bridge*: Townsend, "The Coalition Military Campaign to Defeat the Islamic State in Iraq and Syria," 24.

270   *ISIS used the cadre*: Townsend, "The Coalition Military Campaign to Defeat the Islamic State in Iraq and Syria," 24–25.

270   *mount an audacious attack*: Townsend, "The Coalition Military Campaign to Defeat the Islamic State in Iraq and Syria," 25.

270   *The Iraqis finally resumed*: Townsend, "The Coalition Military Campaign to Defeat the Islamic State in Iraq and Syria," 26.

270   *to Mosul University*: According to a lessons-learned report for the Mosul operation, Iraqi forces recaptured the complex by January 13, 2017. Mosul Study Group, *What the Battle for Mosul Teaches the Force*, No. 17–24 (Fort Leavenworth, KS: U.S. Army University Press, September 2017), 7, https://www .armyupress.army.mil/Portals/7/Primer-on-Urban-Operation/Documents /Mosul-Public-Release1.pdf.

270   *develop chemical weapons*: While ISIS used the university to manufacture chemical stockpiles, it had also stumbled upon a key ingredient for a dirty bomb, radioactive cobalt-60, inside a radiotherapy machine used to treat cancer. Western intelligence watched nervously, waiting for ISIS to attempt to extract the cobalt and create a weapon of mass destruction, but when Mosul University was recaptured, the ISF found it untouched. Confused as to why the cobalt had not been extracted, some experts ventured that ISIS members simply weren't smart enough to find a way to take the machine apart without killing themselves via lethal radiation exposure. Joby Warrick and Loveday Morris, "How ISIS Nearly Stumbled on the Ingredients for a 'Dirty Bomb,'" *The Washington Post*, July 22, 2017, https://www.washingtonpost.com/world/national-security/how-isis-nearly -stumbled-on-the-ingredients-for-a-dirty-bomb/2017/07/22/6a966746-6e31 -11e7-b9e2-2056e768a7e5_story.html.

270   *ISIS set fire*: Campbell MacDiarmid, "Mosul University After ISIL: Damaged but Defiant," *Al Jazeera*, January 26, 2017, https://www.aljazeera.com/features /2017/1/26/mosul-university-after-isil-damaged-but-defiant.

270   *about 240 boats*: Townsend, "The Coalition Military Campaign to Defeat the Islamic State in Iraq and Syria," 24–25.

271   *about five hundred Iraqis killed*: The coalition estimated that 445 Iraqis had been killed and 3,020 injured between February and May in the battle for West Mosul. Total Iraqi casualties for West Mosul were 1,080 killed and 6,190 wounded, compared with 240 killed and 690 wounded for East Mosul. Townsend, "The Coalition Military Campaign to Defeat the Islamic State in Iraq and Syria," 35.

273   *dubbed "Euphrates Shield"*: Kareem Shaheen, "Turkey Sends Tanks into Syria in Operation Aimed at ISIS and Kurds," *The Guardian*, August 24, 2016, https://

www.theguardian.com/world/2016/aug/24/turkey-launches-major-operation
-against-isis-in-key-border-town.

273 *During Obama's last week*: Michael R. Gordon and Eric Schmitt, "Obama's Stark
Options on ISIS: Arm Syrian Kurds or Let Trump Decide," *The New York Times*,
January 17, 2017, https://www.nytimes.com/2017/01/17/world/middleeast/obama
-isis-syria-kurds.html?searchResultPosition=5.

274 *sympathetic to Turkey*: Michael T. Flynn, "Our Ally Turkey Is in Crisis and Needs
Our Support," *The Hill*, November 8, 2016, https://thehill.com/blogs/pundits-blog
/foreign-policy/305021-our-ally-turkey-is-in-crisis-and-needs-our-support.

17. COUNCIL OF WAR

277 *Nobody knew how many*: Stephen J. Townsend, "The Coalition Military Campaign to Defeat the Islamic State in Iraq and Syria 21 AUG 2016–05 SEP 2017,"
declassified command history, September 3, 2017, 15.

277 *The Iraqi plan*: Townsend, "The Coalition Military Campaign to Defeat the
Islamic State in Iraq and Syria," 28.

280 *attacked the Mosul airfield*: Townsend, "The Coalition Military Campaign to
Defeat the Islamic State in Iraq and Syria," 28.

281 *Three days later*: Townsend, "The Coalition Military Campaign to Defeat the
Islamic State in Iraq and Syria," 30–31.

281 *The police's darkest moment*: Townsend, "The Coalition Military Campaign to
Defeat the Islamic State in Iraq and Syria," 31.

282 *They could not directly*: While Iraqi troops could not call in air strikes, Iraqi
or Kurdish officials were located in the strike cells and had to sign off on any
strike along with the approval of the American TEA. Becca Wasser et al., *The
Air War Against the Islamic State: The Role of Airpower in Operation Inherent Resolve* (Santa Monica, CA: RAND Corporation, 2021), 25, https://www.rand.org
/pubs/research_reports/RRA388-1.html.

283 *the entire structure had*: Townsend, "The Coalition Military Campaign to Defeat
the Islamic State in Iraq and Syria," 31.

283 *which accused the United States*: "IS' 'Amaq Reports 1800 Mosul Residents Dead
in American-Iraqi 'Massacres,'" SITE Enterprise, March 21, 2017, https://ent
.siteintelgroup.com/Multimedia/is-amaq-reports-1800-mosul-residents-dead
-in-american-iraqi-massacres.html.

284 *One tactic that ISIS*: The coalition reported the first use of drones by ISIS in East
Mosul on November 9, 2016. The drones were not decisive but were considered highly disruptive, and by the coalition's count there were sixty-two drone
attacks on the ISF between January 24 and February 25, 2017, dropping a variety of munitions, such as 40mm grenades. Townsend, "The Coalition Military
Campaign to Defeat the Islamic State in Iraq and Syria," 27.

284 *ISIS considered their drones*: "Pro-IS Group Releases Infographic on Explosive-
Equipped UAV Results," SITE Enterprise, February 6, 2017, https://ent
.siteintelgroup.com/Chatter/pro-is-group-releases-infographic-on-explosive
-equipped-uav-results.html; "IS Promotes Weaponized UAVs in Naba 67, Claims
Killing and Wounding 39 in Less Than One Week," SITE Enterprise, February
9, 2017, https://ent.siteintelgroup.com/Statements/is-promotes-weaponized-uavs
-in-naba-67-claims-killing-and-wounding-39-in-less-than-one-week.html.

285 *back of an armored truck*: Townsend, "The Coalition Military Campaign to Defeat the Islamic State in Iraq and Syria," 28.

285 *Turning the tables*: Townsend, "The Coalition Military Campaign to Defeat the
Islamic State in Iraq and Syria," 30.

285 *ISIS caught on*: "Jihadist Offers Tips to IS to Overcome Countermeasures to

Drones, VBIEDs," SITE Enterprise, April 14, 2017, https://ent.siteintelgroup
.com/Chatter/jihadist-offers-tips-to-is-to-overcome-countermeasures-to
-drones-vbieds.html.

286   *In early April*: Maggie Haberman, "Jared Kushner Visits Iraq on Invitation
from Joint Chiefs Chairman," *The New York Times*, April 2, 2017, https://www
.nytimes.com/2017/04/02/us/politics/jared-kushner-visits-iraq.html.

286   *the field near the*: In the first grave site, the Emergency Response Division found
40 corpses, and another 334 at a second site before stopping due to the corpses'
decay. Townsend, "The Coalition Military Campaign to Defeat the Islamic
State in Iraq and Syria," 52.

288   *an Iraqi Mi-28*: "IS Reveals Use of Strela Anti-Aircraft Rockets in Mosul Battle
in Naba 78," SITE Enterprise, April 27, 2017, https://ent.siteintelgroup.com
/Periodicals/is-reveals-use-of-strela-anti-aircraft-rockets-in-mosul-battle-in-naba
-78.html.

288   *About 445 Iraqi troops*: Townsend, "The Coalition Military Campaign to Defeat
the Islamic State in Iraq and Syria," 32.

18. THE FINAL DAYS

295   *the notorious prison*: Upon arrival in Badush, PMF forces found a mass grave
containing the corpses of 500 prisoners whom ISIS fighters had executed when
they captured the prison. In 2014, ISIS had executed at least 670 Shiite prisoners after separating them from Sunnis and had held kidnapped Yazidi women
at the prison. Loaa Adel, "Security Forces Find Mass Grave of 500 Bodies in
Badush Prison, Near Mosul," *Iraqi News*, March 11, 2017, http://www.iraqinews
.com/iraq-war/forces-discover-mass-grave-badush-prison/.

295   *Cubs of the Caliphate*: Raya Jalabi, "Cubs of the Caliphate: Rehabilitating Islamic State's Child Fighters," *Reuters*, March 8, 2018, https://www.reuters
.com/article/us-mideast-crisis-iraq-yazidis/cubs-of-the-caliphate-rehabilitating
-islamic-states-child-fighters-idUSKCN1GK0VU.

295   *French jihadists*: Tamer El-Ghobashy, Maria Abi-Habib, and Benoit Faucon,
"France's Special Forces Hunt French Militants Fighting for Islamic State," *The
Wall Street Journal*, May 29, 2017, https://www.wsj.com/articles/frances-special
-forces-hunt-french-militants-fighting-for-islamic-state-1496090116.

297   *lost its protected status*: This loss of protected status occurred slowly, after much
legal review and consideration. While it was *not* in dispute that ISIS was conducting military operations from this location, it took a while to confirm that it
was not still concurrently serving as a hospital.

298   *Townsend gave the go-ahead*: Stephen J. Townsend, "The Coalition Military
Campaign to Defeat the Islamic State in Iraq and Syria 21 AUG 2016–05 SEP
2017," declassified command history, September 3, 2017, 33.

298   *had already engaged*: The Marine gunnery sergeant who had earned a Silver Star
for bravery had used two Javelin anti-tank missiles to destroy an ISIS VBIED,
and in another instance a team of Navy SEALs eliminated a VBIED with an
81mm mortar. Author interview with Marine Raiders.

299   *Free Burma Rangers*: David Eubank, *Do This for Love: Free Burma Rangers in the
Battle of Mosul* (New York: Fidelis Books, 2020).

301   *ISIS had fired mortar*: The coalition counted eight chemical weapons attacks between April 15 and April 25, 2017, that caused forty casualties and one fatality.
Symptoms were reportedly mild, but some casualties included severe chemical
burns and respiratory issues. Townsend, "The Coalition Military Campaign to
Defeat the Islamic State in Iraq and Syria," 31.

302   *had taken the law*: "Video Shows Iraqi Army Throwing ISIS Terrorist Off Cliff,

Shooting Them," *Deccan Chronicle*, July 14, 2017, https://www.deccanchronicle .com/world/middle-east/140717/mosul-victory-video-shows-iraqi-army-throws -isis-terrorist-off-cliff-shoots-them.html.

302 *allowed them to establish*: PMF fighters established their own checkpoints on the border, and some crossed into Syria for a photo op with Iranian-backed pro-regime forces. ISIS made sure to target the PMF outposts, destroying twenty vehicles in one assault on June 20, 2017. Townsend, "The Coalition Military Campaign to Defeat the Islamic State in Iraq and Syria," 33.

306 *ISIS command center*: Townsend, "The Coalition Military Campaign to Defeat the Islamic State in Iraq and Syria," 33.

306 *Iraqi troops finally hoisted*: Townsend, "The Coalition Military Campaign to De-feat the Islamic State in Iraq and Syria," 33.

306 *ISIS blew up the structure*: Falih Hassan and Tim Arango, "ISIS Destroys Al Nuri Mosque, Another Loss for Mosul," *The New York Times*, June 21, 2017, https:// www.nytimes.com/2017/06/21/world/middleeast/mosul-nuri-mosque-isis.html.

306 *ISIS charged that*: "In 'Amaq Video Report, IS Maintains Claim That U.S. Airstrikes Destroyed Great Mosque of Nuri," SITE Enterprise, June 22, 2017, https://ent.siteintelgroup.com/Multimedia/in-amaq-video-report-is-maintains -claim-that-u-s-airstrikes-destroyed-great-mosque-of-nuri.html.

306 *perhaps 150 fighters*: Michael R. Gordon, "No Escape from Mosul, and Unlikely Chance of Surrender," *The New York Times*, July 6, 2017, https://www.nytimes .com/2017/07/06/world/middleeast/mosul-iraq-isis.html?searchResultPosition=2.

307 *ISIS fighters snuck*: Gordon, "No Escape from Mosul, and Unlikely Chance of Surrender."

307 *waves of famished*: Megan Specia and Mona Boshnaq, "Civilians Emerge from Mosul's Rubble Starving, Injured and Traumatized," *The New York Times*, July 3, 2017, https://www.nytimes.com/2017/07/03/world/middleeast/mosul-civilians -escape-isis.html?searchResultPosition=5.

307 *ordering men and boys*: Gordon, "No Escape from Mosul, and Unlikely Chance of Surrender."

307 *ISIS instructed female*: Gordon, "No Escape from Mosul, and Unlikely Chance of Surrender."

308 *The casualties arriving*: Gordon, "No Escape from Mosul, and Unlikely Chance of Surrender."

309 *"I have been with"*: Tim Arango and Michael R. Gordon, "Iraqi Prime Min-ister Arrives in Mosul to Declare Victory over ISIS," *The New York Times*, July 9, 2017, https://www.nytimes.com/2017/07/09/world/middleeast/mosul-isis -liberated.html.

309 *Abadi formally declared*: Arango and Gordon, "Iraqi Prime Minister Arrives in Mosul to Declare Victory over ISIS."

310 *Of the fifty-four neighborhoods*: Arango and Gordon, "Iraqi Prime Minister Ar-rives in Mosul to Declare Victory over ISIS."

310 *The cost of the*: Arango and Gordon, "Iraqi Prime Minister Arrives in Mosul to Declare Victory over ISIS."

311 *610 Iraqi soldiers*: Townsend, "The Coalition Military Campaign to Defeat the Islamic State in Iraq and Syria," 35.

311 *10 bombs*: Townsend, "The Coalition Military Campaign to Defeat the Islamic State in Iraq and Syria," 35.

311 *There were 7,542*: Townsend, "The Coalition Military Campaign to Defeat the Islamic State in Iraq and Syria," 35.

311 *Among the Iraqi Security Forces*: Townsend, "The Coalition Military Campaign to Defeat the Islamic State in Iraq and Syria," 35.

311   *No fewer than 191*: Townsend, "The Coalition Military Campaign to Defeat the Islamic State in Iraq and Syria," 35.

312   *But Townsend sent Abadi*: Townsend, "The Coalition Military Campaign to Defeat the Islamic State in Iraq and Syria," 31.

313   *but after twelve days*: Rukmini Callimachi, "Tal Afar After Liberation from ISIS: Battered but Still Standing," *The New York Times*, September 1, 2017, https://www.nytimes.com/2017/09/01/world/middleeast/tal-afar-mosul-islamic-state.html?searchResultPosition=1.

19. WRATH OF THE EUPHRATES

314   *hundreds of thousands of residents*: Between October 2016 and March 2017, at least 255,000 residents fled Mosul. "As Mosul Displacement Continues, UNHCR Opens New Camps, Expands Appeal," UNHCR, March 17, 2017, https://www.unhcr.org/en-us/news/briefing/2017/3/58cb9f234/mosul-displacement-continues-unhcr-opens-new-camps-expands-appeal.html.

314   *Trump blurted out*: Jonathan Swan, "1 Big Thing: Scoop—Trump to Iraqi PM: How About That Oil?," *Axios*, November 25, 2018, https://www.axios.com/newsletters/axios-sneak-peek-3d9cd027-b3bb-4276-aaba-6e75c5c5aeee.html.

315   *said in its press release*: "Readout of President Donald J. Trump's Call with Prime Minister Haider al-Abadi of Iraq," press release, July 11, 2017, archived on the Trump White House website, https://trumpwhitehouse.archives.gov/briefings-statements/readout-president-donald-j-trumps-call-prime-minister-haider-al-abadi-iraq/.

316   *Obama had flown*: Barack Obama, "President Obama Reviews His Approach to Counterterrorism" (speech, Tampa, FL, December 6, 2016), The White House, https://obamawhitehouse.archives.gov/the-press-office/2016/12/06/remarks-president-administrations-approach-counterterrorism.

317   *Trump vowed*: "Trump: I'd 'Bomb the S**t' out of ISIS," *The Daily Beast*, November 12, 2015, https://www.thedailybeast.com/cheats/2015/11/12/trump-i-d-bomb-the-s-t-out-of-isis.

317   *National Security Presidential Memorandum No. 3*: "Trump Executive Memorandum on Plan to Defeat Islamic State," *VOA News*, January 28, 2017, https://www.voanews.com/a/trump-executive-memorandum-defeat-islamic-state/3697145.html.

318   *McMaster had had*: As a captain, McMaster had commanded Eagle Troop, 2nd Squadron, 2nd Armored Cavalry Regiment, during the Gulf War, providing a screen for the U.S. Army VII Corps as they advanced into Iraq on February 26, 1991, as part of the famed Left Hook. Pushing through a sandstorm, McMaster's unit, which comprised nine M1 Abrams tanks and twelve M3 Bradley fighting vehicles, destroyed fifty Iraqi tanks and twenty-five armored vehicles in twenty-three minutes. McMaster's pursuit of the enemy past his original line of advance at 70 Easting would earn him the Silver Star, the third-highest award for valor in the armed forces. Matthew Cox, "McMaster's Tank Battle in Iraq May Shape Advice in New Role," *Military.com*, February 23, 2017, https://www.military.com/daily-news/2017/02/23/mcmasters-tank-battle-in-iraq-may-shape-advice-in-new-role.html.

318   *McMaster had written*: H. R. McMaster, *Dereliction of Duty: Lyndon Johnson, Robert McNamara, the Joint Chiefs of Staff, and the Lies That Led to Vietnam* (New York: HarperCollins, 1997).

318   *McMaster was edging*: Jim Hickey, a retired Army colonel who had led the hunt for Saddam Hussein and served on the Senate Armed Services Committee, raised the idea of sending McMaster to the White House with Senator Tom

Cotton, a former Army officer who had close ties to the Trump administration. McMaster was at a spirited celebration of the First Troop Philadelphia City Cavalry, one of the U.S.'s oldest military associations, when he was invited to Mar-a-Lago for an audience with Trump himself.

318 *some of the other contenders*: The other candidates included Bob Caslen, the general who had run the small Office of Security Cooperation in Iraq after U.S. troops were withdrawn; Keith Kellogg, a retired Army lieutenant general who had advised Trump during the campaign and was serving as the NSC chief of staff; and John Bolton, the conservative firebrand who had spent his years following the Bush administration firing off op-eds in Washington and writing a book on the threats he saw to U.S. sovereignty. McMaster got a sense of who his competition was when he bumped into Bolton in the men's room during his second day of interviews at the resort. McMaster was selected, but it was clear that Bolton had the support of some of Trump's closest associates, and his footsteps were never far behind.

321 *deploying Army Rangers*: Luis Martinez and Elizabeth McLaughlin, "The US Has Troops in Syria, and Here's What They're Doing," ABC News, April 12, 2017, https://abcnews.go.com/International/us-troops-syria-heres-theyre/story ?id=46020582.

322 *Abu Omar al-Shishani*: "Iraq: ISIL Says Omar Al-Shishani Killed in Air Strike," *Al Jazeera*, July 14, 2016, https://www.aljazeera.com/news/2016/7/14/iraq-isil -says-omar-al-shishani-killed-in-air-strike.

322 *cross Lake Assad*: This is an artificial lake created during the rule of Hafez al-Assad, Bashar's father.

322 *Counter Terrorism Group*: Jack Murphy, "Did Kurdistan's Counter-Terrorist Group Assault the Tabqa Dam in Syria?," SOFREP, May 23, 2017, https:// sofrep.com/news/kurdistans-counter-terrorist-group-assault-taqba-dam-syria/.

323 *But it had helped*: Stephen J. Townsend, "The Coalition Military Campaign to Defeat the Islamic State in Iraq and Syria 21 AUG 2016–05 SEP 2017," declassified command history, September 3, 2017, 40.

323 *and then took the airfield*: The SDF fought for twenty-four hours before capturing the airfield, claiming to have killed seventeen ISIS fighters in the process. ISIS had captured the airfield in 2014 after its garrison of two hundred Syrian soldiers exhausted its ammunition and either fled or surrendered. ISIS unceremoniously executed them in the desert. Andrew Pestano, "Syrian Militia Captures Tabqa Airbase from Islamic State," *UPI*, March 27, 2017, https://www .upi.com/Top_News/World-News/2017/03/27/Syrian-militia-captures-Tabqa -airbase-from-Islamic-State/6641490612667/.

324 *the SDF arranged for engineers*: Townsend, "The Coalition Military Campaign to Defeat the Islamic State in Iraq and Syria," 40.

324 *One was defended*: "Handful of Islamic State Jihadis Stall Push on Raqqa, Syria," *The Australian*, May 11, 2017, https://www.theaustralian.com.au/news/world/the -times/handful-of-islamic-state-jihadis-halt-push-on-raqqa-syria/news-story/51 5542cddab24fb33e6063e7e9ee3152.

324 *When Townsend learned*: Townsend, "The Coalition Military Campaign to Defeat the Islamic State in Iraq and Syria," 40.

324 *"SDF agreed to this"*: Townsend, "The Coalition Military Campaign to Defeat the Islamic State in Iraq and Syria," 40.

325 *only to have ISIS*: ISIS initially occupied Raqqa in 2013 alongside the Islamist coalition Ahrar al-Sham and elements of the Free Syrian Army. Relations were uneasy, and open conflict among the groups was frequent, such as the assassination of the Ahrar al-Sham leader Abu Obeida al-Binnishi at an ISIS checkpoint in September 2013, and the December detention of rebel middleman Ali

al-Alawi. Ahrar al-Sham fighters demanded the freedom of the latter but were kidnapped, and ISIS subsequently attacked the Ahrar al-Sham headquarters in Maskana. The conflict evolved into open warfare, with both al-Qaeda affiliate Jabhat al-Nusra and Ahrar al-Sham besieging ISIS in Raqqa. The siege was broken when Ahrar al-Sham suddenly withdrew its fighters. Lucas Winter, *Raqqa: From Regime Overthrow to Inter-Rebel Fighting* (Fort Leavenworth, KS: Foreign Military Studies Office, 2014), 21–22.

ISIS further consolidated its grip on the city over the course of 2013 and into 2014, launching a VBIED attack on a Free Syrian Army headquarters that killed its leadership and forced the organization out of the city, and forcing Jabhat al-Nusra emir Abu Saad al-Hadrami to flee the city after the execution of three civilians by ISIS in the city square. ISIS again came under attack by the disparate rebel groups in January 2014 and was reduced to holding the Governor's Palace. ISIS emir Abu Omar al-Shishani, located outside the city, signed a truce with Ahrar al-Sham at Jarrah Air Base, but soon broke it and captured the complex for ISIS. ISIS reinforcements subsequently closed the Euphrates bridges into the city from the outside and counterattacked, recapturing the city by January 14 and executing Hadrami. ISIS pushed further, capturing Tal Abyad, Tabqa, and Al-Bab on January 13 and 14. Secure in Raqqa, ISIS issued its first decrees banning smoking and regulating women's clothing on January 23. Charles C. Caris and Samuel Reynolds, *ISIS Governance in Syria*, Middle East Security Report 22 (Washington, DC: Institute for the Study of War, 2014), 11–12, https://www.understandingwar.org/sites/default/files/ISIS_Governance.pdf.

325 *nearly 2,000 fighters*: Townsend, "The Coalition Military Campaign to Defeat the Islamic State in Iraq and Syria," 38.

325 *climbed into an Osprey*: Michael R. Gordon, "U.S. Aid to Syrian Militia Strains Turkish Ties," *The New York Times*, February 24, 2017, https://www.nytimes.com/2017/02/24/world/middleeast/syria-kurds-isis-turkey.html?searchResultPosition=3.

325 *Erdoğan had arranged*: The referendum concerned eighteen amendments that would have revised or repealed seventy-six articles of the Turkish constitution. The amendments largely served to cement the power of the president, and Erdoğan in particular, including abolishing the prime ministry, allowing the president to issue limited decrees with the force of law, allowing the president to dissolve parliament, limiting parliament's ability to conduct oversight of the president, and reducing the number of members in the highest levels of the judiciary, thereby allowing the president to select a larger percentage. Voters approved the referendum by a margin of 51.41 percent to 48.59 percent. Sinan Ekim and Kemal Kirişci, "The Turkish Constitutional Referendum, Explained," Brookings Institution, April 13, 2017, https://www.brookings.edu/blog/order-from-chaos/2017/04/13/the-turkish-constitutional-referendum-explained/; "Turkey Referendum: The Numbers That Tell the Story," *BBC*, April 17, 2017, https://www.bbc.com/news/world-europe-39619354.

326 *whether to arm the Syrian Kurds*: Michael R. Gordon and Eric Schmitt, "Trump to Arm Syrian Kurds, Even as Turkey Strongly Objects," *The New York Times*, May 9, 2017, https://www.nytimes.com/2017/05/09/us/politics/trump-kurds-syria-army.html.

326 *a rare press conference*: James Mattis, Joseph Dunford, and Brett McGurk, "Department of Defense Press Briefing by Secretary Mattis, General Dunford and Special Envoy McGurk on the Campaign to Defeat ISIS in the Pentagon Press Briefing Room," U.S. Department of Defense, May 19, 2017.

326 *his radio call sign*: Speaking at the Air Force Association's Air, Space, and Cyber

Conference in 2017, Secretary of Defense Jim Mattis recounted how he had actually gotten the otherwise intimidating call sign "Chaos." As a regimental commander and colonel at the Marine base in Twentynine Palms, California, he noticed the word "CHAOS" written on the operation officer's whiteboard. When he asked his subordinates why it was there, they reluctantly told him that it was a tongue-in-cheek acronym for "colonel has another outstanding solution." Mackenzie Wolf, "The Origin of Mattis' Call Sign, 'Chaos,'" *Marine Corps Times*, September 21, 2017, https://www.marinecorpstimes.com/news/your -marine-corps/2017/09/21/mattis-explains-the-origin-of-the-call-sign-chaos/.

327 *used the May 19*: Mattis, Dunford, and McGurk, "Department of Defense Press Briefing."

329 *The Russian interlocutors*: Raqqah Study Group, *What the Battle for Raqqah Teaches the Force*, unclassified lessons-learned report issued by the U.S. Army Asymmetric Warfare Group, 29.

329 *U.S. Air Force linguists*: Raqqah Study Group, *What the Battle for Raqqah Teaches the Force*, 20.

329 *After Syrian troops*: Rick Gladstone, "Ancient City of Palmyra Swings Back to Syrian Government Control," *The New York Times*, March 2, 2017, https://www .nytimes.com/2017/03/02/world/middleeast/palmyra-syria-control.html?search ResultPosition=1.

331 *rear of the Syrian plane*: Four F/A-18C Hornets and F/A-18E Super Hornets took off from the USS *George H.W. Bush* for a close air support (CAS) mission on June 18, 2017. Noticing a Russian Air Force Su-35 Flanker circling the Ameri- can CAS flight, one F/A-18E detected another aircraft approaching, which was confirmed to be a Syrian Su-22 Fitter by a nearby E-3 Sentry AWACS plane. Descending to visually identify the jet, Lieutenant Commander Tremel exe- cuted three headbutts, only for the Syrian jet to fire on SDF partners on the ground. Tremel engaged the Su-22, launching an AIM-9X Sidewinder missile that missed, then switching to an AIM-120 AMRAAM, which found its target. The American pilots promptly left Syrian airspace, with two of the Hornets returning to the carrier. The other two, which had not released any munitions, flew to Mosul. Becca Wasser et al., *The Air War Against the Islamic State: The Role of Airpower in Operation Inherent Resolve* (Santa Monica, CA: RAND Corpora- tion, 2021), 270–272, https://www.rand.org/pubs/research_reports/RRA388-1 .html.

331 *The outpost had been*: Nicholas Blanford, "At Remote Desert Garrison in Syria, a US-Iran Confrontation Is Brewing," *The Christian Science Monitor*, June 6, 2017, https://www.csmonitor.com/World/Middle-East/2017/0606/At-remote-desert -garrison-in-Syria-a-US-Iran-confrontation-is-brewing.

331 *bombed a tank*: Townsend, "The Coalition Military Campaign to Defeat the Islamic State in Iraq and Syria," 44.

332 *an Iranian Shaheed-129*: Townsend, "The Coalition Military Campaign to De- feat the Islamic State in Iraq and Syria," 44.

332 *Then, on June 20*: Townsend, "The Coalition Military Campaign to Defeat the Islamic State in Iraq and Syria," 44.

20. ECLIPSE

333 *begun as the Greek city*: Raqqah Study Group, *What the Battle for Raqqah Teaches the Force*, unclassified lessons-learned report issued by the U.S. Army Asym- metric Warfare Group, 9.

333 *tit-for-tat campaign*: Charles C. Caris and Samuel Reynolds, *ISIS Governance in Syria*, Middle East Security Report 22 (Washington, DC: Institute for the

Study of War, 2014), 11–12, https://www.understandingwar.org/sites/default/files/ISIS_Governance.pdf.

334 *dammed the tributaries*: Stephen J. Townsend, "The Coalition Military Campaign to Defeat the Islamic State in Iraq and Syria 21 AUG 2016–05 SEP 2017," declassified command history, September 3, 2017, 41.

334 *draped hundreds of tarps*: Townsend, "The Coalition Military Campaign to Defeat the Islamic State in Iraq and Syria," 38; Raqqah Study Group, *What the Battle for Raqqah Teaches the Force*, 7.

334 *2,500-meter wall*: Raqqah Study Group, *What the Battle for Raqqah Teaches the Force*, 7.

334 *slipped out of the city*: Michael R. Gordon, "ISIS Leaders Are Fleeing Raqqa, U.S. Military Says," *The New York Times*, March 8, 2017, https://www.nytimes.com/2017/03/08/world/middleeast/syria-raqqa-isis.html.

335 *the Australian air force largely*: Australian sources described the pause as a precaution due to the congested airspace around Raqqa. While the pause was temporary, Australian strikes were ultimately limited to Iraq, save for one strike in the MERV on June 23, 2017. Becca Wasser et al., *The Air War Against the Islamic State: The Role of Airpower in Operation Inherent Resolve* (Santa Monica, CA: RAND Corporation, 2021), 188, https://www.rand.org/pubs/research_reports/RRA388-1.html.

336 *burned out the barrels*: Shawn Snow, "Marine Artillery Barrage of Raqqa Was So Intense Two Howitzers Burned Out," *Marine Corps Times*, November 2, 2017, https://www.marinecorpstimes.com/flashpoints/2017/11/02/marine-artillery-barrage-of-raqqa-was-so-intense-two-howitzers-burned-out.

336 *thousand-year-old Harqalah fortress*: Lisa Barrington, "U.S.-Backed Forces Seize Raqqa Ruins; U.N. Sees 'Dire' Situation," *Reuters*, June 7, 2017, https://www.reuters.com/article/uk-mideast-crisis-syria-raqqa-idUKKBN18Y255?edition-redirect=uk; Raqqah Study Group, *What the Battle for Raqqah Teaches the Force*, 7.

336 *pushing into the district of Al-Meshleb*: "US-Backed Fighters Move into ISIS Stronghold Raqqa for the First Time," *The World*, June 6, 2017, https://www.pri.org/stories/2017-06-06/us-backed-fighters-move-isis-stronghold-raqqa-first-time; Raqqah Study Group, *What the Battle for Raqqah Teaches the Force*, 7.

336 *Within a few weeks*: Townsend, "The Coalition Military Campaign to Defeat the Islamic State in Iraq and Syria," 42.

336 *U.S. F-15Es blasted*: Opening two holes in the Old City wall, SDF forces exploited the breach in the east while forces in the west successfully cleared the IED belts that had halted their progress and advanced to the city center. Townsend, "The Coalition Military Campaign to Defeat the Islamic State in Iraq and Syria," 42.

336 *Rushing through the*: Although the SDF managed to establish a foothold, its fighters exploited the gain very slowly, then all at once. One advisor described the scene as follows: "After a few hours, we saw three fighters probe through the gaps. Three turned into six; six turned into 12 . . . It wasn't pretty but it worked." Michael Knights and Wladimir van Wilgenburg, *Accidental Allies: The US–Syrian Democratic Forces Partnership Against the Islamic State* (London: I. B. Tauris, 2021), 146, https://www.washingtoninstitute.org/policy-analysis/accidental-allies-us-syrian-democratic-forces-partnership-against-islamic-state.

336 *On August 14*: "A New Counterattack by the 'Islamic State' Organization East of Al-Raqqa," Syrian Observatory for Human Rights, August 14, 2017, https://www.syriahr.com/en/71898/; Townsend, "The Coalition Military Campaign to Defeat the Islamic State in Iraq and Syria," 43; Raqqah Study Group, *What the Battle for Raqqah Teaches the Force*, 8.

336 *"the circle of hell"*: Quentin Sommerville and Riam Dalati, "The City Fit for No-One," *BBC*, https://www.bbc.co.uk/news/resources/idt-sh/the_city_fit_for_no _one_raqqa_syria_islamic_state_group.

339 *"The SDF offered"*: Raqqah Study Group, *What the Battle for Raqqah Teaches the Force*, 9.

339 *U.S. military documented*: Wasser et al., *The Air War Against the Islamic State*, 193.

340 *"The victory proved"*: Raqqah Study Group, *What the Battle for Raqqah Teaches the Force*, 9.

340 *William Roebuck*: William Roebuck, "Raqqa's Inferno—A Diplomat Reads Dante in Syria," *Foreign Service Journal*, May 2021, https://afsa.org/raqqas -inferno-diplomat-reads-dante-syria.

340 *"We Remain"*: Roebuck, "Raqqa's Inferno."

342 *major policy pronouncement*: Rex Tillerson, "The Way Forward in Syria" (speech, Stanford, CA, January 17, 2018).

342 *opting instead for*: Brian Stelter, "Journalists Outraged by Tillerson's Plan to Travel Without Press," *CNN*, March 10, 2017, https://money.cnn.com/2017/03 /10/media/rex-tillerson-state-department-no-press/.

343 *Laying out the new policy*: Tillerson, "The Way Forward in Syria."

344 *The cost of the fight:* "Weekly Islamic State of Iraq and Syria (ISIS) Cost Report Through June 30, 2017," unclassified Department of Defense cost report, https:// media.defense.gov/2017/Jul/31/2001785287/-1/-1/0/ISIS%20MASTER%20RE PORT%20-%2030JUNE17.PDF.

344 *dispute against Qatar*: Saudi Arabia would eventually lift the blockade in January 2021. Kristian Coates Ulrichsen, "Saudi Arabia Just Lifted Qatar's 43-Month Blockade. How Did This Rift End?," *The Washington Post*, January 8, 2021, https://www.washingtonpost.com/politics/2021/01/08/saudi-arabia-just-lifted -qatars-43-month-blockade-how-did-this-rift-end/.

21. JAZEERA STORM

346 *"Operation Jazeera Storm"*: Alternatively translated as "Jazeera Tempest." "MDC Declared 'Al-Jazeera Tempest' Campaign," Hawar News Agency, September 9, 2017, https://web.archive.org/web/20171111213405/http://en.hawarnews.com /mdc-declared-al-jazeera-tempest-campaign/.

347 *in a 2015 raid*: Barbara Starr and Laura Smith-Park, "Abu Sayyaf, Key ISIS Figure in Syria, Killed in U.S. Raid," *CNN*, May 17, 2015, https://edition.cnn .com/2015/05/17/middleeast/syria-isis-us-raid/.

350 *Trump administration confirmed*: During Pompeo's April 2018 confirmation hearing to be secretary of state, Senator Jeanne Shaheen questioned whether Pompeo, then director of the Central Intelligence Agency, would be able to hold the Russians to task for their interference in the U.S. election. Pompeo responded by noting the attack on the Wagner Group and reported that it had killed several hundred of its men. "Secretary of State Nominee Mike Pompeo Confirmation Hearing, Before the Senate Committee on Foreign Relations," 115th Cong., 2018; Becca Wasser et al., *The Air War Against the Islamic State: The Role of Airpower in Operation Inherent Resolve* (Santa Monica, CA: RAND Corporation, 2021), 116, https://www.rand.org/pubs/research_reports/RRA388-1 .html.

351 *Delta Force commando*: Jared Keller, "The Delta Force Soldier Who Died During a 2018 Raid in Syria Was Actually Killed by Friendly Fire," *Task and Purpose*, July 29, 2019, https://taskandpurpose.com/news/delta-force-friendly-fire-syria/.

352 *That same month*: Dan Mangan, "Rex Tillerson Found Out He Was Fired as Secretary of State from President Donald Trump's Tweet," *CNBC*, March 13,

2018, https://www.cnbc.com/2018/03/13/tillerson-learned-he-was-fired-from-trumps-tweet.html.

352 *obscene epithet*: Secretary Tillerson allegedly referred to President Donald Trump as "a fucking moron" in a Pentagon meeting. Asawin Suebsaeng and Lachlan Markay, "White House Aides Wanted Rex Tillerson to Resign for Calling Trump a 'Fucking Moron,'" *The Daily Beast*, October 4, 2017, https://www.thedailybeast.com/white-house-aides-wanted-rex-tillerson-to-resign-for-calling-trump-a-fucking-moron.

352 *tome on foreign policy*: H. R. McMaster, *Battlegrounds: The Fight to Defend the Free World* (New York: HarperCollins, 2020).

354 *Starting in 2013*: Anne Barnard, Michael R. Gordon, and Jodi Rudoren, "Israel Targeted Iranian Missiles in Syria Attack," *The New York Times*, May 4, 2013, https://www.nytimes.com/2013/05/05/world/middleeast/israel-syria.html.

355 *So sensitive were the attacks*: Israel carried out multiple strikes in Iraq throughout July and August 2019, including a strike that destroyed a weapons depot near the Balad Air Base, and a strike on Amirli that killed two Iranian military commanders. Alissa J. Rubin and Ronen Bergman, "Israeli Airstrike Hits Weapons Depot in Iraq," *The New York Times*, August 22, 2019, https://www.nytimes.com/2019/08/22/world/middleeast/israel-iraq-iran-airstrike.html; Qassim Abdul-Zahra and Lolita Baldor, "Strikes on Iran-Backed Militias Threaten to Destabilize Iraq," *Associated Press*, August 23, 2019, https://apnews.com/article/middle-east-ap-top-news-iran-israel-iraq-06ef6f4d525e408d953f6f31497283aa.

356 *In an August 26*: Jonathan Hoffman, "Statement on Recent Attacks in Iraq," press release, U.S. Department of Defense, August 27, 2019, https://www.centcom.mil/MEDIA/NEWS-ARTICLES/News-Article-View/Article/1944536/statement-on-recent-attacks-in-iraq/.

357 *to move on Afrin*: Mert Ozkan, "Turkey Shells Syria's Afrin Region, Minister Says Operation Has Begun," *Reuters*, January 19, 2018, https://www.reuters.com/article/us-mideast-crisis-syria-turkey/turkey-shells-syrias-afrin-region-minister-says-operation-has-begun-idUSKBN1F80XX.

357 *withdrawal of Russian troops*: Michael Knights and Wladimir van Wilgenburg, *Accidental Allies: The US–Syrian Democratic Forces Partnership Against the Islamic State* (London: I. B. Tauris, 2021), 168, https://www.washingtoninstitute.org/policy-analysis/accidental-allies-us-syrian-democratic-forces-partnership-against-islamic-state.

357 *killed hundreds of Kurds*: Mazloum Abdi would claim that at least two thousand SDF fighters were killed in the offensive. Knights and van Wilgenburg, *Accidental Allies*, 170.

At least ten thousand civilians were displaced in the fighting. "Fighting in Afrin Displaces Thousands, Says Monitor," *Al Jazeera*, March 15, 2018, https://web.archive.org/web/20180627005445/https:/www.aljazeera.com/news/2018/03/turkish-led-assault-syria-afrin-displaced-10000-day-180315181847193.html.

357 *Mazloum's best commanders*: On top of his commanders and troops, Mazloum's best logisticians also left to defend Afrin. The logistician Newroz left to coordinate ammunition supplies in Afrin, and according to one US advisor her leaving alone brought the Deir al-Zour supply chain to a halt. Knights and van Wilgenburg, *Accidental Allies*, 169–170.

358 *near the town of Dashisha*: Rikar Hussein and Zana Omar, "SDF, Iraqis Defend Syrian Border Town from IS," *VOA News*, June 29, 2018, https://www.voanews.com/a/us-backed-syrian-forces-iraqi-army-islamic-state-key-border-town/4460720.html.

358 *hosted by* The Washington Post: Joseph Dunford, "Transformers: Defense with

Joint Chiefs Chairman Gen. Joseph Dunford," *The Washington Post* live event, December 6, 2018, https://www.washingtonpost.com/video/national/transformers-defense-with-gen-joseph-dunford/2018/12/06/85283388-026f-4100-88bc-fb94671081e1_live.html.

359 *Trump said in a video*: Dion Nissenbaum, Nancy A. Youssef, and Vivian Salama, "In Shift, Trump Orders U.S. Troops out of Syria," *The Wall Street Journal*, December 19, 2018, https://www.wsj.com/articles/u-s-military-preparing-for-a-full-withdrawal-of-its-forces-from-northeastern-syria-11545225641.

361 *exit of Brett McGurk*: Jessica Donati and Michael R. Gordon, "President Trump's Envoy in War Against Islamic State Resigns," *The Wall Street Journal*, December 22, 2018, https://www.wsj.com/articles/trumps-envoy-in-war-against-islamic-state-group-resigns-11545498028.

362 *On December 26*: Annie Karni, Mark Landler, and Thomas Gibbons-Neff, "Trump Makes Surprise Visit to American Troops in Iraq," *The New York Times*, December 26, 2018, https://www.nytimes.com/2018/12/26/us/politics/trump-iraq-troops-visit.html.

22. CONTINUING RESOLVE

366 *had ridden on horseback*: Dwight Jon Zimmerman, "21st Century Horse Soldiers— Special Operations Forces and Operation Enduring Freedom," Defense Media Network, September 14, 2021, https://www.defensemedianetwork.com/stories/operation-enduring-freedom-the-first-49-days-4/.

368 *"the SDF's Patton"*: Michael Knights and Wladimir van Wilgenburg, *Accidental Allies: The US–Syrian Democratic Forces Partnership Against the Islamic State* (London: I. B. Tauris, 2021), 168, https://www.washingtoninstitute.org/policy-analysis/accidental-allies-us-syrian-democratic-forces-partnership-against-islamic-state.

368 *with challenging logistics*: After the Turkish intervention in Peace Spring, the United States recognized how easily logistics for the SDF could be brought to a standstill and began contracting trucks to bring supplies directly to the SDF, rather than having the SDF manage all their own supplies. Knights and van Wilgenburg, *Accidental Allies*, 171.

370 *sleeper cells were activated*: Facing bombings and assassinations, including in Raqqa, the Al-Hol refugee camp, and other cities, the SDF took increasingly draconian measures to stymie ISIS cells. Motorcycles were also banned in Al-Hasakah. "Bomb Kills Eight in Syrian City of Raqqa," *Reuters*, April 9, 2019, https://www.reuters.com/article/syria-security-raqqa/bomb-kills-eight-in-syrian-city-of-raqqa-idINKCN1RL1TB; Lamar Erkendi, "IS Changes Modus Operandi in East of Euphrates," *Al-Monitor*, October 2, 2019, https://www.al-monitor.com/originals/2019/10/syria-sdf-ban-niqab-islamic-state-women-attacks.html.

370 *ISIS struck closer*: Army Chief Warrant Officer 2 Jonathan Farmer, Navy Chief Cryptologic Technician Shannon Kent, Defense Intelligence Agency Support Operations Specialist Scott Wirtz, and Arabic interpreter and Valiant Integrated Services contractor Ghadir Taher were killed in the blast. The four Americans were among a total of nineteen people killed. Ben Hubbard and Eric Schmitt, "A Favorite Restaurant in Syria Led ISIS to Americans," *The New York Times*, January 17, 2019, https://www.nytimes.com/2019/01/17/world/middleeast/syria-bombing-manbij-attack.html; Daniella Cheslow, "Defense Department Releases Names of Three U.S. Casualties in Syria Attack," *NPR*, January 18, 2019, https://www.npr.org/2019/01/18/686578315/defense-department-releases-names-of-three-u-s-casualties-in-syria-attack; Jeremy Redmon, "East Point Woman Among 19 Killed in Suicide Bombing in

Syria," *The Atlanta Journal-Constitution*, January 18, 2019, https://www.ajc.com/news/breaking-news/east-point-woman-among-killed-suicide-bombing-syria/auRc0Q17iiIeFYDfpU3kdK/.

370   *a car bomb targeted*: Kyle Rempfer, "ISIS Car Bomb Targets US Troops in Syria One Week After Four Americans Were Killed in Manbij," *Military Times*, January 22, 2019, https://www.militarytimes.com/news/your-army/2019/01/22/isis-car-bomb-targets-us-troops-in-syria-one-week-after-four-americans-were-killed-in-manbij/.

370   *taken up positions*: Rukmini Callimachi, "A Desperate Exodus from ISIS' Final Village," *The New York Times*, February 6, 2019, https://www.nytimes.com/2019/02/06/world/middleeast/isis-baghuz.html.

370   *the fight for Hajin*: Knights and van Wilgenburg, *Accidental Allies*, 175.

371   *beheading or gutting*: In late February, the SDF discovered a mass grave filled with dozens of headless bodies, including women. Mass graves had previously been found in other liberated areas, such as Raqqa. "Severed Heads Found in Mass Grave Near Syria IS Pocket," *Yahoo!News*, February 28, 2019, https://news.yahoo.com/severed-heads-found-mass-grave-near-syria-pocket-164019098.html.

371   *wanted U.S. air and artillery*: There was no shortage of firepower available to the SDF in the battle for Baghuz. The frequency of air strikes led to a noticeable increase in civilian casualties and was augmented by U.S., Iraqi, and French artillery and SDF mortar units. French artillery colonel Francois-Regis Legrier was critical of the SDF's reliance on air strikes due to the increase in civilian casualties. Knights and van Wilgenburg, *Accidental Allies*, 176.

371   *negotiate a way out*: The SDF had initially rejected ISIS requests for safe passage in early February when the operation to clear Baghuz began in earnest. "The International Coalition Continues Its Attack with the SDF on the Last 4 Square Km Remained [*sic*] for the Organization That Is Collapsed Almost Completely amid Fears for the Lives of the Citizens Remaining in the Area," Syrian Observatory for Human Rights, February 9, 2019, https://www.syriahr.com/en/115924/.

     Every time the SDF would restart the offensive, a new tranche of civilians would be discovered or released by ISIS to stop them, such as the sudden discovery of one thousand women and children hidden in caves and tunnels on February 15, 2019. Sarah El Deeb, "Push on Last IS Enclave Blunted by Discovery of Civilians," *Yahoo!News*, February 15, 2019, https://news.yahoo.com/push-last-enclave-blunted-discovery-civilians-130706024.html.

     More than two hundred ISIS fighters would surrender in return for the SDF allowing food trucks to enter Baghuz. "Cornered Islamic State Group Fighters 'Refuse to Surrender to SDF, Seek Exit to Idlib,'" *The New Arab*, February 18, 2019, https://english.alaraby.co.uk/english/news/2019/2/18/islamic-state-group-fighters-refuse-to-surrender-to-sdf.

372   *flood the zone*: In one week, more than thirteen thousand civilians would flee to SDF lines despite the belief that only a few thousand civilians and three hundred fighters remained by the beginning of March. Jeff Seldin, "Final Assault on Last IS Syrian Enclave Underway," *VOA News*, March 1, 2019, https://www.voanews.com/a/final-assault-on-last-is-syrian-enclave-underway/4809749.html.

373   *With the exodus complete*: The SDF would begin their final assault on March 10, confident that no more civilians remained. "US-Backed SDF to Resume Offensive Against IS' Last Syria Enclave," *The New Arab*, March 10, 2019, https://english.alaraby.co.uk/english/news/2019/3/10/sdf-to-resume-offensive-against-is-last-syria-enclave.

374 *An enormous yellow SDF*: "Islamic State Group Defeated as Final Territory Lost, US-Backed Forces Say," *BBC*, March 23, 2019, https://www.bbc.com/news /world-middle-east-47678157.

374 *All told, about fifty thousand*: Rouba El-Husseini, "Syria Force Launches Assault on Last IS Redoubt," *Yahoo!News*, March 1, 2019, https://www.yahoo.com/news /evacuations-syria-holdout-onslaught-005749395.html.

374 *Baghdadi acknowledged*: "Abu Bakr Al-Baghdadi: IS Leader Appears in First Video in Five Years," *BBC*, April 30, 2019, https://www.bbc.com/news/world -middle-east-48098528.

374 *U.S.-manned outposts*: Lolita Baldor, "US, Turkey to Soon Begin Joint Patrols in North Syria," *Associated Press*, October 21, 2018, https://apnews.com/article/7b 13a4c0f7cc47b78200c9a1646c4ad0.

375 *Trump talked with*: Jonathan Marcus, "Trump Makes Way for Turkey Operation Against Kurds in Syria," *BBC*, October 7, 2019, https://www.bbc.com/news/world -middle-east-49956698.

375 *Pentagon ordered the troops*: "Erdogan Says U.S. Troops Started Withdrawal from Northeast Syria After Trump Call," *Reuters*, October 7, 2019, https:// www.reuters.com/article/us-syria-security-turkey-erdogan/erdogan-says -u-s-troops-started-withdrawal-from-northeast-syria-after-trump-call -idUSKBN1WM0M1.

375 *Three days later*: President Erdoğan threw the letter in the trash. Dareh Gregorian and Peter Alexander, "Trump's Extraordinary Letter to Turkey's Erdogan: 'Don't Be a Tough Guy,'" NBC News, October 16, 2019, https://www.nbcnews .com/politics/donald-trump/don-t-be-tough-guy-trump-s-extraordinary-letter -erdogan-n1067746; "Turkey's Erdogan 'Threw Trump's Syria Letter in Bin,'" *BBC*, October 17, 2019, https://www.bbc.com/news/world-middle-east -50080737.

375 *"They didn't help"*: Maanvi Singh, "Trump Defends Syria Decision by Saying Kurds 'Didn't Help Us with Normandy,'" *The Guardian*, October 10, 2019, https:// www.theguardian.com/us-news/2019/oct/09/trump-syria-kurds-normandy.

376 *Pentagon ordered all*: Dion Nissenbaum, Isabel Coles, and Nancy A. Youssef, "'Get the Hell Out of Syria. It's Sand and Blood and Death': Inside America's Chaotic Retreat," *The Wall Street Journal*, October 18, 2019, https://www.wsj .com/articles/get-the-hell-out-of-syria-its-sand-and-blood-and-death-inside -americas-chaotic-retreat-11571421368.

376 *Roebuck explained the plan*: William Roebuck, "Northern Syria: SDF Commander Mazloum Demands Ceasefire or Freedom to Find New Partners," October 10, 2019.

376 *The Turkish military had not*: The beginning of the offensive was largely limited to artillery duels. "Renewed Clashes Between the Kurdish Forces and Pro-Turkey Factions in the North-Eastern Parts of Aleppo Countryside," Syrian Observatory for Human Rights, October 10, 2019, https://www.syriahr.com/en/143264/.

The Turkish army had, however, briefly crossed the border at four points on October 8. Mert Ozkan, "Turkey Opens Ground Assault on Syria's Kurds; U.S. Republicans Turn on Trump," *Reuters*, October 8, 2019, https://www.reuters .com/article/us-syria-security-turkey-usa-idUSKBN1WO05Z.

More than fourteen thousand fighters of the Turkish-backed Syrian militias calling themselves the Syrian National Army had been positioned within the thirty-kilometer security zone to capture the towns of Ras al-Ayn and Tal Abyad and prevent their recapture. Sirwan Kajjo, "Which Syrian Groups Are Involved in Turkey's Syria Offensive?," *VOA News*, October 9, 2019, https://www

.voanews.com/extremism-watch/which-syrian-groups-are-involved-turkeys
-syria-offensive.

376 *"Let me make sure"*: In his cable, Roebuck described Mazloum as uncharacteris-
tically outraged over the situation: "Rising in anger, explosive levels for the normally mild-mannered Mazloum even at the worst of times, he asked again, 'Are
you planning to let Turkey proceed 30km and take our towns and villages?'"
Roebuck, "Northern Syria."

376 *Issuing a rare threat*: Mazloum published an article in *Foreign Policy* explaining
that the SDF had no qualms about turning to Moscow or Damascus for support
if survival was at stake. Mazloum Abdi, "If We Have to Choose Between Com-
promise and Genocide, We Will Choose Our People," *Foreign Policy*, October
13, 2019, https://foreignpolicy.com/2019/10/13/kurds-assad-syria-russia-putin
-turkey-genocide/.

377 *Developments on the battlefield*: Four days into the offensive, Turkish media claimed
that Turkish-backed rebels had severed the M4 highway and captured Ras al-
Ayn, although the latter claim was disputed by the SDF, which launched a counterattack. "SON DAKİKA! Barış Pınarı Harekatı'nda Çok Önemli Gelişme!
Stratejik Noktaya Ulaşıldı," *Sabah*, October 12, 2019, https://www.sabah.com
.tr/gundem/2019/10/12/suriye-milli-ordusu-askerleri-stratejik-m4-kara-yoluna
-ulasti; "Suriye Milli Ordusu, Resulayn'ı Kontrol Altına Aldı," *Timeturk*, October 12, 2019, https://www.timeturk.com/suriye-milli-ordusu-resulayn-i-kontrol
-altina-aldi/haber-1244146; Orhan Coskun and Tom Perry, "Turkish-Led
Forces Advance into Syrian Border Town, Fighting Rages," *Reuters*, October
12, 2019, https://www.reuters.com/article/us-syria-security-turkey-usa/turkish
-forces-intensify-bombardment-around-syrian-town-idUSKBN1WR04D.

377 *Hevrin Khalaf*: Hevrin Khalaf, the thirty-five-year-old secretary general of the
Kurdish Future Party, was pulled from her vehicle at a checkpoint on the M4
highway by Syrian National Army (SNA) fighters, who subsequently beat her,
ripped her hair from her scalp, and shot her five times, leaving her for dead on
the highway. That same day, SNA fighters participated in another battlefield execution, killing one captive who was bound and facedown in the dirt. The SNA
would deny the charge outright. Khalaf's death was felt across the Kurdish diaspora and led to an outpouring of support. Jonathan Vankin, "As Donald Trump
Golfed Saturday, Turkey Said It 'Neutralized' Kurd Leader Hevrin Khalaf,
Executed on Roadside," *Inquisitr*, October 12, 2019, https://www.inquisitr.com
/5689562/donald-trump-golfed-turkey-executed-kurd-hevrin-khalaf/; Joanne
Stocker, "Turkey-Backed Syrian Rebels Kill Kurdish Politician, Execute Prisoners," *The Defense Post*, October 13, 2019, https://www.thedefensepost.com/2019
/10/13/turkey-backed-syrian-rebels-kill-kurdish-politician-execute-prisoners/;
Kareem Khadder, Jennifer Deaton, and Sharif Paget, "Kurdish Politician and
10 Others Killed by 'Turkish-Backed Militia' in Syria, SDF Claims," *CNN*,
October 13, 2019, https://www.cnn.com/2019/10/13/middleeast/syria-turkey
-kurdish-politician-intl/index.html; Michael Bachelard, "This Kurdish Woman's
Death Sparked a Global Outcry. Now We Know How She Died," *The Sydney
Morning Herald*, October 17, 2019, https://www.smh.com.au/world/middle-east
/this-kurdish-woman-s-death-sparked-a-global-outcry-now-we-know-how
-she-died-20191017-p531qs.html; "Kurdish Politician, Other Civilians 'Executed' by Turkey-Backed Group," *Times of Israel*, October 13, 2019, https://
www.timesofisrael.com/kurdish-politician-among-9-civilians-killed-by-turkey
-backed-rebels-monitor/; "Hevrîn Xelef—a Life for the Women's Revolution
and the Freedom of the People of Syria," Women Defend Rojava, October 15,

2019, https://womendefendrojava.net/en/2019/10/14/hevrin-xelef-a-life-for-the
-womens-revolution-and-the-freedom-of-the-people-of-syria/.

377   *leading edge of the*: In one instance that demonstrated the risk to U.S. troops,
American Special Forces based on Mashta al-Nour hill near Kobani were brack-
eted by Turkish mortar fire even though the chairman of the Joint Chiefs of
Staff, General Mark Milley, told reporters that the Turkish Army had U.S. positions down to the grid coordinate. Joseph Trevithick, "U.S. Troops Reportedly
Caught Up in Turkish Artillery Attack in Syria (Updated)," *The Drive*, October
11, 2019, https://www.thedrive.com/the-war-zone/30361/u-s-troops-reportedly
-caught-up-in-turkish-artillery-attack-in-syria.

377   *SDF was blowing up*: David Gauthier-Villars, Vivian Salama, and Dion Nissenbaum, "Turkey Rejects U.S. Call for Immediate Cease-Fire in Syria," *The Wall
Street Journal*, October 16, 2019, https://www.wsj.com/articles/turkey-rejects-u
-s-call-for-immediate-cease-fire-in-syria-11571219662?mod=hp_lista_pos1.

377   *two F-15Es bombed*: Ellen Ioanes, "US Troops Bombed Their Own Anti-ISIS
Headquarters as Turkey-Backed Fighters Closed In During Trump's Hasty Retreat," *Insider*, October 16, 2019, https://www.businessinsider.com/us-bombed
-its-anti-isis-headquarters-as-turkish-troops-advanced-2019-10.

377   *of no use to*: Satellite imagery showed that although the plant was damaged, several structures were largely untouched, including shipping containers and tents
that served as mess halls and living quarters, as well as large clamshell hangars
used to store helicopters by the 160th Special Operations Aviation Regiment.
Tyler Rogoway and Joseph Trevithick, "Satellite Photos Call into Question Impact of U.S. Bombing Its Own Syrian Base After Retreat," *The Drive*, October
22, 2019, https://www.thedrive.com/the-war-zone/30569/satellite-photos-call
-into-question-impact-of-u-s-bombing-its-own-syrian-base-after-retreat.

377   *If the confrontation*: Facing a relentless assault, the SDF announced that guarding prisons was no longer a priority. Mark Townsend, "Kurdish Forces in Syria
Will No Longer Prioritise Guarding Isis Prisons," *The Guardian*, October 12,
2019, https://www.theguardian.com/world/2019/oct/12/kurdish-forces-syria-isis
-prisons-turkish-offensive.

379   *like Franklin Graham*: Elizabeth Dias, "'Shame on Him': Evangelicals Call Out
Trump on Syria," *The New York Times*, October 10, 2019, https://www.nytimes.com
/2019/10/10/us/evangelicals-syria-trump-criticism.html?searchResultPosition=7.

380   *depicting the oil fields*: Courtney Kube and Carol Lee, "Graham and Fox News
Expert Showed Trump a Map to Change His Mind About Syria Withdrawal,"
NBC News, October 22, 2019, https://www.nbcnews.com/news/military/graham
-fox-news-star-showed-trump-map-change-his-mind-n1069901.

380   *Trump reversed course*: Eric Schmitt and Helene Cooper, "Hundreds of U.S. Troops
Leaving, and Also Arriving in, Syria," *The New York Times*, October 30, 2019,
https://www.nytimes.com/2019/10/30/world/middleeast/us-troops-syria-trump
.html.

381   *bases near Manbij*: Thomas Gibbons-Neff and Eric Schmitt, "How the U.S.
Military Will Carry Out a Hasty, Risky Withdrawal from Syria," *The New
York Times*, October 15, 2019, https://www.nytimes.com/2019/10/15/world
/middleeast/turkey-syria-kurds-troops.html; Charlie D'Agata, "Russian Troops
Take Command of U.S. Airbase in Northern Syria," CBS News, November
17, 2019, https://www.cbsnews.com/news/russian-troops-take-command-of-us
-airbase-kobani-northern-syria-2019-11-17/.

381   *set up at Kobani*: Alex Johnson and Emmanuelle Saliba, "Video Shows Russian-
Speaking Man at Abandoned U.S. Base in Syria," NBC News, October 15, 2019,

https://www.nbcnews.com/news/world/video-shows-russian-speaking-man
-abandoned-u-s-base-syria-n1066796.

381 *memorandum of understanding*: Notably, the memorandum also states that Russia
would uphold the Adana Agreement, a 1998 agreement between Turkey and
Syria that obligated Syria to expel the PKK and ensure the security of Turkey's border. "Memorandum of Understanding Between Turkey and Russia on
Northern Syria," *Defense Post*, October 22, 2019, https://www.thedefensepost
.com/2019/10/22/russia-turkey-syria-mou/; Sinam Cengiz, "Why Is the 1998
Adana Pact Between Turkey and Syria Back in the News?," *Arab News*, January
25, 2019, https://www.arabnews.com/node/1441931.

381 *"People said to me"*: David Brennan, "Trump Says U.S. Troops Stayed in Syria
'Because I Kept the Oil,'" *Newsweek*, January 15, 2020, https://www.newsweek
.com/donald-trump-us-troops-syria-oil-bashar-al-assad-kurds-wisconsin-rally
-1482250.

381 *Delta Crescent*: Lara Seligman and Ben Lefebvre, "Little-Known U.S. Firm Se-
cures Deal for Syrian Oil," *Politico*, August 3, 2020, https://www.politico.com
/news/2020/08/03/delta-crescent-energy-syrian-oil-391033.

381 *Bradley fighting vehicles*: Eric Schmitt, "U.S. Sending More Troops to Syria to
Counter the Russians," *The New York Times*, September 18, 2020, https://www
.nytimes.com/2020/09/18/us/politics/us-troops-syria-russia.html.

382 *the SDF's informants*: Tyler Rogoway and Joseph Trevithick, "Everything We
Know and Don't Know About the Raid That Killed ISIS Leader Al Baghdadi
(Updated)," *The Drive*, October 27, 2019, https://www.thedrive.com/the-war
-zone/30690/everything-we-know-and-dont-know-about-the-raid-that-killed
-isis-founder-al-baghdadi.

382 *in honor of Kayla Mueller*: Jennifer Hassan, "Kayla Mueller's Parents Call Baghdadi Raid Named for Their Slain Daughter an 'Amazing Gift,'" *The Washington Post*, October 30, 2019, https://www.washingtonpost.com/world/2019/10/28
/kayla-mueller-was-us-hostage-killed-isis-custody-raid-against-baghdadi-was
-named-her/.

382 *used the deconfliction line*: Alex Hollings, "More Dangerous Than the bin Laden
Raid: Delta Assault Force Flew through Hostile Airspace, Enemy Fire in ISIS
Leader Raid," SOFREP, October 28, 2019, https://sofrep.com/news/more
-dangerous-than-the-bin-laden-raid-delta-assault-force-flew-through-hostile
-airspace-enemy-fire-in-isis-leader-raid/.

382 *The van was later revealed*: Cousins Khalid Mustafa Qurmo and Khalid Abdul
Majid Qurmo died of their wounds, while their friend Barakat Ahmed Barakat
survived but lost his arm and suffered severe leg wounds. A CENTCOM investigation said the civilians had driven toward the helicopter squadron after warning
shots were fired, then turned around back in the direction of Baghdadi's compound, which CENTCOM declared indicated hostile intent. Barakat was left
unable to work despite having five children, and CENTCOM never contacted
him for restitution. Daniel Estrin and Lama Al-Arian, "Syrians Say U.S. Helicopter Fire Killed Civilians During the Raid on Baghdadi," *NPR*, December 3,
2019, https://www.npr.org/2019/12/03/784089600/syrians-say-u-s-helicopter-fire
-killed-civilians-during-the-raid-on-baghdadi; Daniel Estrin, "Pentagon Says
2 Men Killed in Baghdadi Raid Were Combatants but Offers Little Evidence,"
NPR, October 27, 2020, https://www.npr.org/2020/10/27/928161356/pentagon
-says-2-men-killed-in-baghdadi-raid-were-combatants-but-offers-little-pr.

382 *blew a hole in*: Stavros Atlamazoglou, "The Long Reach of America: The Details
Behind the Delta Force Raid," SOFREP, October 28, 2019, https://sofrep.com
/news/the-long-reach-of-america-the-details-behind-the-delta-force-raid/.

383   *two of his children*: Shawn Snow, "CENTCOM Commander Releases Video of
      Raid on Baghdadi Compound, Which Now Looks Like a 'Parking Lot with
      Large Potholes,'" *Military Times*, October 30, 2019, https://www.militarytimes
      .com/news/your-military/2019/10/30/centcom-commander-releases-video-of
      -raid-on-baghdadi-compound-which-now-looks-like-a-parking-lot-with-large
      -potholes/.

383   *Delta Force dog*: The dog, a Belgian Malinois named Conan, would recover
      and get a photo op at the White House with President Trump. Jessica Taylor,
      "Conan, the Military Dog Who Helped Kill ISIS Leader, Honored at White
      House," *NPR*, November 25, 2019, https://www.npr.org/2019/11/25/782653242
      /conan-the-military-dog-who-helped-kill-isis-leader-honored-at-white-house.

383   *buried at sea*: Richard Gonzales, "Head of U.S. Central Command Says ISIS
      Leader Baghdadi Buried at Sea," *NPR*, October 30, 2019, https://www.npr.org
      /2019/10/30/774617578/head-of-u-s-central-command-says-isis-leader
      -baghdadi-buried-at-sea.

383   *ISIS named a new caliph*: Conor Finnegan, "New ISIS Leader Is 'a Nobody,' but
      US Knows 'Almost Nothing' About Him: Official," ABC News, November 6,
      2019, https://abcnews.go.com/International/isis-leader-us-senior-official/story
      ?id=66795150.

383   *Abu Ibrahim al-Hashimi al-Qurayshi*: Reporting by the BBC in 2021 divulged
      previously unknown details about Qurayshi, also known as Abdullah Qardash
      or Hajji Abdullah, a detail confirmed by U.S. intelligence. Qurayshi was born
      in the Turkmen-majority town of Mahlabiya, west of Mosul, as Amir Muham-
      mad Sa'id al-Salbi al-Mawla in 1976, the youngest of seven sons to a father who
      served as Furqan Mosque's imam in Mosul from 1982 to 2001. Qardash be-
      came involved with Ansar al-Islam during mandatory service in Saddam's army
      and eventually joined al-Qaeda in Iraq. Earning degrees in Islamic studies and
      eventually becoming an Islamic judge in Mosul, he was arrested by U.S. forces
      in 2008 and detained at Camp Bucca, where under interrogation he claimed
      he had been chosen as Abu Omar al-Baghdadi's deputy. Baghdadi specifically
      kept Qardash away from the battlefield to protect him as his successor, recog-
      nizing his knowledge of the organization's structure. Qardash initially set up
      an institute to train judges and clergy at al-Imam al-Adham College in Mosul
      alongside Abdul Rahman al-Qaduli, also known as Abu Ali al-Anbari. Anbari
      was killed by U.S. forces in 2016, and other ranking ISIS leaders like Abu Mutaz
      al-Qurayshi, or Muslim Al-Turkmani, Baghdadi's deputy, were killed in U.S.
      air strikes, thus paving the way for Qardash's ascent. When Qardash was
      named as Baghdadi's successor, questions abounded about his lineage, such
      as whether he was a Turkmen, which would disqualify him to be caliph, or an
      Arab descended from the House of the Prophet Muhammad. Qardash cited a
      genealogist to try to prove his Arab ancestry. Feras Kilani, "A Caliph Without
      a Caliphate: The Biography of ISIS's New Leader," *Newlines Magazine*, April
      15, 2021, https://newlinesmag.com/reportage/a-caliph-without-a-caliphate-the
      -biography-of-isiss-new-leader/.

383   *$10 million bounty*: Amanda Macias, "U.S. Doubles Bounty on ISIS Leader to
      $10 Million," *CNBC*, June 24, 2020, https://www.cnbc.com/2020/06/24/mike
      -pompeo-doubles-bounty-on-isis-leader-to-10-million.html.

383   *In December, however*: Michael R. Gordon, "Rocket Attack in Iraq Kills U.S.
      Contractor, Wounds Four U.S. Troops," *The Wall Street Journal*, December 28,
      2019, https://www.wsj.com/articles/rocket-attack-in-iraq-kills-u-s-contractor
      -wounds-four-u-s-troops-11577492632.

383   *After an angry mob*: The retaliatory U.S. strike killed twenty-four militia fighters.

Falih Hassan, Ben Hubbard, and Alissa J. Rubin, "Protesters Attack U.S. Embassy in Iraq, Chanting 'Death to America,'" *The New York Times*, December 31, 2019, https://www.nytimes.com/2019/12/31/world/middleeast/baghdad-protesters-us-embassy.html.

383 *ordered that the Iranian commander*: Isabel Coles and Michael R. Gordon, "U.S. Strike Ordered by Trump Kills Key Iranian Military Leader in Baghdad," *The Wall Street Journal*, January 3, 2020, https://www.wsj.com/articles/leader-of-iranian-revolutionary-guard-s-foreign-wing-killed-11578015855.

384 *Iran struck*: Alissa J. Rubin et al., "Iran Fires on U.S. Forces at 2 Bases in Iraq, Calling It 'Fierce Revenge,'" *The New York Times*, January 7, 2020, https://www.nytimes.com/2020/01/07/world/middleeast/iran-fires-missiles-us.html?searchResultPosition=3.

384 *more than one hundred soldiers*: President Trump dismissed the soldiers' injuries as "headaches," but 109 soldiers were in fact diagnosed with traumatic brain injuries, and 29 of the injured received a Purple Heart. Idrees Ali and Phil Stewart, "More Than 100 U.S. Troops Diagnosed with Brain Injuries from Iran Attack," *Reuters*, February 10, 2020, https://www.reuters.com/article/us-usa-pentagon-tbi-exclusive/exclusive-more-than-100-u-s-troops-diagnosed-with-brain-injuries-from-iran-attack-officials-idUSKBN2041ZK; Gina Harkins, "29 Purple Hearts Approved for Soldiers Injured in Al Asad Missile Attack," *Military.com*, May 4, 2020, https://www.military.com/daily-news/2020/05/04/29-purple-hearts-approved-soldiers-injured-al-asad-missile-attack.html.

384 *nonbinding resolution*: Ahmed Rasheed and Ahmed Aboulenein, "Iraqi Parliament Backs Government Push to Expel Foreign Troops," *Reuters*, January 5, 2020, https://www.reuters.com/article/us-iraq-security-parliament/iraqi-parliament-backs-government-push-to-expel-foreign-troops-idUSKBN1Z407Z.

384 *Trump rebuffed*: "Trump Threatens Iraq with Sanctions If US Troops Are Expelled," *BBC*, January 6, 2020, https://www.bbc.com/news/world-middle-east-51003159.

384 *developed a plan*: Christopher Eng, "Transcript of Oral-History Interview LTG R. Pat White—Commander, CJTF-OIR 2020 September 08," Combined Joint Task Force–Operation Inherent Resolve, unclassified oral history, September 8, 2020, 33.

384 *Trump himself*: Roxana Tiron, Travis Tritten, and Anthony Capaccio, "Trump Orders Troop Drawdown in Iraq, Afghanistan by Jan. 15," *Bloomberg*, November 17, 2020, https://www.bloomberg.com/news/articles/2020-11-17/trump-administration-orders-troop-drawdown-in-iraq-afghanistan.

384 *By March 2020*: Author interview with Nicholas Jones.

386 *bullet ripped through*: Author interview with Nicholas Jones.

386 *Navy Cross*: Corey Dickstein, "Marine Raider Receives Navy Cross for Heroic Acts amid 'Mass Chaos' in Deadly Fight with ISIS in Iraq," *Stars and Stripes*, August 27, 2021, https://www.stripes.com/branches/marine_corps/2021-08-26/marine-raider-navy-cross-jones-isis-iraq-2680739.html.

EPILOGUE

387 *In his September 21, 2021*: Joseph Biden, "Remarks by President Biden Before the 76th Session of the United Nations General Assembly" (Washington, DC, September 21, 2021), The White House, https://www.whitehouse.gov/briefing-room/speeches-remarks/2021/09/21/remarks-by-president-biden-before-the-76th-session-of-the-united-nations-general-assembly/.

387 *At the time of*: Michael R. Gordon, "U.S., Iraq to Agree That Combat Troops Should Leave by End of 2021," *The Wall Street Journal*, July 22, 2021, https://

www.wsj.com/articles/u-s-iraq-to-agree-that-u-s-combat-troops-should-leave-by-end-of-2021-11626975666; Ken Thomas and Michael R. Gordon, "U.S. Combat Role in Iraq to End This Year, Biden Says," *The Wall Street Journal*, July 26, 2021, https://www.wsj.com/articles/u-s-combat-troops-will-leave-iraq-this-year-biden-says-11627326623.

387 *More than forty-eight*: The administration carried out twelve air strikes in Syria and thirty in Iraq between January 1 and May 31. Combined Joint Task Force Inherent Resolve Public Affairs Office, "CJTF-OIR Summary Report, January 2021," April 10, 2021; Combined Joint Task Force Inherent Resolve Public Affairs Office, "CJTF-OIR Summary Report, February 2021," July 6, 2021; Combined Joint Task Force Inherent Resolve Public Affairs Office, "CJTF-OIR Summary Report, March 2021," July 7, 2021; Combined Joint Task Force Inherent Resolve Public Affairs Office, "CJTF-OIR Summary Report, April 2021," July 8, 2021; Combined Joint Task Force Inherent Resolve Public Affairs Office, "CJTF-OIR Summary Report, May 2021," July 9, 2021.

387 *with two air raids*: The first strike was launched in February in response to a rocket attack on the Erbil airport that killed one Filipino contractor, wounded four American contractors, and wounded a Louisiana National Guardsman. The second strike in June was in response to multiple drone attacks on U.S. bases and killed four members of Kataib Sayyed al-Shuhada. Michael R. Gordon, "U.S. Conducts Airstrikes in Syria and Iraq Against Iranian-Backed Militias," *The Wall Street Journal*, June 28, 2021, https://www.wsj.com/articles/u-s-conducts-airstrikes-in-syria-and-iraq-against-iranian-backed-militias-11624835752; Michael R. Gordon and Jared Malsin, "Iran-Backed Militias Fire Rockets in New Attack Aimed at U.S. Forces," *The Wall Street Journal*, June 28, 2021, https://www.wsj.com/articles/iran-backed-militias-threaten-revenge-after-u-s-airstrikes-in-iraq-syria-11624877977; Gordon Lubold, Michael R. Gordon, and Nancy A. Youssef, "Biden Called Off Strike on a Second Military Target in Syria Last Week," *The Wall Street Journal*, March 4, 2021, https://www.wsj.com/articles/a-military-strike-in-syria-shows-biden-team-at-work-11614866795.

390 *A two-star officer*: "Coalition Welcomes New Commander, Continues Mission," news release, U.S. Central Command, September 10, 2021, https://www.centcom.mil/MEDIA/NEWS-ARTICLES/News-Article-View/Article/2771191/coalition-welcomes-new-commander-continues-mission/.

390 *U.S. and allied air*: Becca Wasser et al., *The Air War Against the Islamic State: The Role of Airpower in Operation Inherent Resolve* (Santa Monica, CA: RAND Corporation, 82, 2021), https://www.rand.org/pubs/research_reports/RRA388-1.html.

390 *20 American service personnel*: "U.S. Military Casualties-Operation Inherent Resolve (OIR) Military Deaths," Defense Casualty Analysis System, Department of Defense, https://dcas.dmdc.osd.mil/dcas/pages/report_oir_deaths.xhtml.

391 *The SDF put*: Between 2013 and 2018, a total of 6,759 SDF and YPG fighters were killed, including 1,300 fighting in Turkey, and 10,028 wounded. Michael Knights and Wladimir van Wilgenburg, *Accidental Allies: The US–Syrian Democratic Forces Partnership Against the Islamic State* (London: I. B. Tauris, 2021), 177, 268, https://www.washingtoninstitute.org/policy-analysis/accidental-allies-us-syrian-democratic-forces-partnership-against-islamic-state.

391 *According to the conservative*: "US-Led Coalition in Iraq & Syria," Airwars, https://airwars.org/conflict/coalition-in-iraq-and-syria/.

391 *At the end of 2021*: "Camp Profile—Al Hol, Al-Hasakeh Governorate, Syria, October 2020-Syrian Arab Republic," ReliefWeb, November 26, 2020, https://reliefweb.int/report/syrian-arab-republic/camp-profile-al-hol-al-hasakeh-governorate-syria-october-2020.

391 *conditions so violent*: Department of Defense, Office of the Inspector General, *Operation Inherent Resolve Lead Inspector General Report to the United States Congress, April 1, 2021–June 30, 2021* (Washington, DC: DOD, 2021), 13, https://media .defense.gov/2021/Aug/11/2002828689/-1/-1/1/LEAD%20INSPECTOR%20 GENERAL%20FOR%20OPERATION%20INHERENT%20RESOLVE %20QUARTERLY%20REPORT%20APRIL%201,%202021%20%E2%80 %93%20JUNE%2030,%202021.PDF.

391 *Another 10,000 hardened*: Roughly three thousand to five thousand prisoners are held in each prison in Al-Hasakah and Al-Shaddadi. The SDF also runs detention facilities in Malikiya, Qamishli, and Tabqa on top of ad hoc prisons. Andrew Hanna, "Islamists Imprisoned Across the Middle East," Wilson Center, June 24, 2021, https://www.wilsoncenter.org/article/islamists-imprisoned-across-middle -east.

391 *told his fellow foreign ministers*: Karen DeYoung, "Blinken Says the Number of ISIS Fighters and Family Members Being Held at Detention Camps in Syria Is 'Untenable,'" *The Washington Post*, June 28, 2021, https://www.washingtonpost .com/national-security/binken-isis-prisoners-syria/2021/06/28/a0faa66e-d7f8 -11eb-8fb8-aea56b785b00_story.html.

391 *It still launched*: Department of Defense Inspector General, *Operation Inherent Resolve Lead Inspector General Report to the United States Congress*, 14.

392 *killed two members of*: Department of Defense Inspector General, *Operation Inherent Resolve Lead Inspector General Report to the United States Congress*, 15.

392 *"The U.S. government continued"*: Department of Defense Inspector General, *Operation Inherent Resolve Lead Inspector General Report to the United States Congress*.

392 *the United States had carried out*: In an operation called "Odyssey Lighting," U.S. aircraft launched 495 strikes on ISIS targets in the city of Sirte in a vicious battle that cost the Libyan opposition 712 casualties in return for 660 ISIS dead and 3,000 wounded. Alia Brahimi and Jason Pack, "Tactical Lessons from the Ejection of ISIS from Sirte," Atlantic Council, May 23, 2017, https://www .atlanticcouncil.org/blogs/menasource/tactical-lessons-from-the-ejection-of -isis-from-sirte/; Patrick Markey, "Far from Mosul, Islamic State Close to Defeat in Libya's Sirte," *Reuters*, November 18, 2016, https://www.reuters.com /article/us-libya-security-idUSKBN13D222.

392 *provided reconnaissance for*: U.S. Special Forces on rotation to the Philippines provided intelligence, surveillance, and reconnaissance for the government as they fought for 152 days to recapture the city of Marawi, ultimately leaving more than 950 ISIS fighters dead. "US Joins Battle as Philippines Takes Losses in Besieged City," *CNBC*, June 10, 2017, https://www.cnbc.com/2017/06/10/u-s -special-forces-helping-philippines-troops-in-battle-against-militants-allied-to -islamic-state.html; Ben Brimelow, "ISIS Is Losing Its Grip in Iraq and Syria, but Here Are 9 Places Where It's Still a Threat," *Insider*, November 4, 2017, https://www.businessinsider.com/isis-losing-in-iraq-syria-9-places-where-its -still-a-threat-2017-11#philippines-7.

392 *first emerged in late 2014*: Disgruntled members of the Pakistani Taliban formed ISIS-K in the wake of their leader's death in 2013. ISIS would eventually accept their allegiance on January 26, 2015, and announced it as an official province, or *wilayat*. Harleen Gambhir, "ISIS in Afghanistan," Institute for the Study of War, December 3, 2015, https://www.understandingwar.org/sites/default/files /ISIS%20in%20Afghanistan_2.pdf.

392 *it was estimated to*: Sune Engel Rasmussen, "What Is Islamic State Khorasan Province of Afghanistan?," *The Wall Street Journal*, August 30, 2021, https://www .wsj.com/articles/islamic-state-khorasan-province-afghanistan-11630014893.

393   *During its time in*: Casey Garret Johnson, "The Rise and Stall of the Islamic State in Afghanistan," United States Institute of Peace, November 2016, https://www .usip.org/sites/default/files/SR395-The-Rise-and-Stall-of-the-Islamic-State-in -Afghanistan.pdf; "Islamic State Khorasan (IS-K)," Center for Strategic and International   Studies,   https://www.csis.org/programs/transnational-threats -project/past-projects/terrorism-backgrounders/islamic-state-khorasan.

393   *The group's attack on*: Gordon Lubold and Warren P. Strobel, "U.S. Used a Special Hellfire Missile in Afghanistan Airstrike on Islamic State," *The Wall Street Journal*, August 28, 2021, https://www.wsj.com/articles/u-s-used-a-special-hellfire -missile-in-afghanistan-airstrike-on-islamic-state-11630190876.

393   *attacks on Afghanistan's Shia*: Sune Engel Rasmussen, "Killings of Islamic State Militants Highlight Power Struggle with Afghanistan's Taliban," *The Wall Street Journal*, September 26, 2021, https://www.wsj.com/articles/killings-of -islamic-state-militants-highlight-power-struggle-with-afghanistans-taliban -11632650997.

397   *two brief Army*: Mosul Study Group, *What the Battle for Mosul Teaches the Force*, No. 17–24 (Fort Leavenworth, KS: U.S. Army University Press, September 2017), 7, https://www.armyupress.ar my.mil/Portals/7/Primer-on-Urban -Operation/Documents/Mosul-Public-Release1.pdf; Raqqah Study Group, *What the Battle for Raqqah Teaches the Force*, unclassified lessons-learned report issued by the U.S. Army Asymmetric Warfare Group.

397   *a declassified history*: Stephen J. Townsend, "The Coalition Military Campaign to Defeat the Islamic State in Iraq and Syria 21 AUG 2016–05 SEP 2017," declassified command history, September 3, 2017, 23.

398   *an oral history*: Christopher Eng, "Transcript of Oral-History Interview LTG R. Pat White—Commander, CJTF-OIR 2020 September 08," Combined Joint Task Force–Operation Inherent Resolve, unclassified oral history, September 8, 2020, 33.

398   *several articles*: Ryan Wylie, Aaron Childers, and Brett Sylvia, "Expeditionary Advising: Enabling Iraqi Operations from the Gates of Baghdad Through Eastern Mosul," *Small Wars Journal*, February 22, 2018, https://smallwarsjournal .com/jrnl/art/expeditionary-advising-enabling-iraqi-operations-gates-baghdad -through-eastern-mosul; J. Patrick Work, "Fighting the Islamic State By, With, and Through: *How* Mattered as Much as *What*," *Joint Forces Quarterly* 89 (2018), https://ndupress.ndu.edu/Portals/68/Documents/jfq/jfq-89/jfq-89_56-62 _Work.pdf.

398   *detailed history of*: Becca Wasser et al., *The Air War Against the Islamic State: The Role of Airpower in Operation Inherent Resolve* (Santa Monica, CA: RAND Corporation, 2021), https://www.rand.org/pubs/research_reports/RRA388-1.html.

ACKNOWLEDGMENTS

When I began this book after the Islamic State took Mosul, I understood it would be an ambitious undertaking. The conflict spanned two Middle East countries that were in a state of upheaval. The United States' local partners were an array of "by, with, and through" forces. Internationally, the Americans assembled a broad coalition. Before it was over, the war had spanned three U.S. administrations. In short, the book depended on the cooperation of an extraordinarily large number of people.

They included personnel at all ranks of the U.S. and coalition forces in Iraq and Syria, as well as the U.S. Central Command. They not only agreed to be interviewed on multiple occasions but also allowed me to travel with them around Mosul and in Syria. Senior Iraqi military and civilian officials were generous with their time, as was the Counterterrorism Service, which allowed me to accompany them on two occasions in West Mosul. I also benefited from my interaction with the Kurdistan Regional Government and its Peshmerga commanders, who granted me permission to embed with their forces in Sinjar and during the battle for East Mosul. The Syrian Democratic Forces commander, General Mazloum, received me on one occasion during one of my trips to Syria.

In Washington, Pentagon, State Department, and National

Security Council officials made themselves available as I sought to probe military and diplomatic events. In many cases, these were extensive and repeated interactions. United Nations officials in Iraq helped me understand the scope of the stabilization challenge.

An effort like this also relies on a network of researchers and the support of organizations that are committed to understanding international affairs and national security. Important institutional backing was provided by the Center for a New American Security and the Foundation for the Defense of Democracies. I was also hosted by the Potomac Foundation.

I am also grateful for the support from the Smith Richardson Foundation, which was facilitated by Marin Strmecki, the senior vice president, and Nadia Schadlow when she was a senior program officer at the organization.

A team of experts and dedicated assistants helped me improve the manuscript. Wesley Morgan, author of *The Hardest Place*, whom I first met when he was a teenaged freelancer in Iraq in 2007, drew on his encyclopedic knowledge of the American military's post-9/11 wars to help me hone the descriptions of the role of special operations forces. Michael Brill, a PhD candidate in the Department of Near Eastern Studies at Princeton University with a deep knowledge of the Islamic State's emergence and of the Middle East region, transcribed interviews, translated Arabic documents, and prepared research reports that I drew on in fashioning my chapters.

Ramzy Mardini, a doctoral candidate at the University of Chicago and a scholar on Iraq and the political and sociological factors that gave rise to ISIS, provided valuable input. Chris Gordon assiduously vetted the manuscript and provided editorial advice.

Blake Vieira, my researcher for the final phase of the project, made himself available around the clock and helped run down important details for the text and endnotes. Other researchers who assisted me along the way included Regan Copple, David White, Aaron Hesse, and Eliza Weintraub.

The idea for this project emerged out of a conversation with Andrew Wylie, who served as my agent for two earlier books on conflicts in the region. The telling of this complex tale benefited greatly from the dedication, talent, and patience of the team at Farrar, Straus and Giroux, especially executive editor Alexander Star and assistant editor Ian Van Wye. Nancy Elgin, the production editor, and Janet Renard, the copy editor, labored over the final product.

Finally, I have great appreciation for my family and friends who endured a project that lasted as long as the war itself.

INDEX

A NOTE ABOUT THE AUTHOR

Michael R. Gordon is the national security correspondent for *The Wall Street Journal* and the former chief military correspondent for *The New York Times*. He is the coauthor, with the late general Bernard Trainor, of three definitive histories of the U.S. wars in Iraq: *The Endgame, Cobra II,* and *The Generals' War.*